# LABORATORY MANUAL AND WORKBOOK FOR BIOLOGICAL ANTHROPOLOGY: ENGAGING WITH HUMAN EVOLUTION

K. ELIZABETH SOLURI  COLLEGE OF MARIN

SABRINA C. AGARWAL  UNIVERSITY OF CALIFORNIA, BERKELEY

W. W. NORTON & COMPANY

NEW YORK · LONDON

To all of our students for inspiring us to reach for new heights in our teaching.

Copyright © 2016 by W. W. Norton & Company, Inc.
All rights reserved
Printed in Canada
First Edition

Editor: Eric Svendsen
Developmental Editor: Sunny Hwang
Associate Managing Editor, College: Carla L. Talmadge
Editorial Assistant: Rachel Goodman
Managing Editor, College: Marian Johnson
Managing Editor, College Digital Media: Kim Yi
Associate Director of Production, College: Benjamin Reynolds
Media Editor: Tacy Quinn
Media Project Editor: Jesse Newkirk
Media Editorial Assistant: Marina Rozova
Digital Production: Kristian Sanford
Marketing Manager, Anthropology: Jake Schindel
Designer: Anna Reich
Photo Editors: Trish Marx, Nelson Colon
Permissions Manager: Megan Jackson
Composition: codeMantra
Manufacturing: Transcontinental Interglobe, Beauceville

Permission to use copyrighted material is included alongside the appropriate images.

**ISBN: 978-0-393-91291-3 (pbk.)**

W. W. Norton & Company, Inc., 500 Fifth Avenue, New York, NY 10110

wwnorton.com

W. W. Norton & Company Ltd., 15 Carlisle Street, London W1D 3BS

7 8 9 0

# CONTENTS

**K. Elizabeth Soluri (College of Marin)** received her B.A. from New York University and her M.A. and Ph.D. from the University of California, Berkeley. She has conducted anthropological field and laboratory research across the United States, including work in Valley Forge National Historical Park, Hawaii, and the central California coast. Elizabeth is especially interested in pedagogy and issues of student learning, and her dissertation research focused on redesigning, implementing, and evaluating effective teaching methods for undergraduate anthropology courses, particularly biological anthropology. Elizabeth has taught anthropology courses at several 2-year and 4-year institutions throughout the San Francisco Bay area.

**Sabrina C. Agarwal (University of California, Berkeley)** is an Associate Professor of Anthropology at the University of California, Berkeley. She received her B.A. and M.Sc. from the University of Toronto and her Ph.D. from the same institution, working in both the Department of Anthropology and the Samuel Lunenfeld Research Institute of Mount Sinai Hospital, Toronto. Her research interests are focused broadly upon the age, sex, and gender-related changes in bone quantity and quality, particularly the application of life course approaches to the study of bone maintenance and fragility and its application to dialogues of social identity and embodiment in bioarchaeology. Sabrina has authored several related scholarly articles and edited volumes, most recently the volume (with Bonnie Glencross) *Social Bioarchaeology* (Wiley-Blackwell). She is interested in the philosophies of teaching, and she is actively involved in the pedagogical training of current and future college instructors.

# PREFACE

## FOR INSTRUCTORS
### Active, Engaging, Flexible

The introductory laboratory in biological anthropology can be an inspiring place. It is exciting to see students interact with materials and concepts that may be entirely novel and unfamiliar to them. Of course, it is a challenging place too, a place with many students who enrolled without foreseeing the scientific content and detail of the course. This was the case when we taught introductory biological anthropology at the University of California, Berkeley, and decided to redesign the laboratory portion of the course in 2005. In doing so we had three overarching goals: (1) we wanted to emphasize active student engagement as a way to strengthen learning and long-term retention of course content, (2) we wanted to help students from diverse backgrounds and with varying degrees of experience in anthropology learn the key information about human biology and evolution, and (3) we wanted the lab manual to be simple for instructors to implement in their classes, whether it is used in pieces or as a whole.

We decided to attack this task, both with creativity and with a research and empirical approach emphasizing constant reassessment and improvement. We began simply by creating weekly lab exercises that corresponded with the topics covered in the course and were based on principles of learning from current pedagogy and cognition literature. Then, we spent the next several years trying these lab assignments in classrooms, tweaking them, and testing them again. We also collected empirical data about student engagement, initial learning, and long-term retention of knowledge from the lab component of the course. The data formed the basis for one of the author's (Soluri) doctoral dissertation, which explicitly examined effective pedagogical methods in biological anthropology instruction. With proof of concept at the initial implementation at UC Berkeley, the exercises, questions, and text were then expanded, tested, and refined in additional classroom environments, including community college courses in the San Francisco Bay area. We wanted to make sure our approach would work with as broad an audience as possible.

As a result, we feel this manual has developed into something unique among biological anthropology laboratory manuals.

1. The manual addresses a wide range of topics relevant to introductory biological anthropology courses, including genetics and evolutionary theory, skeletal biology and forensic anthropology, primatology, and paleoanthropology. We provide a balanced approach to the topics that gives students a well-rounded foundation in the discipline. We also present concepts, such as modern human variation, that are central to biological anthropology but are often not emphasized in laboratory texts. In doing this, we help students build the most comprehensive biological anthropology skill set possible. Each of the lab exercises has been designed with real students in mind, and their effectiveness has been tested and fine-tuned over many semesters in real classrooms at various institutions.

2. The authors' concern with employing effective pedagogy has resulted in a distinctive text that explicitly emphasizes a student-centered learning experience. The manual applies active learning pedagogy, which emphasizes the importance of students' hands-on involvement in learning. It is ideal for laboratory contexts where the goal is to foster the development of key skills, as well as content knowledge.

3. The text is exceptional in its further emphasis on cooperative pedagogy, which highlights the importance of student teamwork to complete learning tasks. This approach helps students develop the critical thinking and communication skills that aid them in the biological anthropology classroom and beyond. We have designed the manual's exercises and discussions with cooperative pedagogy in mind, and we encourage instructors to have students work in groups when completing the classroom tasks.

4. We have given additional attention to designing a text that is appropriate for a variety of learning environments and types of learners. Therefore, the exercise format is varied throughout the text, offering a range of activities that target particular learning styles. This variation helps each student to connect with the material, no matter what their learning background. It also allows instructors to choose particular activities suitable for the unique student makeup of each class.

5. Although the units and labs are arranged in the order in which the topics are often covered in classrooms, we have designed them to be modular. Units and labs can be taught in any order that suits the instructor's needs.

6. In addition to its topical breadth, the manual is unusual because of the varied professional experience of its authors. Dr. Soluri's research has focused on the pedagogical aspects of teaching biological anthropology, and she has experience teaching biological anthropology lecture and laboratory courses at large 4-year institutions and community colleges in the United States. Dr. Agarwal's research has focused on bioarchaeology and skeletal analysis, and she has experience teaching biological anthropology lecture and laboratory courses at large and small 4-year institutions in the United States and Canada. Together, their collective research and teaching experience results in a well-rounded text that is appropriate for a wide range of college and university classrooms.

## Organization and Pedagogy

**Four flexible units.** Our text covers a range of biological anthropology topics in sixteen chapters, or labs. The labs are equally distributed into four units, or parts. The first unit (Labs 1–4) focuses on genetics and evolutionary theory. It places biological anthropology in the context of anthropology and science more generally, and it provides information about what evolution is and how it works. The second unit (Labs 5–8) focuses on modern humans. It gives an introduction to the major bones of the human skeleton and teaches some of the skills and methods used by forensic anthropologists. This unit also examines issues of modern human variation and adaptation. The third unit (Labs 9–12) focuses on primatology. It reviews issues of biological classification and highlights similarities and differences in primate anatomy and behavior. The final unit (Labs 13–16) focuses on paleoanthropology. It traces our fossil history from the first primates to modern humans.

As noted earlier, although the units and labs are arranged in the order in which the topics are often covered in classrooms, we have designed them to be modular, and they can be taught in any order. For courses that have fewer class meetings, labs can be combined or eliminated as necessary. For courses that have more class meetings, labs can be divided across multiple class days. Each lab can be treated as a separate entity, allowing the instructor maximum flexibility in scheduling and lesson planning.

**Chapter organization.** Within each lab, there are four primary subsections. The first is the **text section**, providing a written overview of the content for the lab. It can be assigned as reading that reviews course information or introduces it for the first time. The text sections are written in a simple and easy-to-follow format, and they are supported with diagrams, images, and realistic examples to better elucidate points. At the end of the text section of certain labs, we present more advanced concepts that instructors might want to make optional; this material is called out with the heading Exploring Further. The second section is a list of **concept review questions**. These questions target foundational knowledge and are designed to reinforce the learning of basic factual content. They are a good review of the reading portion of the chapter, and they can be assigned as homework to be completed before class or as pre-lab questions to be completed at the start of class. The third section includes a set of **five to ten lab exercises** (depending on the type of content covered and length of the exercises). Instructors can choose to assign all of the exercises in a lab or only a sample, depending on their classroom needs. The exercises emphasize active and cooperative pedagogy and are designed to target higher levels of learning, such as comprehension and analysis. Instructors with access to casts and skeletal elements can easily integrate their own teaching collection with the manual exercises. Instructors who do not have access to casts, or who have gaps in their teaching collection, can direct their students to the images provided in the lab appendices. The final section consists of a list of **critical thinking questions** and tasks. This material often targets the highest levels of learning, such as synthesis and evaluation. It provides students with a review of lab content and a chance to think critically about that content. Instructors can assign this material as follow-up questions completed alongside in-class exercises or outside the classroom. Instructors can also use critical thinking questions and concept review questions as exam questions.

**Art and photo program.** Biological anthropology is a visual discipline and we have tried to illustrate this text in the best possible manner. Every chapter has multiple large and detailed figures and photographs. In most cases, to help students understand the general size of what we picture, we have included scales based on direct measurements of specimens or measurements provided in scientific literature. We strive for accuracy in our drawings and represent many drawings of bones and fossils with an almost three-dimensional appearance. The text has been laid out in a step-by-step manner with use of white space and a double-column design that promotes easy scanning of pages. We provide a map and geological time line on the inside front and back covers.

**Tear-out worksheets.** All worksheets are designed to be torn out and submitted by students with plenty of room for answers. Space for student identification is on every page to aid in grading. Some instructors might also like their students to use the three-hole punch version of this manual. This lets students easily retain worksheets in a binder as they are returned.

### Instructor Supplements (wwnorton.com/instructors)

**Instructor's solutions manual and chapter guidelines.** The entire lab manual is supplemented by special instructor material that gives instructors the information they need to implement the manual in their courses. It presents guidelines for the exercises, including information about materials needed and the approximate length of time suggested for each activity. It also provides instructors with answers to all concept review questions, exercises, and critical thinking questions.

**Image set.** Every image, table, and chart from the book is available for download.

**LMS coursepacks.** Special LMS coursepacks contain versions of selected labs designed to work in your LMS. These facilitate on-line submission of exercises for distance and blended learning students (note that students must have the lab manual for access to images). The coursepack also contains the introductory Concept Review quiz for each chapter, and access to Norton's animation and video resource for biological anthropology.

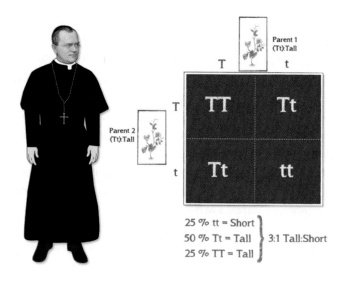

**Low-priced versions and bundle discounts.** This manual is available in a discounted three-hole punch version, as

well as an inexpensive electronic version for your distance learning students. Discounted bundle prices are also available to keep costs reasonable for students. Please contact your W. W. Norton representative for more information.

## FOR STUDENTS

This book is designed to engage you in an exploration of human biology and evolution. The evolution of our species is a vast and complex topic that is studied by biological anthropologists around the world who seek to understand who we are as a species, how we came to be this way, and where we may be headed from here. Biological anthropologists tackle these issues using a range of research questions and methods, and we will investigate these different forms of analysis throughout the text. Each lab in the book includes text that introduces important content information, questions that can be used to test your comprehension of the material, exercises that ask you to think and act like an anthropologist, and critical thinking questions that ask you to combine all of this knowledge in complex and new ways. There is no set order to the labs, and your instructor may choose to present the labs in any order. No matter where you start or finish, the labs will combine to provide a broad picture of the human species and our evolutionary history.

To facilitate your learning, we engage you as active participants. You will complete tasks, answer questions, and think critically about the information presented. You will get the chance to practice some of the comparative and analytical skills used by biological anthropologists, and you will likely begin seeing yourself in a whole new light because of it. We provide you with up-to-date information about major topics in biological anthropology, so that you are gaining the most accurate and current knowledge possible. We also describe issues and examples that are interesting and relevant to your real life. We supply you with high quality photos and drawings of skeletons, fossils, and living animals to illustrate key points and anatomical features throughout the text. Your instructor may then give you access to additional materials, such as skeletal elements and fossil casts, to supplement what you see and learn in the book.

By the end of this book and course, you will be thinking and applying analytical skills like a biological anthropologist. You will have learned more about yourself, your place in the world, and your evolutionary history, and you will be armed with this knowledge as you continue life in and outside of anthropology classrooms.

# ACKNOWLEDGMENTS

We extend our gratitude to the many people who supported us and generously provided their assistance throughout the process of planning, writing, and publishing this book. Among them, Elizabeth would especially like to thank her friends and family who supported her during the development of this project, especially the Soluri, Camp, Schneider, and Hayes/Matsunaga families. Elizabeth extends a special thank you to her husband Tsim, who participated in countless conversations about the book, sharing his ideas and lending his unfailing support every step of the way. Sabrina would like to especially thank Rosemary Joyce, Laurie Wilkie, Ruth Tringham, and Meg Conkey for sharing all their teaching and learning wisdom while formulating ideas for this project. Sabrina also thanks her husband Peter, for his support and encouragement over the years in seeing this book to its fruition.

We greatly appreciate the help and guidance we received from everyone at W. W. Norton & Company. We thank Jack Repcheck for initially approaching us with this opportunity and bolstering us through the early stages of the project. His enthusiasm for the book was contagious and helped get things off the ground. Eric Svendsen took on the project after Jack, and he has expertly steered us through the majority of the writing and publication process. His patience and guidance was instrumental, particularly his insights and assistance during the review, revision, and production processes. We are also indebted to the exceptional editing of Carla Talmadge and Connie Parks, who applied their keen eye to the project from start to finish. We thank Sunny Hwang for her outstanding suggestions for portions of the text and activities, which kept us thinking and exploring new ideas. Rachel Goodman's excellent organization helped keep the process streamlined and efficient. This text is supported by an excellent media and supplement package, and we thank Tacy Quinn and Marina Rozova for their careful work in this area. Numerous people helped compile the wonderful images and figures, including Trish Marx, Nelson Colon, and Lynn Gadson. Ben Reynolds, Sofia Buono, and Fran Daniele carefully oversaw the production process. Ashley Lipps contributed her time and expertise in taking beautiful photographs of much of the skeletal material featured in this text. Tiffiny Tung and Melanie Miller generously shared photographs for inclusion in the text. We extend additional thanks to Alison Galloway, Adrienne Zihlman, and Richard Baldwin (Department of Anthropology at the University of California, Santa Cruz) and Chris Conroy (Museum of Vertebrate Zoology, University of California, Berkeley) for providing access to skeletal material for photographic purposes. Clark Larsen encouraged us and offered valuable advice based on his experience. The project would not have been possible without the outstanding support of the entire W. W. Norton & Company team.

A book of this nature is based on our years of teaching this material in 2- and 4-year institutions in the United States and Canada. We thank all of our undergraduate students—past, present, and future—for inspiring and challenging us. We also thank the numerous graduate students and faculty who have taught with us and shared their classroom experiences and suggestions. In particular, we thank the graduate student instructors at the University of California, Berkeley, who helped us test some of the activities published here: Patrick Beauchesne, Chihhua Chiang, Teresa Dujnic Bulger, Julie Hui, Kari Jones, Ashley Lipps, Andrew Roddick, Arpita Roy, Matthew Russell, and Julie Wesp. Some activities and questions included here were initially produced with the support of a Pedagogy Improvement Grant from the Graduate Student Teaching and Resource Center of the Graduate Division at the University of California, Berkeley, for which we are especially grateful. We also thank the following colleagues for the various forms of pedagogical support and insights they provided: Martin Covington, Terrence Deacon, Bonnie Glencross, Sandra Hollimon, Michelle Hughes Markovics, Rosemary Joyce, Jessica Park, Nicole Slovak, Laurie Taylor, Linda von Hoene, and Barbara Wheeler. We also extend our special thanks to the graduate student teaching assistants, Debra Martin, and Peter Gray at the University of Nevada, Las Vegas, for their test run of the lab manual. Their detailed feedback and ideas were instrumental in shaping the final product.

This book benefited from the feedback and suggestions provided by many reviewers, and we appreciate the time and thought they put into this process.

K. Elizabeth Soluri
Sabrina C. Agarwal

## REVIEWERS

Lise Mifsud, Cuesta College

Tracy Evans, Fullerton College

Marta Alfonso-Durruty, Kansas State University

Alejandra Estrin Dashe, Metropolitan State University

Peter Warnock, Missouri Valley College

Erin Blankenship-Sefczek, Ohio State University

Joshua Sadvari, Ohio State University

Timothy Sefczek, Ohio State University

Arion Melidonis, Oxnard College

Susan Cachel, Rutgers University

Renee Garcia, Saddleback College

Mario Robertson, Santa Ana College

Phyllisa Eisentraut, Santa Barbara City College

Barbara Wheeler, Santa Rosa Junior College

Nancy Cordell, South Puget Sound Community College

Arthur Charles Durband, Texas Tech University

Robert Paine, Texas Tech University

Nasser Malit, The State University of New York at Potsdam

Martin Muller, The University of New Mexico

Charles P. Egeland, The University of North Carolina at Greensboro

Jessica Cade, University of California, Riverside

Sandra Wheeler, University of Central Florida

Lana Williams, University of Central Florida

Michael Pietrusewsky, University of Hawaii

Alan J. Redd, University of Kansas

David Begun, University of Toronto

Jen Shaffer, University of Maryland

Mary S. Willis, University of Nebraska–Lincoln

Peter Gray, University of Nevada, Las Vegas

Debra Martin, University of Nevada, Las Vegas

Cari Lange, Ventura College

Lucas Premo, Washington State University

Robert Renger, Ventura College

# LABORATORY MANUAL AND WORKBOOK FOR BIOLOGICAL ANTHROPOLOGY: ENGAGING WITH HUMAN EVOLUTION

### PART ONE

# GENETICS AND EVOLUTIONARY THEORY

The genetic code for an organism is stored in its DNA. This DNA is coiled with proteins to form chromosomes. Humans have 23 pairs of chromosomes.

# LAB 1: BIOLOGICAL ANTHROPOLOGY AND THE SCIENTIFIC METHOD

## WHAT TOPICS ARE COVERED IN THIS LAB?

- An introduction to the discipline of anthropology
- A discussion of the four fields of anthropology
- A closer consideration of the field of biological anthropology
- A review of science and the scientific method
- An overview of the role of scientific inquiry in biological anthropology research

# LAB 2: GENETICS

## WHAT TOPICS ARE COVERED IN THIS LAB?

- An introduction to the cell parts related to processes of evolution and inheritance
- A look at the importance of cell division for evolution
- A review of DNA replication and protein synthesis

# LAB 3: INHERITANCE

## WHAT TOPICS ARE COVERED IN THIS LAB?

- An overview of Gregor Mendel's research with pea plants
- A consideration of the relationship between dominant and recessive alleles
- A review of genotypes and phenotypes
- An introduction to the production and interpretation of Punnett squares and pedigree diagrams
- A discussion of Mendelian and non-Mendelian traits
- An examination of the ABO blood group in humans to illuminate complex relationships of dominance and recessiveness in real life

# LAB 4: FORCES OF EVOLUTION

## WHAT TOPICS ARE COVERED IN THIS LAB?

- An introduction to the concept of evolution
- A discussion of the role of genetic recombination in evolution
- A review of the primary forces of evolution (mutation, natural selection, genetic drift, and gene flow)
- A consideration of how to determine when evolution is happening, using the Hardy–Weinberg equilibrium

David Marchal/Visuals Unlimited, Inc.

3

Biological anthropologists address a wide range of research topics related to humans and our evolutionary history. This research often includes time in the laboratory and time in the field.

## Lab Learning Objectives

By the end of this lab, students should be able to:

- describe the discipline of anthropology in general, and compare the four fields of anthropology.

- discuss the similarities and differences between the subfields of biological anthropology.

- explain the scientific method and define "scientific theory."

- discuss how biological anthropologists draw on science and scientific techniques in their work.

LAB 1

# Biological Anthropology and the Scientific Method

In Germany, a group of researchers examines modern and ancient human DNA to understand human population movements in the past. Meanwhile, researchers in Ethiopia excavate the fossil remains of some of our relatives who went extinct roughly 4 million years ago. In California, a researcher analyzes 7,000-year-old bones for evidence of changes in bone density related to both biological sex and gender differences during life. At the same time, researchers in Borneo observe orangutans using probing tools to fish for the insects they eat. What do all of these people have in common? They are all conducting biological anthropology research. What does it mean to be a biological anthropologist? What topics do biological anthropologists study? In this lab, we explore answers to these questions.

**anthropology** the study of people

**context** the time, space, environment, historical circumstances, and cultural practices within which a subject of anthropological investigation is situated

**holistic approach** research approach that emphasizes the importance of all aspects of the study subject and requires a consideration of context to gain an understanding of the broader picture

**comparative approach** research approach that emphasizes the importance of comparisons across cultures, times, places, species, etc.

**cultural anthropology** the study of the cultural life of living people, including their cultural practices, beliefs, economics, politics, gender roles, etc.; also called social anthropology

# INTRODUCTION

We begin this lab with an overview of the discipline of anthropology. We discuss the four fields of anthropology, and we pay particular attention to how biological anthropology relates to the other fields of anthropology. We outline the subfields of biological anthropology and consider how they overlap and vary. We also explore science more generally, discussing the scientific method and its role in scientific research. We conclude by examining how biological anthropologists employ the scientific method in their work.

# WHAT IS ANTHROPOLOGY?

**Anthropology**, in the most general sense, refers to the study of people. This can take a variety of forms, including the study of people in the present and people in the past. There are two ideas that are fundamental to all anthropological work. The first idea is the importance of **context**. This includes issues of time, space, unique historical and environmental circumstances, and various culturally specific practices. Context is important to all anthropological work because it shapes what we study. People do not live in a vacuum. Instead, they are inseparable from the context in which they live. For example, if an anthropologist were to fully understand you, they would have to consider your age, where you live, your gender, your life experience, your cultural practices, your family, your place in the broader biological world, and many other factors specific and unique to you. Where you live determines the environmental resources available to you, your food, and possibly your cultural practices. Your cultural practices impact the way you view the world and your place in it. Your biology, such as your sex or age, may impact your place in your culture, and your life experiences often tell the story of all of these factors. It would be impossible to understand you without understanding as much as possible about these other contextual issues. This emphasis on context and how different aspects

of a study subject interrelate and impact one another is often called a **holistic approach**. With a holistic approach, emphasis is placed on seeing the whole picture because anthropology recognizes that numerous factors and contextual issues contribute to what it means to be human.

The second fundamental idea in anthropology is the use of a **comparative approach**. The comparative approach can take many forms, and anthropological comparisons can be the focus of a research project or only a component of a research project. For example, anthropologists often compare different cultural groups, or the same cultural group in different time periods, or people in one region to people in another region, or humans to other species. No matter what anthropologists study, they recognize the importance of considering similarities and differences through comparisons.

Anthropology is unique because it takes into account how people are shaped by their biological and their cultural context, and it explores and compares people in all time periods and regions. Other social sciences, such as psychology and sociology, have minor components of both of these fundamental aspects of anthropology. While many social scientists consider the role of biology and/or culture in human life, most of these disciplines do not emphasize a comparative approach. They study people in the present or people in particular areas of the world. In contrast, anthropological work considers context and employs a broad, comparative perspective.

# FOUR FIELDS OF ANTHROPOLOGY

There are generally four fields of anthropology (**FIGURE 1.1**). These four fields are united by the consideration of culture and an emphasis on the comparative approach, but they vary based on what questions they ask and what materials they study. One field of anthropology is called **cultural anthropology** (often called social anthropology in Europe). Cultural anthropologists study cultural practices, beliefs, economics,

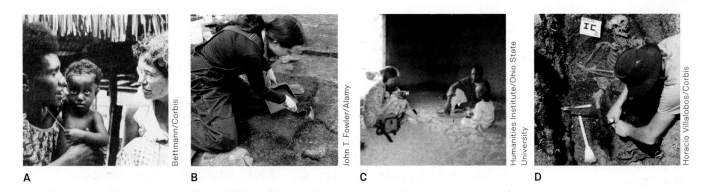

A    B    C    D

**FIGURE 1.1 The Four Fields of Anthropology**
All four fields of anthropology emphasize the importance of context and apply a comparative approach, but they differ in the specific aspects of humanity that they study. Cultural anthropologists (A) study the cultural life of living people. Archaeologists (B) study the cultural life of past people by examining their material remains. Linguistic anthropologists (C) study how people make and use language. Biological anthropologists (D) study human evolution, and their methods of analysis may be applied to help criminal investigations.

politics, gender roles, etc.; they traditionally studied non-Western groups, although this is not always the case in the field today. Cultural anthropologists study living (or recently living) peoples. These anthropologists make observations, conduct interviews, and examine things made by the people being studied (their material culture). For example, a cultural anthropologist might study the seasonal rituals practiced by a particular Native American group. The anthropologist would observe the rituals and the times surrounding the rituals to understand the broader cultural context of the practices. The anthropologist might interview the people involved in the ritual and the people who observe the ritual, and the anthropologist might examine the clothing and materials used in the ritual.

A second field of anthropology is **linguistic anthropology**. Linguistic anthropologists study how people make and use language. Again, linguistic anthropologists tend to research living (or recently living) peoples, and they traditionally studied non-Western populations. Like cultural anthropologists, linguistic anthropologists use observations and interviews to collect data about language production and use. They can also use written documents, where available, and recordings of people speaking the language under study. For example, a linguistic anthropologist might study how language is used differently by men and women in an indigenous group in New Guinea. The anthropologist would

observe people talking with people of their same gender and people not of their same gender. The anthropologist might also interview people about who taught them their language, how they talk to their children of different genders, and how they talk to different people in their community. The anthropologist might also listen to recordings of songs made by earlier researchers studying the same group to see if there are differences in men's and women's singing.

A third field of anthropology is **archaeology**. In Europe, archaeology is sometimes treated as a discipline separate from anthropology. In the United States, however, archaeology is considered a subdiscipline of anthropology, and it is sometimes called anthropological archaeology to highlight this categorization. Archaeologists, like cultural anthropologists, study cultural practices, economics, gender roles, and rituals. However, archaeologists focus on people and cultures in the past. Sometimes they study the distant past, tens of thousands of years ago. Sometimes they study the recent past, maybe only a few decades ago. Archaeologists study both Western and non-Western peoples around the world. Unlike cultural and linguistic anthropology, archaeology primarily examines the material remains left by people to understand their practices and way of life. Material remains are things that are made or modified by people and later recovered by an archaeologist. They include things like remnants of houses

**linguistic anthropology** the study of how people make and use language

**archaeology** the study of the cultural life of past people, as seen through their material remains such as architecture, bones, and tools

and ritual buildings, human bones and burials, tools, animal bones and charred plant parts, ceramic vessels, personal ornaments, statues, clothing, and sometimes historical documents. If archaeologists were studying what Maya people ate in a community in Mexico 1,000 years ago, they would probably try to recover and examine animal and plant remains from meals, ceramic vessels that held food and beverages, areas of the community that were used for food storage or preparation, and any documents that might help them understand food use.

The fourth field of anthropology is called **biological anthropology**. Biological anthropology is traditionally called physical anthropology, with the term "physical" reflecting a traditional focus on the physical measurement of modern humans. Current trends in the field emphasize methods and theories from biology, such as the growing incorporation of DNA analysis. Thus, while both names are acceptable and continue to be used today, we will use "biological anthropology" to reflect anthropologists' increasing use of biological techniques.

Biological anthropology is the study of human evolution, including our biology, our close primate relatives, our fossil ancestry, and our current similarities and differences. Biological anthropologists study people today and in the past. They also study nonhuman species, specifically our living primate relatives and our extinct fossil relatives. They examine a wide range of material, including fossils, living primates, skeletons, and DNA. For example, a biological anthropologist studying the primate capacity for language might examine genes that contribute to language production and comprehension. That same anthropologist could also examine the bones of the skeleton related to language production and/or try to train living primates to produce or understand some form of language. The theme that unifies biological anthropology research is an emphasis on evolution.

One of the things that makes biological anthropology research unusual among the sciences is its emphasis on a **biocultural approach**. This approach recognizes that human biology and culture are closely intertwined and need to

be examined and understood simultaneously. Thus, biological anthropologists consider how stone tool use (culture) impacted past diet and dietary adaptations (biology) or how mating preferences (culture) impact current population isolation and human variation (biology).

## THE SUBFIELDS OF BIOLOGICAL ANTHROPOLOGY

Within biological anthropology, there are several subfields. Each subfield emphasizes different aspects of human evolution and our place in the world. One subfield can be generally referred to as **human biology**. This is a broad subfield that includes research on human genetics, the impact of evolutionary processes on our species, and variation among humans today. This subfield draws heavily on theories and methods from biology. For example, a researcher in human biology might study the evolution of a particular trait, such as adult lactose tolerance. This researcher could explore the impact of different evolutionary processes in shaping this adaptation. He could also consider genetic evidence for the trait, as well as why this trait might vary in human populations today. Another example of human biology research would be a study of energy demands and nutrition in different human populations. The researcher could observe and interview people in different groups to identify what people eat, how regularly they eat, how they spend their time, and how much energy is required for their lifestyle. The researcher would likely take into account differences in age, gender, and social status that may impact energy demands and nutrition.

**Forensic anthropology** is an applied area of biological anthropology that has gained popular attention through the television programs *Bones* and *CSI*. Forensic anthropology is related to human biology because it applies methods of skeletal analysis from biology and anatomy to real-world problems. Forensic anthropologists analyze human skeletons as part of legal investigations. When a criminal investigation uncovers

**biological anthropology** the study of human evolution, including human biology, our close living and extinct relatives, and current similarities and differences within our species; also called physical anthropology

**biocultural approach** research approach that recognizes the close relationship between human biology and culture and attempts to study these two forces simultaneously

**human biology** the study of human genetics, variations within our species, and how our species is impacted by evolutionary processes

**forensic anthropology** the application of knowledge and methods of skeletal analysis to assist in legal investigations

**FIGURE 1.2 Forensic Anthropology**
Forensic anthropologists apply methods of human skeletal analysis to aid criminal investigations. They help identify victims and describe circumstances surrounding death, using clues in human skeletal remains.

a victim that is primarily skeletal, with little soft tissue remaining, investigators call on a forensic anthropologist for assistance **(FIGURE 1.2)**. In some cases, forensic anthropologists are asked to help with investigations of war crimes, natural disasters, and other instances that involve the identification of numerous victims. These anthropologists are experts on the human skeleton and use various methods and techniques to help identify victims and to suggest the circumstances surrounding the victims' deaths.

Another subfield of biological anthropology is called **primatology**. Primatology is the study of living primates **(FIGURE 1.3)**. Primatologists study similarities and differences across primate species, and they try to understand how, why, and when various primate traits evolved. Because humans are primates, this work is used to help understand our broader biological context and evolutionary history. Primatologists draw on biological theories and methods, such as DNA analysis and observations of animals in the wild. Primatologists may also design laboratory experiments to test things such as the ability of primates to perform certain problem-solving tasks or learn language. A primatologist might study chimpanzee social interactions in the wild. In doing this, the researcher would stay near a group of chimpanzees for an extended time, observing and documenting chimpanzee behavior in

various social situations, such as sharing food, having sex, and fighting. This type of information could then be used to help us understand human behavior in similar situations today and in the past.

The final subfield of biological anthropology is called **paleoanthropology**. Paleoanthropology is the study of the anatomy and behavior of humans and our biological relatives in the past **(FIGURE 1.4)**. This subfield uses methods of excavation that are similar to those used by archaeologists, and there is often overlap in the evidence used in paleoanthropology and archaeology. However, archaeologists tend to focus on the modern human species, and paleoanthropologists often focus on our ancient extinct relatives, such as Neanderthals. Paleoanthropologists often deal with the more distant past, even as far back as several million years ago. Paleoanthropologists also focus on the analysis of fossilized skeletal remains and sometimes tools and other artifacts that have been well preserved across long periods. For example, a paleoanthropologist might study when we first diverged from other primates.

**primatology**
the study of living primates, particularly their similarities and differences and why these similarities and differences might exist

**paleoanthropology**
the study of the anatomy and behavior of humans and our extinct relatives

**FIGURE 1.3 Primatology**
Some biological anthropologists, such as Jane Goodall, specialize in primatology.

**scientific method** a cycle of scientific practices that helps scientists to gain knowledge and sparks further scientific inquiries

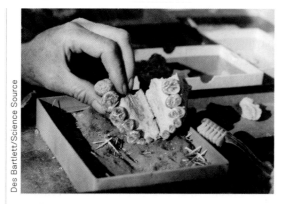
Des Bartlett/Science Source

**FIGURE 1.4 Paleoanthropology**
Paleoanthropologists examine fossilized remains for information about the anatomy and behavior of our extinct relatives.

The paleoanthropologist would collect fossil remains from the relevant time period and analyze their anatomical traits and features to identify the extinct species' relationship to humans and other primates. She might explore what kinds of food our early primate relatives ate by examining fossil teeth and comparing them to modern primate teeth. Work along these lines allows us to trace the evolution of particular human traits, as well as larger evolutionary trends in our history. Paleoanthropologists usually work as part of interdisciplinary teams that bring together researchers such as geologists and paleoecologists who study ancient environments. These interdisciplinary partnerships allow paleoanthropologists to gain a more complete picture of the past they study.

## SCIENCE AND THE SCIENTIFIC METHOD

Science is a way of learning about the world. There are many ways of thinking about the world, but science is different because it relies on observations and tests to accumulate knowledge about aspects of the natural world. These observations and tests must be repeatable and verifiable by other scientists, and scientists in all scientific disciplines use the scientific method to make their observations.

The **scientific method** is a cycle of scientific practices that helps scientists gain knowledge and sparks further scientific inquiries (**FIGURE 1.5**). There are four key stages to this cycle. The first stage is *observation*. A scientist can make observations directly, or they can use observations made by other scientists as part of previous research. For example, a researcher may

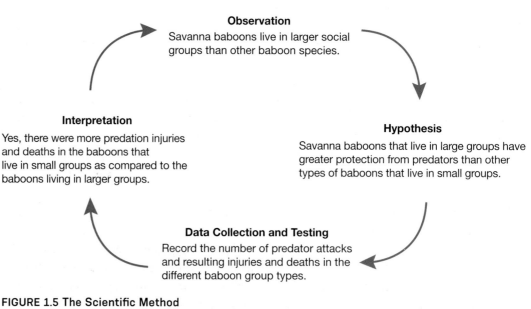

**Observation**
Savanna baboons live in larger social groups than other baboon species.

**Hypothesis**
Savanna baboons that live in large groups have greater protection from predators than other types of baboons that live in small groups.

**Data Collection and Testing**
Record the number of predator attacks and resulting injuries and deaths in the different baboon group types.

**Interpretation**
Yes, there were more predation injuries and deaths in the baboons that live in small groups as compared to the baboons living in larger groups.

**FIGURE 1.5 The Scientific Method**
When conducting research, scientists follow the scientific method. They use previous research and/or new observations to develop hypotheses. They then collect data to test their hypotheses. They use their data to evaluate the hypotheses and make interpretations. These interpretations then serve as the starting point for further research, and the cycle begins again.

**FIGURE 1.6 Savanna Baboons**
Savanna baboons often form larger social groups than baboons that live in forests.

notice that savanna baboons live in larger social groups than other baboon species (**FIGURE 1.6**).

The second stage of the cycle is generating the *hypothesis*. The hypothesis is based on the researcher's observations, and it is a testable explanation of those observations. There can be more than one hypothesis, but the researcher will have to handle them carefully in the next stages of the scientific method to make sure adequate data are collected and evaluated for each hypothesis. To generate a hypothesis, the researcher suggests a testable explanation for their observation. Specifically, it should be written as a statement that if untrue may be disproved (or falsified) by evidence obtained in data collection. For example, following the savanna baboon observation from above, a researcher hypothesizes that savanna baboons that live in large groups have greater protection from predators than other types of baboons that live in small groups. This hypothesis is testable because the researcher can observe the two types of baboons living in different group sizes and collect relevant data about their predation risk and rates of survival.

The third stage of the scientific method is *data collection*. During this stage, the hypothesis is actually tested. Data (or evidence) are collected through experiment or further observations. What type of data are gathered and how the data are collected will depend on the hypothesis being tested. In our baboon example, the researcher must collect data about the number of predator attacks, type of predator attacks, and rates of injury and death in the different baboon group social situations. This kind of data collection is different from traditional experiments that are conducted in laboratories. Laboratory experiments can often be strictly controlled, and the scientist can target particular variables that will be manipulated or kept in check. This makes it possible to identify what causes certain results relatively clearly. It also makes it easy to repeat and verify these experiments and their outcomes. In contrast in the natural world, scientists cannot fully control the research situation, and they often have to work around various environmental barriers, such as bad weather, limited daylight, and skittish research subjects. Even without rigid controls over the study environment, scientists working in these conditions still follow the basic principles of repeatability and verifiability. They closely document each factor that may impact their results, so researchers in the future can repeat the work as closely as possible to test for similar outcomes.

The final stage of the scientific method is *interpretation*. The collected data are used to evaluate the hypothesis. Did the hypothesis adequately explain the early observation? Is there sufficient evidence to support the hypothesis, or should the hypothesis be rejected? In our savanna baboon example, did the researcher find more predation injuries and deaths among the baboons that live in small groups compared

**scientific theory**
a scientific explanation supported by substantial evidence

**social science** a discipline concerned with the study of human society, such as anthropology, psychology, or sociology

to the baboons living in larger groups? Conclusions from this research can then be used as the observations that jump-start another research project in the future. This makes the scientific method an ongoing cycle of knowledge building. Past research feeds current research, which in turn can spark future research with new data and new interpretations.

Because past scientific research becomes the foundation for new research, the scientific method is self-correcting. Later scientists often identify mistakes made in earlier research, and the research can then be performed again. When the same interpretations are supported by evidence from many different researchers and they are widely accepted by the scientific community, they may become a theory. A **scientific theory** is not a guess. It is an explanation supported by substantial evidence. However, this evidence does not mean that a scientific theory is an absolute truth. A scientific theory is still open to reinterpretation and rejection in the face of new evidence. There are several widely accepted scientific theories today, including the theory of evolution (see Lab 4 for more information).

# THE SCIENCE OF BIOLOGICAL ANTHROPOLOGY

Biological anthropologists are scientists. They apply the scientific method to questions about human biology. Because biological anthropologists study human biology in the context of human culture and behavior, biological anthropology is also a **social science**. Biological anthropologists use observations to generate hypotheses, and they accumulate data to evaluate those hypotheses. As previously discussed, some biological anthropology research can be conducted in controlled laboratory settings, similar to how many other scientists implement experiments. Much of the research, however, is conducted by making observations of animals in the wild or observations and analyses of the fossil record. The lack of laboratory experiments does not make biological anthropology unscientific. Remember, the scientific method requires that data are collected to test hypotheses, which is regularly done by biological anthropologists.

# CONCEPT REVIEW QUESTIONS

Name: _____  Section: _____

Course: _____  Date: _____

Answer the following questions in the space provided.

1. What are the *two* fundamental ideas used in anthropology?

2. Which field of anthropology studies the practices, beliefs, economics, politics, and gender roles of living people?

   A. Linguistic anthropology
   B. Archaeology
   C. Biological anthropology
   D. Cultural anthropology

3. Which field of anthropology uses a wide range of data about living and past organisms to study human evolution?

   A. Linguistic anthropology
   B. Archaeology
   C. Biological anthropology
   D. Cultural anthropology

4. Which subfield of biological anthropology uses the fossil record to examine the anatomy and behavior of our relatives in the past?

   A. Forensic anthropology
   B. Paleoanthropology
   C. Human biology
   D. Primatology

5. Which subfield of biological anthropology applies methods of skeletal analysis to study humans in a legal context?

   A. Forensic anthropology
   B. Paleoanthropology
   C. Human biology
   D. Primatology

6. During which stage of the scientific method is the hypothesis evaluated?

   A. Observation
   B. Hypothesis generation
   C. Data collection
   D. Interpretation

7. In the context of the scientific method, what is the hypothesis? How is it different from a scientific theory?

8.  Are scientific theories absolute truths? Why or why not?

9.  Are scientific theories guesses? Why or why not?

10. What is the biocultural approach in biological anthropology?

# LAB EXERCISES

Name: _____   Section: _____

Course: _____   Date: _____

## EXERCISE 1    FIELDS OF ANTHROPOLOGY SCENARIOS

For each of the scenarios below, read the research summary provided and answer the questions that follow with a group of your classmates.

### SCENARIO A

Anthropologists have studied the role of soybean curd and its related by-products in the culture of Hong Kong. The researchers interviewed people about how frequently they ate soybean products, where they ate them (at home or in restaurants), and during what time of day they ate them. The researchers also asked people about how they prepare soybean products, where they obtain soybean products, and any beliefs they might have about the soybean products (such as their nutritional value). The data were used to assess the role of soybean products in the culture. The researchers also considered how this relates to global soybean consumption patterns.

1. What is the primary field of anthropology addressed in this research?

2. Are there any other fields of anthropology addressed in this research?

3. What aspects of context must be considered as part of this research?

4. How might this research contribute to a comparative approach?

### SCENARIO B

An anthropologist has been researching how Native Americans in California were impacted by Spanish missionization from 1776 to 1830. The researcher is particularly interested in how Native Californians may have negotiated their identity and balanced traditional practices with colonial influences. Therefore, the anthropologist excavates material remains from areas where the Native Californians may have gone when they fled the Spanish missions. The material remains include things such as stone tools, shell beads, and historic bottle glass. These materials are analyzed and used in conjunction with historical documents to help the researcher better understand what life was like for the people at that time.

1. What is the primary field of anthropology addressed in this research?

2. Are there any other fields of anthropology addressed in this research?

3. What aspects of context must be considered as part of this research?

4. How might this research contribute to a comparative approach?

**SCENARIO C**

Building on previous research that shows people of different genders often communicate differently, an anthropologist has been studying how gendered communication impacts family interactions. The anthropologist uses recorded conversations from study families' homes. The anthropologist also uses documentary footage of family interactions. The interactions are analyzed for information about gendered communication, power relationships, and connections between various family members.

1. What is the primary field of anthropology addressed in this research?

2. Are there any other fields of anthropology addressed in this research?

3. What aspects of context must be considered as part of this research?

4. How might this research contribute to a comparative approach?

**SCENARIO D**

Anthropologists have been studying Y-chromosome DNA to understand where and when humans first appeared and when they moved into other areas of the world. The Y-chromosome is found only in males, and most of the DNA found on the Y-chromosome is passed directly from fathers to sons. Researchers collect Y-chromosome DNA information from men today and compare the amount of difference seen in the DNA. Greater amounts of genetic difference indicate longer periods of separation between different groups of people because it takes time to accumulate genetic variations. This Y-chromosome DNA research has helped anthropologists to understand our species' origin in Africa and our various migrations to other parts of the world.

1. What is the primary field of anthropology addressed in this research?

2. Are there any other fields of anthropology addressed in this research?

3. What aspects of context must be considered as part of this research?

4. How might this research contribute to a comparative approach?

**EXERCISE 2** **TYPES OF BIOLOGICAL ANTHROPOLOGY SCENARIOS**

For each of the scenarios below, read the research summary provided and answer the questions that follow with a group of your classmates.

**SCENARIO A**

Biological anthropologists have discovered a previously unknown fossil species. The species lived about 4.4 million years ago in Africa. The dating of this fossil species places it closer in time to the last common ancestor of humans and chimpanzees than most other known fossil species. This newly discovered species has an interesting mix of traits. For example, it has adaptations for climbing in trees as well as for walking on two legs on the ground. It does not directly resemble any of the living ape species, which suggests the living ape species (including humans) have each become adapted for their own environmental contexts over time.

1. What is the primary type of biological anthropology addressed in this research?

2. Does the research also touch on topics that might be relevant to researchers in disciplines outside anthropology, such as biology or psychology? If so, which ones?

3. How does this research relate to human evolution? In other words, what can we learn about human evolution from research along these lines?

Biological anthropologists have observed several chimpanzees in western Africa making tools to help them hunt. The chimpanzees were seen modifying branches and sticks into spears. They removed any leaves or small branches to make a smooth shaft. They also chewed on the end of the branches to give them sharp points. They then thrust the sharpened branches like spears into tree trunks, where small primates called galagos make sleeping nests. Although it remains unclear how successful the chimpanzees are in actually killing galagos, multiple members of the chimpanzee group have been observed producing the spears.

1. What is the primary type of biological anthropology addressed in this research?

2. Does the research also touch on topics that might be relevant to researchers in disciplines outside anthropology, such as biology or psychology? If so, which ones?

3. How does this research relate to human evolution? In other words, what can we learn about human evolution from research along these lines?

Biological anthropologists studied the relationship between stress and female reproduction in a rural community in Guatemala. The researchers collected regular urine samples from women over the course of 1 year. Stress hormone and reproductive hormone levels from the samples were measured to determine a possible relationship between stress and reproductive function. Results suggest that stress may negatively impact reproductive health.

1. What is the primary type of biological anthropology addressed in this research?

2. Does the research also touch on topics that might be relevant to researchers in disciplines outside anthropology, such as biology or psychology? If so, which ones?

3. How does this research relate to human evolution? In other words, what can we learn about human evolution from research along these lines?

**SCENARIO D**

Biological anthropologists in Australia were called on to help identify victims of a series of fires. They analyzed the skeletal material for indicators of sex and age, and they compared this information to medical records and other documents to help identify fire victims. The anthropologists worked as part of an interdisciplinary team that was investigating the mass disaster.

1. What is the primary type of biological anthropology addressed in this research?

2. Does the research also touch on topics that might be relevant to researchers in disciplines outside anthropology, such as biology or psychology? If so, which ones?

3. How does this research relate to human evolution? In other words, what can we learn about human evolution from research along these lines?

## EXERCISE 3  BIOLOGICAL ANTHROPOLOGY NEWS ARTICLE DISCUSSION

Your instructor has provided you with a news article related to biological anthropology. Read the article, and answer the following questions with a group of your classmates.

1. What is the overall topic of the article?

2. How does your article relate to human evolution? In other words, what can we learn about human evolution from the article?

3. Who do you think is the target audience for the article?

4. Is the author an expert biological anthropologist? Did the author interview and/or quote an expert biological anthropologist?

5. Is there some information that might be missing from the article? If so, what might have been left out?

6. Based on what you have discussed about this article, what biases and other factors should you consider when following popular media coverage of biological anthropology topics?

## EXERCISE 4   APPLY THE SCIENTIFIC METHOD (HUMAN BIOLOGY)

Work with a group of your classmates to read this scenario and answer the questions that follow.

Previous research shows that some human populations living at extremely high altitudes have larger lungs. Research has also shown that at high elevations the oxygen concentrations are lower, and people in these areas are at risk of not getting enough oxygen.

1. Generate a hypothesis about why people in high altitudes have larger lungs.

2. Describe the type or types of data you would ideally collect to test this hypothesis.

3. Describe what hypothetical data might support the hypothesis. For example, the hypothesis would be supported if we found data that indicated _____ .

4. Describe what hypothetical data might reject the hypothesis. For example, the hypothesis would be rejected if we found data that indicated _____ .

5. If you found data that rejected the hypothesis, how would you rewrite your hypothesis to account for your findings and begin again?

## EXERCISE 5 APPLY THE SCIENTIFIC METHOD (FORENSIC ANTHROPOLOGY)

Work with a group of your classmates to read this scenario and answer the questions that follow.
  Previous research shows that, in humans, the pelvic opening tends to be wider in females than it is in males.

1. Generate a hypothesis about what causes this pattern.

2. Describe the type or types of data you would ideally collect to test this hypothesis.

3. Describe what hypothetical data might support the hypothesis. For example, the hypothesis would be supported if we found data that indicated _____ .

4. Describe what hypothetical data might reject the hypothesis. For example, the hypothesis would be rejected if we found data that indicated _____ .

5.  If you found data that rejected the hypothesis, how would you rewrite your hypothesis to account for your findings and begin again?

<br><br>

**EXERCISE 6**  **APPLY THE SCIENTIFIC METHOD (PRIMATOLOGY)**

Work with a group of your classmates to read this scenario and answer the questions that follow.

Previous research shows chimpanzee males form alliances with one another while chimpanzee females do not. Research has also shown that adult chimpanzee females often split up and go to different areas to feed during the day while adult male chimpanzees spend more time together during the day.

1.  Generate a hypothesis about why chimpanzees behave this way.

<br><br>

2.  Describe the type or types of data you would ideally collect to test this hypothesis.

<br><br>

3.  Describe what hypothetical data might support the hypothesis. For example, the hypothesis would be supported if we found data that indicated _____ .

<br><br>

4.  Describe what hypothetical data might reject the hypothesis. For example, the hypothesis would be rejected if we found data that indicated _____ .

<br><br>

5.  If you found data that rejected the hypothesis, how would you rewrite your hypothesis to account for your findings and begin again?

## EXERCISE 7 APPLY THE SCIENTIFIC METHOD (PALEOANTHROPOLOGY)

Work with a group of your classmates to read this scenario and answer the questions that follow.

Previous research shows that Neanderthals successfully lived in extremely cold environments during the Ice Age in Europe. Research has also shown that toward the end of the Ice Age and around the time that humans moved into Europe, Neanderthals quickly became extinct.

1. Generate a hypothesis about what caused the demise of the Neanderthals.

2. Describe the type or types of data you would ideally collect to test this hypothesis.

3. Describe what hypothetical data might support the hypothesis. For example, the hypothesis would be supported if we found data that indicated _____ .

4. Describe what hypothetical data might reject the hypothesis. For example, the hypothesis would be rejected if we found data that indicated _____ .

5. If you found data that rejected the hypothesis, how would you rewrite your hypothesis to account for your findings and begin again?

## EXERCISE 8    DATA COLLECTION AND INTEROBSERVER ERROR

Have you ever found yourself debating with someone about the size, shape, or color of an object? You think it is a "large" egg, but someone else thinks it is an "extra large" egg. Or, you think the house is painted "moss" green, but someone else thinks the house is painted "avocado" green. These differences of perspective are quite common and can cause real problems in scientific investigations. In science, the difference between how two or more people observe an object or phenomenon is called *interobserver error*. When collecting data, researchers need to consider the possibility of interobserver error and account for it as much as possible, or their results could be skewed and inaccurate.

To explore how dramatic interobserver error can be, complete the following tasks with a group of your classmates.

**STEP 1** Collect the data. Each person in the group takes turns measuring the four objects provided by your instructor. Use the measuring implements your instructor gives you (tape measures, rulers, etc.), and enter your measurements in the appropriate column of the chart. Be sure to keep your measurements to yourself as you go, so you don't influence other people's outcomes.

### INTEROBSERVER ERROR CHART

|  | Observer 1 (Self) | Observer 2 | Observer 3 | Observer 4 |
|---|---|---|---|---|
| Object One |  |  |  |  |
| Object Two |  |  |  |  |
| Object Three |  |  |  |  |
| Object Four |  |  |  |  |

**STEP 2** Evaluate and compile the data. Now, compare and discuss your results with your group members, and enter their results in the appropriate columns of the chart as well.

    1. What differences do you notice?

    2. Why might these differences exist (remember to consider the objects being measured, the tool being used, and the people doing the measuring)?

## EXERCISE 9  DATA COLLECTION AND EVALUATION

Work with a group of your classmates to read this scenario and complete the tasks and questions that follow.

An employee at a shoe store has observed that taller customers have larger shoe sizes than customers who are shorter. She knows that shoe sizes are based on foot length, so she hypothesizes: *Compared to shorter people, taller people have longer feet.* Complete the following steps to apply the scientific method and help the salesperson evaluate her hypothesis.

**STEP 1**  Collect height data. For each person in your group or class, determine the individual's height using tape measures or measuring sticks. *Hint*: It may be easiest to hang a piece of paper on the wall and have each person stand next to the piece of paper. Mark the maximum height (without shoes on) and measure from the floor to that mark on the paper. Make sure only one person does all the measuring, so you avoid interobserver error.

**STEP 2**  Collect foot length data. For each person in your group or class, determine the individual's foot length using tape measures or rulers. *Hint*: It may be easiest to have each person remove a shoe and stand on a piece of paper on the floor. While the person is standing, have another person draw around the outside of the foot, keeping the pencil as close to the foot as possible. Have the person step off the paper and then measure the length of the foot outline from the back of the heel to the tip of the longest toe. Make sure only one person does all the measuring, so you avoid interobserver error.

**STEP 3**  Tabulate the data. Create a list or table for your data that shows the two sets of data for each person (height and foot length). For example, you can re-create the chart below with your own data:

| Name | Height | Foot Length |
|---|---|---|
| Eduardo | 5 ft 10 inches | 10.25 inches |
| Jane | 5 ft 1 inch | 8.75 inches |
| Susan | 5 ft 10 inches | 10 inches |
| Devon | 6 ft | 11 inches |
| Tim | 5 ft 5 inches | 9.25 inches |
| Lily | 5 ft | 9 inches |

**STEP 4**  Interpretation

1. Look for patterns in the data. Describe any patterns you find.

2. Based on the data you collected, is the hypothesis supported or rejected? Why?

# CRITICAL THINKING QUESTIONS

On a separate sheet of paper, answer the following questions.

1. How are cultural anthropology and linguistic anthropology similar? How are they different?

2. How are archaeology and cultural anthropology similar? How are they different?

3. How are archaeology and biological anthropology similar? How are they different?

4. This question may be completed independently or as a group exercise. Find a current news article, or choose one given to you by your instructor, that discusses a biological anthropology topic. Use that article to answer the following questions:
   - What is the overall topic of your article?
   - In which subfield of biological anthropology do you think this topic most belongs?
   - Does the article also touch on topics that might be part of a different field of anthropology (for example, archaeology)? If so, which one?
   - Does the article also touch on topics that might be relevant to researchers in disciplines outside anthropology (biology, psychology, etc.)? If so, which ones?
   - What do your answers to the questions above suggest about the broader significance and relevance of biological anthropology research?

5. In the scientific method, why is it important to generate hypotheses before collecting data?

6. In what way is the scientific method a continuous cycle?

7. How does a nonscientist's view of a theory differ from a scientist's view?

8. This question may be completed individually or as a group exercise. In Exercise 8, you and a group of your classmates collected data on the size of several objects and considered the resulting interobserver error. If you were going to use similar measurement data in a scientific investigation, how might you avoid interobserver error? If you were working with previous data, and there was no way to go back and avoid interobserver error, how might you account for this error in your results and interpretations?

The genetic code for every organism is housed in its DNA.

## Lab Learning Objectives

By the end of this lab, students should be able to:

- describe the basic parts of a cell.

- compare the processes of mitosis and meiosis, including a description of how meiosis relates to evolution.

- describe the components of chromosomes and DNA, including the principle of complementary base pairs.

- explain the process of DNA replication.

- explain the process of protein synthesis, including a comparison of the transcription and translation stages.

# LAB 2

# Genetics

It is early March 1953. James Watson (in his twenties) and Francis Crick (in his thirties) have been working off and on for the last year and a half on an interesting scientific problem. They have been trying to identify the structure of DNA. Research by other scientists has already identified the presence of the biological compounds adenine, thymine, guanine, and cytosine in DNA. Also, these compounds appear to follow some sort of pattern. The quantities of adenine and thymine are the same, and the quantities of guanine and cytosine are the same. Thanks to the hard work of another scientist, Rosalind Franklin (**FIGURE 2.1**), many X-ray photographs have been taken of DNA, and they show that it is a compact, potentially helical structure. These first steps have made a significant contribution to the understanding of DNA's overall shape and components, but many questions still remain. How is so much information kept in such a tiny package, and what could explain the paired quantities of the adenine, thymine, guanine, and cytosine molecules?

In a laboratory at the University of Cambridge in England, Watson and Crick have been trying to answer these questions. After months and months, and a few frustrating missteps, Watson has arrived to the laboratory with a new idea. What if the adenine and thymine bond together in the structure and the guanine and cytosine bond together? This would certainly explain their similar quantities, but is it real or another false lead?

**29**

A                                              B

**FIGURE 2.1 DNA Pioneers**
Much of what we know about DNA and genetics today is possible because
of the work of researchers like Rosalind Franklin (A) and James Watson
and Francis Crick (B) who discovered the underlying structure of DNA.

**prokaryote** organism
(such as a bacterium)
that has a cell
without a nucleus
and is often made of
only a single cell

**eukaryote** organism
(such as a plant or
animal) that is made
of many cells that
have cell nuclei

**nucleus** the area
inside a eukaryotic
cell that contains
most of the cell's
DNA

**DNA
(deoxyribonucleic
acid)** the chemical
that acts as the
genetic blueprint for
an organism

**nuclear DNA** the
DNA found in the
nucleus of the cell

**organelle** a type of
cell part with its
own function, like an
organ of the body

**mitochondria** cell
organelles that
produce energy for
the cell and that
contain their own
DNA

**mitochondrial DNA
(mtDNA)** the DNA
found in mitochondria
that is passed from
mothers to offspring

Watson and Crick get to work building, measuring, and refining a model of DNA based on this idea (and other ideas pieced together over the course of the past year). The model they construct takes the shape of a double helix with bonded pairs of adenine–thymine and guanine–cytosine running along the core. Their excitement mounts, and over the coming days, weeks, and months, their structure is verified by other scientists and supported by further X-ray photography. Watson and Crick (with the help of numerous other researchers) have just revolutionized our understanding of life on Earth! Their work earns them a Nobel Prize, and it forms the foundation of our modern understanding of genetics and the passing of traits between generations. Understanding these concepts allows us to better understand how evolution happens, and in this lab we review these foundational genetics concepts with this in mind.

## INTRODUCTION

We begin this lab with an introduction to cells, the basic building blocks of life. This includes a review of the parts of the cell related to genetics and inheritance and an examination of how cells divide and replicate. We also take a close look at the importance of cell division for evolution. We then focus on DNA—the genetic code passed from one generation to the next. We consider how DNA replicates and how it codes for proteins in the body.

## WHAT IS A CELL?

Cells are the most basic units of life. All living organisms are made of cells. Some organisms, such as bacteria, are made of only one cell. The cells of bacteria do not have a cell nucleus, and these organisms are called **prokaryotes**. Other organisms, such as plants and animals, are made of many cells. The cells of plants and animals have a cell nucleus, and these organisms are called **eukaryotes**. We will focus on eukaryotic cells because they are the cells found in humans, as well as other animals and plants.

Some of the major parts of eukaryotic cells are the nucleus, the mitochondria, the cytoplasm, and the cell membrane (**FIGURE 2.2**). The **nucleus** stores genetic information in the form of **DNA (deoxyribonucleic acid)**. This **nuclear DNA** holds almost all of the organism's genetic information, which together with environmental influences determines the appearance and behavior of an organism. Outside the nucleus, there are various other organelles. **Organelles** are cell parts that have different functions, similar to the special functions of different organs in the body. The *endoplasmic reticulum* is an organelle that holds *ribosomes*, which are important organelles for the production of the body's proteins. **Mitochondria** are organelles that produce "chemical power" for the cell. They take in nutrients and turn them into energy for the cell. Interestingly, mitochondria have their own DNA, separate from the DNA found in the cell nucleus. This DNA is called **mitochondrial DNA (mtDNA)**. This mtDNA has been very useful in attempts to track human lineages and relationships in the past because it is passed directly from a mother to her offspring. The nucleus and the cell organelles, such as mitochondria, are all suspended in the cell in a fluid called *cytoplasm*. Cytoplasmic fluid helps give cells their shape. All of these cell parts are held together by the *cell membrane*. This membrane is a barrier that separates the cell from its surroundings. The membrane is semipermeable, meaning some things can pass through the membrane while others cannot.

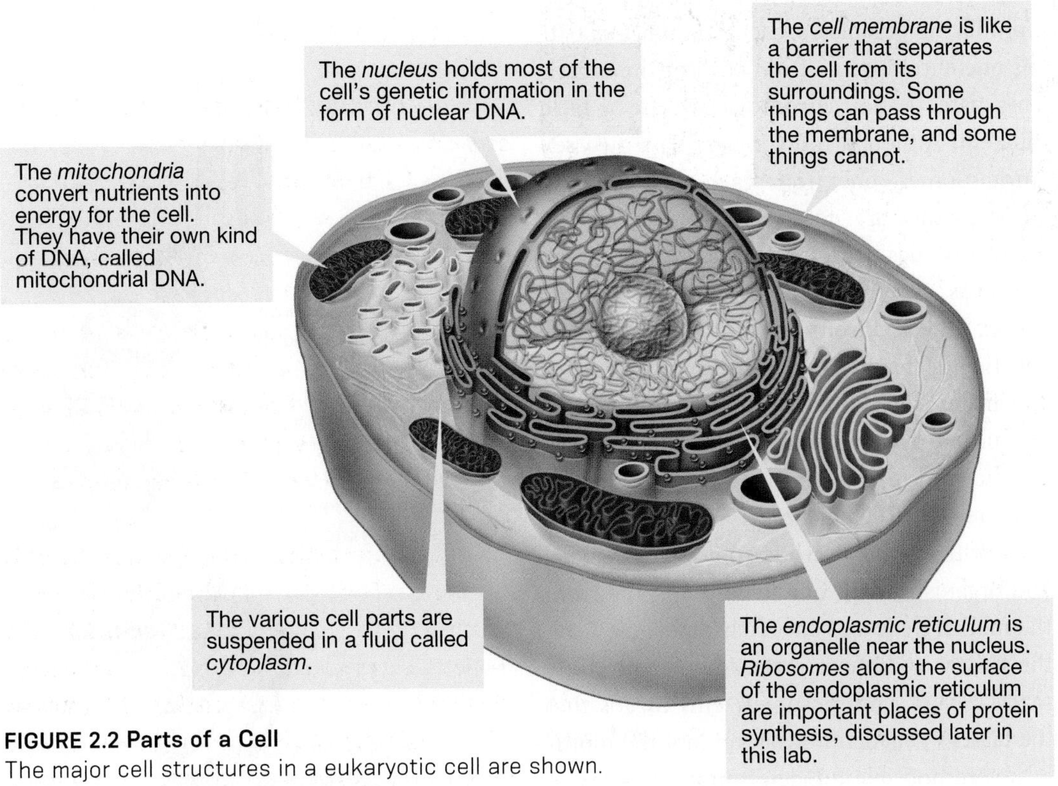

The *nucleus* holds most of the cell's genetic information in the form of nuclear DNA.

The *cell membrane* is like a barrier that separates the cell from its surroundings. Some things can pass through the membrane, and some things cannot.

The *mitochondria* convert nutrients into energy for the cell. They have their own kind of DNA, called mitochondrial DNA.

The various cell parts are suspended in a fluid called *cytoplasm*.

The *endoplasmic reticulum* is an organelle near the nucleus. *Ribosomes* along the surface of the endoplasmic reticulum are important places of protein synthesis, discussed later in this lab.

**FIGURE 2.2 Parts of a Cell**
The major cell structures in a eukaryotic cell are shown.

# THE GENETIC CODE

The DNA found inside the cell nucleus is the genetic information or blueprint for the organism. DNA is a chemical that is organized into **chromosomes** in the nucleus (**FIGURE 2.3**). These chromosomes are like long threads. A chromosome usually occurs as a single fiber called a **chromatid**, but chromatids can duplicate and occur in pairs when a cell is about to divide (see below). Chromosomes have an area that is contracted, called a **centromere**. The centromere can be located toward the end of the chromatid or in the middle, depending on the chromosome. This variation makes centromere position a useful tool for identifying chromosomes. Different species have different numbers of chromosomes, but the number of chromosomes found in an organism is not an indicator of an organism's complexity. For example, humans have 46 chromosomes, chimpanzees have 48 chromosomes, and turkeys have 82 chromosomes. None of these organisms is more or less complex than the others.

## Types of Chromosomes

There are two types of chromosomes: the autosomes and the sex chromosomes. The **autosomes**, or non-sex chromosomes, exist in homologous pairs. **Homologous pairs** are sets of matching chromosomes with similar types of genetic information, similar lengths, and similar centromere positions. In sexually

Centromeres

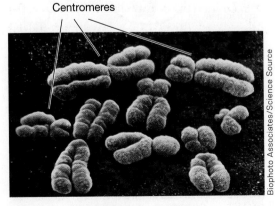

Biophoto Associates/Science Source

**FIGURE 2.3 Chromosomes**
These chromosomes made of paired chromatids show the diversity of chromosome size and shape. Also, note the different centromere locations on different chromosomes.

**chromosome** a tightly coiled strand of DNA within the cell nucleus

**chromatid** a single chromosome fiber that duplicates and occurs in pairs when a cell is about to divide

**centromere** the contracted area of a chromosome, whose position varies from one chromosome to the next, useful in distinguishing chromosomes

**autosome** a chromosome other than one of the sex chromosomes

**homologous pair** a set of matching chromosomes with similar types of genetic information, similar lengths, and similar centromere positions

**sex chromosome**
one of the two different chromosomes (X and Y) involved in the determination of an organism's biological sex

**X chromosome** the larger of the two sex chromosomes, having genetic information related to a wide range of traits

**Y chromosome** the smaller of the two sex chromosomes, having genetic information that codes primarily for traits related to maleness

**nucleotide** a set of linked phosphate, sugar, and nitrogen base molecules in DNA

**adenine** one of the nitrogen bases in DNA; its complement is thymine

**thymine** one of the nitrogen bases in DNA; its complement is adenine

**guanine** one of the nitrogen bases in DNA; its complement is cytosine

**cytosine** one of the nitrogen bases in DNA; its complement is guanine

reproducing organisms, each homologous pair has one chromosome from each of the organism's parents. **Sex chromosomes** are a little different. Although most people have two sex chromosomes, one from each parent, these chromosomes are not truly homologous like the autosomes. The two different sex chromosomes determine an organism's biological sex. The **X chromosome** is larger and has genetic information important to both females and males, such as genes that allow for color vision. The **Y chromosome** is smaller and has genetic information that codes primarily for traits related to "maleness." Generally, organisms with two X chromosomes are female, and organisms with one X chromosome from the mother's egg and one Y chromosome from the father's sperm are male. Importantly, only males have Y chromosomes. This means that the father's genetic information, not the mother's, is responsible for determining the sex of offspring. Only the inheritance of the father's Y chromosome can result in a male offspring. This is particularly interesting when considering that in many cultures, in the past and today, women are held responsible for the successful production of male heirs.

## DNA Structure

The genetic information on chromosomes is found in their DNA. The DNA has a double-helix shape, similar to a twisting ladder or spiral staircase. The sides of the ladder are formed by phosphates and sugars. The rungs of the ladder are made of nitrogen bases. Each set of linked phosphate, sugar, and nitrogen base molecules is called a **nucleotide**. The nucleotides on the two sides of the helix are held together by bonds between the nitrogen bases. There are four possible bases in DNA: **adenine**, **thymine**, **guanine**, and **cytosine**. These bases, often abbreviated A, T, G, and C, form complementary base pairs because each one only bonds with one of the other bases. Adenine and thymine always bond together, and guanine and cytosine always bond together **(FIGURE 2.4)**.

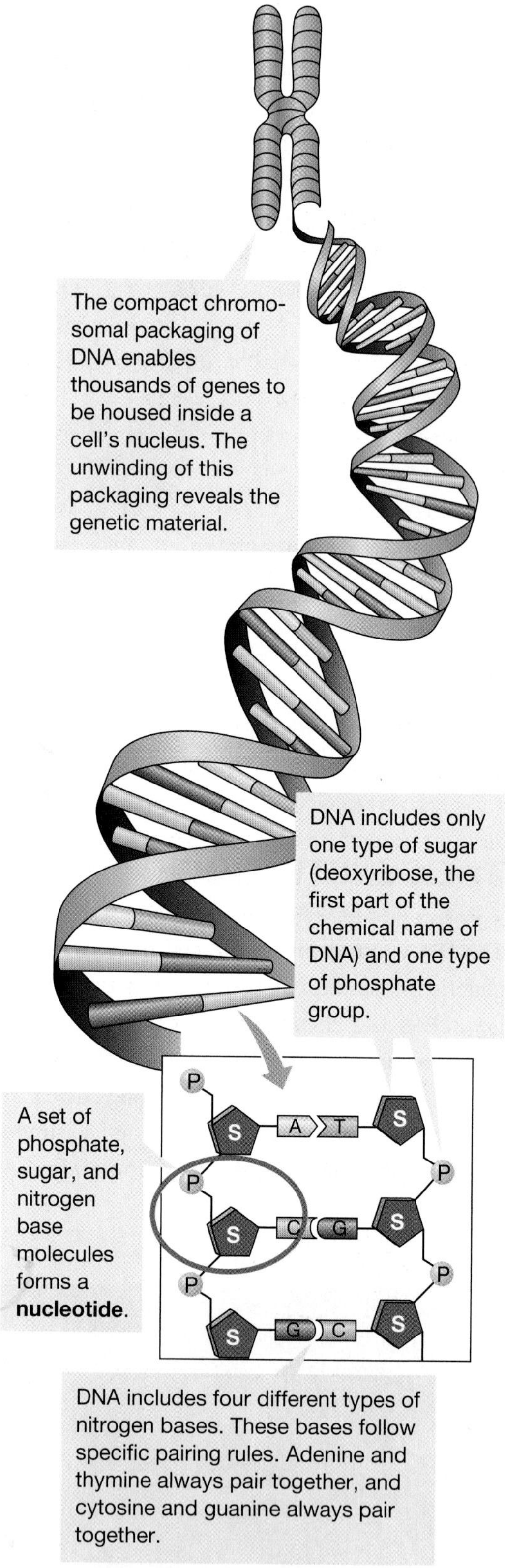

The compact chromosomal packaging of DNA enables thousands of genes to be housed inside a cell's nucleus. The unwinding of this packaging reveals the genetic material.

DNA includes only one type of sugar (deoxyribose, the first part of the chemical name of DNA) and one type of phosphate group.

A set of phosphate, sugar, and nitrogen base molecules forms a **nucleotide**.

DNA includes four different types of nitrogen bases. These bases follow specific pairing rules. Adenine and thymine always pair together, and cytosine and guanine always pair together.

**FIGURE 2.4 DNA Structure**
DNA resembles a twisted ladder, called a double helix. The rungs of the ladder are formed by the nitrogen bases. The sides of the ladder are formed by the phosphates and sugars.

## Genes and Alleles

Sections of DNA that code for particular traits are called **genes**, and each gene has alternate versions, called **alleles**. For each trait, there are multiple alleles (gene variations). Often, there are even multiple genes for a trait, which multiplies the number of alleles and variations. The genes for each trait are arranged as part of larger sequences of genes for many traits (**FIGURE 2.5**). These long gene sequences are the long strands of twisting DNA that make chromosomes. Chromosomes hold the genetic code that determines how our bodies look and function. The chromosomes act in particular ways during cell division to make sure the right amount of genetic information is passed into the replicated cells.

## Representing the Genetic Code: Karyotypes

An individual or species' chromosomal makeup is often represented in a **karyotype**—a picture of the chromosomes, numbered and laid out in their homologous pairs. Karyotypes are produced by staining chromosomes such that some bases (adenine and thymine) show as different colors than other bases (guanine and cytosine). The chromosomes are then matched to their homologous partners based on similarities in size, centromere location, and dye pattern. The

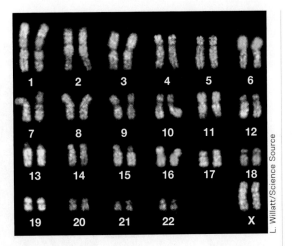

L. Willatt/Science Source

**FIGURE 2.6 Human Karyotype**
This human karyotype shows 46 chromosomes, arranged in 23 homologous pairs and laid out from largest to smallest. Note the sex chromosomes are placed at the end of the karyotype. This individual has two X chromosomes, so she is female.

homologous chromosomes are arranged and numbered in size order, from largest to smallest. In humans, this results in 23 pairs of chromosomes of different sizes (**FIGURE 2.6**). The sex chromosomes are often distinguished from the autosomes and placed at the end of the karyotype, despite their relatively larger size. Karyotypes can be used for a variety of purposes, including identifying chromosomal anomalies or comparing chromosomal information across species for classification purposes.

# DNA REPLICATION

**DNA replication** is the process that allows for the duplication of genetic information. It is the important first step in the cell division processes discussed below. During DNA replication, a strand of DNA is copied, resulting in two identical strands where there was previously one. The replication process is very simple (**FIGURE 2.7**). First, the DNA strand is unzipped by an enzyme when replication needs to occur. The bonds holding the two sides of the DNA ladder together weaken and allow the two sides to separate. This exposes the nitrogen bases that were previously bonded together. Second,

**gene** a section of DNA that codes for a particular trait

**allele** an alternate version of a gene

**karyotype** the picture of an individual's stained chromosomes, arranged in homologous pairs and laid out in order from largest to smallest

**DNA replication** the process whereby DNA is copied

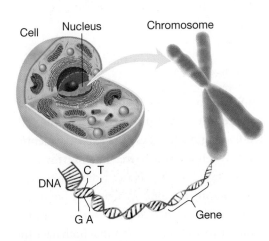

**FIGURE 2.5 The Organization of Genetic Material**
Sequences of genes form long DNA strands. The DNA strands coil to form the chromosomes in the cell nucleus.

**FIGURE 2.7 DNA Replication**

Because all of the bases in a sequence of DNA follow strict pairing rules, one side of a DNA strand can act as the blueprint for a complete strand during DNA replication. The existing nitrogen bases will attract complementary free-floating nucleotides.

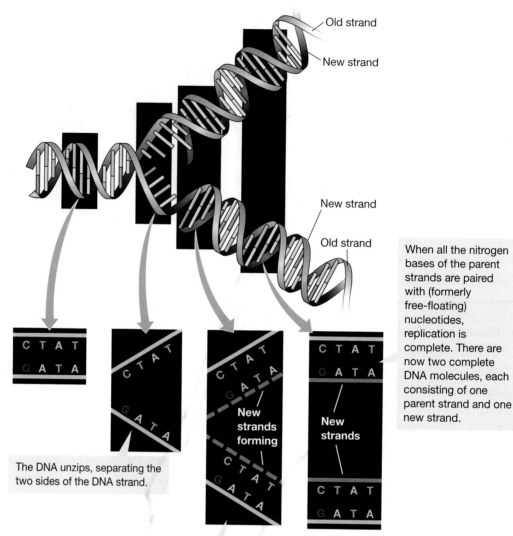

Old strand

New strand

New strand

Old strand

When all the nitrogen bases of the parent strands are paired with (formerly free-floating) nucleotides, replication is complete. There are now two complete DNA molecules, each consisting of one parent strand and one new strand.

C T A T
G A T A

C T A T
G A T A

New strands forming

C T A T
G A T A

New strands

C T A T
G A T A

C T A T
G A T A

The DNA unzips, separating the two sides of the DNA strand.

Free-floating nucleotides bond with the exposed nitrogen bases. This bonding follows the pairing rules, with adenine and thymine bonding together and cytosine and guanine bonding together.

free-floating nucleotides in the cell (sets of phosphates, sugars, and nitrogen bases) line up with the exposed sides of the DNA strand. The nucleotides and nitrogen bases bond, making a two-sided strand of DNA.

Because all of the bases in a sequence of DNA follow strict pairing rules, one side of a DNA strand can act as the blueprint for a complete strand. Each base on a side of DNA can determine which free-floating nucleotides are bonded to make a complete, two-sided DNA strand. Imagine there is a DNA strand with a bond between adenine and thymine. When this

strand separates for replication, the adenine and thymine are exposed and open for bonding with free-floating nucleotides. The exposed adenine can only bond with a free-floating thymine, and the exposed thymine can only bond with a free-floating adenine. When these bonds are formed with the free-floating nucleotides, the result is two sections of DNA that both have the same adenine–thymine bond. This structured pairing happens for each of the exposed sets of bases along the DNA strand, and each exposed base matches with its appropriate free-floating nucleotide until the strand is duplicated.

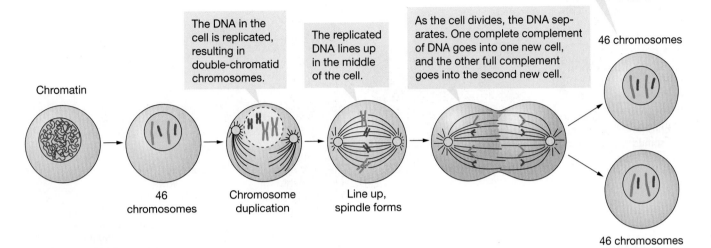

The DNA in the cell is replicated, resulting in double-chromatid chromosomes.

The replicated DNA lines up in the middle of the cell.

As the cell divides, the DNA separates. One complete complement of DNA goes into one new cell, and the other full complement goes into the second new cell.

Each new cell has a full set of DNA, with 23 pairs of chromosomes.

Chromatin

46 chromosomes

46 chromosomes

46 chromosomes

Chromosome duplication

Line up, spindle forms

46 chromosomes

**FIGURE 2.8 Mitosis**
The process of cell division that takes place in somatic cells is called mitosis. It involves one cell division, and it results in two daughter cells that are exact copies of the original cell.

# CELL DIVISION

Humans have two different types of cells: somatic cells and gametes. **Somatic cells** are called body cells because they are the cells that make up our different body parts. Hair, organs, bone, fat, and other body parts are made of somatic cells. **Gametes** are called sex cells because they are the cells involved in sexual reproduction. Males have sperm, and females have ova (eggs). New cells are produced in our bodies through a process called cell division. Generally, cell division in somatic cells occurs through **mitosis**, and cell division in gametes happens through **meiosis**.

In humans, mitosis begins with the 46 single-chromatid chromosomes in the somatic cell. The chromosomes duplicate via DNA replication to form double-chromatid chromosomes. These chromosomes align in the middle of the cell in single file. Then, the chromosomes split in half at their centromeres and each chromatid goes to different sides of the cell. The cell then pinches in at the middle, leaving two cells that each have a complete set of 46 single-chromatid chromosomes. This process begins with one cell and ends with two daughter cells that are both exact replicas of the original

cell (**FIGURE 2.8**). The process of mitosis creates new somatic cells, which allows for growth and repair of damaged tissue in the body.

Meiosis is a little different (**FIGURE 2.9**). Meiosis begins with a gamete-forming cell containing 46 single-chromatid chromosomes that replicate to form double-chromatid chromosomes. As in mitosis, these chromosomes then line up in the center of the cell, this time with their homologous partner. The homologous chromosomes in this stage of meiosis can exchange genetic information with their partner. This is called **crossing-over** because genetic information is exchanged from one chromosome to the other chromosome (Figure 2.9B). After crossing-over, the chromosomes divide for the first time. The double-chromatid chromosomes do not split in half as they do in mitosis at this stage. Instead, the chromosomes remain intact, and the different members of homologous pairs move to different ends of the cell. Then, the cell pinches in and creates two cells, called daughter cells. Remember that because of the crossing-over that occurred earlier, some genetic information has been exchanged, leading to new combinations of genes that were not present before. This means the daughter cells are not identical

**somatic cell** a non-sex cell that makes up different body parts; also called body cell

**gamete** a sex cell (in humans, sperm or egg)

**mitosis** the process of cell division that occurs in somatic cells

**meiosis** the process of cell division that produces gametes

**crossing-over** the stage in meiosis during which genetic information is exchanged between the two chromosomes in a homologous pair

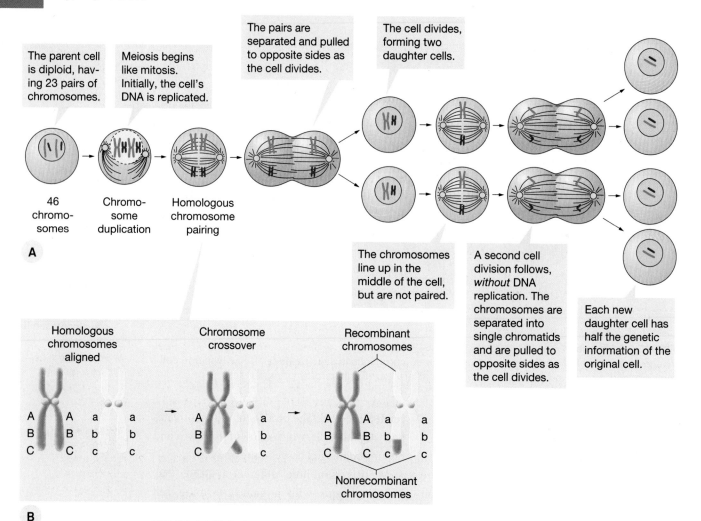

The parent cell is diploid, having 23 pairs of chromosomes.

Meiosis begins like mitosis. Initially, the cell's DNA is replicated.

The pairs are separated and pulled to opposite sides as the cell divides.

The cell divides, forming two daughter cells.

46 chromosomes

Chromosome duplication

Homologous chromosome pairing

**A**

The chromosomes line up in the middle of the cell, but are not paired.

A second cell division follows, *without* DNA replication. The chromosomes are separated into single chromatids and are pulled to opposite sides as the cell divides.

Each new daughter cell has half the genetic information of the original cell.

Homologous chromosomes aligned

Chromosome crossover

Recombinant chromosomes

A A a    a
B B b    b
C C c    c

A        a
B        b
C        c

A        a
B        b
C        c

A A a    a
B B b    b
C C c    c

Nonrecombinant chromosomes

**B**

**FIGURE 2.9 Meiosis and Crossing-over**
(A) The process of cell division that takes place to make gametes is called meiosis. It involves two cell divisions, and it results in four daughter cells that have half the genetic information of the original cell. (B) Early in meiosis, homologous pairs of chromosomes line up in the middle of the cell and swap genetic information during a process called crossing-over.[1]

**genetic recombination** the mixing of genetic information into new combinations that occurs during meiosis

to each other nor to the original cell. The two daughter cells then undergo a second division. The double-chromatid chromosomes move to the center of the cell. The double-chromatid chromosomes then split at their centromeres, as in mitosis. The single-chromatid chromosomes move to opposite sides of the cell, and the cell pinches at the middle, leaving two cells. Because there were two daughter cells after the first division that then divided again, meiosis results in a total of four daughter cells. Each of the four cells has 23 single-chromatid chromosomes (half the genetic information of the original cell) (Figure 2.9A). The process of meiosis creates gametes (sperm and ova in humans), which are necessary for sexual reproduction.

Meiosis is very important to evolution because it results in **genetic recombination**. This does not mean that entirely new genes are created. It means that the existing genes are mixed up in new combinations. As the chromosomes cross over and the cell is divided, new combinations of genetic information are formed. For example, even though two traits are carried on the same chromosome, they may not necessarily be inherited together. If one of those traits is exchanged with the homologous chromosome during crossing-over, the two traits

[1] Adapted from OpenStax College. 2014. Concepts of biology. OpenStax CNX. cnx.org/contents/b3c1e1d2-839c-42b0-a314-e119a8aafbdd@8.49. Textbook content produced by OpenStax College is licensed under a Creative Commons Attribution License 3.0 license.

become separated. When the cell divides, the two traits will end up in different daughter cells and will not be inherited together. This leads to variation, and variation plays a key role in evolution. At the same time, each daughter cell in meiosis carries only half of a parent's possible genes. So, if a person only has one offspring, only half of their genes will be passed to the next generation. If a person has two offspring, there is a greater likelihood of passing on more of their possible genes; however it is not guaranteed that the parent's entire genome is represented in those two offspring. Remember, the parent's genes are going to be recombined during each meiosis event. There will be some overlap in genes that are passed to both of the offspring, and there will be some genes that are passed only to one offspring and not the other offspring. Even if a person has 100 offspring, some of their genes will never be passed to their children. This variation in genetic recombination and genetic representation across generations is central to evolution.

## PROTEIN SYNTHESIS

DNA is the template for proteins in our body. Proteins are chemicals that form and regulate tissues in the body, and they are the physical expression of our genetic code. Proteins themselves are made of amino acids that are produced by the body or obtained through certain foods. The number and combination of amino acids control the kind of protein that is formed. The amino acids that are produced in the body are defined by the DNA sequence. So, a sequence of DNA codes for a specific sequence of amino acids, which determines a protein. This process of determining proteins from a DNA sequence is called **protein synthesis**.

There are two primary steps to protein synthesis. The first step is called **transcription**. Nuclear DNA cannot leave the cell nucleus, so the DNA must be transcribed to another form that can leave the nucleus and code for proteins elsewhere **(FIGURE 2.10)**. Transcription, then, is basically a copying process. In fact, it

begins very similarly to DNA replication. First, the DNA strand unzips, exposing the two sides of the strand. The exposed bases on one side of the strand attract free-floating nucleotides. However, these nucleotides are not DNA nucleotides. They are **ribonucleic acid (RNA)** nucleotides. RNA is similar to DNA, except that its sugar is slightly different and, instead of thymine, RNA has uracil. Uracil bonds with adenine in RNA, just like thymine bonds with adenine in DNA. The cytosine and guanine in RNA bond with each other, as in DNA. The exposed bases on the template strand of the unzipped DNA strand bond with the appropriate free-floating RNA nucleotides, following the same matching principles seen in DNA replication. This forms a strand of RNA called **messenger RNA (mRNA)**. The mRNA separates from the DNA and moves outside the nucleus to the cell cytoplasm, and the original DNA strand stays inside the nucleus and closes back up (Figure 2.10A).

The second step of protein synthesis is called **translation**. During translation, the RNA is translated (or interpreted) to form a sequence of amino acids that forms a specific protein. Having moved into the cytoplasm, the mRNA now attaches to ribosomes, the organelles where protein synthesis occurs. Inside the cytoplasm there is another form of RNA called **transfer RNA (tRNA)**. The tRNA contains triplets of bases called **anticodons**. These free-floating tRNA molecules seek out complementary mRNA triplets called **codons**. Again, the basic rules of base pairing apply. Each mRNA codon is a series of three bases that will only match the appropriate series of bases in the complementary tRNA anticodon. For example, an mRNA codon of adenine-guanine-uracil will match with a tRNA anticodon of uracil-cytosine-adenine. Each tRNA molecule carries a specific amino acid that corresponds to its anticodon. The series of mRNA codons are read in order, like you read a line of text on a page. As each mRNA codon is read, the tRNA with the appropriate anticodon and amino acid are brought over. These amino acids then link together in long chains to make proteins (Figure 2.10B).

**protein synthesis** the process of determining proteins from a DNA sequence

**transcription** the first step of protein synthesis where nuclear DNA is transcribed into messenger RNA that can leave the cell nucleus

**RNA (ribonucleic acid)** a chemical that is similar to DNA, except it contains uracil instead of thymine; it plays vital roles in the process of protein synthesis

**messenger RNA (mRNA)** the RNA formed in the first stage of protein synthesis (transcription) that brings the genetic information from the cell nucleus to the ribosome

**translation** the second step of protein synthesis where RNA is translated (or read) to form a sequence of amino acids that forms a protein

**transfer RNA (tRNA)** the RNA that helps form the amino acid chains in the second stage of protein synthesis (translation)

**anticodon** a triplet of bases in transfer RNA

**codon** a triplet of bases in DNA (or messenger RNA)

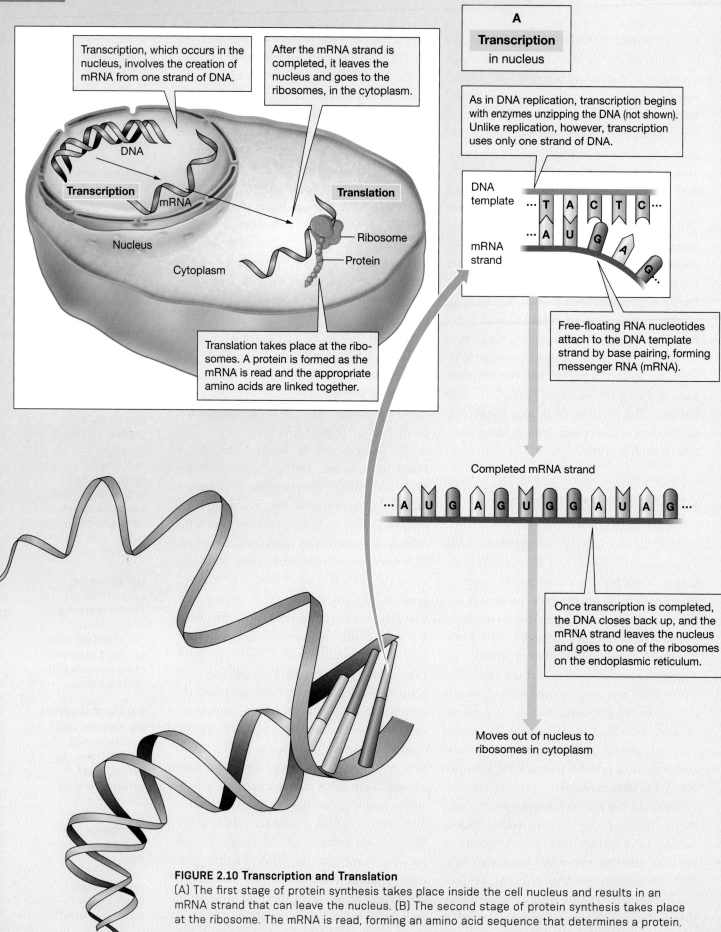

Transcription, which occurs in the nucleus, involves the creation of mRNA from one strand of DNA.

After the mRNA strand is completed, it leaves the nucleus and goes to the ribosomes, in the cytoplasm.

DNA

**Transcription**

mRNA

Nucleus

**Translation**

Cytoplasm

Ribosome

Protein

Translation takes place at the ribosomes. A protein is formed as the mRNA is read and the appropriate amino acids are linked together.

**A**

**Transcription**
in nucleus

As in DNA replication, transcription begins with enzymes unzipping the DNA (not shown). Unlike replication, however, transcription uses only one strand of DNA.

DNA template

... T A C T C ...

mRNA strand

... A U G A G ...

Free-floating RNA nucleotides attach to the DNA template strand by base pairing, forming messenger RNA (mRNA).

Completed mRNA strand

... A U G A G U G G A U A G ...

Once transcription is completed, the DNA closes back up, and the mRNA strand leaves the nucleus and goes to one of the ribosomes on the endoplasmic reticulum.

Moves out of nucleus to ribosomes in cytoplasm

**FIGURE 2.10 Transcription and Translation**
(A) The first stage of protein synthesis takes place inside the cell nucleus and results in an mRNA strand that can leave the nucleus. (B) The second stage of protein synthesis takes place at the ribosome. The mRNA is read, forming an amino acid sequence that determines a protein.

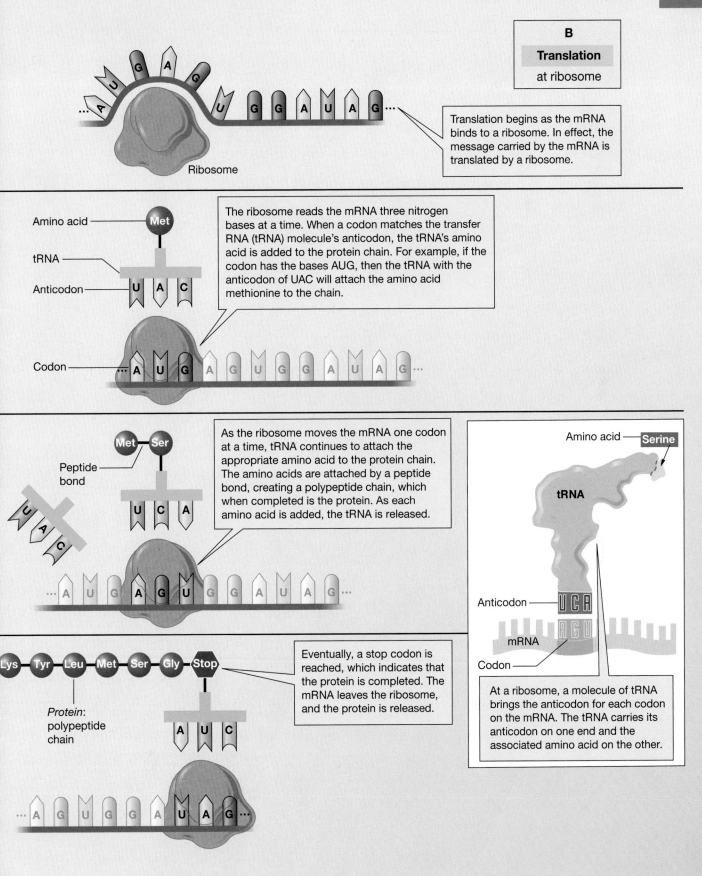

**B**

**Translation**

at ribosome

Translation begins as the mRNA binds to a ribosome. In effect, the message carried by the mRNA is translated by a ribosome.

Ribosome

Amino acid — Met

tRNA

Anticodon — U A C

The ribosome reads the mRNA three nitrogen bases at a time. When a codon matches the transfer RNA (tRNA) molecule's anticodon, the tRNA's amino acid is added to the protein chain. For example, if the codon has the bases AUG, then the tRNA with the anticodon of UAC will attach the amino acid methionine to the chain.

Codon — ...A U G A G U G G A U A G...

Met — Ser

Peptide bond

U C A

U A C

...A U G A G U G G A U A G...

As the ribosome moves the mRNA one codon at a time, tRNA continues to attach the appropriate amino acid to the protein chain. The amino acids are attached by a peptide bond, creating a polypeptide chain, which when completed is the protein. As each amino acid is added, the tRNA is released.

Amino acid — Serine

tRNA

Anticodon — UCA

mRNA

Codon

At a ribosome, a molecule of tRNA brings the anticodon for each codon on the mRNA. The tRNA carries its anticodon on one end and the associated amino acid on the other.

Lys — Tyr — Leu — Met — Ser — Gly — Stop

*Protein*: polypeptide chain

A U C

Eventually, a stop codon is reached, which indicates that the protein is completed. The mRNA leaves the ribosome, and the protein is released.

...A G U G G A U A G...

# CONCEPT REVIEW QUESTIONS

Name: _____     Section: _____

Course: _____     Date: _____

Answer the following questions in the space provided.

1.  What is the difference between a prokaryote and a eukaryote?

    *prokaryote does not have a nucleus*

2.  Which of the following cell parts produces energy for the cell and has its own DNA?

    A.  Nucleus
    B.  Cytoplasm
    C.  Cell membrane
    D.  Mitochondria *(circled)*

3.  What do the two members of a homologous chromosome pair have in common?

    *Centro*

4.  Following the rules of complementary base pairing, which of these DNA bases could successfully bond with adenine?

    A.  Thymine
    B.  Guanine
    C.  Adenine
    D.  Cytosine

5.  Following the rules of complementary base paring, which of these RNA bases could successfully bond with adenine?

    A.  Thymine
    B.  Uracil
    C.  Cytosine
    D.  Adenine

6.  Variations of the same gene are called _____*Alleles*_____.

7.  Mitosis occurs in which type of cell?

    *Somatic*

8.  Meiosis occurs in which type of cell?

    *gamete*

9.  The genetic information that moves from the nucleus to the cytoplasm of a cell during protein synthesis is called

    A.  mDNA.
    B.  tRNA.
    C.  mRNA. *(circled)*
    D.  tDNA.

10. During protein synthesis, the amino acids are transported by

    A.  mDNA.
    B.  tRNA. *(circled)*
    C.  mRNA.
    D.  tDNA.

# LAB EXERCISES

Name: _____    Section: _____

Course: _____    Date: _____

## EXERCISE 1    CREATING AND INTERPRETING KARYOTYPES

Your instructor has provided you and a group of your classmates with the stained chromosomes from person Z. Follow these steps to create person Z's karyotype and answer the questions.

**STEP 1**  Match each chromosome to its homologous partner (remember to look for similar size, centromere location, and staining patterns).

**STEP 2**  Arrange the chromosome pairs in order from largest to smallest.

**STEP 3**  Match the sex chromosomes provided by your instructor.

1.  How many autosomes does person Z have? How many sex chromosomes?

2.  Is person Z male or female? Why?

**COMPARING KARYOTYPES**

Work with a group of your classmates to review the two karyotypes and answer the questions.
Note the karyotypes provided depict single chromosomes, rather than homologous pairs.

1. Describe two things the karyotypes have in common.

2. Describe two things that differ between the karyotypes.

3. Which karyotype is from a human? How do you know this?

4. Which karyotype is from a chimp? How do you know this?

**PHASES OF MITOSIS**

The phases of mitosis depicted are out of order. Work with a group of your classmates to number the phases based on their correct order, beginning with number 1.

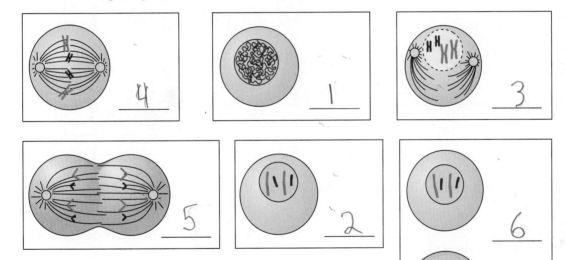

**PHASES OF MEIOSIS**

The phases of meiosis depicted are out of order. Work with a group of your classmates to number the phases based on their correct order, beginning with number 1.

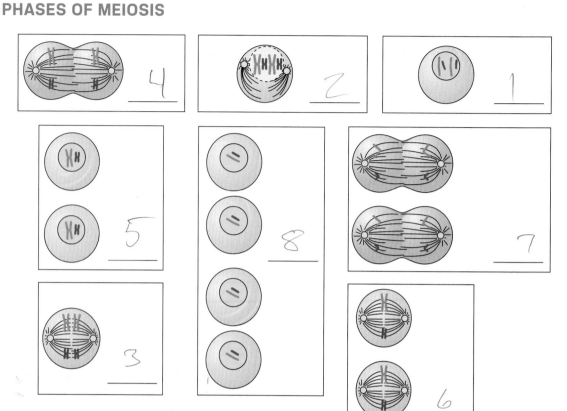

**MITOSIS AND MEIOSIS COMPARISON**

Work with a group of your classmates to review the cell division processes in Exercises 3 and 4 (or the diagrams of mitosis and meiosis from Figures 2.8 and 2.9). Use the information to compare the two processes of cell division and complete the following chart and questions.

For each of the descriptions on the left, place a mark in the appropriate cell division column on the right.

|  | Mitosis | Meiosis |
|---|---|---|
| Occurs in Gamete-Forming Cells |  |  |
| Occurs in Somatic Cells |  |  |
| Has One Cell Division |  |  |
| Has Two Cell Divisions |  |  |
| Results in Two Daughter Cells |  |  |
| Results in Four Daughter Cells |  |  |
| Results in Daughter Cells with Half the Original Cell's Genetic Material |  |  |
| Results in Daughter Cells That Are Exact Copies of the Original Cell |  |  |

1. Which process of cell division allows for growth and repair of damaged tissue?

2. Which process of cell division produces cells necessary for reproduction?

3. Which process results in recombination of genetic material?

## EXERCISE 6    RECOMBINATION

For this exercise, use the cards provided in the lab Appendix or at the very back of this manual on heavier paper. There are five pairs in the set, distinguished by different colors (a pair of white cards, a pair of blue cards, a pair of yellow cards, etc.). Each color pair represents a section of DNA from a particular chromosome.

| Color of Card Pair | Chromosome Represented |
|---|---|
| Blue | Chromosome 4 |
| Red | Chromosome 7 |
| Yellow | Chromosome 10 |
| Green | Chromosome 15 |
| White | Chromosome 20 |

Within a color pair, one card is labeled "Parental" and the other is labeled "Recombinant." These cards represent some of the DNA an offspring may inherit. If an offspring inherits the parental version of a chromosome card, the DNA was *not* recombined and was transmitted in its original form. If an offspring inherits the recombinant version of a chromosome card, the DNA was recombined and was transmitted in its new form.

**STEP 1**  Separate your pairs of cards into five piles, based on the color on their backs. Pick up the two blue cards and shuffle them. Then, lay both blue cards facedown on the table next to each other. Repeat this process with the other color pairs until all five sets have been shuffled and laid out facedown next to each other.

**STEP 2**  Randomly select one card from each color pair until you have five different colored cards. These five cards represent the versions of the DNA that were passed to Offspring 1. Turn the five cards over to see which versions of the chromosomes Offspring 1 inherited. For each chromosome color, indicate whether Offspring 1 inherited the parental or recombinant form in the following chart.

**STEP 3**  Replace the five cards you selected. Reshuffle them with their color partners, and lay them facedown again in their color pairs. Repeat step 2 to determine the versions of the chromosomes inherited by Offspring 2. Write your results in the chart.

**STEP 4**  Continue replacing, shuffling, and reselecting cards for additional offspring until your chart is complete. (*Note*: If you have time, you may run the results for 10 offspring total.)

| | Offspring 1 | Offspring 2 | Offspring 3 | Offspring 4 | Offspring 5 |
|---|---|---|---|---|---|
| Blue | | | | | |
| Red | | | | | |
| Yellow | | | | | |
| Green | | | | | |
| White | | | | | |
| Total Percentage Recombinant | | | | | |

**STEP 5** For each offspring, determine what percentage of the group of five chromosomes was inherited in a new, recombined form. (*Note*: 1/5 = 20%, 2/5 = 40%, 3/5 = 60%, etc.) Write your answers in the space provided in the last row of the chart.

**STEP 6** Evaluate your results.

    1. Do all offspring from the same parents inherit the same versions of the available genetic material? Why or why not?

    2. How many offspring inherited all 100% of their parent's original DNA?

    3. How does recombination impact genetic variation in future generations?

## EXERCISE 7   DNA REPLICATION

Work with a partner to complete this exercise.

**STEP 1** Review the imaginary strand of DNA below. Note the complementary base pairs.

A G C A A T C C G T C T T G G
T C G T T A G G C A G A A C C

**STEP 2** To begin replicating this strand of DNA, draw the two sides of the strand separating.

**STEP 3** Now, draw the free-floating bases linking up with the separate sides. Remember to follow the rules of complementary base pairing.

**STEP 4** Draw the two resulting DNA strands.

## EXERCISE 8  MAKING PROTEINS

Work with a partner to complete this exercise. You will use the DNA strand from Exercise 7 to make the protein for which it codes.

**STEP 1**  Draw the original DNA strand from Exercise 7 below.

**STEP 2**  Draw the DNA strand separating down the middle (as in the beginning of DNA replication).

**STEP 3**  Draw the free-floating RNA bases linking up with the *top* side of the DNA strand. Remember to follow the rules of complementary base pairing and to account for the special RNA base, uracil.

**STEP 4**  Draw the new mRNA strand *and* the rezipped DNA strand. Label which strand stays in the nucleus *and* which strand moves to the ribosome.

**STEP 5**  Draw the free-floating tRNA anticodons attracted by the mRNA codons in the ribosome. Be sure to follow the rules of complementary base pairing.

**STEP 6** Review the mRNA codons and tRNA anticodons in your drawing above. Remember, each tRNA anticodon will bring a specific amino acid, as indicated by the mRNA codon sequence. Use the mRNA codons and the amino acid chart provided to help you write the amino acid sequence for this RNA strand in the space below.

## CHART OF AMINO ACIDS BY mRNA CODONS

| | | | |
|---|---|---|---|
| UUU...Phenylalanine | UCU...Serine | UAU...Tyrosine | UGU...Cysteine |
| UUC...Phenylalanine | UCC...Serine | UAC...Tyrosine | UGC...Cysteine |
| UUA...Leucine | UCA...Serine | UAA...Stop codon | UGA...Stop codon |
| UUG...Leucine | UCG...Serine | UAG...Stop codon | UGG...Tryptophan |
| CUU...Leucine | CCU...Proline | CAU...Histidine | CGU...Arginine |
| CUC...Leucine | CCC...Proline | CAC...Histidine | CGC...Arginine |
| CUA...Leucine | CCA...Proline | CAA...Glutamine | CGA...Arginine |
| CUG...Leucine | CCG...Proline | CAG...Glutamine | CGG...Arginine |
| AUU...Isoleucine | ACU...Threonine | AAU...Asparagine | AGU...Serine |
| AUC...Isoleucine | ACC...Threonine | AAC...Asparagine | AGC...Serine |
| AUA...Isoleucine | ACA...Threonine | AAA...Lysine | AGA...Arginine |
| AUG...Methionine; Start codon | ACG...Threonine | AAG...Lysine | AGG...Arginine |
| GUU...Valine | GCU...Alanine | GAU...Aspartate | GGU...Glycine |
| GUC...Valine | GCC...Alanine | GAC...Aspartate | GGC...Glycine |
| GUA...Valine | GCA...Alanine | GAA...Glutamate | GGA...Glycine |
| GUG...Valine | GCG...Alanine | GAG...Glutamate | GGG...Glycine |

1. Which steps in the exercise re-created the transcription stage of protein synthesis?

2. Which steps in the exercise re-created the translation stage of protein synthesis?

3. Why is it necessary for RNA to be involved in protein synthesis? In other words, why is DNA unable to synthesize proteins on its own?

On a separate sheet of paper, answer the following questions.

1. This question may be completed independently or as a group exercise. You have learned that humans have 46 total chromosomes, and chimpanzees have 48 total chromosomes. Use other textbooks in biological anthropology and biology (or reputable online resources) to find the number of chromosomes in other organisms. Give an organism with considerably more chromosomes than humans. Give an organism with considerably fewer chromosomes than humans. Did your findings surprise you? What did your research suggest about the relationship between chromosome number and organism complexity?

2. Why don't the sex chromosomes have true homologous partners like the autosomes?

3. This question may be completed independently or as a group discussion. What do you think might happen if a person had two X chromosomes and one Y chromosome? Would this person be male or female? What would they look like?

4. Why is it important that mitosis result in daughter cells that are exact copies of the original cell's 46 chromosomes?

5. Why is it important that meiosis result in daughter cells that have half of the original cell's chromosomes?

6. How are RNA and DNA similar? How are they different?

7. Describe the difference between the transcription step and the translation step in protein synthesis.

8. Repeat Exercises 7 and 8, using this DNA strand:

   C G T T A A C T G A C G G A C
   G C A A T T G A C T G C C T G

# APPENDIX:
# LAB EXERCISE RESOURCES

## Exercise 6 Recombination

Cut along the dotted lines to separate the cards.

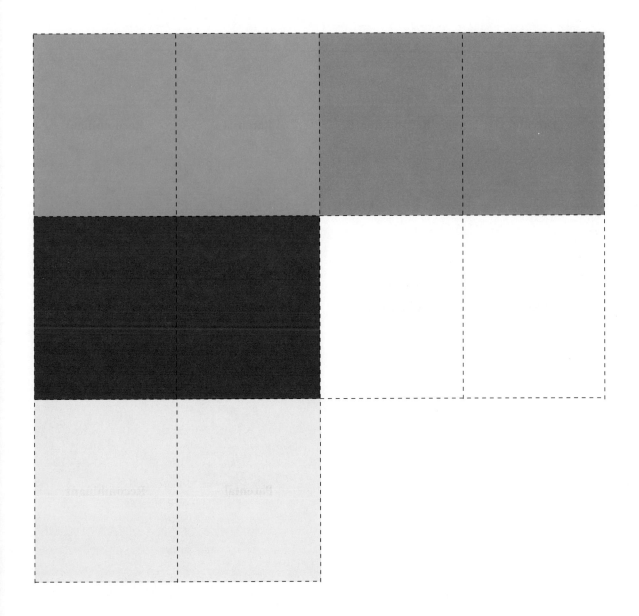

| Parental | Recombinant | Parental | Recombinant |
| Parental | Recombinant | Parental | Recombinant |
| | | Parental | Recombinant |

Courtesy of Teresa Soluri

Courtesy of Sabrina Agarwal

These photos show author (Soluri) with her sister, father, and brother and author (Agarwal) with her mother. Note that family members often resemble one another and share physical features in common.

## Lab Learning Objectives

By the end of this lab, students should be able to:

- describe the work of Gregor Mendel, including the types of data he collected and the laws derived from this research (the law of segregation and the law of independent assortment).

- describe the relationship between dominant and recessive alleles and the relationship between genotypes and phenotypes for traits.

- draw and interpret Punnett squares and pedigree diagrams.

- compare Mendelian and polygenic traits, using examples from humans.

- discuss the complexities of inheritance exemplified by the ABO blood group in humans.

LAB 3

# Inheritance

All her life, Dr. Soluri—one of the authors of this text—has been told that she has her father's eyes. When she looks at pictures of herself standing next to her father and siblings, the similarities in their features do appear pronounced. The same is true for Dr. Agarwal—the other author of this text—who bears a strong resemblance to her mother. Is this an optical illusion? Do people only see familial similarities because they have been told for so long that they exist? Or do people really share some physical traits in common with their family? If we share traits with our parents, how does this come to be? And why do siblings sometimes have the same traits? This lab touches on these issues, allowing us to answer some of these questions and explore larger issues of population changes over time.

# INTRODUCTION

In this lab, we begin with early research on inheritance—the passing of traits from one generation to the next—conducted by Gregor Mendel. We then consider the relationship between dominant alleles and recessive alleles and the relationship between genotypes and phenotypes. We also discuss different ways of representing inheritance using Punnett squares and pedigree diagrams. We distinguish between Mendelian and polygenic traits, using examples of these traits in humans. We conclude with a look at the ABO blood group in humans as an example of how issues of inheritance play out in real life.

# GREGOR MENDEL

In the mid-1800s, an Augustinian friar named **Gregor Mendel** conducted a series of tests in a monastery located in the present-day Czech Republic. He crossbred pea plants in the monastery garden and tracked the expression of different characteristics across multiple generations. Some of the traits he studied included flower color, stem length, and pea color (**FIGURE 3.1**). For each of these traits, he identified two possible forms. Flowers were purple or white; stems were tall or short; peas were yellow or green. He noticed that there were regular outcomes when plants with different traits were bred. This allowed him to identify two key principles.

The first of Mendel's principles is the **law of segregation**. Many people assumed that traits from two parents were blended in their offspring. This would mean that if a tall pea plant and a short pea plant were bred, we would expect their offspring plants to have an intermediate height. However, Mendel recognized that this was not the case. Most of the offspring plants he observed were, in fact, tall plants. Mendel interpreted this to mean that traits are controlled by distinct units. These units occur in pairs, with one inherited from the mother and one inherited from the father. This means that the units for the traits (what we now know as *genes*) appear separately in the sex cells of the parents and are brought together in the offspring. The units are segregated and then reunited.

The second principle is the **law of independent assortment**. Mendel noticed that the pea

**Gregor Mendel** a European monk who conducted tests on pea plants and identified two important principles of classification

**law of segregation** the particles (or genes) for traits appear separately in the (sex cells of) parents and are then reunited in an offspring

**law of independent assortment** the particles (or genes) for different traits are sorted (and passed on) independently of one another

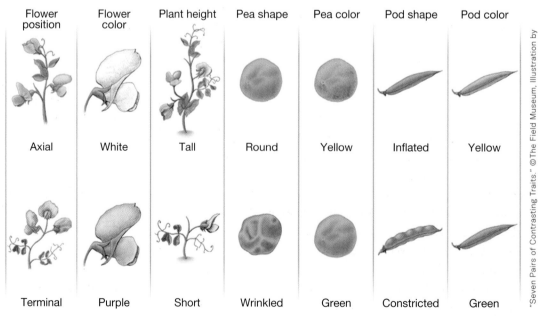

**FIGURE 3.1 Mendel's Pea Plants**
Gregor Mendel studied these traits in pea plants. Through this work, he identified two important laws about inheritance.

"Seven Pairs of Contrasting Traits." ©The Field Museum, Illustration by Greg Mercer. Reprinted with permission.

plant traits were often inherited separately from one another. For example, not all tall plants had yellow seeds. This meant that the units for these traits were sorting independently of one another in the offspring. Today, we understand that this occurs during the process of meiosis. When gametes are formed, the alleles for one trait segregate into the daughter cells independently of the alleles for another trait. This is particularly the case with genes found on different chromosomes. In contrast, when genes are located on the same chromosome, they are more likely to be inherited together and serve as exceptions to the law of independent assortment.

Mendel's work was largely ignored at the time of its publication. It was not until several decades later, in the early 1900s, that his work was rediscovered and integrated with the growing understanding of genetics. Today, we know that genes control traits in much the same way that Mendel theorized some sort of unit controls traits. We also know that these genes are segregated in the sex cells during meiosis, as Mendel's law of segregation suggested. Finally, we also now know that Mendel's law of independent assortment is accurate. If the genes for traits are found on different, nonhomologous chromosomes, they will be independently sorted during meiosis when the nonhomologous chromosomes move to the new cells.

## DOMINANCE AND RECESSIVENESS

When conducting his pea plant tests, Mendel noticed that some versions of a trait were more likely to appear in the next generation than others. For example, when mating a purple flower plant and a white flower plant, the offspring plants usually had purple flowers. Mendel had discovered that some versions of the traits were **dominant**, while other versions were **recessive**. When we combine this with our understanding of genetics today, we recognize that some alleles (alternate forms of a gene) are dominant over other alleles. This does not mean that the dominant alleles are better, stronger, or more

common in the population. It simply means that the dominant alleles mask the effects of the recessive alleles. For example, the tall stem allele is dominant over the short stem allele in pea plants. The presence of a tall stem allele will automatically mask a short stem allele because tallness will manifest itself and obscure shortness. This means that even if you have a pea plant that has one tall allele and one short allele, the plant will look like a tall plant.

## GENOTYPE AND PHENOTYPE

This relationship between dominant and recessive alleles highlights an important distinction between the level of genetic makeup and the level of gene expression. An organism's actual genetic material (the alleles they carry) is considered their **genotype**. This genotype is written in a way that indicates the dominant or recessive alleles present. Let's return to our short and tall pea plants. The dominant allele is for tallness, so it will be represented by a *T* in our example. The recessive allele is for shortness, so it will be represented by a *t* in our example. Remember, one allele will be inherited from the mother, and one allele will be inherited from the father. Each plant should have two alleles for the tallness trait. If a plant has two dominant alleles for the trait, its genotype is written as *TT*, indicating each of the dominant alleles present. This plant is considered to be **homozygous dominant** for the trait because it has two of the same dominant alleles. If a plant has two recessive alleles, its genotype is *tt*. This plant is considered to be **homozygous recessive** for the trait because it has two of the same recessive alleles. If a plant has one dominant allele and one recessive allele, its genotype is *Tt*. This plant is considered to be **heterozygous** for the trait because it has a mix of alleles (one of each variation).

These same rules for writing genotypes apply to other traits, as well. The capital letter indicates the dominant allele, and the lowercase letter indicates the recessive allele. Whenever possible, the same letter is used for both alleles.

**dominant** a dominant allele masks the effects of other alleles for a trait; may also be used in reference to dominant traits or dominant phenotypes

**recessive** a recessive allele is masked by a dominant allele for a trait; may also be used in reference to recessive traits or recessive phenotypes

**genotype** the specific alleles an organism has for a trait

**homozygous dominant** an organism's genotype for a trait when it has two dominant alleles for the trait (such as *RR*)

**homozygous recessive** an organism's genotype for a trait when it has two recessive alleles for the trait (such as *rr*)

**heterozygous** an organism's genotype for a trait when it has one dominant allele and one recessive allele for a trait (such as *Rr*)

**phenotype** the physical expression of an organism's genotype for a trait

**Punnett square** the method of diagramming inheritance where parent genotypes are used to estimate the probability of various genotypes in a potential offspring

That letter is usually the first letter of the dominant version of the trait, such as *T* for the pea plant tallness trait. However, because some letters look similar in their capitalized and lowercase forms, they are avoided when possible. For example, the letter *M* is often avoided when writing genotypes.

The genotype represents the molecular level of genetic makeup, but the physical expression of this genetic material happens at a different level. The actual expression of an organism's genetic material is their **phenotype**. For our tall and short pea plants, there are two possible phenotypes: the dominant phenotype (tall) and the recessive phenotype (short). The homozygous dominant plant will have the dominant phenotype (tall) because it only has dominant alleles to be expressed. The heterozygous plant will also have the dominant phenotype (tall) because the expression of the recessive allele is masked by the dominant allele. The homozygous recessive plant will be the only plant that actually has the recessive phenotype (short) because it is the only plant that lacks the dominant allele.

If you know an organism's genotype for a trait, you can determine its phenotype for that trait, as we did with the tall and short pea plants. It is a bit more difficult to infer genotype from phenotype. If you have an organism with the recessive phenotype, you can be confident that it has the homozygous recessive genotype. However, if you have an organism with the dominant phenotype, the organism could have the homozygous dominant genotype or the heterozygous genotype for the trait. Determining the genotype in these situations requires more information about the organism's relatives. We will explore this further when we discuss pedigree diagrams below.

## PUNNETT SQUARES

There are two possible ways to diagram inheritance. The first is the **Punnett square**, which was devised in the early 1900s by a British biologist named Reginald Punnett. The Punnett square diagrams the possible genotypic outcomes for the mating of two organisms. In the diagram, one parent's genotype is written above the boxes, and the other parent's genotype is written to the left of the boxes. The boxes are then completed with the possible allele combinations for an offspring. For example, in the Punnett square shown in **FIGURE 3.2**, one pea plant parent is homozygous dominant (*TT*) for the tallness trait. The other pea plant parent is heterozygous (*Tt*) for the trait. The boxes indicate the possible genotypes for one of their offspring. In the box at the top left, there are two dominant alleles, one from each parent. The same is true for the box at the top right. The box at the bottom left has one dominant allele from one parent and one recessive allele from the other parent. The box at the bottom right has the same possible genotype. This means there is a 50% chance the offspring would be homozygous dominant for the trait and a 50% chance the offspring would be heterozygous.

Punnett squares show genotypes, but you can use this information to determine phenotypes as well. In the example given, both parents have the dominant phenotype. Based

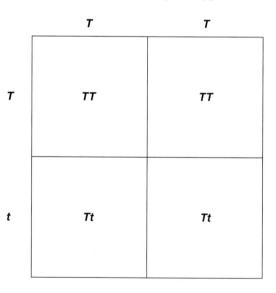

**FIGURE 3.2 Punnett Square for Mendelian Trait *T* (Tallness in Pea Plants)**
If a homozygous dominant individual (*TT*) mates with a heterozygous individual (*Tt*), there is a 50% chance they will have an offspring who is homozygous dominant (*TT*) and a 50% chance they will have an offspring who is heterozygous (*Tt*).

on the genotype possibilities for their offspring, we can also say that there is a 100% chance their offspring will have the dominant phenotype.

It is important to remember that the Punnett square is showing you possible outcomes for one mating. It is not showing what outcome would happen if the parents had further offspring. However, the Punnett square (and corresponding outcome chances) would be the same for each separate mating. In the example in Figure 3.2, each time the parents mate there is a 50% chance of a homozygous dominant offspring and a 50% chance of a heterozygous offspring. Even if the parents have four offspring, they could all be homozygous dominant for the trait because the chances are the same for each separate mating.

## PEDIGREE DIAGRAMS

Another way of representing inheritance is through the **pedigree diagram**. Pedigree diagrams show multiple generations of real, related organisms. This is different from the Punnett square, which only shows one real generation (the parents) and one potential generation (the possibilities for a single offspring). Pedigree diagrams also show phenotypes for a trait, rather than genotypes. While genotype can be inferred from this information, we cannot always be 100% confident in that inference.

Pedigree diagrams include several symbols to represent the real individuals involved. Squares are used to represent males. Circles are used to represent females. Mated pairs are linked by a horizontal line between their symbols. Offspring are then drawn as descending from their parents' mated pair. When an individual's shape is shaded (colored in), the individual expresses the trait in question. When the shape is left uncolored, the individual does not express the trait in question. This means either dominant or recessive traits may be shaded in the diagram, depending on what trait is represented. For example, in a diagram for the dominant freckles trait, individuals who have freckles (the dominant phenotype) will be shaded in the diagram.

In a diagram for the recessive trait of attached earlobes, individuals who have lower earlobes that attach to the side of the head (the recessive phenotype) will be shaded in the diagram.

In the sample pedigree diagram in **FIGURE 3.3**, individuals A, D, and G are male. Individuals B, C, E, and F are female. Individuals A and B mated and had two offspring (individuals C and D). Individual D mated with individual E, and they had two offspring (individuals F and G). This sample pedigree diagram shows a family of people and their phenotypes for the freckles trait. In humans, having freckles is dominant over not having freckles, so the shaded individuals express freckles (in this case the dominant phenotype). Individuals B, C, and D have the dominant phenotype, and individuals A, E, F, and G have the recessive phenotype.

Even though pedigree diagrams do not directly show genotypes, we can infer genotypes based on the information found in the diagrams. In our example pedigree, we can confidently say that individuals A, E, F, and G all have the homozygous recessive genotype (*ff*)

**pedigree diagram**
the method of diagramming inheritance that shows the phenotypes of individuals from multiple generations in a family

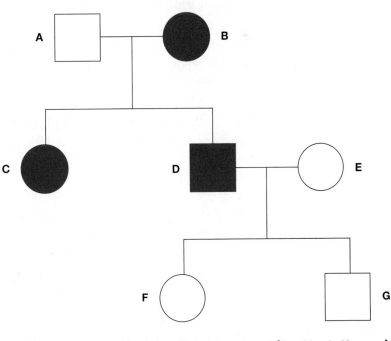

**FIGURE 3.3 Pedigree Diagram for Mendelian Trait *F* (Freckles in Humans)** Squares represent males, and circles represent females. Shapes that are colored in reflect individuals who are affected by (or express) the trait. Shapes that are uncolored reflect individuals who are not affected by (or do not express) the trait. In this example, person E is a female who does not express the trait and has the recessive phenotype (no freckles).

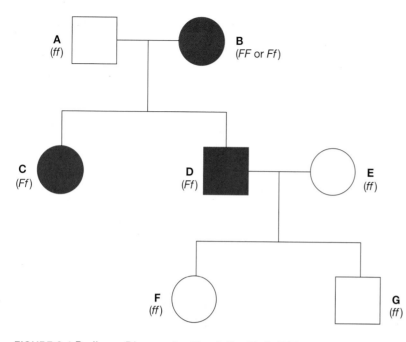

A
(ff)

B
(FF or Ff)

C
(Ff)

D
(Ff)

E
(ff)

F
(ff)

G
(ff)

**FIGURE 3.4 Pedigree Diagram for Mendelian Trait _F_ (Freckles in Humans) with Genotypes Added**
In this version of the pedigree diagram from Figure 3.3, the genotypes have been added. Note that, in some cases, only one genotype is possible, but in other cases, multiple genotypes are possible based on the available information.

**Mendelian trait** trait controlled by one gene (although there may be multiple alleles for that one gene)

**genetic locus** the location of a gene on a chromosome

for freckles because they all have the recessive phenotype (**FIGURE 3.4**). The only way an individual can have the recessive phenotype is if they have the homozygous recessive genotype.

Determining the genotype for the other individuals is more challenging. First, individual C must have the heterozygous genotype (_Ff_) because she has a homozygous recessive father. This father would have passed on a recessive allele to individual C. Because individual C has the dominant phenotype, we know she must also have at least one dominant allele. Therefore, we know individual C is heterozygous because she has one recessive allele from her father and one dominant allele from her mother (Figure 3.4). Second, because individual D is individual C's brother, the same line of thinking can also be used to determine that individual D is also heterozygous (_Ff_) for the trait. Even if we did not know about individual D's parents, we could still use the information about his offspring to come to the same conclusion. Individual D must be heterozygous for the trait because he has homozygous recessive offspring. This indicates that he has a recessive allele in his genotype that was

passed on to his offspring (Figure 3.4). Lastly, individual B presents an interesting challenge. Even using the information we have about her offspring, we cannot be sure if individual B is homozygous dominant (_FF_) or heterozygous. Either genotype, when mated with individual A (who is homozygous recessive), could result in the offspring genotypes and phenotypes already determined (Figure 3.4).

## MENDELIAN TRAITS AND POLYGENIC TRAITS

Generally, there are two kinds of traits in humans: Mendelian traits and polygenic traits. **Mendelian traits** are traits that are controlled by one gene. There are multiple alleles for the gene, but only one **genetic locus** (location of a gene on a chromosome) is involved. For this reason, Mendelian traits are sometimes said to follow a "simple" pattern of inheritance. Humans have some Mendelian traits. For example, attachment of the lower earlobe to the side of the head is a Mendelian trait. The unattached earlobe allele is dominant, and the attached earlobe allele is recessive. Another Mendelian trait in humans is the hitchhiker's thumb (**FIGURE 3.5**). The non-hitchhiker's thumb allele is dominant, and the hitchhiker's thumb allele is recessive. Freckles on the face are also inherited in Mendelian fashion. Freckles are dominant and the lack of freckles is recessive.

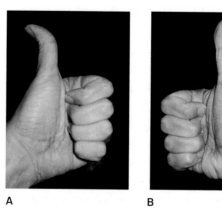

A                    B

K. Elizabeth Soluri

**FIGURE 3.5 Hitchhiker's Thumb**
One of the few Mendelian traits in humans is for hitchhiker's thumb (A), which is recessive to normal, non-hitchhiker's thumb (B).

While humans certainly have some Mendelian traits, most of our traits are actually **polygenic traits**. Polygenic traits are controlled by alleles at multiple genetic loci. Often many genes are involved, and the phenotypic expression is complex (more like a continuum of expression). Human stature is a good example of this. We do not just have "short" or "tall" people in any given population. Rather, there is a continuum of different heights ranging from short to tall. Skin color, hair color, and eye color are other examples of polygenic traits in humans.

## ▶▶▶ EXPLORING FURTHER

**The ABO Blood Group**  We have focused on Mendelian traits with one dominant allele and one recessive allele, like the tall and short pea plants. However, Mendelian traits often have more complex dominance relationships between the alleles involved. The classic example of this in humans is the ABO blood group system.

There are different types of cell surface markers, called **antigens**, found on the surface of our red blood cells. In general, antigens are any substances (such as bacteria or enzymes, or fragments thereof) that trigger an immune response. Blood group antigens are either sugars or proteins. The antigens expressed on a red blood cell determine an individual's blood type. The main two blood groups are called ABO (with blood types A, B, AB, and O) and Rh (with Rh-positive and Rh-negative blood types). In the ABO blood system there are two cell surface markers or antigens: antigen A and antigen B (**FIGURE 3.6**). We know that the A and B blood antigens are sugars, but not much is known about their function in the body today or in our evolutionary past.

The alleles for these antigens are found at one genetic locus, which means ABO blood type is a Mendelian trait. A person can inherit the A antigen allele, the B antigen allele, or the O allele (which manifests as having neither antigen on the blood cell surface).

This makes six possible genotypes for the ABO blood system:

- A person can be *AA*, with the A antigen allele inherited from both parents.

- A person can be *AO*, with the A antigen allele inherited from one parent and the O allele inherited from the other parent.

- A person can be *BB*, with the B antigen allele inherited from both parents.

- A person can be *BO*, with the B antigen allele inherited from one parent and the O allele inherited from the other parent.

- A person can be *AB*, with the A antigen allele inherited from one parent and the B antigen allele inherited from the other parent.

- A person can be *OO*, with the O allele inherited from both parents.

**polygenic trait** trait controlled by alleles at multiple genetic loci

**antigen** (in ABO blood group system) the cell surface marker found on red blood cells that relates to an individual's ABO blood type and triggers antibody reactions to a foreign blood antigen

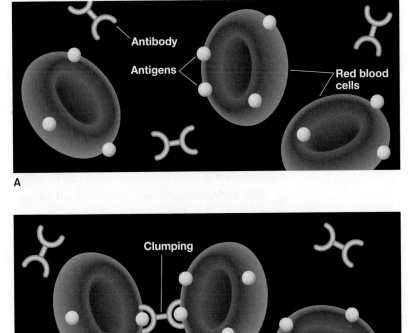

**FIGURE 3.6 ABO Blood Antigens and Antibodies**
The A and B blood antigens are found on the surface of the red blood cells. When foreign blood antigens are introduced to the body via the transfusion of incompatible blood, antibodies are produced (A). The antibodies attach to the antigens and cause the blood cells to clump, which can restrict blood flow (B).

**codominant** when multiple alleles are expressed in the phenotype, without one being clearly dominant over the other

**antibody** protein that attacks antigens directly or marks them for attack by other parts of the immune system

Interestingly, there are only four corresponding phenotypes or blood types:

- People with the *AA* genotype and the *AO* genotype have A antigens on their red blood cells, giving them the A blood type as their phenotype.

- People with the *BB* and *BO* genotypes have B antigens on their red blood cells, giving them the B blood type as their phenotype.

- People with the *AB* genotype have both A antigens and B antigens on their red blood cells, giving them the AB blood type as their phenotype.

- People with the *OO* genotype do not have either type of antigen on their red blood cells, giving them the O blood type as their phenotype.

This discrepancy in the number of possible genotypes and phenotypes suggests the ABO blood group has a complex pattern of dominance and recessiveness. The A antigen allele is dominant over the O allele. The O allele does not result in antigens, but the presence of the A allele in a heterozygous individual will result in the production of the A antigens, giving *AO* individuals the A blood phenotype. The B antigen allele is also dominant over the O allele, with *BO* individuals having the B blood phenotype. The only individuals with a true O blood type are homozygous for the O allele, further suggesting the O allele is recessive. The relationship between the A antigen allele and B antigen allele is particularly interesting. These two alleles are what we call **codominant**. When the two alleles appear together, as in *AB* individuals, both alleles are expressed in the phenotype. One is not dominant over the other; they are equally dominant.

While much of the function of these red blood cell antigens is still unknown, we do know that exposure to foreign blood antigens triggers a dangerous response from the immune system that can be fatal. The body differentiates between its normal antigens (self-antigens) and foreign antigens. In the case of many antigens, such as bacteria, this triggers a protective reaction from the immune system. The body produces **antibodies**, which are special proteins that attack the antigens directly or mark them for attack by other parts of the immune system. This allows the body to neutralize and fight off infections. In the case of the blood surface antigens, the body identifies any foreign blood antigens and produces antibodies to combat them (Figure 3.6). The antibodies attach to the antigens and cause the blood cells to clump together. The coagulated blood does not travel smoothly through the blood vessels, and the body cannot get the blood and oxygen it needs. This can result in death.

Because of the antibody response to foreign blood antigens, it is essential that we know an individual's blood genotype and phenotype for successful blood transfusions to occur. Individuals who have the A blood type can receive blood from people who also have the A blood type because the antigens are the same. Individuals who have the B blood type can receive blood from people who also have the B blood type because their antigens are the same. However, a person with the A blood type cannot receive blood from a person with the B blood type (and vice versa) because it introduces foreign blood antigens that will trigger an immune response.

A person who has the O blood type can only receive blood from someone who has the O blood type. Someone with O blood doesn't have either type of antigen, so both the A and the B antigens are considered foreign and trigger an immune response. However, O blood is considered to be the universal donor blood. It doesn't have either antigen, so it will not introduce a foreign antigen to the body of a recipient. Anyone can receive blood from a person with the O blood type.

A person who has the AB blood type can receive blood from anyone, making them the universal recipient. A person with AB blood can receive blood from someone else who also has AB blood, but they can also receive blood from someone who has A blood or someone who has B blood. Because the A antigen allele and the B antigen allele are codominant, a person with AB blood has both types of antigens in their body. When A blood is introduced, it is accepted because the A antigen is already present. The same is true for the introduction of B blood. The introduction of O blood is also successful because it does not have any antigens that cause clumping.

The complex relationships of dominance and recessiveness among these different antigen alleles create a complicated picture of blood group genotypes and phenotypes, and these genotypes and phenotypes must be understood in order to successfully transfuse blood. The blood type alleles also seem to have unusual distributions across populations worldwide. We will return to this in Lab 8 when we discuss human variation.

# CONCEPT REVIEW QUESTIONS

Name: _____     Section: _____

Course: _____     Date: _____

Answer the following questions in the space provided.

1. Name two pea plant traits studied by Gregor Mendel.

2. Define genotype.

3. Define phenotype.

4. Why would a pea plant that is heterozygous for the tallness trait have the dominant phenotype?

5. A pea plant with the recessive phenotype for tallness would have which of the following genotypes?
   A. *TT*
   B. *tt*
   C. *Tt*
   D. *TT* or *Tt*

6. A pea plant with the dominant phenotype for tallness would have which of the following genotypes?
   A. *TT*
   B. *tt*
   C. *Tt*
   D. *TT* or *Tt*

7. What is the difference between a Mendelian trait and a polygenic trait?

8. Which of the following is a polygenic trait in humans?
   A. Hitchhiker's thumb
   B. Earlobe attachment
   C. Skin color
   D. Freckles

9. In the ABO blood system, what is/are the possible genotypes for a person who has the A blood type?

10. In the ABO blood system, what is/are the possible genotypes for a person who has the O blood type?

# LAB EXERCISES

Name: _____    Section: _____

Course: _____    Date: _____

## EXERCISE 1   CREATING PUNNETT SQUARES

Work in a small group or alone to complete this exercise. Trait *F* is the Mendelian trait for freckles, where *F* is dominant over *f*.

- Timmy is homozygous dominant for trait *F*.
- Timmy mates with Sally who is heterozygous for trait *F*.
- Timmy's father *and* Timmy's mother are *both* heterozygous for trait *F*.
- Timmy's maternal grandmother (mother's mother) is homozygous recessive for trait *F*.
- Timmy's maternal grandfather (mother's father) is homozygous dominant for trait *F*.

Use the information provided to complete the three separate Punnett squares below:

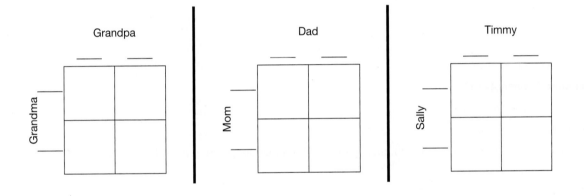

## EXERCISE 2   CREATING PEDIGREE DIAGRAMS

Working in a small group or alone, review the information about Timmy's family from Exercise 1. Use this information to create a pedigree diagram for trait *F* in his family. Be sure to include all three generations and all six people described. Use the space below.

**INTERPRETING PUNNETT SQUARES**

Work in a small group or alone to complete this exercise. This is a Punnett square for trait *R*, showing two parents mating. Trait *R* is the Mendelian trait in humans for tongue rolling. The allele for the ability to roll the tongue (*R*) is dominant over the allele for the inability to roll the tongue (*r*).

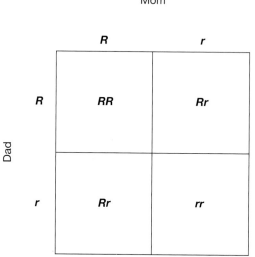

1. What is the mother's genotype? _____
2. What is the mother's phenotype? _____
3. What is the father's genotype? _____
4. What is the father's phenotype? _____
5. What is the probability of their daughter Maria having each of the possible genotypes and phenotypes?

6. Are you 100% sure of the parents' phenotypes? Are you 100% sure of Maria's phenotype? If not, which are problematic? Why?

7. Are you 100% sure of the parents' genotypes? Are you 100% sure of Maria's genotype? If not, which are problematic? Why?

## EXERCISE 4 INTERPRETING PEDIGREE DIAGRAMS

Work in a small group or alone to complete this exercise. This is a pedigree diagram for trait *R* in a family. Trait *R* is the Mendelian trait in humans for tongue rolling. The allele for the ability to roll the tongue (*R*) is dominant over the allele for the inability to roll the tongue (*r*).

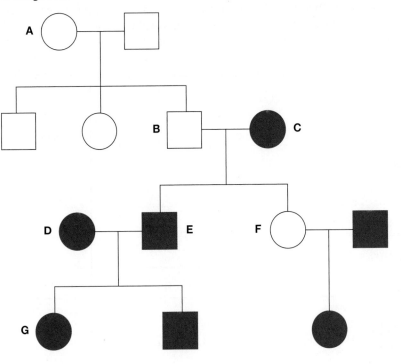

Complete the following chart using the pedigree diagram.

| Person | Genotype | Phenotype |
|--------|----------|-----------|
| A | | |
| B | | |
| C | | |
| D | | |
| E | | |
| F | | |
| G | | |

1. Are you 100% sure of the phenotypes? If not, which are problematic? Why?


2. Are you 100% sure of the genotypes? If not, which are problematic? Why?

## EXERCISE 5    MENDELIAN TRAITS IN HUMANS 1

While most human traits are polygenic, the traits in the chart below have traditionally been considered Mendelian traits. More recent research has disputed the single-gene nature of some of these traits, but for the purpose of this exercise, assume that the following traits are Mendelian.

Work with a partner to help each other determine your own phenotypes and possible genotypes for these traits. Write your answers in the chart. (*Note:* A "cleft chin" is a chin with a slight indentation in the middle. "Attached earlobes" are earlobes that are fully attached to the side of the head, rather than unattached earlobes that have a lower section that is free-hanging away from the side of the head. A "widow's peak" is a hairline that dips down in the middle of the forehead to form a V-shape, rather than a non-widow's peak hairline that runs horizontally straight along the forehead.)

| Mendelian Trait | Your Phenotype | Your Possible Genotype(s) |
|---|---|---|
| Cleft Chin (Dominant) | | |
| Freckles (Dominant) | | |
| Attached Earlobes (Recessive) | | |
| Hitchhiker's Thumb (Recessive) | | |
| Widow's Peak (Dominant) | | |

## EXERCISE 6    MENDELIAN TRAITS IN HUMANS 2

Some people can taste phenylthiocarbamide (PTC) and similar substances, but some people cannot. PTC tasting is a simple Mendelian trait in humans, where tasting ($T$) is dominant over nontasting ($t$).

Your instructor has distributed two taste strips: a control strip and a PTC strip.

**STEP 1**  Make sure to dispose of any candy, gum, or cough drops you may be chewing.

**STEP 2**  Differentiate the two taste strips by labeling them C (for control) and P (for PTC).

**STEP 3**  Touch the control strip to your tongue. Do not eat the strip. What do you taste? This is the taste of the paper, without any added substances.

**STEP 4**  Touch the PTC strip to your tongue. Do not eat the strip. What do you taste?

**STEP 5**  Discuss your results with several of your classmates. Based on your experience answer the following questions:

  1.  Are you a PTC taster? Do you have the dominant phenotype or the recessive phenotype?

  2.  What is your possible genotype(s)?

  3.  How do you compare to other people?

**EXERCISE 7  THE ABO BLOOD SYSTEM**

Work with a small group or alone to answer the following questions about the ABO blood system and blood type compatibility.

1. Can a person with type A blood successfully receive a transfusion from a person who has type O? Why or why not?

2. Can a person with type A blood successfully receive a transfusion from a person who has type B? Why or why not?

3. Can a person with type O blood successfully donate their blood to a person who has type AB? Why or why not?

4. Can a person with type B blood successfully donate their blood to a person who has type O? Why or why not?

5. Can a person with type AB blood successfully donate their blood to a person who has type A? Why or why not?

**EXERCISE 8  DIHYBRID CROSS**

So far, you have worked on Punnett squares that show monohybrid crosses—probabilities for an offspring from two parents involving a *single* trait, such as tongue rolling. When conducting his research, Mendel devised something known as a dihybrid cross, which allowed him to consider *two* different traits. Mendel's work on dihybrid crosses in pea plants helped him realize that traits are inherited separately (the law of independent assortment).

**SCENARIO A**

Here is an example of a dihybrid cross with Mendel's pea plants. Consider two traits in pea plants: tallness (*T*) and flower color (*P*). Tallness (*T*) is dominant over shortness (*t*), and purple flowers (*P*) are dominant over white flowers (*p*). If a plant that is heterozygous for tallness (*Tt*) and homozygous recessive for flower color (*pp*) is mated with a plant that is homozygous dominant for tallness (*TT*) and for flower color (*PP*), what are the probabilities for the offspring's genotypes?

**STEP 1**  The first step is to determine the parents' genotypes. Here, one plant is *Ttpp* and the other is *TTPP*.

**STEP 2**  Next, we have to determine all the possible gametes each plant might contribute. To do this, we write down the *T* and *P* combinations that may be present in each plant's gametes.

>  » In plant 1, the possible gametes are *Tp, Tp, tp,* and *tp.*

>  » In plant 2, the possible gametes are *TP, TP, TP,* and, *TP.*

**STEP 3**  Last, we mate these possible gametes in a large Punnett square:

**Plant 1: *Ttpp***

|                   | ***Tp*** | ***Tp*** | ***tp*** | ***tp*** |
|-------------------|----------|----------|----------|----------|
| ***TP***          | *TTPp*   | *TTPp*   | *TtPp*   | *TtPp*   |
| ***TP***          | *TTPp*   | *TTPp*   | *TtPp*   | *TtPp*   |
| ***TP***          | *TTPp*   | *TTPp*   | *TtPp*   | *TtPp*   |
| ***TP***          | *TTPp*   | *TTPp*   | *TtPp*   | *TtPp*   |

(row label: **Plant 2: *TTPP***)

In this example, the results are as follows:

>  » There is a 50% chance of an offspring that is *TTPp*.

>  » There is a 50% chance of an offspring that is *TtPp*.

>  » On the phenotypic level, there is a 100% likelihood that the offspring will be tall and have purple flowers.

**SCENARIO B**

For this exercise work alone or in a small group to complete the dihybrid cross and questions that follow. Consider two traits in humans: freckles (*F*) and widow's peak (*W*). Having freckles (*F*) is dominant over not having freckles (*f*), and having a widow's peak (*W*) is dominant over not having a widow's peak (*w*).

- Suzy is heterozygous for freckles and widow's peak.
- Jose is homozygous recessive for freckles and widow's peak.
- Suzy and Jose are about to have a baby, and they are curious about the likelihood that the child will inherit these traits.

**STEP 1**  Enter Suzy's and Jose's genotypes in the Punnett square.

**STEP 2**  Enter Suzy's and Jose's possible gametes in the shaded rows and columns.

**STEP 3**  Complete the Punnett square and answer the following questions.

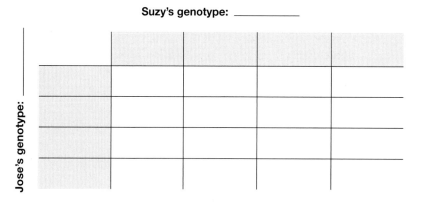

**Suzy's genotype:** _____

Jose's genotype: _____

1. What is the likelihood that Suzy and Jose's child will have freckles but will not have a widow's peak?

2. What is the likelihood that Suzy and Jose's child will not have freckles but will have a widow's peak?

3. What is the likelihood that Suzy and Jose's child will have freckles and a widow's peak?

4. What is the likelihood that Suzy and Jose's child will not have freckles or a widow's peak?

# CRITICAL THINKING QUESTIONS

On a separate sheet of paper, answer the following questions.

1. This question may be completed independently or as a group discussion. Describe the two laws of inheritance put forward by Gregor Mendel. For each, also describe how you think modern genetics has clarified or supported these early concepts.

2. This question may be completed independently or as a group exercise. Use the Punnett squares you completed in Exercise 2 to answer the following questions.

   • Timmy was homozygous dominant for trait *F*. Looking at the Punnett square for his parents' mating, what was the probability of Timmy having a different genotype? What was the probability of Timmy having a different phenotype?

   • Timmy's mother was heterozygous for trait *F*. Looking at the Punnett square for the grandparents' mating, what was the probability of Timmy's mother having a different genotype? What was the probability of Timmy's mother having a different phenotype?

3. Complete the following chart comparing Punnett squares and pedigree diagrams. For each characteristic, indicate whether Punnett squares, pedigree diagrams, or both are applicable by placing a mark in the appropriate column.

| | Punnett Square | Pedigree Diagram |
|---|---|---|
| Shows One Mating at a Time | | |
| Shows Multiple Generations at a Time | | |
| Shows Phenotypes | | |
| Requires You to Infer Phenotypes | | |
| Shows Genotypes | | |
| Requires You to Infer Genotypes | | |
| Shows Real Individuals | | |
| Shows Potential Individuals | | |

4. Review the chart you completed in Exercise 5 of your Mendelian traits. For any traits where you are unsure about your genotype, interview your biological parents and siblings to find out their phenotypes. Like you would in a pedigree diagram, use your family members' answers to help you more clearly identify your own genotype(s) for the traits.

5. This question may be completed independently or as a group discussion. Review your results from the dihybrid cross in Exercise 8. Did the inheritance of one trait impact the likelihood of inheriting the other trait? For example, was Suzy and Jose's child more likely to have a widow's peak if it also had freckles? How does the relationship between the two traits support Mendel's law of independent assortment?

6. This question may be completed independently or as a group exercise. Miss Primrose breeds dogs to show in competitions. Her prized female dog, named Stella, recently had an unexpected litter of puppies. Two of the puppies have an unusual coat color called agouti, where each hair has numerous dark and light bands and a dark tip. Miss Primrose specifically bred Stella with another prize-winning dog named Max, but neither Stella or Max have the agouti fur trait. Miss Primrose suspects that Stella may have been secretly impregnated by a stray dog she has seen in their neighborhood who does have an agouti coat. Miss Primrose collected the following research and pedigree information on Stella and Max:

   - The nonagouti coat trait (*N*) is dominant over the agouti coat trait (*n*).

   - Stella does not have an agouti coat.

   - Neither of Stella's parents has an agouti coat.

   - Stella's maternal grandfather does not have an agouti coat, but Stella's maternal grandmother does have an agouti coat.

   - Max does not have an agouti coat.

   - Max's mother does not have an agouti coat, but Max's father does have an agouti coat.

   Based on this information, is it possible that Max is the father of this litter of puppies? Why or why not? (*Hint*: It might be helpful to make a pedigree diagram of Stella's and Max's families, so you can determine their genotypes and the possibility of their having agouti puppies.)

Charles Darwin was the naturalist aboard the HMS *Beagle* on a trip around the world in the 1830s. The voyage included stops in the Galapagos Islands, where Darwin's observations of variations in finches, tortoises, and other animals fueled his development of the theory of natural selection.

## Lab Learning Objectives

By the end of this lab, students should be able to:

- define evolution.

- describe mutation and how it relates to genetic variation.

- describe the forces of evolution (natural selection, genetic drift, and gene flow).

- apply the Hardy–Weinberg equation to determine if a trait is undergoing evolution in a population.

LAB 4

# Forces of Evolution

It is October 2, 1836, and the HMS *Beagle* has just returned to Falmouth, Cornwall, England, after a 5-year voyage around the world. Captain Robert FitzRoy commanded the ship with the purpose of conducting surveys of the South American coast and improving on existing charts and maps of the area. Charles Darwin served as the naturalist on the voyage, collecting information about and samples of various plants, animals, and geological features encountered during the trip. Darwin's experiences have gotten him thinking, and upon his return, he will begin to review his extensive notes and samples from the field. With this data and the influence of other contemporary and past scientists, Darwin will develop a theory that will revolutionize science and the way humans perceive the world. He will form an explanation for how we got to be the way we are and how we relate to other organisms past and present. He will devise a theory of evolution known as natural selection. Today, we know that natural selection, as described by Darwin, is a great force that drives evolutionary change. We also recognize that there are multiple processes in addition to natural selection that can bring about evolution. Each of these processes have played (and continue to play) an important role in our own evolutionary history. This lab explores these evolutionary processes to help us further examine our own evolutionary context.

**evolution** change in allele frequency

# INTRODUCTION

We begin with a consideration of evolution in general. We then examine the various processes that drive evolution: mutation, natural selection, genetic drift, and gene flow. For each of these processes, we review the basic concept and how it works, with an eye toward examples in human populations. We conclude by exploring how to determine if evolution is happening.

## WHAT IS EVOLUTION?

In population biology, we define and measure **evolution** as a change in allele frequency. This has several important implications. First, we are discussing alleles, which means we are discussing the *genetic* level, not just the phenotypic level. Because of the complex relationships that often exist between dominant and recessive alleles, evolution may be occurring subtly at the genetic level without us realizing it at the phenotypic level. This is particularly the case with polygenic traits, where multiple genetic loci are in play at one time.

Second, evolution involves allele *frequencies*. These are ratios of different alleles for a trait. As such, they are always calculated for groups, not individuals. This means evolution occurs at the population level, not at the level of the individual.

Third, because evolution is about allele frequencies, evolution occurs in *traits*. Within a population at any given time, some traits may be evolving while others remain the same. It is not that the population is evolving. Instead, it is a trait (or suite of traits) that is evolving within a population.

Finally, evolution is a *change* in allele frequency. This means that evolution occurs across multiple generations. To measure a change in a population's allele frequency for a trait, we must be examining the population over time, from one generation to the next. If a population has an allele frequency of *x* for a trait, the only way to determine if evolution is occurring or has occurred is to examine the preceding generation or the offspring generation. If either of these generations has a different allele frequency (*y*), we can say that the frequency is changing and evolution is occurring or has occurred.

Changes in allele frequencies occur all the time in all organisms. But what causes these changes? How do we explain evolution? There are multiple factors or mechanisms that can bring about changes in allele frequencies. These mechanisms of evolution are often called the "forces of evolution" because they drive evolutionary changes. Although we discuss them separately here, multiple forces of evolution often act simultaneously in real life **(FIGURE 4.1)**.

## GENETIC RECOMBINATION

In Lab 2, we discussed the process of cell division in gamete-forming cells, called meiosis. Remember, during meiosis genes from homologous chromosomes cross over and are recombined. This *genetic recombination* results in variation by forming new combinations of genetic material. No new genetic material is created, but new combinations of existing genetic material are produced. Recombination is not considered one of the traditional forces of evolution, but it plays an important role in creating variation, which is the raw material for evolutionary processes.

***Example*** Imagine that a person is heterozygous for the Mendelian freckle trait **(FIGURE 4.2)**. During meiosis, the chromosome that holds the freckle gene lines up with its homologous partner. The first chromosome carries the dominant allele for the trait, and the homologous chromosome carries the recessive allele. These two alleles are exchanged during a crossing-over event. This creates a slightly different collection of genetic material on those chromosomes. The first chromosome now has the recessive allele for the freckle trait, and the

**FIGURE 4.1 Darwin's Finches**
Charles Darwin noted variation among the finches on the Galapagos Islands. These observations helped him as he developed his theory of natural selection. Today, we have even more evidence in support of Darwin's early ideas.

Ryan M. Bolton/Shutterstock

Stubblefield Photography/Shutterstock

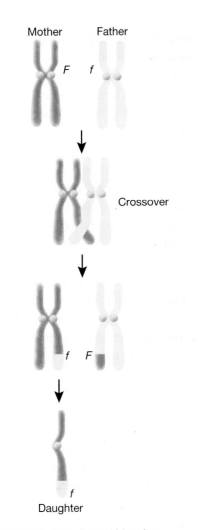

**FIGURE 4.2 Genetic Recombination**
Genetic recombination can cause minor genetic variations between generations. In the example depicted here and described in the text, a daughter receives a slightly different combination of genes than was found in her mother's corresponding chromosome.

# FORCES OF EVOLUTION— MUTATION

While recombination results in new combinations of genetic material, it does not produce new genes. The only source of entirely new genetic material is **mutation**. Most mutations occur during DNA replication. Usually this process copies the DNA perfectly, but sometimes there are errors, or mutations. If the errors occur in DNA segments that do not code for traits or play a role in regulating genes, the errors have no real effect. However, sometimes the errors occur in coding DNA and can have a profound impact. While mutations can occur in cells throughout the body, the mutations that impact evolution occur only in gametes (reproductive cells such as the sperm and egg). Remember, these mutations are the only ones that may be passed to the next generation.

Mutations can be very small genetic changes. If a single base pair of DNA is altered, it changes the corresponding codon. This can sometimes result in a different amino acid, which may result in a different protein. These kinds of mutations are called **point mutations** because they occur at a single point in the DNA strand. **Sickle-cell anemia** is an example of a point mutation. One base pair is substituted by another, and the sickle-cell allele is formed. Expression of this mutated gene produces misshapen red blood cells that cause blockages in blood vessels (for more information on the sickle-cell trait, see Lab 8).

Mutations can also be much larger errors. During the process of meiosis, a large section of a chromosome can be moved elsewhere on the chromosome, or it can be moved to a completely different chromosome. Sometimes whole chromosomes can be duplicated, resulting in an extra chromosome. This is the case with **Down syndrome**, where there is an extra chromosome 21. Other times, a whole chromosome can be lost, leaving the organism with one fewer chromosome. This is the case with **Turner syndrome**, where there is a single X chromosome and no other sex chromosome.

**mutation** change in the genetic code that creates entirely new genetic material

**point mutation** a mutation that occurs at a single point (nitrogen base) in a DNA strand

**sickle-cell anemia** a disease that results from the sickle-cell allele

**Down syndrome** a chromosomal disorder that results from an extra chromosome 21

**Turner syndrome** a chromosomal disorder that results from having a single X chromosome without another sex chromosome

homologous partner now has the dominant allele for the freckle trait. The first chromosome ends up in a gamete that produces an offspring. The resulting daughter has a slightly different combination of genetic material on this chromosome than her mother. The mother had the dominant allele for the freckle trait along with the other genes found on this chromosome. The daughter has the recessive allele for the freckle trait along with the other genes. While the mother and daughter's chromosomes are very similar, there are minor variations, like the switch in the freckle allele, as a result of crossing-over in meiosis.

**Charles Darwin**
often considered
the father of
evolutionary
thinking, he devised
the theory of natural
selection to explain
the process of
evolution in the
natural world

**natural selection**
the theory outlined
by Charles Darwin
to explain evolution:
it argues that
some traits are
more suited to
an organism's
particular
environmental
context and are
therefore passed
on preferentially
into the next
generation, and
these traits become
more common
in successive
generations,
resulting in
evolutionary shifts
in populations

We do not know all of the causes of mutations. Sometimes they are caused by external factors, like exposure to radiation or specific chemicals. However, most mutations seem to be spontaneous, with no known cause. Also, while we often associate the word mutation with negative things, mutations are not always harmful. Many mutations are neutral or even advantageous.

No matter what their cause, mutations create new genetic material, such as entirely new alleles. The variations created by mutation can then be acted on by other evolutionary processes. Thus, mutation works in concert with other forces to bring about evolutionary changes.

## FORCES OF EVOLUTION— NATURAL SELECTION

In 1859, **Charles Darwin** published *On the Origin of Species*. This work presented his ideas about evolution and outlined his theory of **natural selection**. This theory offers an explanation for how evolution occurs. Since Darwin's original work, the theory of natural selection has been repeatedly refined to include our growing knowledge of genetics. However, the basic outline of the theory remains the same. The theory of natural selection states that beneficial alleles increase in frequency over time in a population because of increased survival and reproduction of individuals with those alleles. Let's look more closely at the mechanism behind natural selection.

First, there is always variation in a trait (and thus the alleles that code for them) within a population. Not everyone in the population will have the same versions of the trait or allele. Second, there is a tendency toward overreproduction compared to the limited availability of resources. In general, more offspring are produced than can be supported by the resources present. This causes competition for resources. These resources include such things as food, shelter, and access to mates. Resources are always limited. They may be distributed unevenly in an environment or limited seasonally, or there may be some resources that are better (for example, more nutritious or safer) than other resources. At any given time, members of a population are competing for access to these resources. Third, because of this competition, some versions of a trait will be better suited to the environmental context than other versions. That is, some versions will be advantageous, for example, helping the organism access food or reproduce efficiently. Other versions will be disadvantageous, perhaps limiting access to food or hindering reproduction. Finally, the organisms with the more helpful traits will outreproduce the other organisms and pass their helpful traits on to the next generation. Over many generations, the population as a whole will have more of the helpful traits.

Importantly, natural selection emphasizes traits and alleles, not the individuals carrying those traits and alleles. It is the traits that are advantageous or disadvantageous, and the traits are passed to the next generation. Also, natural selection highlights the importance of the trait frequency changing over multiple generations, thus incorporating the definition of evolution.

*Example* Over 50,000 years ago a group of mammoths (*Mammuthus columb*) swam approximately 4 miles from the California coast to an island due west in the Pacific Ocean. As the Ice Age came to an end, ice caps and glaciers melted, and sea levels rose around the world. This island became four separate, smaller islands (known today as the California Channel Islands). The available food for the mammoths became more limited. This was particularly problematic in the winter because the mammoths could not migrate to different territories when their local food was scarce. In these times of limited food, mammoths that had smaller body sizes were able to outcompete their larger counterparts **(FIGURE 4.3)**. The smaller mammoths needed less food to survive, and their shorter limbs allowed them to climb the steep terrain efficiently. These mammoths were able to survive and produce more small-bodied offspring. Over many generations, the entire population became smaller, and a new species of dwarf mammoths (*Mammuthus exilis*) arose by 13,000 years ago. These dwarf mammoths were less than half the size of their mainland ancestor; they stood around 4–6 feet high at the shoulder and weighed around 1 ton.

Remember, advantageous traits are not necessarily traits for strength, vitality, wit, etc. For example, in the dwarf mammoths described above, smallness was advantageous. Advantageous traits are simply traits that help **reproductive success** (the production of offspring). Similarly, disadvantageous traits are not necessarily injurious or fatal. A disadvantageous trait is merely a trait that limits reproductive success.

## FORCES OF EVOLUTION— GENETIC DRIFT

Sometimes allele frequencies change randomly. This process is called **genetic drift**. It is helpful to think of this like a statistics problem. Imagine there is a population where there are an equal number of dominant and recessive alleles represented. You might think that if these individuals mate, there will be an equal number of dominant and recessive alleles in the second generation. However, when you think of flipping a coin you realize this is not necessarily the case. When you flip a coin, there is a 50% chance each time you flip it that you will get a coin with heads facing up. There is also a 50% chance you will get a coin with tails facing up. The results of one coin flip are independent of the results of the next coin flip; this 50% chance is the same *each time* you flip the coin. If a coin is flipped 10 times, it is possible that the results will be 10 heads or 10 tails in a row. This outcome is unlikely, but it is possible.

Similar patterns emerge in mating. If two heterozygous individuals mate, there is a 50% chance the mother will pass on her dominant allele and a 50% chance she will pass on her recessive allele. The same is true for the father. However, if the individuals produce four

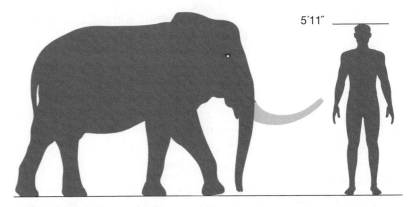

**FIGURE 4.3 Pygmy Mammoth**
Although mainland mammoths were about 14 feet tall on average, pygmy mammoths on the Channel Islands averaged only 4.5 to 7 feet tall, making them closer in size to a modern human. Their small size was selectively favored on the islands where there was less food available to support large-bodied mammoths.

offspring, it is entirely possible that the mother will pass on her recessive allele all four times and the father will pass on his recessive allele all four times. While this is less likely, it is still possible. We could start with a population of two heterozygous individuals and end up with a second generation of all homozygous recessive individuals. This is called genetic drift, as over multiple generations, a population's allele frequency may shift away from the original population's allele frequency.

At the same time, not every individual will have the same number of offspring, and this, too, can cause a random shift in allele frequencies. Imagine that one individual named Devon has five offspring, and another individual named Shalyce has zero offspring. Devon's genetic material will be overrepresented in the second generation, and Shalyce's genetic material will be underrepresented in the second generation. Therefore, there will be a slight shift in the population's allele frequency, with more of Devon's alleles going forward.

There is also a special kind of genetic drift called the **founder effect** [FIGURE 4.4]. The founder effect occurs when only a small number of individuals from a larger population are involved in producing the next generation. This can happen when a large percentage of a population dies (for example, from famine or war) and only a few individuals are left to reproduce.

**reproductive success** the successful production of viable (fertile) offspring

**genetic drift** the changes in allele frequencies that occur randomly, due to factors like differential reproduction and sampling errors

**founder effect** a special type of genetic drift that occurs when a subset of a larger population founds the next generation due to substantial population loss or population movement

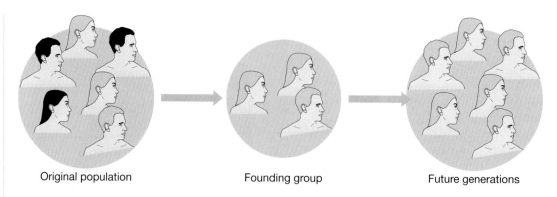

Original population          Founding group          Future generations

**FIGURE 4.4 The Founder Effect**
A particular type of genetic drift, called the founder effect, occurs when only a subset of a larger population is involved in producing future generations. Depending on the traits carried by the founding group, the future generations can be very different from the original population.

It can also happen when a small group of individuals leave the original population to live somewhere else. These individuals then reproduce in isolation from the rest of the original population's gene pool. In cases of the founder effect, the "founders" (the individuals involved in reproduction separate from the original, larger population) do not necessarily represent the original, larger population's allele frequency. So, when these founders reproduce, they do not generate the original population's allele frequency, and in effect they jump-start genetic drift. When a small founding population does not have the original population's gene frequency, this can lead to what is called a **genetic**

**bottleneck**, meaning that some of the original genetic diversity is entirely lost.

*Example*  In 1608, French settlers moved to the St. Lawrence River area and established a colony at Quebec City (**FIGURE 4.5**). Within approximately 70 years, 2,600 settlers had moved to the region. These settlers from France came from a variety of regions, but most came from major Atlantic seaports and areas near Paris. Thus, the founding population was a small sample of the original, larger population of France. Today's French-Canadian population in the region is largely descended from this small founding population, and because of this founding history, French-Canadians have higher rates of certain diseases than other populations. For example, Tay-Sachs disease is more common in French-Canadians than in most other groups. This disease is caused by a genetic mutation that must be inherited from both parents. People with Tay-Sachs disease lack a particular protein that is necessary for breaking down a chemical in nerve cells. The lack of this protein causes deafness, blindness, seizures, and other neurological symptoms; it results in death by around age 6. The Tay-Sachs mutation was more common in the founding settler population than the overall population of France. Because French-Canadians are largely descended from this biased founding population, they are more likely to carry this disease than many other populations. This is the founder effect.

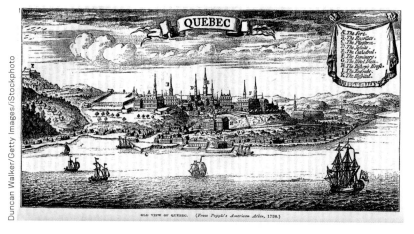

**FIGURE 4.5 Colonial Quebec City**
Early colonists in Quebec City were a small sample of the larger French population at that time. Many of today's French-Canadians in the area are descended from this group of founders, and they have a higher rate of certain genetic traits because these traits were more common in their biased founding ancestors than in the larger French population.

Duncan Walker/Getty Images/iStockphoto

# FORCES OF EVOLUTION— GENE FLOW

A final factor in changing allele frequencies is a process called **gene flow**. Gene flow refers to situations where genes are exchanged between previously isolated populations. If individuals in population A and population B do not normally mate with one another, populations A and B are considered to be reproductively isolated. Now, if some individuals from population A do mate with individuals from population B, gene flow has occurred between the populations (**FIGURE 4.6**).

*Example*   Slavery was legal in the United States from colonial times until the ratification of the Thirteenth Amendment of the U.S. Constitution in December 1865. During this period, it is estimated that hundreds of thousands of people were forcibly captured in Africa and transported to America, where they were enslaved and forced to work for Americans of European descent. Although legal restrictions discouraged marriages and mating relationships between the enslaved Africans and European-Americans, sexual relationships were common (and often forced on the enslaved people). The African-American people of today are descended in part from these relationships, and their DNA shows signs of this mixing of genetic information. The African-American population has elevated contributions of European Y-chromosome DNA (inherited through the male lineage) and African mitochondrial DNA (mtDNA) and X-chromosome DNA (both inherited through the female lineage). This pattern of sex-linked genetic markers supports countless historical accounts of sexual relationships involving European-American men and enslaved African women. Thus, the African-American population today carries a combination of African and European genes because of the gene flow that occurred many generations ago.

Gene flow can have particularly dramatic consequences when one population has genetic material not found in the other population or when one population is much larger than the other. For example, imagine population X and population Y are interbreeding for the first time and gene flow is underway. Population X has genes for blue eyes that are not found in population Y, but because of gene flow these traits will be introduced to population Y for the first time. This will dramatically alter the future allele frequencies of population Y because this new genetic material will now be present. Also, if population X is ten times the size of population Y, then the genes from population X may be found in higher numbers in future generations than the genes from population Y. This will also change the future allele frequencies of population Y because there will now be more genes from population X present.

**genetic bottleneck** substantial loss of genetic diversity (as in many founder effect situations)

**gene flow** the exchange of genes between previously isolated populations that begin to interbreed

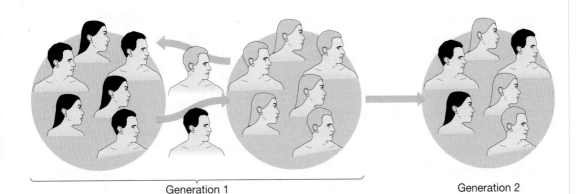

Generation 1                    Generation 2

**FIGURE 4.6 Gene Flow**
Two populations (one with only dark hair and one with only light hair) interbreed. In future generations, both the dark hair and the light hair genes are present.

**Hardy–Weinberg equation** the equation ($p^2 + 2pq + q^2 = 1$) outlined by Godfrey Hardy and Wilhelm Weinberg to predict the probable genotype frequencies of a Mendelian trait in the next generation

*[handwritten notes: p = frequency of Dom Allele B; q = frequency of recc Allele b]*

# HARDY–WEINBERG EQUILIBRIUM

We have discussed what evolution is and how it happens, but how can we tell when it is happening? In the early 1900s, both Godfrey Hardy (an English mathematician) and Wilhelm Weinberg (a German physician) recognized not all traits are evolving all the time. Sometimes, a trait is stable, or in a state of equilibrium. They identified seven key conditions that were necessary for this stability:

1. No mutation is occurring.
2. No natural selection is occurring.
3. No gene flow is occurring.
4. The population is infinitely large.
5. Mating within the population is random.
6. All members of the population mate.
7. All members of the population produce the same number of offspring.

If all of these conditions are true, then the genotype frequencies for the trait should be the same from one generation to the next. The trait is in equilibrium and not evolving.

With this in mind, Hardy and Weinberg developed an equation to predict the probable genotype frequencies of a Mendelian trait in the next generation:

$$p^2 + 2pq + q^2 = 1$$

The **Hardy–Weinberg equation** is used for simple Mendelian traits that are determined by one gene with two alleles. When analyzing a trait with one dominant allele and one recessive allele, $p$ is the frequency of dominant alleles for the trait, and $q$ is the frequency of recessive alleles for the trait. Therefore, $p + q = 1$ because the total number of alleles must account for the entire 100% of the gene pool. The chance of being homozygous dominant is $p^2$, the chance of being homozygous recessive is $q^2$, and the chance of being heterozygous is $2pq$. The whole population must be the sum of all the possible genotypes, so $p^2 + 2pq + q^2$ must equal 1 (or 100%).

*Example 1* Consider the Mendelian pea plant trait for stem height discussed in Lab

3. For this trait, stem tallness $T$ is the dominant allele and stem shortness $t$ is the recessive allele. In one population of pea plants, 60% (0.6) of the alleles are dominant ($T$) and 40% (0.4) are recessive ($t$) **(FIGURE 4.7)**. We plug

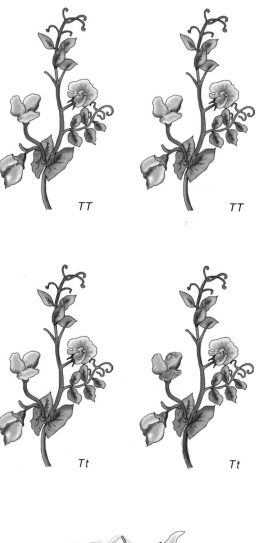

**FIGURE 4.7 Hardy–Weinberg Example 1**
In this population of pea plants, there are two homozygous dominant plants for tallness ($TT$), two heterozygous plants ($Tt$), and one homozygous recessive plant ($tt$). This means 60% (6 out of 10) of the tallness alleles in the population are dominant ($T$) and 40% (4 out of 10) are recessive ($t$). Using the Hardy–Weinberg equation, we can now determine what the allele frequency should be in the next generation, and we can compare this to actual data to assess whether evolution is underway.

this information into the Hardy–Weinberg equation:

$$p = 0.6 \qquad q = 0.4$$
$$p^2 + 2pq + q^2 = 1$$
$$(0.6)^2 + 2(0.6 \times 0.4) + (0.4)^2 = 1$$
$$0.36 + 2(0.24) + 0.16 = 1$$
$$0.36 + 0.48 + 0.16 = 1$$

We have determined that the genotype frequencies in the second generation should be 0.36 (36%) *TT*, 0.48 (48%) *Tt*, and 0.16 (16%) *tt*. If these frequencies are seen in the next generation, the tallness trait is said to be in equilibrium, or not currently evolving. If these frequencies are *not* seen in the next generation, the trait *is* evolving.

The Hardy–Weinberg equation can also be used to examine a trait with two alleles that are codominant. In this case, *p* is the frequency of one allele (for example, allele *R*), and *q* is the frequency of the other allele for the trait (for example, allele *S*). The chance of being homozygous for allele *R* (*RR*) is $p^2$; the chance of being homozygous for allele *S* (*SS*) is $q^2$; and the chance of being heterozygous (*RS*) is 2*pq*. As is the case with a trait that is not codominant, the whole population here must still be the sum of all the possible genotypes, so $p^2 + 2pq + q^2$ must equal 1 (or 100%).

***Example 2*** Imagine a plant population where flower color is a Mendelian trait with two codominant alleles coding for white flowers (*W*) and red flowers (*R*). The flowers on these plants may be white (*WW*), red (*RR*), or speckled with white and red (*WR*). In this population, 75% (0.75) of the alleles are for white (*W*) and 25% (0.25) are for red (*R*) **(FIGURE 4.8)**. We plug this information into the Hardy–Weinberg equation:

$$p = 0.75 \qquad q = 0.25$$
$$p^2 + 2pq + q^2 = 1$$
$$(0.75)^2 + 2(0.75 \times 0.25) + (0.25)^2 = 1$$
$$0.5625 + 2(0.1875) + 0.0625 = 1$$
$$0.5625 + 0.375 + 0.0625 = 1$$

**FIGURE 4.8 Hardy–Weinberg Example 2**
In this population of plants, there are four homozygous plants for white flowers (*WW*), one heterozygous plant with speckled flowers (*WR*), and one homozygous plant for red flowers (*RR*). This means 75% (9 out of 12) of the alleles in the population are for white flowers (*W*) and 25% (3 out of 12) are for red flowers (*R*). Using the Hardy–Weinberg equation, we can now determine what the allele frequency should be in the next generation, and we can compare this to actual data to assess whether evolution is underway.

We have determined that the genotype frequencies in the second generation should be 0.5625 (56.25%) *WW*, 0.375 (37.5%) *WR*, and 0.0625 (6.25%) *RR*. As in the previous example, if these frequencies are seen in the next generation, the trait is said to be in equilibrium (not evolving). Again, if these frequencies are *not* seen in the next generation, the trait *is* evolving. In this way, the Hardy–Weinberg equation can be used to determine if a trait is evolving (or has evolved) in a population.

The Hardy–Weinberg equation provides a useful tool for examining evolutionary changes across generations. Consider the inheritance diagrams discussed in Lab 3. Punnett squares give valuable information about the probable outcomes for the mating of two individuals, and pedigree diagrams provide helpful information about the inheritance of a trait across numerous individuals from multiple generations within a family. The Hardy–Weinberg equation allows us to predict probable genotypes, as in the Punnett square, but it goes a step further and takes into account entire populations, rather than just two individuals.

Hardy and Weinberg's work also illustrates an important issue regarding the relationship between dominant and recessive alleles. We often assume that dominant alleles are stronger, more common, and more likely to be inherited than recessive alleles. In fact, the word "dominant" is used only to indicate that the allele is more likely to be physically expressed than an alternate (recessive) form of the gene. This likelihood of expression is completely separate from the likelihood of inheriting the allele. Remember from Lab 3 that the level of gene expression (phenotype) is different from the level of genetic makeup (genotype). When a heterozygous individual produces an offspring, he or she is equally likely to pass on the recessive allele or the dominant allele. The Hardy–Weinberg equation further confirms this principle. In the equation, dominant alleles do not hold a special place as the most frequent alleles, and dominant alleles and recessive alleles are equally likely to become less common in a population over time.

It is important to remember that the Hardy–Weinberg equation is based on a hypothetical state of equilibrium, where all seven of the conditions noted above are true. In reality, this rarely, if ever, happens. One or more of these conditions almost always does not apply, and traits are usually evolving.

# CONCEPT REVIEW QUESTIONS

Name: _____    Section: _____

Course: _____    Date: _____

Answer the following questions in the space provided.

1. How do we measure and define evolution?

2. True or false? Evolution occurs at the level of the individual.

3. True or false? Evolution occurs in traits.

4. True or false? Evolution occurs in a single generation.

5. The only source of entirely new genetic material is

   A. natural selection.
   B. mutation.
   C. recombination.
   D. genetic drift.

6. Which of the following is *not* a key component of natural selection?

   A. Traits for strength and vitality are favored over other traits.
   B. Random variation exists for every trait in a population.
   C. There will always be competition for resources.
   D. Those with advantageous traits will outreproduce others.

7. The founder effect is a specific type of

   A. gene flow.
   B. meiosis.
   C. genetic drift.
   D. mutation.

8. List two of the seven key conditions necessary for a trait to be in equilibrium.

9. In the Hardy–Weinberg equation, what does $p$ stand for?

10. In the Hardy–Weinberg equation, what does $q$ stand for?

# LAB EXERCISES

Name: _____    Section: _____

Course: _____    Date: _____

## EXERCISE 1   MUTATION

Work in a small group or alone to complete this exercise. In Lab 2, Exercise 7, you determined the amino acid sequence for the following strand of DNA:

A G C A A T C C G T C T T G G
T C G T T A G G C A G A A C C

That strand has mutated. It is now:

A G C A A C C C G T C T T G G
T C G T T G G G C A G A A C C

Use your knowledge of mutation and protein synthesis to answer these questions:

1. What mutation has occurred?

2. Will this mutation have a real effect? Why or why not? (*Hint*: You may want to try Exercise 8 from Lab 2 again, using the mutated DNA strand to make the mutated protein.)

## EXERCISE 2   NATURAL SELECTION ACTIVITY 1

Work in a small group to complete this exercise. In this exercise, you will simulate a case of natural selection in a predator–prey situation.

**STEP 1** Set up the predators. There is variation in predatory feeding apparatuses in this population. Each group member will choose one of the available predator feeding apparatuses: fork, spoon, knife, or four fingers (with your thumb taped to your hand, so you cannot use it). You will each also take a cup, which will represent the predator's mouth. Your goal will be to use your feeding apparatus to collect food and put it in your mouth.

**STEP 2** Set up the prey in the environment. Your instructor has provided you with different types of prey that vary in size and shape. You should have 100 of each prey type. Your instructor has provided a delineated habitat for you to use. Distribute your prey evenly in this habitat, and be sure to mix the prey so each type is found throughout the habitat.

**STEP 3** Establish your hypotheses:

1. Which prey type do you think will be the most fit and avoid capture more often than the other prey types?

2. Which predator do you think will be the most fit and succeed in capturing the most prey?

**STEP 4** Simulate hunting session 1. Distribute yourselves (the predators) around the habitat full of prey. You will be given 60 seconds to hunt for prey. You must pick up the prey with your feeding apparatus, and place it into your cup (your predator's mouth). Your cup must remain flat on the table or ground at all times and cannot be used to help you scrape or scoop up prey. You may hunt prey that is being hunted by other predators. Set a timer for 60 seconds (or use a watch to monitor the time), and begin hunting.

**STEP 5** Record your results. After the end of your 60 seconds of hunting, record the number of prey collected by each predator in the appropriate chart. Be sure to identify which prey you have designated as prey 1, 2, and 3 in the chart. Set these captured prey aside. They are dead and will not produce offspring.

**STEP 6** Reestablish the predators. The predators that collected more prey are well-fed and producing offspring. The predator that collected the least amount of prey is underfed and will not produce offspring. This underfed predator will not participate in future hunts, but the group member should still follow along and record the outcomes of the others' hunts in his or her work. In addition, if any predators have broken their feeding apparatus, they are also underfed and do not produce offspring. They will sit out from future hunts but continue recording results.

**STEP 7** Reestablish the environment. Only the prey that have survived the hunt can reproduce. Determine the number of survivors for each prey type. Add in enough of each surviving prey type to double their numbers in the next generation. Be sure to distribute them evenly in the habitat.

**STEP 8** Repeat steps 4 through 7 for two more hunting sessions. Continue to eliminate underfed predators and double-up surviving prey. Be sure to keep track of your results in the charts provided for each hunting session.

## HUNTING SESSION 1

| | Fork | Knife | Spoon | Fingers | Total Prey |
|---|---|---|---|---|---|
| Prey 1 _____ | | | | | |
| Prey 2 _____ | | | | | |
| Prey 3 _____ | | | | | |
| Total | | | | | |

## HUNTING SESSION 2

|                | Fork | Knife | Spoon | Fingers | Total Prey |
|----------------|------|-------|-------|---------|------------|
| Prey 1 _____ |      |       |       |         |            |
| Prey 2 _____ |      |       |       |         |            |
| Prey 3 _____ |      |       |       |         |            |
| Total          |      |       |       |         |            |

## HUNTING SESSION 3

|                | Fork | Knife | Spoon | Fingers | Total Prey |
|----------------|------|-------|-------|---------|------------|
| Prey 1 _____ |      |       |       |         |            |
| Prey 2 _____ |      |       |       |         |            |
| Prey 3 _____ |      |       |       |         |            |
| Total          |      |       |       |         |            |

**STEP 9** Use your results to answer the remaining questions:

3. Which prey was the best adapted? What data do you have to support this?

4. Which predator was the best adapted? What data do you have to support this?

5. In what ways does this activity demonstrate the process of natural selection and its consequences?

## EXERCISE 3   NATURAL SELECTION ACTIVITY 2

Work in a small group to complete this exercise. You have a cup of beans in front of you with 20 white beans and 20 red beans. These beans represent the alleles for a simple Mendelian trait, where red is dominant ($R$) and white is recessive ($r$). The cup holds the alleles for an entire population (the gene pool).

**STEP 1**  Create a population from the gene pool. Randomly pull out pairs of two beans, and lay them out in front of you. Each pair of beans represents one individual's genotype for this trait. You should have a total of 20 pairs of beans (20 individuals in the population). Record the genotypes of the individuals (pairs of beans) in the first table.

| Individual | Genotype | Individual | Genotype |
|---|---|---|---|
| 1 | | 11 | |
| 2 | | 12 | |
| 3 | | 13 | |
| 4 | | 14 | |
| 5 | | 15 | |
| 6 | | 16 | |
| 7 | | 17 | |
| 8 | | 18 | |
| 9 | | 19 | |
| 10 | | 20 | |

1. How many recessive alleles are present in your overall population?

2. How many dominant alleles are present in your overall population?

**STEP 2**  Simulate an environmental change that affects the population. A drastic new change in the environment makes the homozygous recessive genotype *lethal*. Set aside all of your homozygous recessive pairs. These individuals have died and will no longer contribute to the next generation.

**STEP 3**  Create the descendant population from the survivors. The rest of the gene pool continues mating, and each couple produces enough offspring to replace themselves in the next generation. So, put the alleles (beans) back into the gene pool (cup), and randomly draw out new genotypes (pairs of beans) for the next generation. Record the genotypes of this generation in the second table. (*Note:* You may not need all the rows in the table.)

| Individual | Genotype | Individual | Genotype |
|---|---|---|---|
| 1 | | 11 | |
| 2 | | 12 | |
| 3 | | 13 | |
| 4 | | 14 | |
| 5 | | 15 | |
| 6 | | 16 | |
| 7 | | 17 | |
| 8 | | 18 | |
| 9 | | 19 | |
| 10 | | 20 | |

3.  How many recessive alleles are present in your overall population now?

4.  How many dominant alleles are present in your overall population now?

**STEP 4** Assess the effect of the environmental change on future generations. The homozygous recessive genotype is still lethal. Continue removing homozygous recessive genotypes and remating the resulting gene pool for another generation. Record the genotypes of this third generation in the third table. (*Note*: You may not need all the rows in the table.)

| Individual | Genotype | Individual | Genotype |
|---|---|---|---|
| 1 | | 11 | |
| 2 | | 12 | |
| 3 | | 13 | |
| 4 | | 14 | |
| 5 | | 15 | |
| 6 | | 16 | |
| 7 | | 17 | |
| 8 | | 18 | |
| 9 | | 19 | |
| 10 | | 20 | |

5. How many alleles of each kind are present in your overall population this time?

6. What is happening to the recessive allele?

7. What might eventually happen in this population if the new environment does not revert to the original and the homozygous recessive genotype continues to be lethal?

## EXERCISE 4 THE FOUNDER EFFECT

Work in a small group to complete this exercise. You have a cup of beans in front of you with 20 white beans and 20 red beans. These beans represent the alleles for a simple Mendelian trait, where red is dominant ($R$) and white is recessive ($r$). The cup holds the alleles for an entire population (the gene pool).

**STEP 1** Assess the gene pool.

1. How many alleles of each kind are present in your overall population?

**STEP 2** Select the surviving subpopulation. Randomly draw out five genotypes (pairs of beans) that will survive an ecological catastrophe. Record the genotypes of these five individuals.

| Individual | Genotype |
|---|---|
| 1 | |
| 2 | |
| 3 | |
| 4 | |
| 5 | |

2. How many of each allele type are represented in this surviving population?

3. As this surviving population mates, and the population increases again, will it differ from the original, larger population? Why or why not?

**STEP 3** Select a second subpopulation. Return your alleles (beans) back to the gene pool (cup). Now, let's say only two individuals survive the catastrophe. Randomly draw out two genotypes that survive. Record the genotypes in the table.

| Individual | Genotype |
|------------|----------|
| 1 | |
| 2 | |

4. How many of each allele type are represented in this surviving population?

5. Does this founding group differ from the first founding group above? Why or why not?

6. Does this founding group differ from the original, larger population? Why or why not?

7. How might the size of the founding group impact the effects of genetic drift?

## EXERCISE 5 GENE FLOW

Work in a small group to complete this exercise. You have a cup of beans in front of you with 20 white beans and 24 red beans. These beans represent the alleles for a simple Mendelian trait, where red is dominant ($R$) and white is recessive ($r$). In 1997, a self-isolated group of people living on a small island was joined by a group of explorers from a nearby island.

**STEP 1** Create the original, self-isolated population. The self-isolated population consists of six males. Three of them are homozygous recessive, two are heterozygous, and one is homozygous dominant. Pull out the appropriate genotypes and set them in front of you.

1. How many recessive alleles are present in this self-isolated population?

2. How many dominant alleles are present in this self-isolated population?

**STEP 2** Create the explorer population, keeping the males and females separate. The explorer population consists of two males and eight females, all of whom are homozygous dominant for the same Mendelian trait.

3. How many recessive alleles are present in this explorer population?

4. How many dominant alleles are present in this explorer population?

**STEP 3** Create the descendant population. Everyone on the island found their perfect mate and decided to have two children. Being sure to keep the male and female alleles separate, mix up the male alleles together, and mix up the female alleles together. Create the next generation by taking one allele from the males and combining it with one allele from the females until 16 new individuals (pairs of alleles) are sitting in front of you. Record their genotypes in the table.

| Individual | Genotype | | Individual | Genotype |
|---|---|---|---|---|
| 1 | | | 9 | |
| 2 | | | 10 | |
| 3 | | | 11 | |
| 4 | | | 12 | |
| 5 | | | 13 | |
| 6 | | | 14 | |
| 7 | | | 15 | |
| 8 | | | 16 | |

5. How many recessive alleles are present in this descendant population?

6. How does this vary from the number of recessive alleles present in the explorer population?

7. How many dominant alleles are present in the descendant population?

8. How does this vary from the number of dominant alleles in the original, self-isolated population?

9. What long-term effects can gene flow have on any two populations that are exchanging genes?

## EXERCISE 6   HARDY–WEINBERG EQUILIBRIUM

Work in a small group or alone to complete this exercise. In human population X, consider the simple Mendelian trait for freckles. *F* is the dominant allele and *f* is the recessive allele. Individuals who are homozygous dominant (*FF*) or heterozygous (*Ff*) for the trait express freckles. Individuals who are homozygous recessive (*ff*) for the trait do not express freckles. In this population, 30% (0.3) of the alleles are recessive (*f*) and 70% (0.7) are dominant (*F*).

1. Use the Hardy–Weinberg equation to determine the genotype frequencies we should *expect* in the next generation. Be sure to show your work.

2. You have collected data on the *observed* genotype frequencies of the next generation. They are: 60% *FF*, 30% *Ff*, and 10% *ff*. Based on these observations and your expectations, is this trait currently evolving in this population? Why or why not?

# CRITICAL THINKING QUESTIONS

On a separate sheet of paper, answer the following questions.

1. Describe the circumstances under which mutation *will* have a real evolutionary effect. Describe the circumstances under which mutation *will not* have a real evolutionary effect.

2. This question may be completed independently or as a group discussion. Describe a hypothetical scenario of natural selection for a trait. Be sure to describe each of the key elements (such as how the trait varies in the population, how the trait factors into resource competition, and how the trait frequency changes over multiple generations).

3. This question may be completed independently or as a group discussion. Describe a hypothetical scenario of the founder effect for a trait where substantial genetic variation is lost (causing a genetic bottleneck). Be sure to describe each of the key elements (such as why the founder effect event occurs, why genetic information is lost, and how the trait frequency changes over multiple generations).

4. This question may be completed independently or as a group discussion. Describe a hypothetical scenario of gene flow for a trait. Be sure to describe each of the key elements (such as the trait frequency in the two populations prior to gene flow, why gene flow occurs, and the consequences of the gene flow event in future generations).

5. In human population A, hitchhiker's thumb is a simple Mendelian trait. For this trait, *N* is the dominant allele and *n* is the recessive allele. Individuals who are homozygous dominant (*NN*) or heterozygous (*Nn*) express non-hitchhiker's thumbs. Individuals who are homozygous recessive (*nn*) express hitchhiker's thumbs. In this population, 90% (0.9) of the alleles are dominant (*N*) and 10% (0.1) are recessive (*n*).

   Use the Hardy–Weinberg equation to determine the genotype frequencies we should *expect* in the next generation. Be sure to show your work.

   You have collected data on the *observed* genotype frequencies of the next generation. They are 70% *NN*, 20% *Nn*, and 10% *nn*. Based on these observations and your expectations, is this trait currently evolving in this population? Why or why not?

6. The flu vaccine (administered as a shot or a nasal spray) is made of a combination of different types of influenza viruses that research indicates will be most common during the upcoming season. For each type of influenza, there are numerous specific viruses that can be selected for use in the vaccine. The vaccine works by introducing small amounts of these influenza viruses to the body. This stimulates the immune system to create antibodies against these specific viruses that help protect the individual from becoming infected with these viruses. Each year, the specific viruses used in the vaccine will vary. Based on what you know of evolution, why might this be the case? Why can't we reuse the same vaccine (and combination of viruses) from year to year?

### PART TWO

# MODERN HUMANS

Bones vary depending on species, sex, age, diet, locomotion, and many other factors. We can examine bones to learn more about humans, how we vary, and how we compare to other species.

# LAB 5: INTRODUCTION TO THE SKELETON

## WHAT TOPICS ARE COVERED IN THIS LAB?

- An examination of bone's function in the body and the different types of bone
- A look at how the bone cells work together to make and resorb bone in the body
- An introduction to the types of bones and key features of bone
- An orientation to the skeleton and important directional terminology

# LAB 6: BONES OF THE SKELETON

## WHAT TOPICS ARE COVERED IN THIS LAB?

- A review of the major bones of the axial skeleton and their defining traits
- A review of the major bones of the appendicular skeleton and their defining traits

# LAB 7: BIOARCHAEOLOGY AND FORENSIC ANTHROPOLOGY

## WHAT TOPICS ARE COVERED IN THIS LAB?

- An overview of bioarchaeology and the methods used by bioarchaeologists to study past humans
- An introduction to the methods used by forensic anthropologists

# LAB 8: MODERN HUMAN VARIATION

## WHAT TOPICS ARE COVERED IN THIS LAB?

- A consideration of the biological and cultural basis for "race"
- Modern human adaptation and variation, with particular attention given to:
  - » Skin color
  - » Altitude adaptations
  - » Climatic adaptations (Allen's and Bergmann's rules)
  - » ABO blood system allele frequency distributions
  - » Lactose tolerance
  - » The sickle-cell trait

SIU/Visuals Unlimited, Inc.

When looking at an X-ray, we notice that the exterior edge of the bone appears to be whiter than the inside. This coloration reflects the different composition of the exterior and interior tissue of individual bones.

LAB 5

# Introduction to the Skeleton

## Lab Learning Objectives

By the end of this lab, students should be able to:

- explain the major functions of bone.

- describe the types of bone tissue.

- discuss the bone remodeling process and why it occurs.

- use overall bone shape, bone features, and directional terminology to describe bones.

- differentiate between the axial and appendicular parts of the skeleton.

Many of us have had bones in our bodies X-rayed to check for damage and fractures following an injury. Even if you have not seen an X-ray of your own bones, you have probably seen an X-ray of someone else's bones on television, in books, or online. When looking at an X-ray, have you ever wondered why the bone appears brighter white toward the exterior and darker toward the interior? Does it reflect some difference in the density or the structure of the bone tissue? This lab explores the basics of bone biology and provides answers to these questions and more.

Biological anthropologists often work with skeletal material, comparing humans and nonhuman primates, analyzing fossil materials, or examining human remains in forensic settings. As such, biological anthropologists need to have an understanding of bone, its function, and its tissue structures. Biological anthropologists also must be able to describe the relative position and orientation of bones within the skeletons of different primates, and this lab presents the relevant terminology and concepts necessary for these descriptions.

**connective tissue**
body tissue made of
cells, fibers (such as
collagen fibers), and
extracellular matrix

**cartilage** a type of
flexible connective
tissue found at
the joints between
bones and in the
nose and ear

**articulation** a
meeting between
bones in the body

**fibrous joint** a joint
united by irregular,
fibrous connective
tissue that allows
for little to no
movement

**cartilaginous joint**
a joint united by
cartilage that allows
some movement

**synovial joint** a
highly mobile joint
held together by
ligaments and
irregular connective
tissue that forms a
fluid-filled articular
capsule

# INTRODUCTION

In this lab, we begin with an overview of the skeletal system and consideration of the various functions bone plays in the body. We then examine the types of bone tissues and bone cells, and we explore how bone cells work together to make, resorb, and maintain the bones of the body. We also discuss how bones can be generally distinguished by their features and shapes. We conclude with an orientation to the skeleton. We differentiate between the axial and appendicular parts of the skeleton and review important directional terminology.

# BONE FUNCTION

Bones play two key roles in our bodies. First, the bones of the skeleton have a *structural function*. They act like the wood frame of a house. The muscles attach to the bones, like drywall is attached to wood studs. This gives the muscles the structural support they need and provides a system of levers the muscles can use to move the body. The framing of a house also provides a protected area where the plumbing and the electric wiring can be erected. Many of the bones in our bodies act as similar protective structures. For example, the rib cage forms a protected area for many vital organs, like the heart and lungs.

The second major function of the skeleton is a *physiological function*, meaning the skeleton is an essential part of the normal and healthy functioning of the body. Inside the bones, there is a soft tissue called bone marrow. There are two types of bone marrow in the center of bones: red marrow and yellow marrow. The red marrow is tissue that is capable of producing blood cells for the rest of the body. The yellow marrow is made up of mostly fat cells, and the amount of yellow marrow increases as adults age. In addition, our bones also store important nutrients. In particular, the bones store calcium and phosphorus. When these nutrients are needed elsewhere in the body, they can be released from the bones and sent where necessary. By producing blood cells and storing fat

and key nutrients, the skeleton plays a vital role in supporting the overall health of the body.

# THE SKELETAL SYSTEM AND BONE TISSUE

Bone and cartilage are two types of **connective tissue** in the skeletal system. Connective tissue is made up of cells, fibers (mostly elastic collagen fibers), and extracellular matrix. **Cartilage** is a flexible connective tissue due to its abundance of collagen fibers, but it has no direct blood supply. Cartilage is found in many parts of the human body, including the joints between bones, the ear, the nose, and the bronchial tubes in the airways. In an embryo, the skeleton is made up almost entirely of cartilage that is replaced by bone tissue during growth and development. Once the growth period is completed, most of the cartilage in the skeleton is replaced by bone, except in a few places where it is retained into adulthood, such as in the rib cage and on the surface of joints.

Joints are **articulations**, places where two bones meet or *articulate with* one another. The articular surfaces of each bone in a joint are smooth. During life, the articular ends of the bones are separated from each other by a layer of cartilage that helps the joint withstand mechanical impact and movement. There are many joints in the human body, and they are classified by their amount of movement and the type of tissue that connects them. The three main types of joints are fibrous joints, cartilaginous joints, and synovial joints. **Fibrous joints** are united by short, irregular, fibrous connective tissue, and they allow for little or no movement (examples are the suture joints between the flat skull bones). **Cartilaginous joints** are united by cartilage and permit a little movement (such as the joints between vertebrae in the spine, formed by intervertebral disks). **Synovial joints** are the most mobile joints and allow a variety of movements (such as the knee or shoulder joint). The bones of synovial joints are held together along their outer surfaces by ligaments and dense, irregular connective tissue that forms an

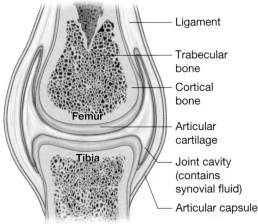

**FIGURE 5.1 The Human Knee**
At the knee joint, a typical synovial joint, the femur (thighbone) articulates with the tibia (shinbone). Notice the bones are held together by ligaments.

articular capsule around it (**FIGURE 5.1**). Unlike in fibrous and cartilaginous joints, there is a small gap, the joint space, between the articular surfaces of the bones in a synovial joint. The capsule is filled with a slippery lubricant called synovial fluid, which flows into the joint space and helps healthy joints move easily.

Bone is a much more rigid connective tissue compared to cartilage. Bones of the skeletal system work together with many other systems in the body, such as the muscular system and the circulatory system. Approximately one-third of bone tissue is made of organic components, and two-thirds is made of inorganic components. The organic material includes proteins like collagen, which helps make up the matrix surrounding the cells in the bone. The inorganic material is primarily made of carbonated apatite. This is a mineral made up of calcium, phosphate, and fluoride. While the inorganic components are important for the structural integrity of the bone, the collagen fibers also contribute significantly to the strength and resilience of the bone.

There are two main types of bone: woven bone and lamellar bone. **Woven bone** is unorganized bone, primarily seen in immature bone. Juvenile skeletons that are still growing and

developing have a lot of woven bone. However, adults can also have woven bone. For example, if a person has broken a bone, they will have woven bone at the site of the injury, as the bone tries to fill in and repair the break. The other type of bone, **lamellar bone**, is mature bone. An adult's skeleton, when not injured or healing, is made of lamellar bone.

Within lamellar bone, there are two types of bone tissue: cortical bone and trabecular bone (**FIGURE 5.2**). **Cortical bone** is the compact tissue that makes up the outside surface of bone. It often appears solid and smooth. In contrast, the **trabecular bone** is the spongy or honeycomb-like tissue that makes up the inside of the bone. It appears less solid and rougher than cortical bone, but it is more metabolically active due to the greater amount of surface area in the honeycomb-like structure.

On a microscopic scale, there are three main types of bone cells: osteoblasts, osteocytes, and osteoclasts. Each of these bone cell types has a different primary function. The **osteoblasts** are responsible for forming bone, the **osteocytes** are responsible for bone maintenance, and the **osteoclasts** are responsible for removing bone. These bone cells work together in a constant process called bone remodeling.

**woven bone** a type of bone that is unorganized and primarily found in immature bone

**lamellar bone** a type of organized, mature bone

**cortical bone** the compact tissue that forms the outside surface of lamellar bone

**trabecular bone** the spongy (honeycomb-like) tissue that forms the inside of lamellar bone

**osteoblast** a bone cell responsible for forming bone

**osteocyte** a bone cell responsible for bone maintenance

**osteoclast** a bone cell responsible for removing bone

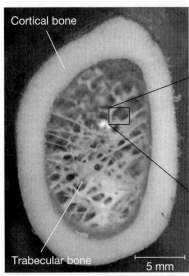

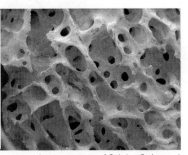

Image courtesy of Sabrina C. Agarwal

Image courtesy of Sabrina C. Agarwal

**FIGURE 5.2 Bone Tissue**
In cross section, mature bone shows cortical bone on the exterior and trabecular bone on the interior. Notice the honeycomb appearance of trabecular bone.

**bone remodeling**
the process of bone resorption and re-formation

# BONE REMODELING

How is bone made and resorbed? Throughout our lives, our bones are constantly resorbed and re-formed. In fact, approximately every 10 years our skeleton is completely replaced by new bone tissue. This process of bone resorption and re-formation is called **bone remodeling** (FIGURE 5.3). In this process, the osteoclast bone cells remove and resorb bone. These osteoclasts are large cells with multiple nuclei. They act almost like cleaning pads that scrub away old bone. Then, the osteoblast bone cells come in to make (or build) new bone. As the osteoblasts become trapped in the bone tissue as it mineralizes, they become osteocyte bone cells. These osteocytes are the living bone cells that are then left responsible for maintaining the bone tissue.

There are many reasons why this bone remodeling process happens in the skeleton. The first is to allow for normal *growth and development*. As we age from birth to adulthood, our skeletons need to grow, and many osteoblast

cells lay down tissue to allow for this expansion and growth of bones.

The second reason why bone remodels is to *extract important nutrients* from the skeleton. Remember, bones store nutrients like calcium and phosphorus. When those nutrients are needed elsewhere in the body, bone remodeling begins. Tiny gaps are removed from the bone to release the trapped nutrients. The tiny gaps are then filled in, and the bone is built back up.

A third reason why bone remodeling happens is to *repair damage* that occurs to the bone. This damage can be large-scale damage, like a bone fracture. But even if you have never had a fracture, your skeleton is still full of small-scale microdamage from everyday use. Like a road that slowly accumulates pits and small cracks, the bones accumulate similar microscopic damage every day. Also, like a road, if that minor damage goes unrepaired, it can lead to much worse damage. In a road, it can result in potholes and much larger cracks. In your skeleton, neglecting the microdamage can decrease the strength and health of the bone. Thus, in healthy bone, the cells work together continuously to repair damage on multiple scales.

A final reason why bone remodels is to *meet the functional and biomechanical challenges* of the bone. A simple phrase is used to highlight this relationship between bone remodeling and the functional needs of the skeleton: "Use it or lose it." If you use a part of your body a lot, the muscles in that area will grow larger. When you have larger muscles, you need larger bones for their attachment. So, when you *use* a body part a lot, the corresponding muscle and bone grow bigger. Bone remodeling drives this bone growth. At the same time, if you do not use a part of your body enough, the muscles in that area will become smaller. When there are smaller muscles, less bone is needed for their attachment. So, when you don't use a body part enough, you *lose* muscle and bone mass. Bone remodeling also drives this bone loss.

We see the use it or lose it principle in our lives all the time. For example, you may have noticed that your ring sizes are slightly larger on the hand you write with because you use this

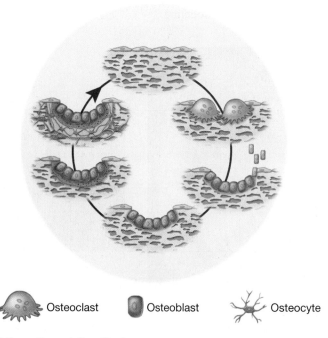

Osteoclast    Osteoblast    Osteocyte

**FIGURE 5.3 Bone Remodeling Cycle**
In the bone remodeling cycle, the osteoclasts remove and resorb bone. Then, the osteoblasts build up new bone. Trapped osteoblasts become living bone cells (called osteocytes) that maintain bone.

hand more frequently. More extreme examples of this principle are found in athletes and astronauts. Athletes often use one arm more than another (think of baseball pitchers or tennis players). The bone of the arm that is used more will be larger. Astronauts are an opposite example. After spending extended times in outer space, astronauts often lose significant muscle and bone mass because of the lack of mechanical force on their muscles and bones in the zero gravity environment.

# DISTINGUISHING BONES: SHAPES

Vertebrate organisms have a large number of different bones. Humans, for example, have a total of 206 bones. With so many bones, how do we distinguish between them? One way to do this is by looking at their overall shape. The bones of the human skeleton can be classified into four different categories based on their shape: long bones, short bones, flat bones, and irregular bones.

**Long bones** are made of a central shaft with distinct, slightly larger ends on each side (**FIGURE 5.4**). The long bones, joints, and associated muscles work together to help the arms and legs achieve their maximum potential when engaged in daily activities, such as bearing weight, facilitating movements like flexion and extension, and carrying loads. In particular, having longer muscles in the arms and legs allows for a greater range of motion, and these longer muscles require longer bones for support and extension. A classic example of a long bone is the femur in our thigh. It has a long shaft in the middle and two distinct ends. Importantly, while the femur is a measurably long and large bone (typically the largest bone in the human body), not all long bones are large. For example, the long bones of the hand and fingers are much smaller than the femur, but they are still considered long bones based on their shape and how they grow. During growth, the ends of the long bones (called the *epiphyses*) have growth plates that separate the ends from the shaft to

allow the bone to grow in length until the end of puberty (see Lab 7 for more information).

In contrast to long bones, **short bones** do not have a clear shaft. Instead, short bones are more cube-like in shape, with similar width and length dimensions (**FIGURE 5.5**). These short bones are often found in compact areas, and the presence of multiple, tightly packed short bones limits the range of motion in that area. The bones of the wrist (the carpals) are classic short bones. They are cube-like, appearing relatively similar on most sides, and there are several of them compacted in a small area, which limits mobility and gives stability within the wrist.

**Flat bones** are thin, plate-like bones that make up a small proportion of the bones in the body (**FIGURE 5.6**). They have a layer of trabecular bone sandwiched between two thin layers of flat cortical bone. Flat bones may serve as broad areas for muscle attachment (as in the shoulder blade, or scapula) or as plate-like protection for delicate structures (as in the bones of the skull, or cranium).

**Irregular bones** do not readily fit into any of the other three categories. They have complex

**FIGURE 5.4
A Long Bone**
The human femur (thighbone) is a typical long bone. Notice the elongated shape with a middle shaft and two distinct ends.

**long bone** a bone with an elongated middle shaft and distinct, slightly larger ends

**short bone** a bone with a cube-like shape, with similar width and length dimensions

**flat bone** a bone with a layer of trabecular bone sandwiched between two thin layers of flat cortical bone

**irregular bone** a bone with a complex shape that is not easily classified as long, short, or flat

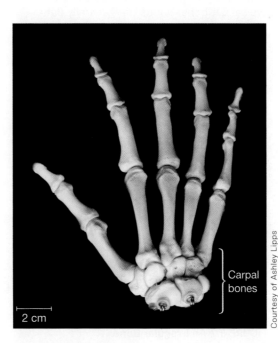

Courtesy of Ashley Lipps

**FIGURE 5.5 A Short Bone**
Human carpals (wrist bones) are typical short bones. Notice the cube-like shape. Remember, though, that the hand and finger bones (the metacarpals and phalanges) are long bones, despite their small size.

**projection** an area of bone that protrudes from the main bone surface

**sagittal crest** a ridge of bone along the midline of the cranium that allows for the attachment of extra-large chewing muscles

and varied shapes **(FIGURE 5.7)**. The bones of the spine, called vertebrae, are good examples of irregular bones. They are clearly not long bones because they do not have anything resembling

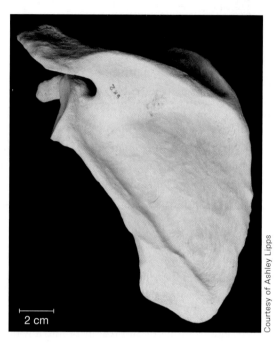

2 cm

**FIGURE 5.6 A Flat Bone**
The human scapula (shoulder blade) is a typical flat bone. Notice the generally flat shape that allows for extensive muscle attachment.

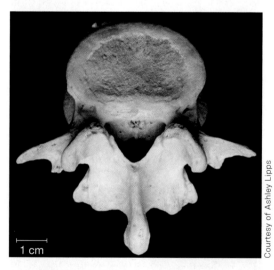

1 cm

**FIGURE 5.7 An Irregular Bone**
A human vertebra (back bone) is a typical irregular bone. It does not easily fit into the other shape categories. It is not elongated, cube-like, or flat. It has a unique, irregular shape.

a shaft. We can also rule out a classification of vertebrae as flat bones because they are too thick and fat to be part of the plate-like group of bones. At first they might appear to be short bones because of the cube-like shape of the vertebral body. However, on closer consideration, it becomes apparent that the specialized spines sticking out of the vertebrae (that serve to anchor key ligaments of the spine) make the overall shape of the bones highly unusual and less cube-like. The vertebrae don't qualify as long bones, short bones, or flat bones; therefore, they are placed in the catchall category of irregular bones.

## DISTINGUISHING BONES: FEATURES

Distinguishing between bones does not stop with overall shape. Multiple bones can be placed into each of the shape categories (long, short, flat, and irregular). How can we further distinguish the bones within these broad categories? Another way to describe bones is by using the marks and features on them. Remember, bone is a responsive tissue, so influences from surrounding tissues, such as changes in attaching muscles, will leave marks on the skeleton. Because each bone will have slightly different markings depending on how it relates to and interacts with other nearby tissues, we can use the markings (bone features) to help us further identify specific bones.

There are numerous specific types of bone features, but we will focus on three major types: (1) projections; (2) depressions, fossae, and grooves; and (3) foramina and canals. **Projections** are areas of bone that stick out from the rest of the bone surface. These bumps or ridges vary in size and usually serve as sites for muscle and tendon attachment. An extreme example of a projection is the **sagittal crest (FIGURE 5.8)**. This is an extra ridge of bone that runs along the midline of the cranium in some primates, like gorillas. It allows for the attachment of extra-large chewing muscles.

Courtesy of Ashley Lipps

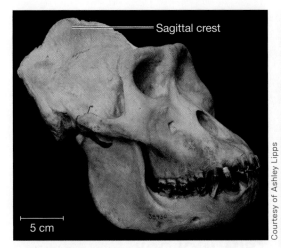

Sagittal crest

Courtesy of Ashley Lipps

**FIGURE 5.8 Sagittal Crest**
The sagittal crest on a gorilla is an example of a bone projection. It is an area of bone that projects from the surface of the cranium (skull) and allows for the attachment of large chewing muscles.

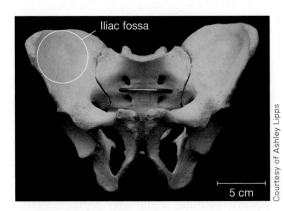

Iliac fossa

5 cm

Courtesy of Ashley Lipps

**FIGURE 5.9 Iliac Fossa**
The iliac fossa on the anterior surface of the ilium (upper portion of the pelvis) is an example of a bone fossa. It is an indented area of bone where the iliac muscle attaches.

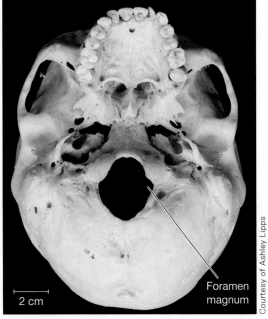

2 cm

Foramen magnum

Courtesy of Ashley Lipps

**FIGURE 5.10 Foramen Magnum**
The foramen magnum on the underside of a human cranium (skull) is an example of a bone foramen. It is a large hole in the cranium that allows the brain to connect to the spinal cord.

**Depressions**, **fossae**, and **grooves** are indentations on the bone surface that often accommodate nerves, blood vessels, muscles, or other structures. For example, there is a large indentation called the iliac fossa on the anterior of the ilium (the upper bone of the pelvis) **(FIGURE 5.9)**. This indentation accommodates the iliac muscle, which attaches in that area.

**Foramina** and **canals** are holes in the bone. Foramina (singular is *foramen*) are usually simple holes, while canals are often narrow, tubular channels in bone, like tunnels. These holes in the bone are usually associated with nerves or vessels. For example, the **foramen magnum** is the large hole at the base of the cranium **(FIGURE 5.10)**. It allows for the brain stem (descending from inside the cranium) to connect to the spinal cord (inside the vertebral column).

# AXIAL SKELETON AND APPENDICULAR SKELETON

Now that we have talked about the different types of bone shapes and features, it is important to contextualize this information with an overall orientation to the skeleton. The human skeleton can be divided into two parts: the axial skeleton and the appendicular skeleton **(FIGURE 5.11)**. The **axial skeleton** is comprised of all of the bones that are along the midline (or central axis) of the body. This includes the bones of the cranium, the mandible, the rib cage, and

**depression** a hollow or depressed area of a bone

**fossa (fossae,** plural) a shallow depression in a bone

**groove** a furrow along the surface of a bone

**foramen (foramina,** plural) a hole in a bone

**canal** a narrow tunnel or tubular channel in a bone

**foramen magnum** the large hole at the base of the cranium that allows the brain to connect to the spinal cord

**axial skeleton** the bones that lie along the midline (central axis) of the body

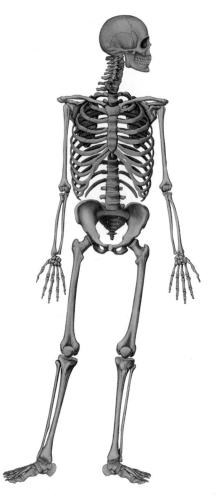

**FIGURE 5.11 The Axial and Appendicular Skeletal Elements**
In the human skeleton, the bones that run along the midline (central axis) of the body are considered axial bones (red). The bones that make up the limbs (appendages) are considered appendicular bones (green).

**appendicular skeleton** the bones of the appendages (arms and legs)

**superior** relative location higher on the body's axis

**inferior** relative location lower on the body's axis

**medial** relative location closer to the midline of the body

**lateral** relative location farther from the midline of the body

the vertebral column. All of these bones lie on the central axis of the body.

The **appendicular skeleton** is comprised of all of the bones of the appendages (arms and legs). This includes the bones of the arm, wrist, and hand, as well as the bones of the leg, ankle, and foot. Importantly, bones are considered to be part of an appendage if they are essential to the function of that appendage. This means there are some bones that appear to lie on the central axis but are actually part of the appendicular skeleton. For example, the hip bones (or pelvis) might appear to be the base of the body's midline, as if it were part of the axial skeleton. However, the primary function of the pelvis is to act as an area of muscle attachment for leg muscles. This makes the pelvis part of the appendicular skeleton. Similarly, the clavicle and scapula, bones that help make up the shoulder, appear to be on the midline of the body. However, these two bones are primarily involved with arm muscle attachment and stability, making them part of the appendicular skeleton.

## DIRECTIONAL TERMINOLOGY

In addition to distinguishing between the axial and appendicular parts of the skeleton, it is also possible to describe the location and position of bones (and other bony parts or features) using directional terminology. These terms all make up pairs of opposites, where the two terms in a pair describe two alternate positions, and each term must be used in relation to other parts of the body. For example, a bone may not simply be called superior, but it can be said to be positioned more superiorly in relation to another bone. Most of these positions are relative to the midline or different sides of the body.

**Superior** and **inferior** are used to refer to relative positions along the central, longitudinal axis of the body in the anatomical position (**FIGURE 5.12**). Bones that are superior are located higher on this axis (closer to the top of the head) than bones that are inferior. For example, the cervical vertebrae (in the neck) are superior to the lumbar vertebrae (in the lower back).

Medial and lateral are used to refer to positions relative to the midline of the body, but they are different from superior and inferior (Figure 5.12). With superior and inferior, the focus is on a position along the central axis. However, with medial and lateral, the focus is on what is closer or further from the central axis. **Medial** refers to being closer to the midline, and **lateral** refers to being farther from the midline (more to the side). For example, the little toe is lateral to the big toe.

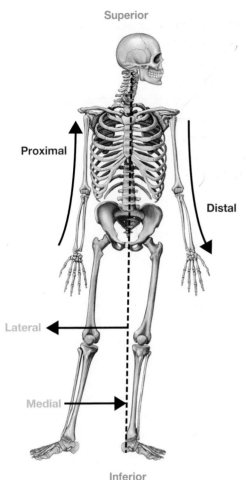

**FIGURE 5.12 Superior–Inferior, Medial–Lateral, and Proximal–Distal**
Directional terminology describes the relative position of bones in the skeleton. Notice that bones higher along the central axis are more superior, and bones lower along this axis are more inferior. Lateral bones are further from the central axis (like those in the pinky toe), while medial bones are closer to this axis (like those in the big toe). Lastly, if a bone (or end of a bone) is closer to the trunk, it is more proximal. If the bone (or end of a bone) is further from the trunk, it is more distal.

Proximal and distal are also used to refer to positions relative to the middle of the body, but here the emphasis is on being toward the trunk or away from the trunk (Figure 5.12). These terms are often used to describe different ends of bones, particularly in the arms and legs. The **proximal** end is the end nearest to (in greatest proximity with) the trunk. The **distal** end is the end that is farthest (most distant) from the trunk. For example, the shoulder end of the humerus (the

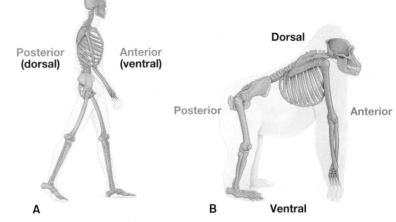

**FIGURE 5.13 Anterior–Posterior and Ventral–Dorsal**
Notice in the human (A), the front of the body is both the anterior and the ventral side, and the back of the body is both the posterior and the dorsal side. In the ape (B), the underside of the body (closest to the ground) is the ventral side; the top of the body (closest to the sky) is the dorsal side; the front of the body (closer to the face) is the anterior side; and the rear of the body is the posterior side.

upper arm bone) is the proximal end, and the elbow end of the humerus is the distal end.

Anterior and posterior are used to refer to sides of the body (**FIGURE 5.13**). **Anterior** refers to the front, and **posterior** refers to the back. Thus, an anterior surface of a bone is the surface that faces the front of the body. The posterior surface of a bone is the surface that faces the back of the body. For example the anterior surface of the cranium is made up of the face bones, and the posterior surface is made of the bone at the back of the skull, called the occipital bone. Similarly, when a bone feature has an anterior position, it is located closer to the front of the bone. If the feature has a posterior position, it is located closer to the back of the bone. For example, the eye sockets are positioned more anteriorly on the skull than the foramen magnum.

In the case of other vertebrates, the terms dorsal and ventral are also used to refer to sides of the body (Figure 5.13). **Dorsal** refers to the back, and **ventral** refers to the belly side. You can think of dolphins that have a dorsal fin on their backs. In humans, these terms are synonymous to anterior (front) and posterior (back). The ventral surface of a bone is the same as the anterior surface, and the dorsal surface of a bone is the same as the posterior surface.

**proximal** relative location closer to the trunk of the body

**distal** relative location farther away from the trunk of the body

**anterior** relative location toward the front of the body

**posterior** relative location toward the rear of the body

**dorsal** relative location toward the back of the body

**ventral** relative location toward the belly of the body

# CONCEPT REVIEW QUESTIONS

Name: _____  Section: _____

Course: _____  Date: _____

Answer the following questions in the space provided.

1. Describe one of the main functions of the skeleton inside the body.

2. What are the two main types of bone tissue in lamellar bone?

3. True or false? Approximately 2/3 of the skeleton is made of organic components.

4. Which type of bone cell is responsible for making bone?
   A. Osteoblast
   B. Osteoclast
   C. Osteodon
   D. Osteocyte

5. Which type of bone cell is responsible for removing bone?
   A. Osteodon
   B. Osteocyte
   C. Osteoblast
   D. Osteoclast

6. Describe one reason why bone remodels.

7. You are examining a bone that has a shaft in the middle and distinct ends on each side. What type of bone is this?
   A. Flat bone
   B. Long bone
   C. Irregular bone
   D. Short bone

8. A hole in the bone that is associated with a nearby nerve or vessel is usually called a
   A. depression.
   B. fossa.
   C. foramen.
   D. projection.

9. Name one bone that is part of the appendicular skeleton.

10. Compared to the cervical (neck) vertebrae, the lumbar (lower back) vertebrae are positioned more

    A. anteriorly.
    B. inferiorly.
    C. ventrally.
    D. laterally.

# LAB EXERCISES

Name: _____     Section: _____

Course: _____     Date: _____

## EXERCISE 1   BONE REMODELING

Work with a small group or alone to complete the following exercise:

1.  Describe a hypothetical situation of the "use it" portion of the use it or lose it principle. Description of the situation/behavior:




    Explanation for why *more* bone is present under these circumstances:




2.  Describe a hypothetical situation of the "lose it" portion of the use it or lose it principle. Description of the situation/behavior:




    Explanation for why *less* bone is present under these circumstances:

EXERCISE 2   **BONE SHAPES**

Work with a small group or alone to complete the following exercise. For each of the bone shapes, choose a different color. Be sure to consider which colors might stand out well against one another. Indicate your color choices in the spaces provided:

- Long bones = _____
- Flat bones = _____
- Short bones = _____
- Irregular bones = _____

Now, classify each of the bones on the skeleton diagram (to the right) as one of the four bone shapes. Color each bone on the diagram the appropriate color based on your choices above.

EXERCISE 3   **BONE FEATURES**

Work with a small group to complete this exercise. Use the skeletal material provided by your instructor (or the pictures in the lab Appendix) to complete the following tasks:

1.  Examine the cervical vertebra (neck vertebra) depicted. Locate the features in bold described below, and write the corresponding letters in the blanks provided on the image.

    A.  The **transverse foramen** (one on each side of the vertebra) transmits the vertebral arteries that give blood to the brain.

    B.  The posterior end of the vertebra has a **spinous process** to which muscles and ligaments attach.

    C.  The foramen posterior to the body of the vertebra creates the **vertebral canal** for the spinal cord to pass through when the vertebrae are stacked up on each other in the spine.

2.  Examine the humerus (upper arm bone) depicted. Locate the features in bold described below, and write the corresponding letters in the blanks provided on the image.

    A.  On the posterior side of the distal end of the humerus, there is a feature called the **olecranon fossa**. This is where the elbow-forming projection of the ulna (one of the lower arm bones) sits when the lower arm is extended.

    B.  The medial side of the distal humerus has a small projection you can feel on the inside of your arm, called the **medial epicondyle**.

    C.  On the shaft of the humerus, there is a projection (called the **deltoid tuberosity**) where the deltoid muscle attaches.

3.  Examine the sacrum, shinbone (tibia), and hip bone (pelvis) depicted. For each bone, identify if the bone feature indicated by a red circle is a projection, depression/groove, or foramen/canal.

    A.

    B.

    C.

EXERCISE 4   **AXIAL AND APPENDICULAR SKELETON**

Work with a small group or alone to complete this exercise. Review the skeleton diagram from Exercise 2 above.

1.  On the diagram, draw *circles* around bones that are part of the axial skeleton.

2.  On the diagram, draw *boxes* around bones that are part of the appendicular skeleton.

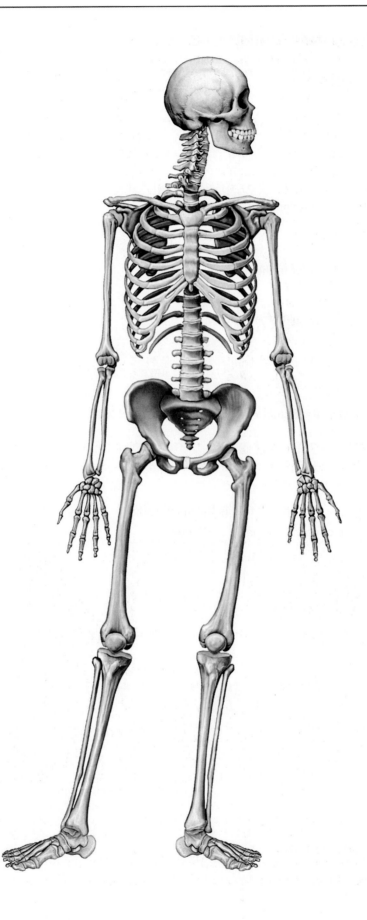

## EXERCISE 5  DIRECTIONAL TERMINOLOGY

Work with a small group or alone to complete the following exercise. Use the skeletal material provided by your instructor (or the diagram in the lab Appendix) to answer the questions below.

1. Name three (3) bones that are proximal to the carpals.

2. Name two (2) bones that are anterior to the occipital bone.

3. Name one (1) bone that is superior to the temporal bone.

4. Name four (4) bones that are distal to the femur.

5. Name one (1) bone that is posterior to the sternum.

6. Name one (1) bone that is inferior to the cervical vertebrae.

7. Draw a circle around the toe of each foot that is the most medial.
8. Draw a box around the toe of each foot that is most lateral.

On a separate sheet of paper, answer the following questions.

1. This question may be completed independently or as a group discussion. The skeleton is an integral part of the body. It works with other major body systems to help the body function and stay healthy. The bones are also shaped by their relationships with other body systems. How does the skeleton specifically work with and relate to the muscular system? How does the skeleton specifically work with and relate to the circulatory system? (Be sure to consider things like bone remodeling and bone features, as well as general bone function.)

2. Under what circumstances would an adult have woven (or unorganized) bone?

3. This question may be completed independently or as a group discussion. Review your work in Exercise 1 above. Describe an additional hypothetical situation of the "use it" portion of the "use it or lose it" principle. Be sure to describe the situation/behavior and explain why more bone is present under these circumstances. Also, describe an additional hypothetical situation of the "lose it" portion of the "use it or lose it" principle. Be sure to describe the situation and behavior and explain why less bone is present under these circumstances.

4. This question may be completed independently or as a group discussion. Use the skeleton diagram from Exercise 2 (p. 117) to help you visualize the different bone shapes in the human body. Why are short bones well suited to an area like the wrist? Why are long bones more suited to areas like the lower arm?

5. Why is a bone like the scapula (or shoulder blade) considered part of the appendicular skeleton and not the axial skeleton?

6. This question may be completed independently or as a group activity. Use directional terminology to describe the relationship between the following pairs of bones in the *human* skeleton. Use the skeleton diagram provided in the lab Appendix for Exercise 5 to help you.

   Cranium–pelvis                    Femur–tarsals

   Tibia–fibula                      Pinky toe phalanges–big toe phalanges

   Sternum–thoracic vertebrae        Occipital–frontal

   Radius–humerus                    Lumbar vertebrae–cervical vertebrae

7. This question may be completed independently or as a group discussion. Consider the mandibular canal pictured here. It is located inside the mandible (lower jawbone), extending posteriorly from the mental foramen. Based on what you know of bone features, what do you think this canal is for? Why would we need a hollow space in this area of this bone?

Mandibular canal

Mental foramen

# APPENDIX: LAB EXERCISE IMAGES

## Exercise 3 Bone Features

1. Cervical vertebra

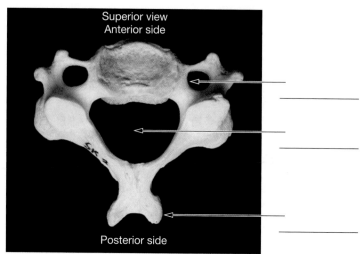

Courtesy of Ashley Lipps

2. Left humerus (upper arm bone)

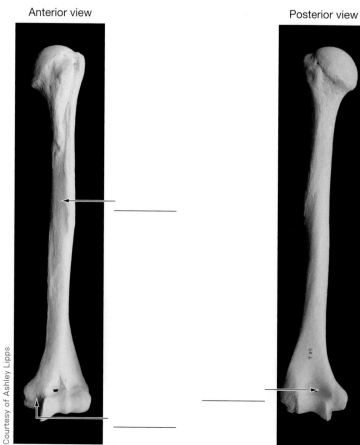

Courtesy of Ashley Lipps

3. Sacrum, shinbone (tibia), and hip bone (pelvis)

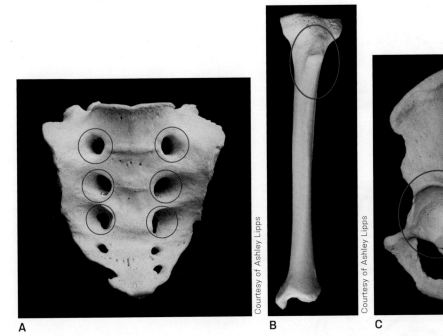

A

B

C

Courtesy of Ashley Lipps

Courtesy of Ashley Lipps

Courtesy of Ashley Lipps

# Exercise 5 Directional Terminology

Selected Bones of the Human Skeleton

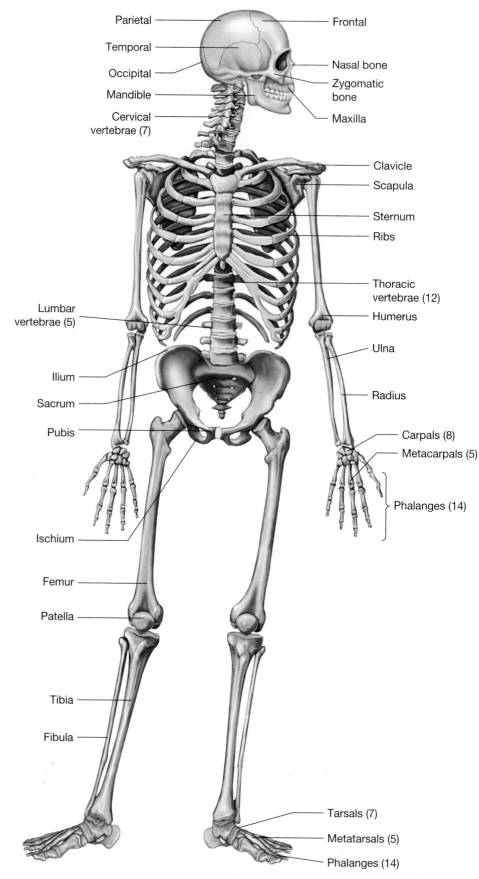

Parietal — Frontal

Temporal

Occipital — Nasal bone

Mandible — Zygomatic bone

Cervical vertebrae (7) — Maxilla

Clavicle

Scapula

Sternum

Ribs

Thoracic vertebrae (12)

Lumbar vertebrae (5) — Humerus

Ulna

Ilium

Sacrum — Radius

Pubis

Carpals (8)

Metacarpals (5)

Phalanges (14)

Ischium

Femur

Patella

Tibia

Fibula

Tarsals (7)

Metatarsals (5)

Phalanges (14)

A children's song called "Skeleton Bones" orients children to the parts of the human body such as the bones of the foot and leg. Biological anthropologists need a more in-depth, scientific understanding of the skeleton for their work.

LAB **6**

# Bones of the Skeleton

## Lab Learning Objectives

By the end of this lab, students should be able to:

- identify the major bones of the human skeleton, using their defining features.

- identify the teeth of the human skeleton, using their defining features.

- compare different bones and discuss how any observable similarities or differences relate to functional similarities or differences.

Many people are familiar with the song "Dem Bones," (also called "Skeleton Bones"). The verses of this song describe the placement of bones in our bodies:

*With the toe bone connected to the foot bone,*
*And the foot bone connected to the ankle bone,*
*And the ankle bone connected to the leg bone, . . .*

This makes for a fun classroom game where children can sing the song and point to the various areas of the body, and it is a great way for small children to learn the different parts of the body. But this is clearly a simplified description of the bones of the skeleton. There are actually multiple toe bones, and in fact there are multiple foot bones, ankle bones, and leg bones as well. Biological anthropologists must have an accurate and detailed understanding of the skeleton. This allows us to better understand skeletal similarities and differences among living primate species, and it provides us the knowledge we need to analyze fossilized skeletal material from our extinct relatives. In addition, a comprehensive understanding of the human skeleton is essential in the applied field of forensic anthropology. This lab lays the groundwork for these tasks by exploring some of the fundamentals of human skeletal anatomy.

**cranium** the skull
without the jawbone

**frontal bone** the
most anterior bone
of the cranium

**brow ridge** a bony
ridge located above
the eye orbits

**parietal bone** one
of the pair of bones
posterior to the
frontal bone that
forms the top of the
cranium

# INTRODUCTION

This lab closely examines the major bones of the skeleton (**FIGURE 6.1**). We begin with a consideration of the bones in the axial skeleton, and we then turn to the bones of the appendicular skeleton. For each bone, we discuss the relative location and position of the bone within the body, as well as the identifying features on each bone.

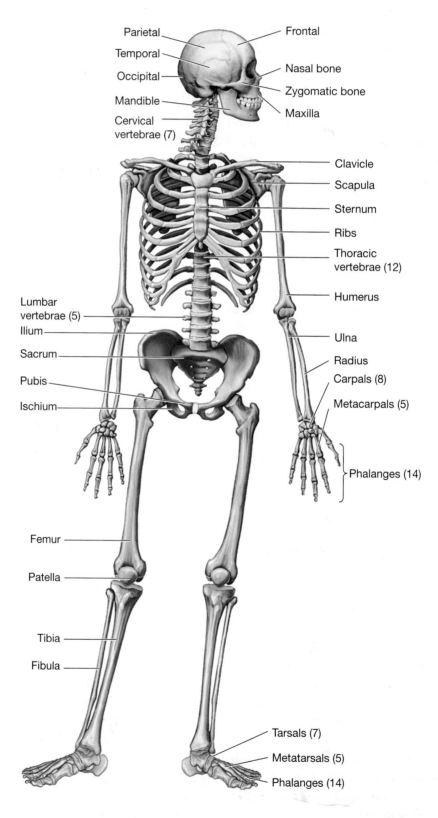

Parietal
Temporal
Occipital
Mandible
Cervical
vertebrae (7)

Frontal
Nasal bone
Zygomatic bone
Maxilla

Clavicle
Scapula
Sternum
Ribs
Thoracic
vertebrae (12)

Humerus

Lumbar
vertebrae (5)
Ilium
Sacrum
Pubis
Ischium

Ulna
Radius
Carpals (8)
Metacarpals (5)

Phalanges (14)

Femur

Patella

Tibia

Fibula

Tarsals (7)
Metatarsals (5)
Phalanges (14)

**FIGURE 6.1 The Human Skeleton**
The major bones in the human
skeleton are labeled.

# PART 1: THE AXIAL SKELETON

Remember, the *axial skeleton* is comprised of the bones that lie along the midline (or axis) of the body. We will discuss each of the major bones along this axis in humans, beginning at the superior end of the body and working our way down.

## The Cranium and Mandible

The skull (the entire bony structure of the head and jaw) is perhaps the most complex element of the skeleton. The **cranium** (or skull without the jawbone, or mandible) houses many of the key organs of the senses as well as the brain. The skull is also of major interest to biological anthropologists, as it is critical in age and sex determinations and is a key structure in understanding the evolutionary history of primates. Although it appears to be a single, complex structure, the cranium is actually made of many smaller bones that fuse together as we grow (**FIGURE 6.2** and **FIGURE 6.3**). It is important to understand the different bones of the cranium because they have different features and functions.

One of the most anterior bones of the cranium is the **frontal bone**, also called just the *frontal* (Figures 6.2A and 6.3A). This bone is what makes up our foreheads and the superior (top) part of our eye sockets (*eye orbits* or just *orbits*). The frontal bone is one of the largest and thickest cranial bones. It is distinguished by a number of key landmarks, including the *supraorbital foramen* (or sometimes a *notch*), which is a small hole above each eye orbit for blood vessels and nerves; and the *frontal eminences* (or *bosses*), which are the paired, raised areas on the bony forehead (**FIGURE 6.4**). Two other important landmarks are the *supraorbital margins*, which are the upper edges of the orbits, and the **brow ridge** (or *superciliary arches*), which are the bony ridges above the orbits that are often larger in males than females.

Posterior to the frontal bone are the paired **parietal bones**, or *parietals* (Figures 6.2B and 6.3B). There is one on each side that forms the superior and lateral sides of the cranium. The parietals are square-shaped bones that have overall uniform thickness. They are the largest bones of the braincase.

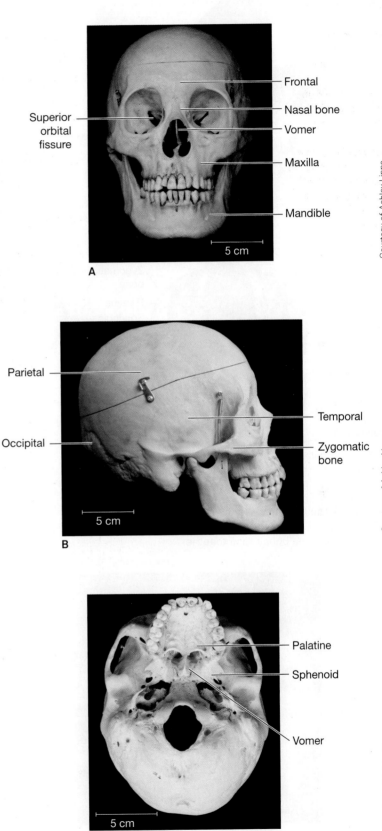

Courtesy of Ashley Lipps

Courtesy of Ashley Lipps

Courtesy of Ashley Lipps

**FIGURE 6.2 The Cranium**
(A) Frontal view, (B) lateral view, and (C) basilar (underside) view of a human skull. Note the major bones labeled.

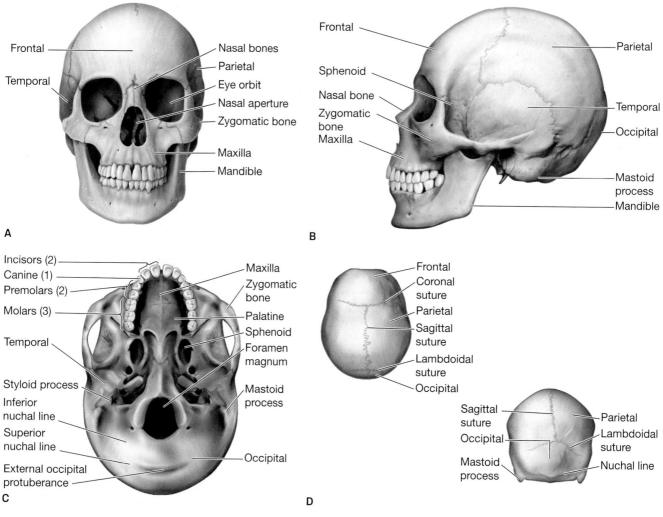

**FIGURE 6.3 The Cranium**

(A) Frontal view, (B) lateral view, and (C) basilar (underside) view of the human skull. (D) Sutures form where cranial bones fuse together.

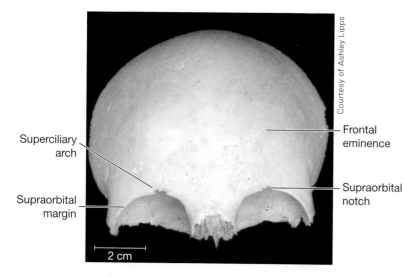

Courtesy of Ashley Lipps

**FIGURE 6.4 The Frontal Bone**

Anterior or ectocranial view of a human frontal bone. Note the important features that distinguish this bone.

The **occipital bone**, or *occipital*, forms the posterior surface and base of the skull (Figures 6.2B and 6.3B), and it has a number of key landmarks (**FIGURE 6.5**). The *foramen magnum* is the large opening through which the brain stem passes to enter the vertebral canal. The *occipital condyles* are two projections with oval articular (joint) surfaces on either side of the foramen magnum. They articulate with the first cervical vertebra in the neck. Just superior to each of the occipital condyles are the *hypoglossal canals*, which are small openings on either side of the foramen magnum for the 12th cranial nerves that innervate the tongue. On the external surface of the occipital, we also see the horizontal *nuchal lines*, which are bony ridges to which the neck (or nuchal) muscles attach. We also find the *external occipital protuberance*, which looks like a bump on the midline of the external surface of the occipital. Highly variable in size, it is often larger in males than females.

Inferior to the parietal bones are the **temporal bones**, or *temporals*, one on each side of the cranium (Figures 6.2B and 6.3B). The temporal bones form the upper portion of the jaw joint and also house the organs and delicate bones for hearing. The temporal bone has a number of key features on the outside (or ectocranial) surface (FIGURE 6.6A). The flat, smooth area of the bone is called the *squamous portion*. It articulates superiorly with the parietal bone. The *zygomatic process* is a thin projection that forms half of the zygomatic arch (what we can feel as our cheekbone). The **zygomatic arches** form a space for the jaw muscles, which attach to the mandible below and the temporal bones above. The zygomatic arches are important because they vary in size depending on a primate's dietary adaptations. The small depression seen just below the root of the zygomatic process is called the *mandibular fossa*. This is where the mandible articulates and forms the *temporomandibular joint (TMJ)* during life. The small external opening or hole just behind the mandibular fossa is the opening to the external ear canal and is called the *external auditory* (or *acoustic*) *meatus*. Posterior to the auditory meatus is the **mastoid process**, which is a small bony bump you can feel just below and behind your ear. The mastoid process is a point of attachment for neck muscles that rotate, flex, and extend the head. Males often have larger mastoid processes than females.

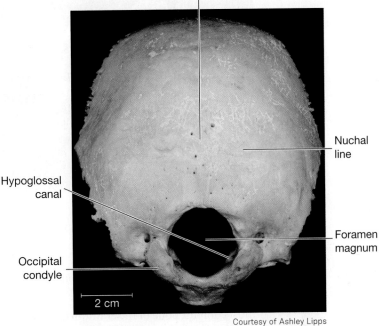

External occipital protuberance

Hypoglossal canal

Occipital condyle

Nuchal line

Foramen magnum

2 cm

Courtesy of Ashley Lipps

**FIGURE 6.5 The Occipital Bone**
Posterior or ectocranial view of a human occipital bone with important features labeled.

On the inside (or endocranial side) of the temporal bone, we see the inner *petrous portion* (FIGURE 6.6B). This petrous portion (or pyramid) is a dense region that encloses the fragile organs and tiny bones for hearing. The ear bones are called the **auditory ossicles**, and they are the smallest bones in the human body (FIGURE 6.7). On each side of the cranium, there are three bones: the *malleus* (hammer), the *incus* (anvil), and the *stapes* (stirrup). The malleus is connected to the eardrum, and the remaining bones are located more medially in each ear.

**occipital bone** the bone that forms the back and base of the cranium

**temporal bone** one of the pair of bones inferior to the parietal bone on each side of the cranium

**zygomatic arch** cheekbone area formed by numerous small bones, allowing a space for the jaw muscles that attach to the mandible below and the temporal bone above

**mastoid process** the bony projection located posterior to the ear that allows for the attachment of neck muscles

**auditory ossicles** the three tiny bones that help form each middle ear

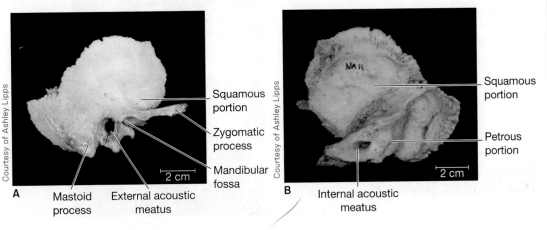

Courtesy of Ashley Lipps

Squamous portion

Zygomatic process

Mandibular fossa

**A**    Mastoid process    External acoustic meatus

Courtesy of Ashley Lipps

Squamous portion

Petrous portion

2 cm

**B**    Internal acoustic meatus

**FIGURE 6.6 The Temporal Bone**
(A) Lateral (ectocranial) view and (B) medial (endocranial) view of a human right temporal bone.

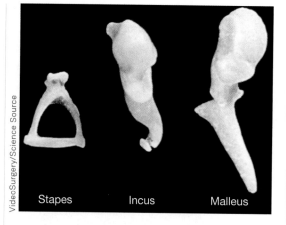

**FIGURE 6.7 The Ear Ossicles**
Note the differences in shape among the three human ear bones (or ossicles).

The **sphenoid bone**, or *sphenoid*, is a bat- or butterfly-shaped bone, and it is perhaps the most complex bone of the cranium **(FIGURE 6.8)**. It is difficult to see in its entirety in the skull because it sits deep between the cranial vault and the face bones. However, you can see parts of it from the side of the cranium or by looking inside the orbits. The sphenoid has many small openings that conduct important cranial nerves and blood vessels for the face. There are four basic parts of the sphenoid bone: the pterygoid plates, the body, and the greater and lesser wings. The *pterygoid plates* can only be seen from below or from the side of the cranium. They are thin plates of bone that serve as sites of muscle attachment. The *body* is the substantial portion of the bone lying on the midline. It has a saddle-like depression on it called the *sella turcica*, which holds the hormone-secreting pituitary gland. There are two *greater wings* (one on each side). They are anterior to the temporal bones and can be seen through the eye orbits. There are also two *lesser wings*, which are much smaller and provide partial support for the anterior of the brain. Because of its location in the cranium, the sphenoid also has two other features associated specifically with the eye. The *superior orbital fissures* are long fissures between the lesser and greater wings. These fissures are visible in the eye orbit (see Figures 6.2A and 6.3A), and they allow nerves and blood vessels to connect to the eye. The small, round opening superior to each orbital fissure is called the *optic foramen*, which is the opening to the *optic*

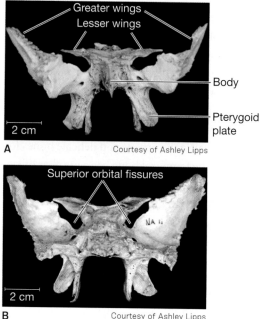

**FIGURE 6.8 The Sphenoid Bone**
(A) Anterior view and (B) posterior view of a human sphenoid bone. Note the important features that distinguish this bone.

*canal*. This canal accommodates the optic nerve and blood vessels as they pass to the eye.

The **ethmoid**, or *ethmoid bone*, is a small, delicate, cube-shaped bone. It is centered along the midline between the frontal and sphenoid bones. Due to its position in the skull, it articulates with many bones. It forms the medial wall of the eye orbits and the roof of the nasal cavity. Several features can be seen in the disarticulated bone **(FIGURE 6.9)**. The *cribriform*

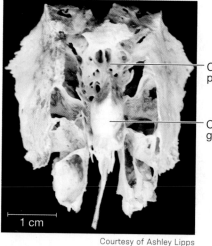

**FIGURE 6.9 The Ethmoid**
Note the important features that distinguish a human ethmoid.

**sphenoid bone** the butterfly-shaped bone between the cranial vault and face

**ethmoid** the small, cube-shaped bone between the frontal and sphenoid bones in the cranium

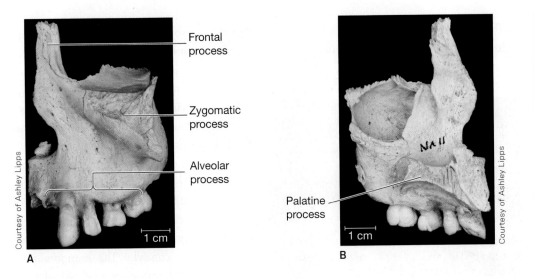

Frontal process

Zygomatic process

Alveolar process

Palatine process

Courtesy of Ashley Lipps

A    B

**FIGURE 6.10 The Maxilla**
(A) Anterior view and (B) posterior view of a human left maxilla with important features labeled.

**maxilla** (**maxillae**, plural) one of the pair of bones that forms the face and holds the upper teeth

**palatine** one of a pair of bones that forms part of the hard palate in the mouth

**zygomatic bone** one of the bones that forms the zygomatic arch

**nasal bone** one of a pair of small bones that forms the bridge of the nose

**vomer** a small, thin bone inside the nasal cavity

*plate* is a horizontal area of bone that forms the roof of the nasal cavity. It looks like a sieve with many tiny perforations that allow the olfactory nerves to pass from the nose to the brain. The small projection perpendicular to the cribriform plate is the *crista galli*. This is where a part of the outer covering of the brain attaches. The olfactory bulbs (organs for smell) sit on the cribriform plate on either side of the crista galli.

The **maxillae** (**maxilla**, singular) are a pair of bones (one on each side of the face) that hold the roots of the upper (maxillary) teeth. These bones form the face, the floor of the nasal cavity and orbits, and the roof of the mouth (hard palate) (Figures 6.2A and 6.3A). There are four key features of the maxilla (**FIGURE 6.10**). The *alveolar process* is the inferior portion that contains the teeth; the *zygomatic process* forms part of the cheek; the *palatine process* forms most of the hard palate and floor of the nasal cavity; and the long, thin *frontal process* articulates with the frontal bone and other facial bones.

The **palatines**, or *palatine bones*, are a pair of small, L-shaped bones that sit just posterior to the palatine processes of the maxillae (**FIGURE 6.11**). They form the most posterior part of the hard palate.

The **zygomatic bones** are a pair of bones that lie between the maxillae and the temporal bones (Figures 6.2B and 6.3A). They form the

most prominent part of the cheeks. The *temporal process* articulates with the temporal bone, the *maxillary process* articulates with the maxilla, the *frontal process* articulates with the frontal bone, and the *infraorbital margin* forms the lower outside (inferolateral) corner of the orbits (**FIGURE 6.12**).

The **nasal bones** are small, rectangular bones that lie along the midline, just below the frontal bone. They form the bony bridge of the nose (Figures 6.2A and 6.3A).

The **vomer** is a small, thin, plow-shaped bone that is located in the midline of the nasal cavity and forms the inferior part of the nasal septum (Figures 6.2A and 6.2C).

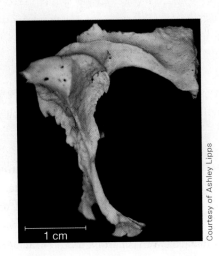

Courtesy of Ashley Lipps

**FIGURE 6.11 The Palatine**
Posterior view of a human left palatine.

Courtesy of Ashley Lipps

**inferior nasal concha (conchae,** plural) one of a pair of scroll-like bones inside the nasal cavity

**mandible** the bone that holds the lower teeth and is primarily responsible for chewing, also called the jawbone

**suture** an immovable fibrous joint between the individual bones of the cranium

**fontanelle** a soft spot on a baby's head where the space at the suture joints is particularly big

The **inferior nasal conchae** are a pair of delicate, scroll-like bones found inside the nasal cavity inferior to the ethmoid. Sometimes called the *turbinate bones*, they are important in moistening inhaled air **(FIGURE 6.13)**.

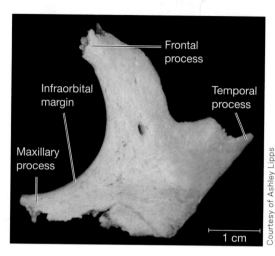

**FIGURE 6.12 The Zygomatic Bone**
Anterior view of a human left zygomatic bone.

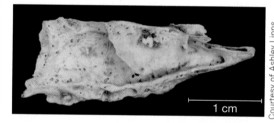

**FIGURE 6.13 The Inferior Nasal Concha**
Lateral view of a human left inferior nasal concha.

The lower jawbone, or **mandible**, sits below the anterior of the cranium (Figures 6.2 and 6.3). It is primarily responsible for chewing, so it holds the lower teeth and includes areas for the attachment of chewing muscles **(FIGURE 6.14)**. The main part of the mandible is its horizontal *body,* which is thick and strong to support the teeth. A *vertical ramus* extends upward on each side of the mandible, and the end of each vertical ramus is marked by a mandibular condyle. The *mandibular condyles* are round processes that articulate with the fossa on the temporal bones to make the *temporomandibular joint (TMJ)*. On each side of the mandible, anterior and superior to the vertical ramus, there is another bony projection called the *coronoid process*. This is a thin, flat, triangular-shaped eminence that serves as an attachment site for a chewing muscle. The protuberance in the midline of the mandible is called the *mental protuberance* (or *eminence*) and forms the bony chin.

All of the individual bones of the cranium articulate together by means of immovable fibrous joints called **sutures**. When we are born, the spaces between the sutures are not completely fused to allow for growth of the brain and cranium. Some of the spaces between these suture joints are so big that there are noticeable soft spots on the superior and posterior surfaces of babies' heads, which are called **fontanelles**. There are cartilaginous membranes here that will eventually grow and harden into bone **(FIGURE 6.15)**. The different sutures have different names. The *metopic suture* (or *frontal suture*) runs down the center of the frontal bone. The *sagittal suture* is seen along the midline of the skull between the parietal bones. The *coronal suture* lies between the frontal bone and the parietal bones. The *lambdoidal suture* separates the occipital bone from the two parietal bones, and the *squamosal suture* is between the temporal and the parietal bones. There are also many other smaller sutures that are simply named after the

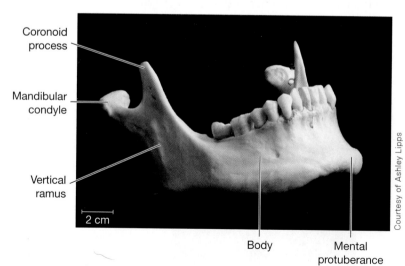

**FIGURE 6.14 The Mandible**
Anterolateral view of a human mandible with important features labeled.

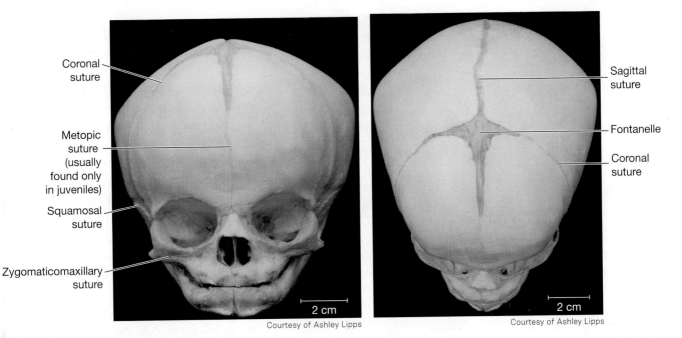

Coronal suture

Metopic suture (usually found only in juveniles)

Squamosal suture

Zygomaticomaxillary suture

2 cm

Courtesy of Ashley Lipps

Sagittal suture

Fontanelle

Coronal suture

2 cm

Courtesy of Ashley Lipps

**FIGURE 6.15 The Newborn Cranium**
We are born with spaces between our cranial sutures, such as those seen in a newborn cranium. These spaces are called fontanelles.

bones they run between, such as the *zygomaticomaxillary suture*, which runs between the zygomatic and maxilla bones, or the *frontonasal suture* that is the small suture between the frontal and nasal bones.

## The Hyoid Bone

The **hyoid bone** is a small, U-shaped bone suspended in the throat below the cranium. It is unusual because it does not articulate with any other bones. However, it does articulate (via ligaments) with numerous cartilages that form the *larynx*, which is involved in swallowing and speech. The hyoid has three main parts (**FIGURE 6.16**). The *body* is the larger, central area of the bone; the *greater horns* form the posterior ends; and the *lesser horns* are small projections on the superior surface of the body. All of these areas allow for various muscle attachments that help move the larynx and tongue.

## The Dentition

The teeth are referred to as the **dentition**, and although they are considered part of the digestive system, we will discuss them here because of their utility for biological anthropologists.

They relate to our dietary adaptations, can be used to help classify us and our living and fossil relatives, and can indicate aspects of our social behavior. The teeth also preserve better than other parts of the body in the fossil record. This means we often rely on them when identifying and understanding fossil species.

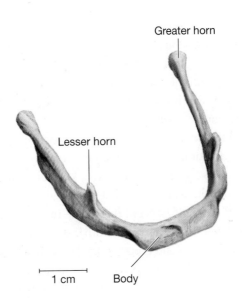

Greater horn

Lesser horn

1 cm    Body

**FIGURE 6.16 The Hyoid Bone**
Superior view of a human hyoid bone.

**hyoid bone** the small, U-shaped bone suspended in the throat below the cranium

**dentition** the teeth

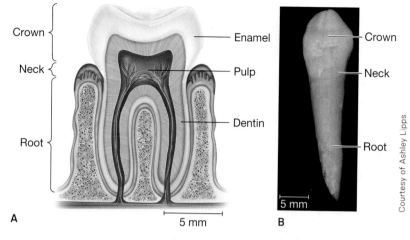

Crown

Neck

Root

Enamel

Pulp

Dentin

5 mm

A

Crown

Neck

Root

5 mm

B

Courtesy of Ashley Lipps

**FIGURE 6.17 Tooth Structure**
(A) Cross section of the human tooth, showing major regions. (B) Human canine tooth, showing major areas visible from the exterior of the tooth.

**enamel** the hard mineralized tissue on the exterior surface of a tooth

**dentin** a calcified tissue found inside a tooth, beneath the enamel surface

**deciduous teeth** the first set of teeth, also called baby teeth, that are later replaced by permanent teeth

**permanent teeth** the second set of teeth, also called adult teeth, that replace the earlier deciduous teeth

**incisors** the spatula-shaped teeth at the front of the mouth

**canine** a pointy tooth between the incisors and premolars

**premolar** tooth with two cusps, between the canines and molars

Each tooth shares the same basic structure **(FIGURE 6.17)**. The three main regions of the tooth are the crown, the neck, and the root. The *crown* is the area we see above the gum line, the *neck* is the constricted area just below the crown, and the *root* is the area that extends below the gum line and anchors the tooth. The exterior of the crown is covered by a hard substance called the **enamel**, which is made up mostly of minerals and is the hardest substance in the human body. This is the tooth's protective covering. A layer of dentin lies beneath the enamel. The **dentin** contains a slightly higher proportion of organic material than the enamel, so it is softer and more subject to decay. However, dentin is still largely inorganic and provides support for the tooth. The central area of the tooth is the *pulp*, which is a soft tissue that contains nerves and blood vessels.

Like most mammals, we have two sets of dentition during the course of our lives. Humans in particular have 20 **deciduous teeth**, which are also called baby teeth because they are the first teeth that come in when we are babies. We then have another set of 32 teeth that grows in and replaces the deciduous teeth as we get older. These teeth, commonly called the adult teeth, are the **permanent teeth**.

In each set of teeth, there are four different types of teeth **(FIGURE 6.18)**. These tooth types vary in their position, shape, and function.

The teeth at the anterior of the mouth are the **incisors**. The incisors are used primarily for biting, and they are spatula-shaped. Behind the incisors are the **canines**. The canines in some animals, such as carnivores, are for shredding. In primates, however, they mostly relate to aggressive threat displays and male competition behaviors. The canines are generally cone-shaped. After the canines, we find the **premolars**, which are used for chewing. These teeth are sometimes called bicuspids because they each have two cusps on the chewing surface. A **cusp** is a projection on the chewing surface of the tooth that is usually rounded or slightly pointed. The teeth in the posterior of the mouth are the **molars**. Like the premolars, the molars are used for chewing. The molars are generally similar to premolars but tend to be larger, squarer, and have more cusps.

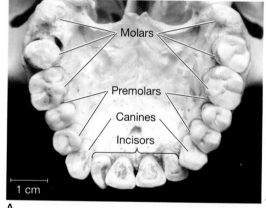

Molars

Premolars

Canines

Incisors

1 cm

A

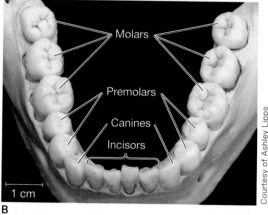

Molars

Premolars

Canines

Incisors

1 cm

B

Courtesy of Ashley Lipps

**FIGURE 6.18 The Dentition**
Note the different tooth types in the (A) maxillary and (B) mandibular dentition.

## Dental Formulas

Different species of animals will have different numbers of each kind of tooth. Species that are closely related tend to have the same numbers of each kind of tooth, so determining tooth numbers is an important tool used in classification. The numerical count of the different tooth types in a species is called the **dental formula**. To determine a species' dental formula, you must focus on one quadrant of the mouth of an individual at a time. You would begin with an upper quadrant, either the upper right or the upper left. You then count the number of each type of tooth in the quadrant, working from the anterior of the mouth toward the posterior. You write these numbers in order, separating them with periods. You then do the same for the corresponding lower quadrant of the mouth. For example, if you first used the upper right quadrant, you now examine, count, and write down the tooth numbers in the lower right quadrant. Again, be sure to separate the numbers with periods. The two sets of numbers are then written on top of each other, such that the upper quadrant numbers are above the lower quadrant numbers. Many species will have the same counts in the top and bottom, so their dental formula can be simplified to only one set of numbers (the top or bottom). However, in some species the counts may vary by one or two teeth in the top and bottom, so both sets of numbers must be reported.

Let's use the dentition in Figure 6.18 to practice determining a dental formula. We will begin in the upper right quadrant. When we count the teeth from anterior to posterior, we find two incisors, one canine, two premolars, and three molars. We find the same numbers when we count from anterior to posterior in the lower right quadrant: two incisors, one canine, two premolars, and three molars. This is written as follows:

2.1.2.3
2.1.2.3

Or, because the top and bottom are the same, the dental formula can be simplified to 2.1.2.3. This is the dental formula for humans and our close primate relatives. So, if you count your own teeth in a mirror, you will probably find you have this dental formula. If you have had your wisdom teeth removed (or if you never had any), your teeth will not represent the typical dental formula for our species because you will have only two molars, instead of three. The wisdom teeth are the third molars and are the last to erupt. They usually come in during your late teens or early twenties. As a species, we tend to have three molars in each quadrant of our mouth. However, it is becoming increasingly common for some people (in populations with access to dental care) to have the third molars removed because they do not have enough room in their mouths for them.

## The Vertebral Column

As we work our way down the body from the cranium, we first encounter the vertebral column. The **vertebral column** is the vertical stack of bones that comprise what we commonly call our backbone. This includes the 24 individual vertebrae, the sacrum, and the coccyx. These bones protect the spinal cord as it runs from the base of the cranium to the lower body. In humans, the vertebral column takes an unusual S-shape, due to a curve in the neck and a curve in the lower back (**FIGURE 6.19**). This is an adaptation we have to help with our unique form of bipedal locomotion (see Lab 14 for more information).

The **vertebrae** (**vertebra**, singular) are the irregularly shaped bones that make up most of the vertebral column. They are separated by *intervertebral discs*, which form cartilaginous joints that allow for mobility and also cushion and absorb shock in the spine. In general, the vertebrae share the same basic structures (**FIGURE 6.20**). They have a large, cylindrical area called the *body* that extends anteriorly. The *vertebral arch* extends posteriorly from the body. This arch forms an opening called the *vertebral foramen*, which holds the spinal cord. On either side of the vertebral arch, *transverse processes* extend laterally. On the posterior surface of the vertebral arch, there is a *spinous process* that extends out along the midline. These various processes help with muscle attachment and/or articulation with other bones.

**cusp** a rounded (or slightly pointed) projection on a tooth's chewing surface

**molar** a large, multicusped tooth at the back of the mouth

**dental formula** a numerical count of the different tooth types in an animal

**vertebral column** the row of bones that form the backbone

**vertebra** (**vertebrae**, plural) an irregularly shaped bone that is part of the vertebral column

**cervical vertebra**
one of the seven vertebrae (C1–C7) that form the neck

**atlas** the unusually shaped C1, a vertebra that works with the axis to allow for head movement and rotation

**axis** the unusually shaped C2, a vertebra that works with the atlas to allow for head movement and rotation

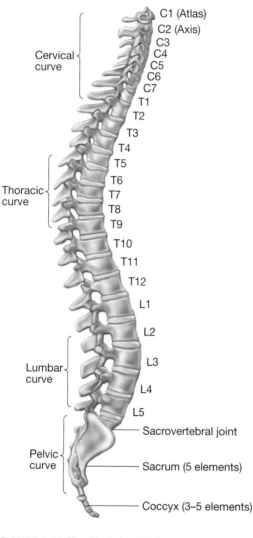

**FIGURE 6.19 The Vertebral Column**
Lateral view of the human vertebral column. Note the different types of vertebrae and the curvature of different areas of the spine. These curves give humans a uniquely shaped vertebral column, as discussed in greater detail in Lab 14.

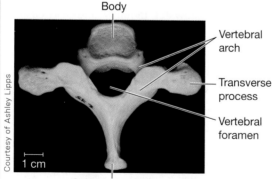

**FIGURE 6.20 Typical Vertebrae**
A thoracic vertebra (superior view) represents a typical human vertebra. Note the major bony features that are shared by most vertebrae.

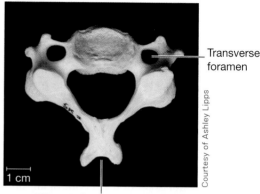

**FIGURE 6.21 Typical Cervical Vertebrae**
Superior view of a typical cervical vertebra. Note the major bony features that are shared by most cervical vertebrae.

There are three types of vertebrae superior to the pelvis; they are differentiated based on their position in the vertebral column and their function. The **cervical vertebrae** are found in the neck. They are the smallest vertebrae in humans. There are seven cervical vertebrae, and they are numbered based on their order from the most superior to the most inferior. Thus, C1 (cervical 1) is the most superior cervical vertebra, and C7 is the most inferior cervical vertebra. The cervical vertebrae have some unusual features **(FIGURE 6.21)**. On the cervical vertebrae, each transverse process has a *transverse foramen* that allows arteries to pass through the neck to supply blood and oxygen to the brain. In addition, most cervical vertebrae have short spinous processes with *bifurcated* (or *forked*) *ends*, meaning the end splits into two separate branches. The first two cervical vertebrae are particularly unusual. The first cervical vertebra (C1) is called the **atlas (FIGURE 6.22)**. Unlike other vertebrae, it does not have a body. Instead, it has an *anterior arch* and a *posterior arch* that give it a ring-like shape. It also has a *superior articular facet* on each of the transverse processes. These facets articulate with the protruding *occipital condyles* at the base of the cranium. The second cervical vertebra (C2) is called the **axis (FIGURE 6.23)**. The axis has a small body with a perpendicular structure called the *odontoid process* (or *dens*),

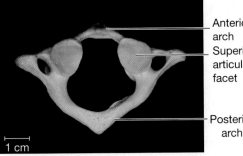

Courtesy of Ashley Lipps

Anterior arch
Superior articular facet
Posterior arch

**FIGURE 6.22 The Atlas**
Superior view of a human atlas. Note the important features that distinguish it from other cervical vertebrae.

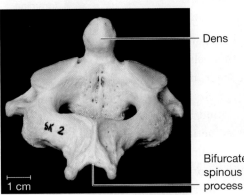

Courtesy of Ashley Lipps

Dens

Bifurcated spinous process

**FIGURE 6.23 The Axis**
Posterior view of a human axis, with important features that distinguish it from other cervical vertebrae labeled.

which extends superiorly. This structure acts as the pivot on which the atlas rotates. These two cervical vertebrae work together to allow for head movement and rotation, which is why they have unusual shapes that provide more mobility.

Interestingly, almost all mammals have seven cervical vertebrae, no matter how long their necks. For example, humans, giraffes, and cows all have seven cervical vertebrae. Giraffes do not have a longer neck because they have more cervical vertebrae than other mammals. Rather, their cervical vertebrae are larger and longer than those of many other mammals.

Inferior to the cervical vertebrae are the **thoracic vertebrae**, which form the backbone in the chest area. There are twelve thoracic vertebrae, numbered T1 (most superior) to T12

(most inferior), and they articulate to ribs. In addition to being a little larger than cervical vertebrae, the thoracic vertebrae can be distinguished by a few key features (**FIGURE 6.24**). On each side of the body of a typical thoracic vertebra, there are two *costal facets*, with one being more superior and the other being more inferior along the vertebral body. These facets articulate with the heads of the ribs. In addition, the spinous processes on thoracic vertebrae are usually long and oriented so that they point downward and overlap one another. However, the lowest thoracic vertebrae have spinous processes that more closely resemble those of lumbar vertebrae.

Lastly, inferior to the thoracic vertebrae are the **lumbar vertebrae**. There are five lumbar vertebrae, numbered L1 (most superior) to L5 (most inferior). These are the largest vertebrae in humans because they support the weight of the upper body. They are relatively generalized and lack the special features

**thoracic vertebra** one of the 12 vertebrae (T1–T12) that articulate with ribs in the chest area

**lumbar vertebra** one of the five vertebrae (L1–L5) that form the lower back

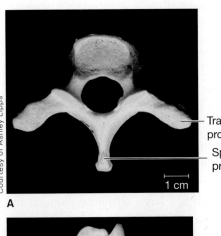

Courtesy of Ashley Lipps

Transverse process
Spinous process

**A**

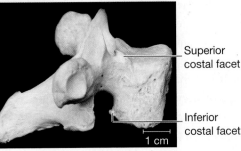

Courtesy of Ashley Lipps

Superior costal facet

Inferior costal facet

**B**

**FIGURE 6.24 The Thoracic Vertebrae**
(A) Superior view and (B) lateral view of a human thoracic vertebra. Note the important features that distinguish it from other types of vertebrae.

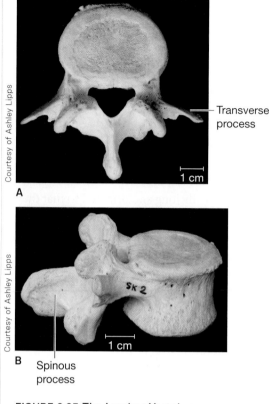

Courtesy of Ashley Lipps

**A**

Transverse process

1 cm

Courtesy of Ashley Lipps

**B** Spinous process

1 cm

**FIGURE 6.25 The Lumbar Vertebrae**
(A) Superior view and (B) lateral view of a human lumbar vertebra, with important features that distinguish it from other types of vertebrae labeled.

articulates with the last lumbar vertebra (L5), and the inferior surface of the sacrum articulates with the superior surface of the coccyx. The **coccyx** is a small bone that anchors a few muscles and ligaments **(FIGURE 6.27)**. It is formed by the fusion of three to five rudimentary vertebrae (the *coccygeal vertebrae*), and it is known commonly as the tailbone because it is the remnant of a vestigial tail that is lost seen in the other vertebrae **(FIGURE 6.25)**. For example, lumbar vertebrae do not have the transverse foramen found in cervical vertebrae or the costal facets found in thoracic vertebrae. Lumbar vertebrae also have short, blunt spinous processes.

The remainder of the vertebral column is made of two bones: the sacrum and the coccyx. The **sacrum** is a large, triangular bone at the base of the vertebral column **(FIGURE 6.26)**. Overall, the bone curves slightly, creating a concave anterior surface and convex posterior surface; and it has numerous, small holes (called *sacral foramina*) that allow for the passage of nerves and blood vessels. The sacrum is comprised of five vertebrae that begin fusing together in the teen years and are fully fused in adults. The flared sides of the sacrum (called *alae*; *ala*, singular) are formed by the fusion of the transverse processes, and they articulate with the ilia on the pelvis to form the *sacroiliac joints*. The superior surface of the sacrum

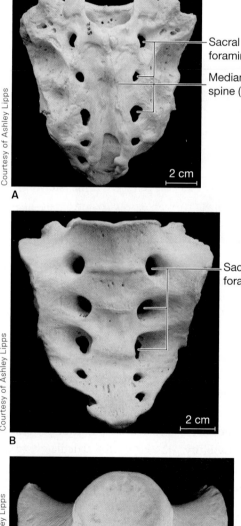

Courtesy of Ashley Lipps

**A**

Sacral foramina

Median spine (crest)

2 cm

Courtesy of Ashley Lipps

**B**

Sacral foramina

2 cm

Courtesy of Ashley Lipps

**C**

Ala

2 cm

**FIGURE 6.26 The Sacrum**
(A) Anterior view, (B) posterior view, and (C) superior view of a human sacrum. Note the important features that distinguish this bone.

**sacrum** the large, triangular bone at the base of the vertebral column and between the two hip bones

**coccyx** a small bone that articulates to the inferior end of the sacrum, also called the tailbone

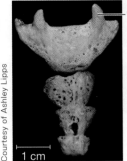

Cornua

FIGURE 6.27 The Coccyx
Posterior view of a human coccyx.

1 cm

very early in our embryonic development. The *cornua* project from the superior surface of the coccyx and articulate with the sacrum.

## The Ribs and Sternum

The vital organs of the chest, such as the heart and lungs, are enclosed and protected by the thoracic cage, or rib cage (FIGURE 6.28). The posterior of the thoracic cage is formed by the articulation of the ribs with the thoracic vertebrae. The ribs then curve around to the anterior, where they attach to the sternum (via cartilage) to form the anterior of the thoracic cage.

The **sternum** (commonly called the breast-bone) is formed by three bones that fuse together later in life (FIGURE 6.29). The most superior of these bones is the *manubrium*. It is a triangular-shaped bone that has a *clavicular notch* on each side to articulate with the clavicles. It also has a *jugular notch* in the center that can be felt just at the base of your throat. The second bone of the sternum, the *sternal body*, is inferior to the manubrium. It is more elongated and oval-shaped. It has *costal notches* along each side, where the ribs articulate (via cartilage). The most inferior bone is the *xiphoid process*. It is the cartilaginous inferior point of the sternum that becomes mineralized into bone later in life.

There are twenty-four **ribs** arranged in pairs, with twelve ribs on each side of the thoracic cage (FIGURE 6.30). All of these ribs articulate with the thoracic vertebrae posteriorly, but they do not all articulate with the sternum anteriorly. The first seven pairs of ribs are called *true ribs* because they articulate with the sternum directly via *costal cartilage*. The next three pairs

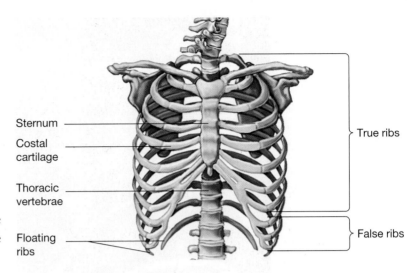

Sternum
Costal cartilage
Thoracic vertebrae
Floating ribs
True ribs
False ribs

FIGURE 6.28 The Thoracic Cage
Anterior view of a human thoracic cage (or rib cage). Note the different bones that make up this important structure.

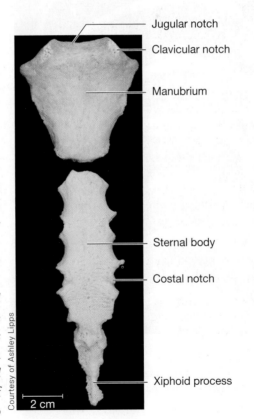

Jugular notch
Clavicular notch
Manubrium
Sternal body
Costal notch
Xiphoid process

2 cm

FIGURE 6.29 The Sternum
Anterior view of a human sternum, showing the three bones that fuse to form this bone.

of ribs are called *false ribs* because they join with the costal cartilage of the ribs above, rather than directly to the sternum. The last two pairs of ribs do not connect to the sternum at all, so they are called *floating ribs*. These floating ribs

**sternum** bone formed by the fusion of three separate bones in the chest, also called the breastbone

**rib bone** one of the 12 long bones that form each side of the rib cage (or thoracic cage)

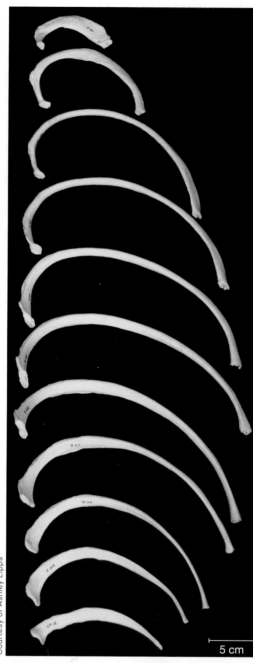

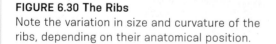

**FIGURE 6.30 The Ribs**
Note the variation in size and curvature of the ribs, depending on their anatomical position.

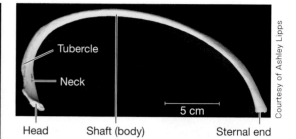

**FIGURE 6.31 Typical Rib**
Superior view of a typical human left rib. Note the important features that ribs share.

The main part of the rib is called the *shaft* (or *body*). The shaft is the elongated, flat area that curves around to the anterior of the thoracic cage. While the superior (top) of this shaft is rounded, the inferior (underside) of this shaft has a sharp, tapering edge. This can be helpful when trying to determine to which side of the body a rib belongs. You can identify the sharp surface (underside) and can then orient the rib correctly to determine if it is from the right or left side of the thoracic cage.

# PART 2: THE APPENDICULAR SKELETON

Now that we have discussed the bones of the axial skeleton, we turn to the bones of the appendicular skeleton. Remember, the *appendicular skeleton* is comprised of the bones that form the appendages (arms and legs) on each side of the body. This includes some bones that appear to be along the body's axis but are considered appendicular because they are functionally tied to the appendages. We discuss each of the major bones of the human appendicular skeleton, beginning with the upper limb.

## The Clavicle

The **clavicle** is commonly referred to as the collarbone. It helps to stabilize the shoulder, providing structural support and areas for muscle attachment. In general, the clavicle is a slightly curved (somewhat S-shaped) bone

are sometimes considered to be a specific kind of false ribs. All ribs share the same key features (**FIGURE 6.31**). They have a *head* on the posterior end that articulates with the body of a thoracic vertebra, and they have a *tubercle* along the *neck* of the rib that articulates with the transverse process of the same thoracic vertebra.

**clavicle** a slightly curved bone that helps stabilize each shoulder, also called the collarbone

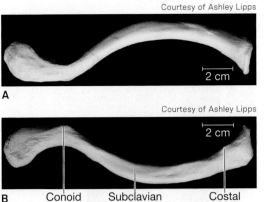

2 cm

**A**

2 cm

**B**     Conoid     Subclavian     Costal
       tubercle       groove       tuberosity

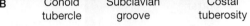

**FIGURE 6.32 The Clavicle**
(A) Superior view and (B) inferior view of
a human left clavicle. Note the important
features that distinguish this bone.

**(FIGURE 6.32).** You can feel the curve in your own clavicle if you run your fingers along it from one end to the other. The medial end of the clavicle is rounded, and it articulates with the sternum. The lateral end of the clavicle is flatter, and it articulates with the scapula. The *conoid tubercle* is an area for ligament attachment located on the lateral end of the posteroinferior surface. There is also a long, shallow depression (called the *subclavian groove*) that runs along the inferior side of the clavicle's central shaft. This area accommodates nearby blood vessels. Finally, on the medial inferior end, there is a rough surface called the *costal tuberosity* for the attachment for another ligament.

## The Scapula

The **scapula** is commonly called the shoulder blade **(FIGURE 6.33)**. It is a large, flat, triangular bone. It is fairly mobile, and you can feel it move around on your back as you move your arm. In humans and some other primates, the scapula is positioned on the posterior surface of the rib cage. In other primates and animals, the scapula is often positioned more to the side of the rib cage (see Lab 12 for more information). Each edge of the triangular scapula has a name. The *superior border* runs along the superior edge; the *vertebral border* runs along the medial edge, parallel to the vertebral column; and the *axillary border* runs along the lateral edge, near the armpit. On the posterior surface of the scapula,

there is a ridge of bone that runs roughly parallel to the superior border. This ridge is called the *scapular spine*. At the lateral edge of the spine, there is a projection called the *acromion process*, which articulates with the clavicle. Near the acromion process along the superior border, there is another large projection called the *coracoid process* that is an area for arm muscle attachment. Where the axillary and superior borders meet, there is a round depression called the *glenoid fossa*. This shallow depression articulates with the head of the humerus (upper arm bone) to form the highly mobile shoulder joint.

Coracoid process

Superior
border

Vertebral
(medial)
border

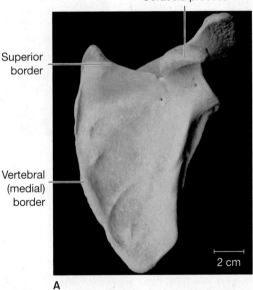

2 cm

**A**

Scapular spine

Acromion
process

Glenoid
fossa

Axillary
(lateral)
border

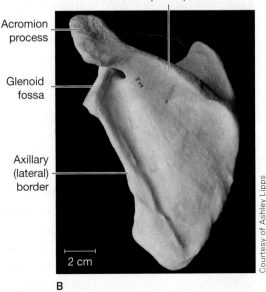

2 cm

**B**

**scapula** a large, flat bone that forms part of each shoulder joint, also called the shoulder blade

**FIGURE 6.33
The Scapula**
(A) Anterior view and (B) posterior view of a human left scapula, with important features labeled.

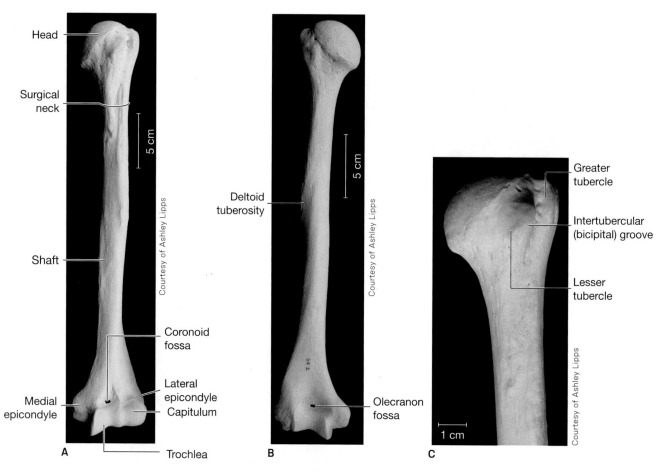

**FIGURE 6.34 The Humerus**
(A) Anterior view, (B) posterior view, and (C) close-up of the proximal end of a human left humerus. Note the important features that distinguish this bone.

## The Humerus

The upper arm bone is called the **humerus** and is a typical long bone (**FIGURE 6.34**). The proximal end of the humerus is called the *head*. It has a rounded shape, and it is the part of the humerus that articulates with the glenoid fossa of the scapula. Near the head of the humerus, there are two important projections. The *lesser tubercle* is the more anterior and smaller of the two, while the *greater tubercle* is more posterior and larger. Both tubercles are areas for muscle attachment. Between these two projections, there is an indentation called the *intertubercular* (or *bicipital*) *groove*. This groove accommodates a tendon of the biceps muscle. Below the head, there is an area called the *surgical neck*, which joins the head to the shaft. Further down the shaft of the bone on the lateral surface, there is an area called the *deltoid tuberosity*, which is where the deltoid muscle attaches.

At the distal end of the humerus, there are several key features. The *capitulum* is a rounded projection on the lateral side, and it articulates with the radius (a lower arm bone). The *trochlea* is an area that is shaped like a spool of thread. It is medial to the capitulum and articulates with the ulna (the other lower arm bone). Lateral (and slightly proximal) to the capitulum is a projection called the *lateral epicondyle*. A slightly larger projection, called the *medial epicondyle*, is positioned medial (and slightly proximal) to the trochlea. Both epicondyles are areas for ligament and/or muscle attachment for the lower arm. In addition to these various projections, the distal end of the humerus has two pronounced depressions. The *olecranon fossa* is a large depression on the posterior surface, and the *coronoid fossa* is a smaller depression on the anterior surface. Both of these depressions articulate with the ulna as part of the elbow joint.

**humerus** the upper bone in each arm

## The Radius and Ulna

The lower arm is made up of two long bones: the radius and the ulna (**FIGURE 6.35**). The proximal ends of both the radius and the ulna articulate with the humerus. The distal ends of these two lower arm bones articulate with the carpals to form the wrist. With your arm at your side and the palm of your hand facing forward, the **radius** is the more lateral and shorter of the two lower arm bones (**FIGURE 6.36**). Its proximal end has a round depression called the *head*, which articulates with the capitulum of the humerus. Below the head, there is a projection on the anteromedial surface called the *radial tuberosity*. It is an area of attachment for the biceps muscle. Between the head and the radial tuberosity, the bone is constricted (narrower) in an area called the *neck* of the radius. The *shaft* of the radius extends from the neck to the distal end of the bone. At the distal end, there is a sharply pointed area called the *styloid process* on the lateral side of the bone.

With your arm at your side and the palm of your hand facing forward, the **ulna** is the more medial and longer of the two lower arm bones (Figure 6.35). It has a unique, wrench-shaped proximal end formed by several key features (**FIGURE 6.37**). The *olecranon process* is a large projection that accommodates muscle attachment and fits in the olecranon fossa of the humerus when the arm is extended. This is the large bony area that we often think of as the tip of our elbow. Just below the olecranon fossa, there is an area called the *trochlear notch*, which is a C-shaped notch that articulates with the rounded trochlea of the humerus. At the base of the trochlear notch on the anterior surface, there is a pointy projection called the *coronoid process* that articulates with the coronoid fossa of the humerus. The ulna articulates with the radius at the *radial notch*, which is located on the lateral end of the coronoid process. As with the radius, the main length of the ulna is called the *shaft*, and the distal end is marked by a pointy projection called a *styloid process*. However, in the ulna, the styloid process is located on the medial side of the bone, rather than the lateral side.

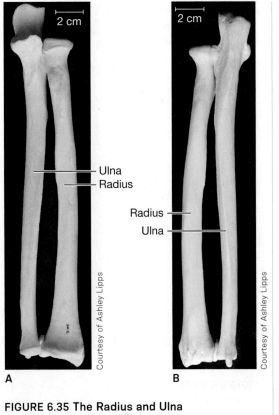

A            B

Ulna
Radius

Radius
Ulna

**FIGURE 6.35 The Radius and Ulna**
(A) Anterior view and (B) posterior view of a human left radius and ulna in anatomical position.

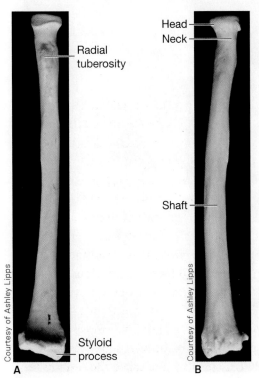

Radial tuberosity

Head
Neck

Shaft

Styloid process

A            B

**FIGURE 6.36 The Radius**
(A) Anterior view and (B) posterior view of a human left radius. Note the important features that help to distinguish this bone.

**radius** the more lateral of the two lower bones in each arm

**ulna** the more medial of the two lower bones in each arm

**carpal** one of the eight short bones of each wrist

**metacarpal** one of the five bones that form the palm of each hand

**phalanx** (**phalanges,** plural) one of the fourteen bones that form the fingers and toes on each hand or foot

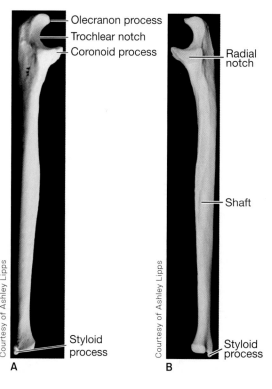

FIGURE 6.37 The Ulna
(A) Lateral view and (B) medial view of a human left ulna, with important features labeled.

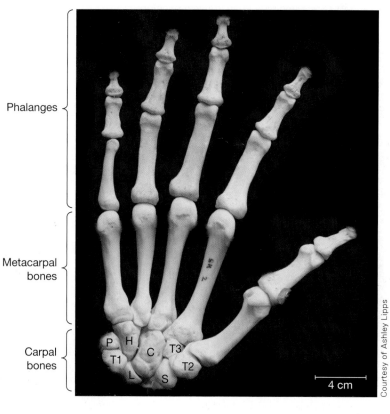

FIGURE 6.38 The Bones of the Hand and Wrist (Right Hand)
Palmar view of the bones of the right hand and wrist in anatomical position. Carpals: S = scaphoid, L = lunate, T1 = triquetral, P = pisiform, T2 = trapezium, T3 = trapezoid, C = capitate, H = hamate.

## The Bones of the Wrist and Hand

The bones of the wrist and hand take three basic forms: carpals (wrist bones), metacarpals (palm or hand bones), and hand phalanges (finger bones) **(FIGURE 6.38)**. There are eight **carpals** in each hand. They are typical short bones, appearing generally cube-like in shape **(FIGURE 6.39)**. They provide support and limit mobility in the wrist area. They are positioned such that they form two rows, with four bones in each row. The proximal row includes (from lateral to medial) the *scaphoid*, the *lunate*, the *triquetral* (or *triquetrum*), and the *pisiform*. The distal row includes (again from lateral to medial) the *trapezium*, the *trapezoid*, the *capitate*, and the *hamate*. Notice that while all of these bones have a general cube shape, they do vary in exact shape and size.

The bones of the hand, or palm, are called the **metacarpals** **(FIGURE 6.40)**. There are five metacarpals in each hand, with one metacarpal corresponding with each finger. The metacarpals are numbered from 1 to 5, with 1 corresponding to the thumb and 5 corresponding to the pinky finger. The proximal end of a metacarpal is somewhat square-shaped and concave, and it articulates with one or more rounded carpal surfaces. In humans, the proximal ends of metacarpals 2 through 5 also articulate with the adjacent metacarpals. The distal end of a metacarpal is more rounded, and it articulates with a phalanx (finger bone).

The finger bones are called **phalanges** (**phalanx**, singular). The thumb has only two

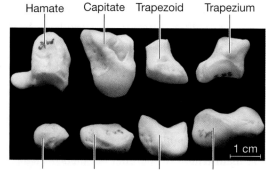

FIGURE 6.39 The Carpals
Note the similarities and differences among individual human left carpal bones.

phalanges, but the other fingers each have three phalanges (**FIGURE 6.41**). From the metacarpal to the fingertip, the three phalanges of each finger are referred to as the proximal phalanx, the intermediate phalanx, and the distal phalanx. The thumb has only a proximal phalanx and a distal phalanx; it lacks the intermediate phalanx. In general, the hand phalanges get smaller as they approach the fingertip, with the proximal phalanges being the largest and the distal phalanges being the smallest. The distal phalanges have flattened distal ends that correspond to the pads on our fingertips.

## The Pelvis

Having considered the upper limb, we now turn to the lower limb. The pelvis (or *pelvic girdle*) appears to be one large bone, but it is actually composed of three bones. The posterior is formed by the sacrum, which is considered part of the axial skeleton. The sides and anterior are formed by the two **ossa coxae** (**os coxa**, singular), also called **innominate bones** or hip bones (**FIGURE 6.42**). The ossa coxae articulate with the sacrum posteriorly at the *sacroiliac joints*, and they articulate to each other anteriorly at the *pubic symphysis joint*. Each os coxa is in turn formed by the fusion of three bones: the ilium, the ischium, and the pubis. The **ilium** is the large, blade-like area that you can feel when you put your hands on your hips. The **ischium** forms the underside upon which we sit. The **pubis** is the anterior region, and it is the area where the two ossa coxae articulate with one another.

The pelvis is an important area for muscle attachment, such as for the gluteal muscles that help move the leg and stabilize the body during locomotion. The pelvis is also useful for determining an individual's sex because it varies considerably between males and females. Because

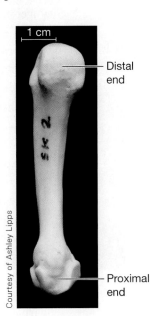

1 cm

Distal end

Proximal end

Courtesy of Ashley Lipps

**FIGURE 6.40 The Metacarpals**
Anterior view of a typical human left metacarpal bone. Note the difference between the proximal and distal ends.

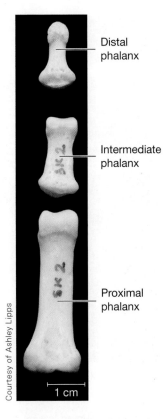

Distal phalanx

Intermediate phalanx

Proximal phalanx

1 cm

Courtesy of Ashley Lipps

**FIGURE 6.41 The Finger Bones**
Anterior view of the three hand phalanges (or finger bones) from one left finger. The four fingers each have three phalanges, such as those here. The thumb has only two phalanges.

**os coxa** (**ossa coxae**, plural) one of the pair of bones that form the side and front of the pelvis, resulting from the fusion of the ilium, ischium, and pubis; also known as the **innominate bone**

**ilium** (**ilia**, plural) the large, blade-like area of each os coxa (hip bone)

**ischium** the bone that forms the underside (posteroinferior side) of an os coxa

**pubis** the bone that forms the front (anterior) of an os coxa, also called the pubic bone

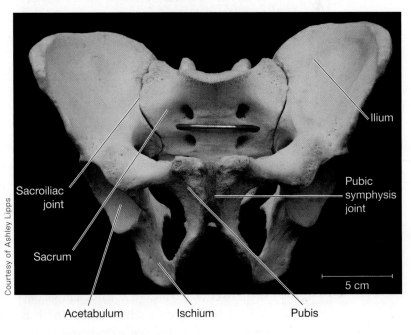

Sacroiliac joint

Sacrum

Ilium

Pubic symphysis joint

Acetabulum          Ischium          Pubis

5 cm

Courtesy of Ashley Lipps

**FIGURE 6.42 The Pelvic Girdle**
Note the different bones that form an articulated human pelvic girdle (anterior view).

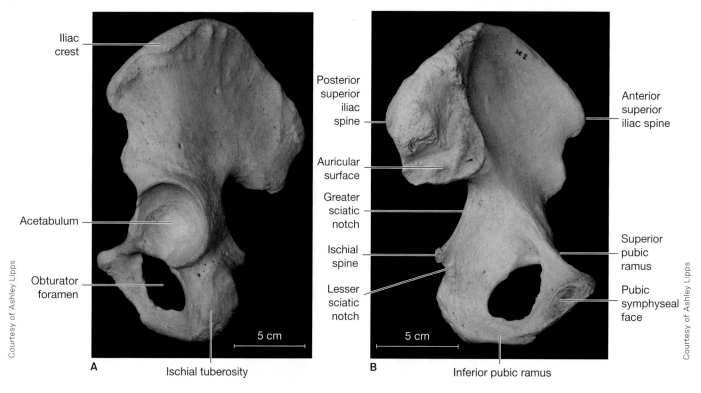

Iliac crest

Posterior superior iliac spine

Auricular surface

Greater sciatic notch

Ischial spine

Lesser sciatic notch

Anterior superior iliac spine

Acetabulum

Obturator foramen

Superior pubic ramus

Pubic symphyseal face

5 cm

5 cm

**A**

Ischial tuberosity

**B**

Inferior pubic ramus

**FIGURE 6.43 The Os Coxa**
(A) Lateral view and (B) medial view of a human left os coxa. Note the important features of the ilium, ischium, and pubis, the three bones that fuse to form each hip bone.

there are numerous significant features in the pelvis, we discuss them for each bone, beginning with the features of the ilium **(FIGURE 6.43)**. On the medial surface of the ilium, there is an ear-shaped area called the *auricular surface*. This is where the os coxa articulates with the sacrum to form the sacroiliac joint. The superior edge of the ilium is called the *iliac crest*. This is an attachment area for numerous abdominal muscles. The *anterior superior iliac spine* is found at the anterior end of the iliac crest, and the *posterior superior iliac spine* is found at the posterior end of the iliac crest. Both are areas for muscle attachment. The *greater sciatic notch* is located inferior to the posterior superior iliac spine, and it accommodates muscles and nerves that run through the pelvis to the lower limb. The *acetabulum* is the large, cup-like depression on the lateral surface of the os coxa. It is located anterior and slightly inferior to the greater sciatic notch, and it is the area of the pelvis that articulates with the femur head to form the hip joint. It is also the area where the ilium, ischium, and pubis fuse together.

There are additional important features on the ischium (Figure 6.43). Posterior to the acetabulum and inferior to the greater sciatic notch, we find the *ischial spine*. The *lesser sciatic notch* is then located just inferior to the ischial spine, and it accommodates an important leg muscle. The large, rough area of bone just below the lesser sciatic notch is called the *ischial tuberosity*. It forms the posteroinferior corner of the pelvis, and it is an attachment point for several leg muscles.

Finally, on the pubis, we see other important features (Figure 6.43). The *superior pubic ramus* joins the pubis to the ilium in the acetabulum, and the *inferior pubic ramus* joins the pubis to the ischium. Together with the ischium, these two rami form a large hole, called the *obturator foramen*, which allows for the passage of nerves and blood vessels between the pelvis and leg. The *pubic symphysis* is the relatively immobile cartilaginous joint where the pubis bones of the two ossa coxae articulate. The surface of the pubis that is involved in this articulation is called the *pubic symphyseal face*, and it is an important area used to estimate age from a skeleton.

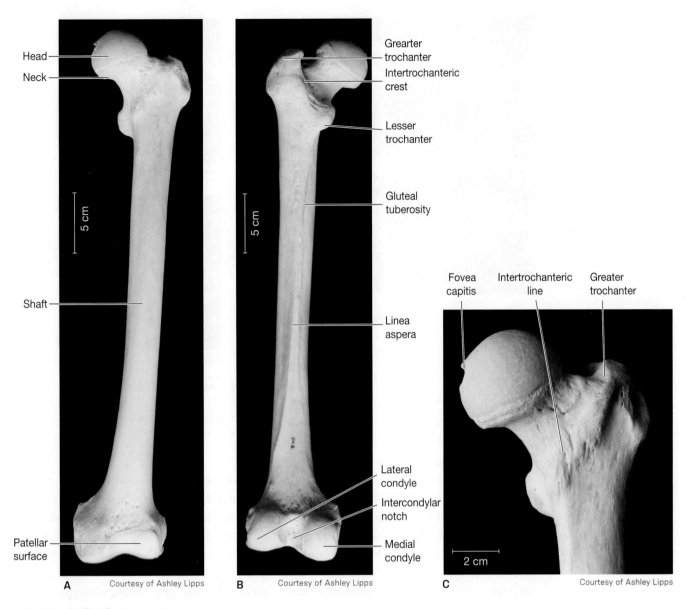

Head
Neck
5 cm
Shaft
Patellar surface
**A** Courtesy of Ashley Lipps

Grearter trochanter
Intertrochanteric crest
Lesser trochanter
Gluteal tuberosity
5 cm
Linea aspera
Lateral condyle
Intercondylar notch
Medial condyle
**B** Courtesy of Ashley Lipps

Fovea capitis
Intertrochanteric line
Greater trochanter
2 cm
**C** Courtesy of Ashley Lipps

**FIGURE 6.44 The Femur**
(A) Anterior view, (B) posterior view, and (C) close-up of the anterior proximal end of a human left femur. Note the important features that distinguish this bone.

## The Femur and Patella

The large and heavy thigh bone is called the **femur (FIGURE 6.44)**. The proximal end of the femur has a round *head* that articulates with the acetabulum of the pelvis. The head of the femur has a small depression in the center, called the *fovea capitis*. An important ligament runs between here and the acetabulum to help keep the femur in place in the hip joint. Below the head, there is a constricted area, called the *neck* of the femur, which joins the head and shaft. On the lateral side of the proximal end of the femur, there is a large projection called the *greater trochanter*. This is a muscle attachment

site for gluteal muscles that originate on the pelvis. Just below where the femur neck meets the shaft on the posterior surface, there is another projection called the *lesser trochanter*. This is an area of attachment for muscles from the pelvis and lower back. Between the greater and lesser trochanters on the posterior surface of the femur, there is a raised ridge called the *intertrochanteric crest*. Between the trochanters on the anterior surface, there is a less pronounced line in the bone called the *intertrochanteric line*. Extending down the femur shaft from the greater trochanter, there is an area called the *gluteal tuberosity* on the posterior, lateral

**femur** the bone that forms the thigh of each leg

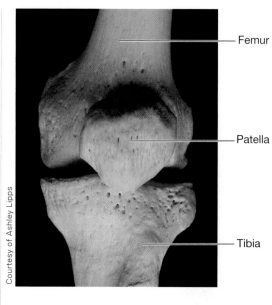

Courtesy of Ashley Lipps

**FIGURE 6.45 The Patella and Femur**
Anterior view of a human left patella, femur, and tibia in anatomical position.

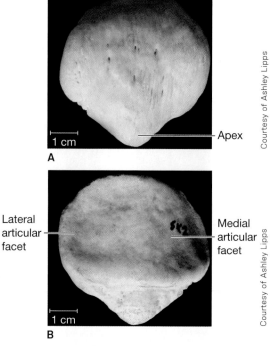

Courtesy of Ashley Lipps

**FIGURE 6.46 The Patella**
(A) Anterior view and (B) posterior view of a human left patella. Note the important features that distinguish this bone.

surface. This can be a pronounced projection or appear as simply a rough area of the bone. As its name suggests, the gluteal tuberosity is an area for gluteal muscle attachment. Beginning at the inferior end of the gluteal tuberosity and extending down much of the posterior shaft surface, there is a ridge of bone called the *linea aspera* that is an important area for the attachment of the hamstring muscles. There are two large, rounded projections at the distal end of the femur. The more medial projection is called the *medial condyle*, and the more lateral projection is called the *lateral condyle*. These two condyles articulate with the proximal end of the tibia (shinbone) to form the knee joint. On the posterior surface between these two condyles, there is a depression called the *intercondylar fossa* or *notch*. On the anterior surface between the condyles, there is a depression called the *patellar surface*, which is where the patella (kneecap) articulates and moves back and forth during knee movement.

The **patella** (commonly called the kneecap) is a small bone that is somewhat triangular in shape. The patella is the largest sesamoid bone in the body. A sesamoid bone is a bone that is embedded within a tendon and is typically very tiny. The patella articulates with the patellar surface on the anterior side of the distal femur (**FIGURE 6.45**). It moves up and down along this surface as the knee moves, helping to both protect the knee and facilitate its function. The patella has three key features (**FIGURE 6.46**). The distal tip of the patella comes to a slight point, called the *apex*. On the posterior surface, the patella has two depressions that articulate with the distal surface of the femur. The medial depression is called the *medial articular facet*, and the lateral depression is called the *lateral articular facet*.

## The Tibia and Fibula

The lower leg is comprised of two long bones: the tibia and the fibula. The **tibia** is commonly called the shinbone, and it is the thicker and more medial of the two lower leg bones (**FIGURE 6.47**). The proximal end of the tibia is marked by a relatively flat surface, called the *tibial plateau*, which articulates with the distal end of the femur (**FIGURE 6.48**). The medial side of the tibial plateau is formed by the *medial condyle*, and the lateral side of the tibial plateau is

**patella** the small, slightly triangular bone that helps form each knee joint, also called the kneecap

**tibia** the larger and more medial of the two bones in each lower leg, also called the shinbone

**fibula** the thinner and more lateral of the two bones in each lower leg

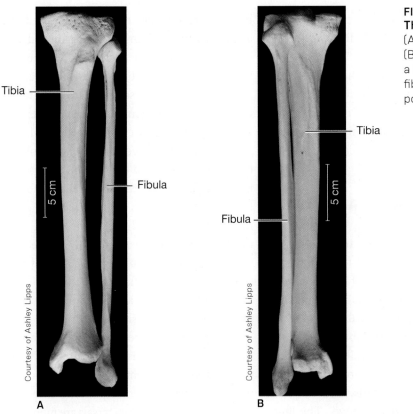

Tibia

Fibula

5 cm

Courtesy of Ashley Lipps

**A**

Tibia

Fibula

5 cm

Courtesy of Ashley Lipps

**B**

**FIGURE 6.47**
**The Tibia and Fibula**
(A) Anterior view and
(B) posterior view of
a human left tibia and
fibula in anatomical
position.

formed by the *lateral condyle*. These condyles are separated by a small, raised area called the *intercondylar eminence*. Toward the posterior of the lateral condyle, there is a small facet called the *superior fibular articular facet*, which is where the proximal ends of the tibia and fibula articulate. Inferior to the tibial plateau on the anterior surface, there is a projection called the *tibial tuberosity* that is an area of attachment for the quadriceps muscle. Along the anterior surface of the central tibia shaft, there is a sharp crest of bone. This is called the *anterior crest*, and it is the area of bone you can feel when you run your fingers down your shin. At the distal end of the tibia, there is a projection on the medial side called the *medial malleolus*. This is the large knob of bone you can feel on the inside of your ankle. On the lateral side of the distal tibia there is an *inferior fibular articular surface* (or *fibular notch*), which is where the distal ends of the tibia and fibula articulate.

The **fibula** is the thinner and more lateral of the two lower leg bones (Figure 6.47). Unlike the tibia, the fibula is not involved in the knee joint. At the proximal end, the fibula

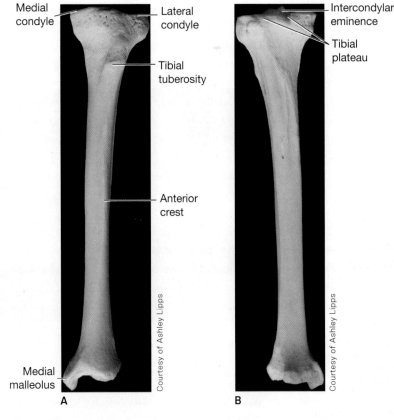

Medial condyle

Lateral condyle

Tibial tuberosity

Anterior crest

Medial malleolus

Courtesy of Ashley Lipps

**A**

Intercondylar eminence

Tibial plateau

Courtesy of Ashley Lipps

**B**

**FIGURE 6.48 The Tibia**
(A) Anterior view and (B) posterior view of a human left tibia. Note the important features that distinguish this bone.

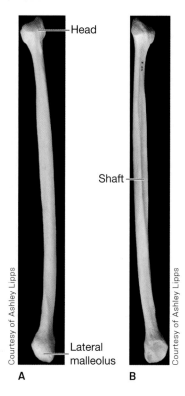

Head

Shaft

Lateral
malleolus

A          B

**FIGURE 6.49 The Fibula**
(A) Anterior view and (B)
posterior view of a human left
fibula, with important features
labeled.

has a rounded *head* that articulates with the tibia **(FIGURE 6.49)**. The *shaft* of the fibula is long and thin. The distal end of the fibula is somewhat flatter than the rounded head, and it is marked by a projection at the tip of the bone called the *lateral malleolus*. This projection is the knob of bone you can feel on the outside of your ankle.

### The Bones of the Ankle and Foot

Similar to the wrist and hand, the bones of the ankle and foot take three basic forms: tarsals (ankle bones), metatarsals (foot bones), and phalanges (toe bones) **(FIGURE 6.50)**. There are seven **tarsals** in each foot, and, like the carpals, they are generally cube-like in shape **(FIGURE 6.51)**. However, tarsals are larger than carpals, and they are not positioned in two rows. The largest tarsal bone is the *calcaneus*, which forms the heel of the foot. The second

largest tarsal is the *talus* (often called the astragalus in nonhumans). It is medial and superior to the calcaneus and articulates with the tibia and fibula to form the ankle. The third largest tarsal is the *cuboid*. It lies between the calcaneus and metatarsals and is the most regularly cube-shaped tarsal. The *navicular* is positioned medial to the cuboid, between the talus and the remaining tarsals— the cuneiforms. There are three cuneiforms: the *medial cuneiform*, the *intermediate cuneiform*, and the *lateral cuneiform* (listed from most medial to most lateral). Notice that while most of these bones have a general cube shape, they vary considerably in their exact shape and size. The calcaneus and talus have particularly unusual shapes.

The bones of the foot are called the **metatarsals**. The foot is laid out similarly to the hand. There are five metatarsals in each foot, with one metatarsal corresponding with each toe **(FIGURE 6.52)**. The metatarsals are numbered from 1 to 5, with 1 corresponding to the big toe (or **hallux**) and 5 corresponding to the pinky

---

**tarsal** one of the
seven short bones
that form each ankle

**metatarsal** one of
the five bones that
form each foot

**hallux** the biggest
and most medial of
the toes on each
foot

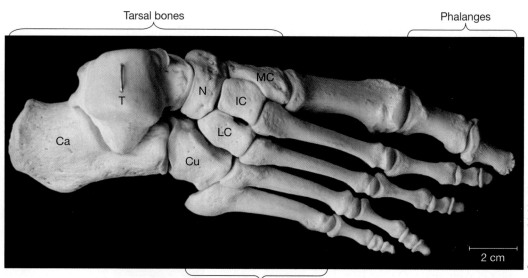

Tarsal bones

Phalanges

Metatarsal bones

2 cm

**FIGURE 6.50 The Bones of the Foot and Ankle (Right)**
Superior view of the bones of the human right foot and ankle in anatomical position. Tarsals: Ca = calcaneus, T = talus, N = navicular, Cu = cuboid, MC = medial cuneiform, IC = intermediate cuneiform, LC = lateral cuneiform.

toe. The proximal end of a metatarsal is somewhat square-shaped and concave, and it articulates with a complementary tarsal surface. The distal end of a metatarsal is more rounded, and it articulates with a phalanx. In humans, the first metatarsal (for the hallux) is much thicker than the other metatarsals.

Like the finger bones, the toe bones are called toe phalanges (phalanx, singular). Again, the layout and organization of the toe bones is similar to the finger bones (**FIGURE 6.53**). The hallux has only two phalanges, but the other toes each have three phalanges. From the metatarsal to the ends of the toes, the three phalanges of each toe are referred to as the proximal phalanx, the intermediate phalanx, and the distal phalanx. The hallux has only a proximal phalanx and a distal phalanx; it lacks the intermediate phalanx. In general, the toe phalanges get smaller as they approach the end of the toe. In humans, the toe phalanges are usually smaller than their counterparts in the fingers.

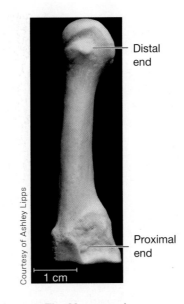

**FIGURE 6.52 The Metatarsals**
Anterior view of a typical human left metatarsal. Note the difference between the proximal and distal ends.

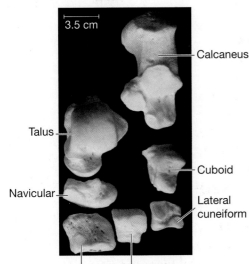

**FIGURE 6.51 The Tarsals**
Note the similarities and differences among the individual human left tarsal bones.

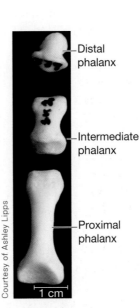

**FIGURE 6.53 The Toe Bones**
Anterior view of the three human left toe phalanges (or toe bones) from one toe. The four toes each have three phalanges, such as those here. The hallux (big toe) has only two phalanges.

# CONCEPT REVIEW QUESTIONS

Name: _____     Section: _____

Course: _____     Date: _____

Answer the following questions in the space provided.

1. Name the bone that forms the posterior (back) of the cranium.


2. Name the four types of teeth found in primates.



3. Which of the following bones is found in the neck?

   A. Cervical vertebra
   B. Sacrum
   C. Lumbar vertebra
   D. Thoracic vertebra

4. Which of the following bones articulates with ribs?

   A. Sacrum
   B. Lumbar vertebra
   C. Cervical vertebra
   D. Thoracic vertebra

5. How many ribs articulate directly with the sternum? How many ribs articulate with the sternum indirectly? How many ribs do not articulate with the sternum at all?



6. Name the three bones that articulate with the humerus



7. How many phalanges are in the typical human hand?

   A. 8
   B. 14
   C. 15
   D. 5

8. Name the three fused bones that comprise each side of the ossa coxae.



9. Name the three bones that articulate with the femur.



10. True or false? The carpals are found in the ankle area.

# LAB EXERCISES

Name: _____  Section: _____

Course: _____  Date: _____

## EXERCISE 1  CRANIUM

Work with a small group or alone to complete this exercise.

### PART A

Refer to the skeletal material provided by your instructor (or the human cranium pictures in the lab Appendix). Some of the major bones of the cranium have been assigned numbers. For each number, provide the appropriate bone name in the space below:

1.                                    5.

2.                                    6.

3.                                    7.

4.

### PART B

Refer to the skeletal material provided by your instructor (or the human cranium pictured in the lab Appendix) and label (or identify) the following key features of the cranium:

1. External auditory (acoustic) meatus

2. Mental protuberance

3. Mastoid process

4. Alveolar process

5. Foramen magnum

6. Occipital condyle

## EXERCISE 2  DENTITION

Work with a small group or alone to complete this exercise. Refer to the skeletal material provided by your instructor (or the mystery animal dentition picture in the lab Appendix) to calculate the dental formula for the animal and write it in the space provided.

Dental formula:

## EXERCISE 3  VERTEBRAL COLUMN

Work with a small group or alone to complete the following exercise.

### PART A

Refer to the skeletal material provided by your instructor (or the human vertebral column diagram in the lab Appendix). The major bones of the vertebral column have been assigned numbers. For each number, provide the appropriate name in the space below:

1.                                              4.

2.                                              5.

3.

### PART B

Refer to the skeletal material provided by your instructor (or the typical human vertebra pictured in the lab Appendix) and label the following key features on the vertebra:

1. Vertebral body                          3. Spinous process

2. Vertebral foramen                       4. Transverse process

### PART C

Refer to the skeletal material provided by your instructor (or the three vertebrae pictured in the lab Appendix) to answer the following questions.

1. Which mystery vertebra is a cervical vertebra? Describe two features that helped you determine this.

2. Which mystery vertebra is a thoracic vertebra? Describe two features that helped you determine this.

3. Which mystery vertebra is a lumbar vertebra? Describe two features that helped you determine this.

## EXERCISE 4 THORACIC CAGE (RIB CAGE)

Work with a small group or alone to complete this exercise. Refer to the skeletal material provided by your instructor (or the human rib cage pictured in the lab Appendix) and label the following bones of the rib cage:

1. Manubrium

2. Sternal body

3. Xiphoid process

4. True ribs

5. False ribs

6. Floating ribs

## EXERCISE 5 UPPER LIMB

Work with a small group or alone to complete the following exercise.

### PART A

Refer to the skeletal material provided by your instructor (or the human upper limb picture in the lab Appendix). The major bones have been numbered. For each number, provide the appropriate name in the space provided.

1.

2.

3.

4.

5.

6.

### PART B

Refer to the skeletal material provided by your instructor (or the human humerus pictured in the lab Appendix) and label the following key features of the humerus:

1. Head

2. Lesser tubercle

3. Greater tubercle

4. Intertubercular groove

5. Lateral epicondyle

6. Medial epicondyle

7. Olecranon fossa

8. Coronoid fossa

### PART C

Review the bones of the hand provided by your instructor or depicted in Figure 6.38. Describe two things that make the first finger (the thumb) different from the other fingers.

## EXERCISE 6    LOWER LIMB

Work with a small group or alone to complete the following exercise.

### PART A

Review the skeletal material provided by your instructor (or the human pelvis pictured in the lab Appendix). The major bones and features have been numbered. For each number, provide the appropriate name in the space provided.

1.                                      5.

2.                                      6.

3.                                      7.

4.

### PART B

Refer to the skeletal material provided by your instructor (or the human lower limb picture in the lab Appendix). The major bones have been numbered. For each number, provide the appropriate bone name in the space provided.

1.                                      4.

2.                                      5.

3.                                      6.

### PART C

Review the skeletal material provided by your instructor (or the human femur pictured in the lab Appendix) and label the following key features of the femur:

1. Head                                 5. Lateral condyle

2. Neck                                 6. Medial condyle

3. Greater trochanter                   7. Patellar surface

4. Lesser trochanter

### PART D

Review the bones of the foot provided by your instructor or depicted in Figure 6.50. Describe two things that make the first toe (the big toe) different from the other toes.

# CRITICAL THINKING QUESTIONS

On a separate sheet of paper, answer the following questions.

1. This question may be completed independently or as a group discussion. Why do you think there are so many bones in the cranium? Why do you think we are born with separate cranial bones that later fuse together as we grow and develop?

2. This question may be completed independently or as a group discussion. Review the vertebral column from Exercise 3. What similarities and differences do you notice between the three major types of vertebrae? Why might these similarities exist? Why might these differences exist? Humans do not have tails, so we do not have caudal vertebrae (the vertebrae that comprise the tail). However, many other primates do have these vertebrae. Based on what you know about the other kinds of vertebrae, what do you expect caudal vertebrae to look like? Compare your estimation to images of caudal vertebrae in your classroom, online, or in books. How accurate was your estimation?

3. This question may be completed independently or as a group discussion. The ribs articulate to the sternum through lengths of costal cartilage. This means much of the anterior side of the rib cage is cartilage. Why do you think it is important that so much of the rib cage is made of cartilage and not bone?

4. This question may be completed independently or as a group discussion. Review the upper limb from Exercise 5. Compare the shoulder joint and the elbow joint. What do you notice is similar? What do you notice is different? How do these similarities and differences relate to similarities and differences in the function and mobility of these joints?

5. This question may be completed independently or as a group discussion. Review the upper limb from Exercise 5 and the lower limb from Exercise 6. Consider the joints, the types of bones, and the overall layout of the bones. What do you notice is similar? What do you notice is different? How do these similarities and differences relate to similarities and differences in the function and mobility of these appendages?

6. This question may be completed independently or as a group discussion. The human hands and feet have similar types and numbers of bones. However, the hands and feet appear very different. What physical differences do you notice between the hands and feet? How might these differences relate to differences in the function of these body parts? Would you expect other primates to have hands and feet that differed like this? Why or why not?

# APPENDIX: LAB EXERCISE IMAGES

## Exercise 1 Cranium

A.

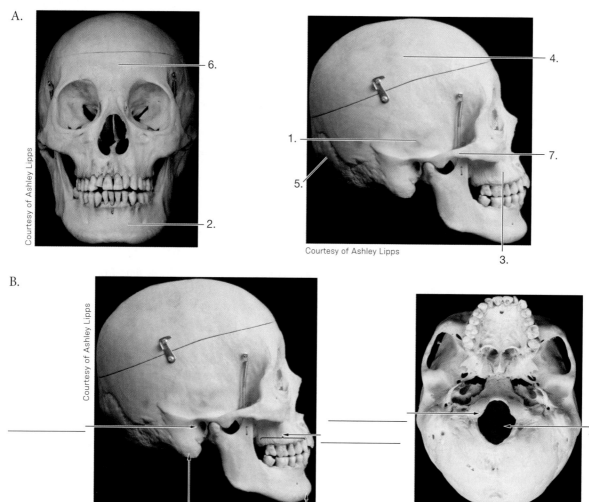

Courtesy of Ashley Lipps

Courtesy of Ashley Lipps

B.

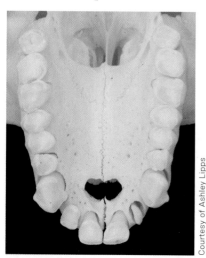

Courtesy of Ashley Lipps

Courtesy of Ashley Lipps

Courtesy of Ashley Lipps

## Exercise 2 Dentition

Courtesy of Ashley Lipps

Note: The lower dentition is identical to the upper dentition seen here.

# Exercise 3 Vertebral Column

A.

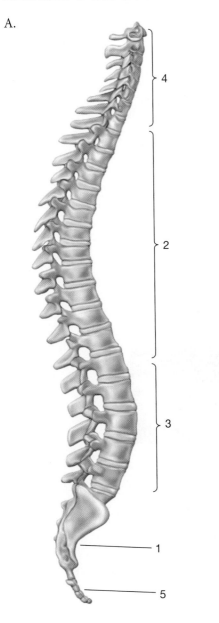

B.

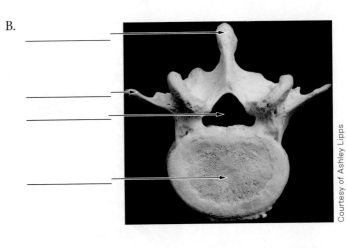

Courtesy of Ashley Lipps

C.

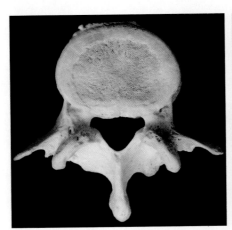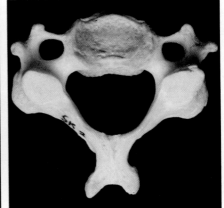

A          Courtesy of Ashley Lipps    B          Courtesy of Ashley Lipps    C          Courtesy of Ashley Lipps

## Exercise 4 Thoracic Cage (Rib Cage)

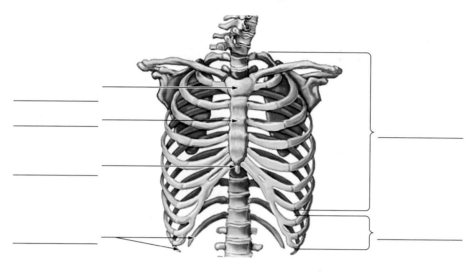

## Exercise 5 Upper Limb

A.

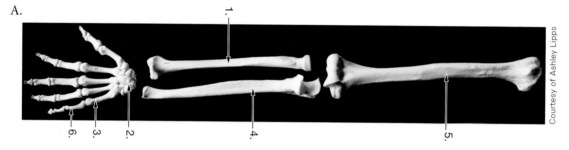

Courtesy of Ashley Lipps

B.

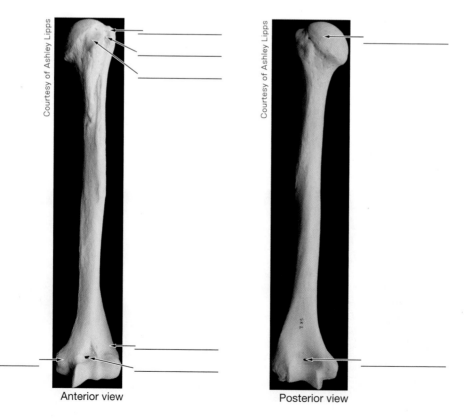

Anterior view

Posterior view

# Exercise 6 Lower Limb

A.

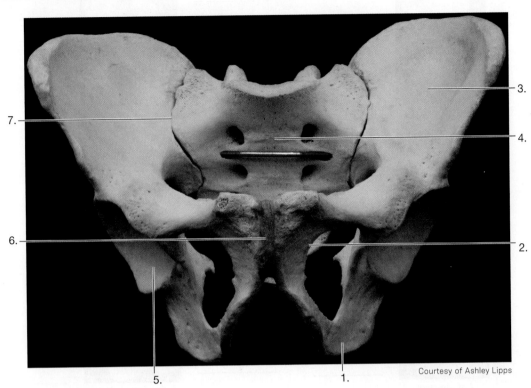

7.

3.

4.

6.

2.

5.

1.

Courtesy of Ashley Lipps

B.

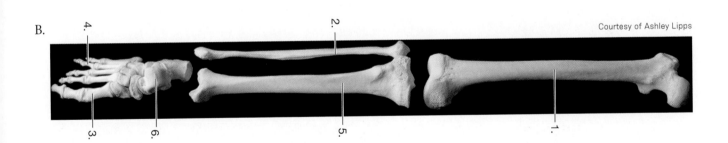

4.

2.

Courtesy of Ashley Lipps

3.

6.

5.

1.

C.

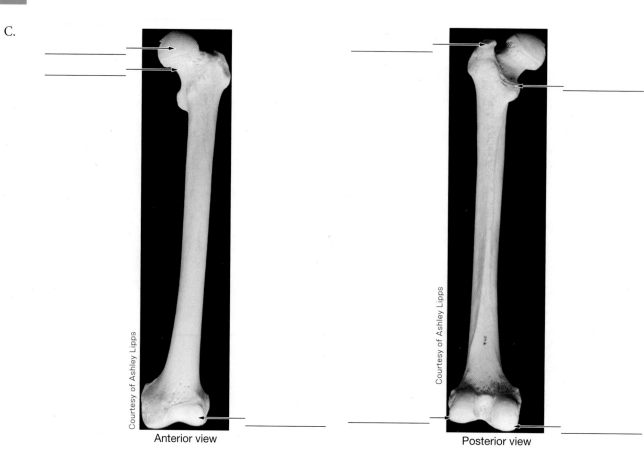

Anterior view

Posterior view

Courtesy of Ashley Lipps

The conditions in the Amazon rainforest lead to rapid decomposition, and human remains in this area are often mostly skeletal (with little soft tissue). In these cases, a forensic anthropologist may be called upon to assist in police investigations.

## Lab Learning Objectives

By the end of this lab, students should be able to:

- discuss the similarities and differences between forensic anthropology and bioarchaeology.

- distinguish between human and animal bone.

- determine the minimum number of individuals represented by a bone assemblage.

- estimate likely sex and age at death of individuals based on their bones.

- make stature estimations based on measurements from long bones.

- identify and distinguish between key types of antemortem and perimortem pathology.

- discuss methods for determining likely ancestry from skeletal material.

LAB 7

# Bioarchaeology and Forensic Anthropology

In August 2006, two tourists were reported missing in the Ecuadorian area of the Amazon jungle. Between December 2006 and March 2007, dismembered human remains were recovered from three separate locations in the area. The body parts were highly decomposed, with little soft tissue available for identification or analysis. Because of this, a forensic anthropologist was called in to assist with the examination of the human remains. Using expert knowledge of the human skeleton, the forensic anthropologist was able to identify the victims and reconstruct some of the circumstances surrounding their deaths.

The anthropologist identified that the remains belonged to two separate individuals. From here, the anthropologist tried to reconstruct the identity of the victims. She identified the sex, age, and stature (height) of the victims, as well as some unique characteristics, such as the individuals' dental health and history. Based on this research, the victims were successfully identified as the two missing tourists. In addition, the anthropologist studied marks on the bones and learned that the victims had been dismembered using a chain saw. This information, along with other forensic evidence (such as fibers and possible murder weapons recovered from the scene), will be used in the trial of the suspected perpetrators.

**bioarchaeology** the study of skeletal remains from archaeological contexts

Although coroners and other related experts have a valuable understanding of human soft tissue, there are sometimes situations where soft tissue evidence is limited or unavailable. In these situations, understanding the nuances of the human skeleton can be particularly useful. In this lab, we examine how forensic anthropologists use skeletal remains to reconstruct a victim's identity and the circumstances surrounding his or her death. We also discuss how bioarchaeologists use similar pieces of information from skeletons to reconstruct information about individuals and populations in the past.

## INTRODUCTION

This lab closely explores the procedures and methods used by bioarchaeologists and forensic anthropologists. We begin with an introduction to the field of bioarchaeology. We then turn to the related field of forensic anthropology. For both, we consider the primary steps in analyzing the skeletal remains of individuals. For each step, we review the techniques used and the key skeletal elements needed. We also discuss more detailed aspects of forensic anthropology protocol that can obtain more specific information and lead to the identification of an individual(s). Both bioarchaeology and forensic anthropology, and the methods associated with them, are important parts of the discipline of biological anthropology. Many biological anthropologists are employed in these fields, and work along these lines has been popularized through hit television series and best-selling novels.

## WHAT IS BIOARCHAEOLOGY?

**Bioarchaeology** is the study of human skeletal remains from archaeological sites (**FIGURE 7.1**). Bioarchaeologists are not involved in contemporary legal cases; they are more broadly interested in understanding the past lifeways of historic and prehistoric people through the analysis of their skeletons. Bioarchaeological studies attempt to reconstruct past human activities, diet, disease, and overall health patterns. Because bioarchaeologists apply methods of skeletal analysis to archaeological contexts, they bridge the gap between biological anthropology and archaeology. Similar to many other fields, bioarchaeology is often interdisciplinary and overlaps with other disciplines, such as demography, chemistry, and medicine. How much information bioarchaeologists can learn from archaeological skeletal remains depends on the state of preservation; preservation is affected by multiple factors, including how old the remains are and in what type of environment they are buried. Also, it is important to note that the study of ancient skeletal remains carries important ethical and legal issues. In many countries, including the United States, there are laws that protect the rights of descendant communities and their religious beliefs and cultural heritage over the study and disturbance of skeletal remains. Bioarchaeologists are always keenly aware of their ethical responsibilities and the need to treat human remains with respect.

Photo courtesy of Melanie Miller

**FIGURE 7.1 Bioarchaeology**
Bioarchaeologists, such as Melanie Miller seen here, use methods of skeletal analysis to understand what life was like for past (archaeological) populations. This excavation focused on 5,000-year-old skeletons in Ubate, Colombia. The researcher used gloves, a face mask, and aluminum foil packets to avoid contaminating the DNA recovered from the archaeological context.

The bioarchaeologist compiles as much information as possible from ancient skeletal remains to reconstruct the life of the individual (age at death, sex, signs of disease, etc.). Ultimately, however, the bioarchaeologist is also interested in reconstructing the lives of groups of people and communities, not just individuals. They study the life histories of archaeological populations to get a sense for how the larger group lived and to answer broader questions: Were there differences between the way males and females lived, between the way young people and old people lived, or between people of different statuses? Bioarchaeologists apply many of the same methods and techniques as forensic anthropologists, and when presented with archaeological skeletal remains, they follow many of the same protocol steps.

## WHAT IS FORENSIC ANTHROPOLOGY?

**Forensic anthropology** is the branch of biological anthropology that applies specialized methods of skeletal analysis to human skeletal remains during the course of legal investigations. For example, if a victim was buried for many years or a victim's body was severely burned, much of the victim's soft tissue would no longer be available. At times such as these, a forensic anthropologist is called on to analyze the remaining skeletal material. The primary job of the forensic anthropologist in these situations is to build a profile that will help in identifying the victim and, if possible, help in determining the circumstances surrounding the victim's death.

Although popular television shows and books suggest that forensic anthropologists spend all of their time investigating individual victims, this is not always the case. Forensic anthropologists often work on cases of mass death, such as genocide, war crimes, and natural disasters. In addition, many forensic anthropologists participate in investigations only part-time. They spend the rest of their time teaching or conducting research.

When a forensic anthropologist is investigating skeletal material in legal contexts, they follow a protocol that lays out steps in a meaningful order to help them identify an individual. Often, one step cannot be accurately completed without the completion of prior steps. These steps include determining the age, sex, and stature of the individuals, as well as examining indications of pathology before death and estimating the amount of time since death.

## METHODS USED IN THE ANALYSIS OF SKELETAL REMAINS

Many of the steps and methods used in the analysis of skeletal remains are the same for forensic and archaeological contexts. Typically, once the basic steps in analysis are complete, additional methods are used to gain more specific and specialized information. For example, chemical analysis (isotope analysis) may be used to get data on the diet of archaeological populations, analysis of skeletal morphology or modification can be used to infer lifestyle or cultural behaviors, or DNA analysis may be used to help identify individual forensic victims. We discuss here the primary first steps taken in analyzing skeletal material.

Some Key Steps in Analyzing Human Skeletal Remains

1. Distinguish between human and animal bone.
2. Determine the minimum number of individuals present.
3. Determine the sex of each individual.
4. Determine the age at death for each individual.
5. Estimate the stature of each individual.
6. Identify pathology or stress indicators for each individual.

Additional Steps Specifically in Forensic Contexts

7. Determine the ancestry of each individual.
8. Calculate the postmortem interval.

**forensic anthropology** the application of knowledge and methods of skeletal analysis to assist in legal investigations

**assemblage** a collection of material (such as bones and/or artifacts) recovered from a forensic context or an archaeological or paleoanthropological site

**minimum number of individuals (MNI)** the minimum number of individuals that could be represented by the skeletal elements recovered

# DISTINGUISHING HUMAN VERSUS ANIMAL BONE

There are many human bones that resemble the bones of other animals. For example, the bones of a human hand and the bones of a bear paw are very similar **(FIGURE 7.2)**. This means that human bones can be mistaken for other animals and vice versa. This is even more likely to occur when the skeletal material is fragmented and incomplete. It is important for both bioarchaeologists and forensic anthropologists to make sure they are working with human bone before they proceed with their analysis. There are two considerations when determining if a bone is human.

First, you must consider the size. Is a bone the appropriate size to be that of a juvenile or adult human? Even though there is a lot of variation in human size, there are many animals that are considerably larger or smaller. For example, cows are very large and have large, robust bones. This robusticity is clear even in some bone fragments, so it can be used to differentiate cow bones from more gracile (slender) human bones. Similarly, dog bones are relatively gracile but smaller than human bones.

This smallness can be used to differentiate them from larger human bones.

The second consideration is unique human adaptations. For example, humans have chins and foreheads whereas other animals do not. If a mandibular fragment is found with a chin, it must be human. Similarly, if a tall, vaulted frontal bone is found, it must be human. We also have a series of specialized adaptations for our bipedal locomotion (walking upright on two limbs) that make our skeletons unusual (see Lab 14 for more details). If a bone is found with any of these adaptations, it must be human.

# DETERMINING THE MINIMUM NUMBER OF INDIVIDUALS

In most bioarchaeological contexts and in many forensic contexts, the recovered bones are from multiple individuals. It is then up to the bioarchaeologist or forensic anthropologist to determine how many people are actually represented by the bones in the **assemblage** (collected material). Because there are many bones in the human body that could be recovered, it is often impossible to determine *exactly* how many people are represented. Instead, biological anthropologists focus on determining the **minimum number of individuals (MNI)** possibly represented by the bone assemblage. This gets us closer to the number of individuals without overestimating the number. It also helps the researcher to distinguish skeletal elements from different people and focus further analysis on separate individuals. There are three steps to this process.

## Step One: Are there any bones that are unique in the human body?

There are certain bones that are unique in the human body, such as the mandible—there is only one. Because there is only one mandible in each human, if your assemblage has two

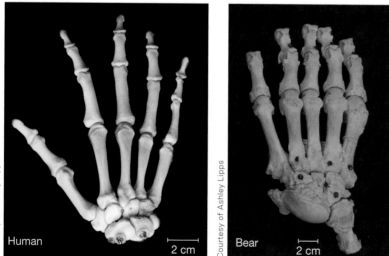

*Courtesy of Ashley Lipps* Human 2 cm

*Courtesy of Ashley Lipps* Bear 2 cm

**FIGURE 7.2 Human or Nonhuman?**
Some human skeletal elements are very similar to those of other animals. For example, this human hand is similar to this bear paw. The bioarchaeologist or forensic anthropologist must be able to distinguish when they are working with human bone.

mandibles, you must have *at least* two people. You could have more than two people because there could be people whose mandibles were removed or destroyed. But you definitely have at least two people.

## Step Two: Are there any bones that are from the same side of the body?

Some bones in the human body are not unique, but they are sided. For example, the human body has two femur bones; the femur is not a unique bone. But the right femur and the left femur are different; the femur is sided (**FIGURE 7.3**). If your site has two right femurs, you know you have at least two individuals. Again, you could have more individuals whose right femurs are not present, but you know you have at least two individuals.

## Step Three: Can you match any of the bones to the same individual?

The final step is trying to match the bones together. Imagine that your assemblage has two right femurs and two right pelvises. Based on step two, you would think you have four individuals. However, it is possible that at least one of your right femurs and one of your right pelvises belong to the same individual. Because of this possibility, biological anthropologists try to match bones together that may belong to the same person (**FIGURE 7.4**). Bones that appear to join with each other (such as the right femur and pelvis) can be articulated to see if they fit correctly. If they do, the femur and pelvis belong to the same person, not to two different people. Biological anthropologists will also determine if multiple bones might belong with each other based on their preservation condition, age, sex, or pathology. Bones from the same body and skeletal area are often in a similar state of preservation and of similar age and sex. The bones may also show the same disease or pathology if they are found in a similar part of the body or if the pathology is spread throughout the body.

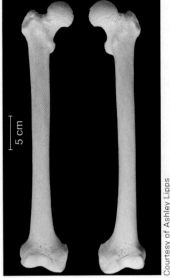
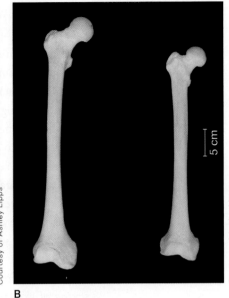

**FIGURE 7.3 One Person or Two?**
Bones like the femur are paired in the human body. If a biological anthropologist has a right femur and a left femur (A), they might be from the same person. However, if a biological anthropologist has two right femurs (B), she knows she is examining at least two individuals.

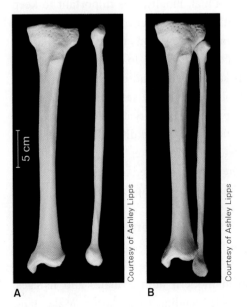

**FIGURE 7.4 One Person or Two?**
When a biological anthropologist recovers two bones that might articulate together, such as the tibia and fibula (A), he or she must try to articulate them to see if they match. If the two bones articulate correctly (B), they probably came from the same person. If the two bones do not articulate correctly due to differences in size or shape, they probably came from two different people.

# DETERMINING SEX

After determining that the bones in question are indeed human and estimating the number of individuals, one of the first things that a bioarchaeologist or forensic anthropologist must determine is the biological sex of the individual(s) in question; this is called **sexing**. Determining sex from skeletal remains is based on **sexual dimorphism**, which is the variation between adult male and adult female bodies. In the case of sexual dimorphism in the skeleton, we are specifically looking at differences in bone morphology (size and shape). It is important to remember that the sexing of skeletons is relative and exists on a continuum: an individual is more male or less male or more female or less female. It is not a cut-and-dry determination with only two choices. Further, sexing determines the likely biological sex of an individual, but it does not speak to the sexual orientation or gender of an individual. Finally, it is important to keep in mind that sex determination can only be done on adult skeletons (individuals that are postpubescent). Prior to this age, the skeleton is still growing and developing; many of the biologically based sex differences, which develop later in puberty due to hormones, are not yet present or are difficult to determine. Sex determination takes two primary forms: sex determination based on size and sex determination based on shape.

## Sex Determination Based on Size

In general, there is a slight size difference between modern human males and females, with males tending to be larger. Males tend to be taller than females, so they tend to have longer bones than females. Males tend to be heavier and more muscular than females, so they tend to have more robust bones and rugged bony features than females. Of course, there are always individuals that do not follow this general pattern. There are taller, more muscular females and shorter, more gracile males.

Further, populations differ in their average skeletal size and amount of sexual dimorphism (see Lab 8 for more information about human variation). This is why sex determination is not cut-and-dry.

The cranium is often used in sex determination based on size. In general, cranial features and areas of muscle attachment are more pronounced and robust in males than in females (**FIGURE 7.5**). For example, males have more pronounced or larger features such as *brow ridges* and larger areas of muscle attachment like larger *mastoid processes*. In addition, the *superior margin of the eye orbit* in males is usually rounded and blunt, but it is sharper in females. Males also tend to have a square-shaped *mandible* and chin, and females tend to have a rounder mandible and pointed chin. Lastly, males tend to have slightly larger and more pronounced *canine teeth*, while females have smaller and less pronounced canines.

## Sex Determination Based on Shape

There are also differences between male and female skeletons based on functional differences between the sexes. The sexes have evolved to complement one another in sexual reproduction; therefore, they have functional differences related to their different roles in the reproductive process. Specifically, females can give birth, so the female bony pelvis must accommodate the passing of a fetus during childbirth. Males cannot give birth, and their pelvises cannot accommodate the passing of a fetus.

Looking more closely at the pelvis, we see a number of specific traits that vary between females and males due to this functional difference (**FIGURE 7.6**). For example, generally the female *pubic bone* is more rectangular, while the male pubic bone is more triangular. The *subpubic angle* (the angle formed below the pubic symphysis) is wider in females, and the angle is sharper and narrower in males. The *greater sciatic notch* (a notch on

**sexing** the process of determining the likely sex of an individual based on skeletal remains

**sexual dimorphism** the physical differences between mature males and females of a species

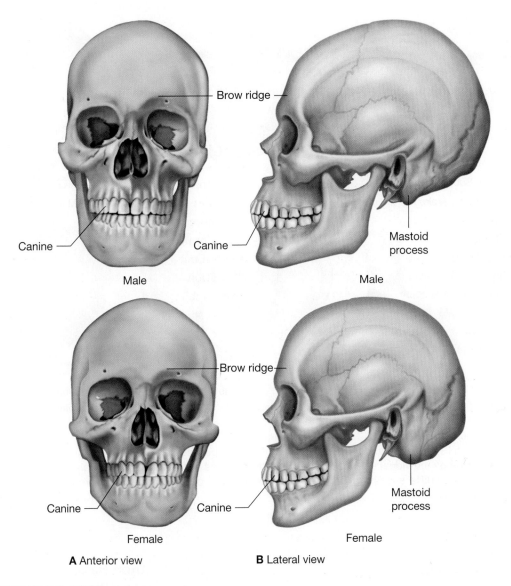

**FIGURE 7.5 Cranial Sexing**
(A) Anterior and (B) lateral views of human skulls show cranial features used to determine an individual's probable sex. Numerous cranial features vary in size between males and females, with males generally being more robust.

the inferior side of the ilium bone) is narrower from top to bottom (superoinferiorly) and deeper from front to back (anteroposteriorly) in females, such that it resembles a boomerang in shape. In males, the greater sciatic notch is deeper from top to bottom (superoinferiorly) and narrower from front to back (anteroposteriorly), giving it a candy cane shape. In addition, the *pelvic opening* (the large hole in the center of the pelvis that is formed by the articulation of the two ossa coxae and the sacrum) is wider in females and narrower in males. The larger female pelvic opening allows for the fetus to pass through the pelvis during childbirth. Passing through the birth canal is also facilitated by the position of the *coccyx* (tailbone) in females. In males, this bone curves ventrally (anteriorly) and partially obstructs the pelvic opening. In females, the bone is positioned more dorsally (posteriorly), and the female pelvic opening is less obstructed than it is in males.

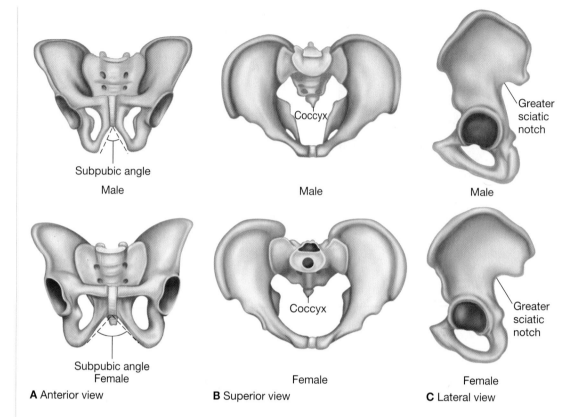

Subpubic angle
Male

Male

Greater sciatic notch

Male

Coccyx

Subpubic angle
Female

Coccyx

Female

Greater sciatic notch

Female

**A** Anterior view

**B** Superior view

**C** Lateral view

**FIGURE 7.6 Pelvic Sexing**
(A) Anterior, (B) superior, and (C) lateral views of human pelvises show pelvic features used to determine an individual's probable sex. Several features will differ between males and females. These differences primarily relate to the female's ability to give birth through the pelvic opening.

**aging** the process of estimating an individual's age at death based on skeletal remains

**juvenile** a physically immature individual whose body is still growing and developing

**adult** an individual that has reached physical maturity

**ossification** the process of bone mineralization and fusion that occurs as an individual develops into a physically mature adult

**epiphyseal fusion** the process of ossification where the shaft and ends of a long bone fuse together, the extent of which can be used to age a juvenile skeleton

**diaphysis** the central area of a long bone that forms separately and fuses with the ends of the bone during growth and development

**epiphysis** (epiphyses, plural) the area at the end of a long bone that forms separately and fuses with the middle of the bone during growth and development

# DETERMINING AGE AT DEATH

After separating out individuals and determining their biological sex, both bioarchaeologists and forensic anthropologists typically move to determining the age of those different individuals; this is called **aging**. Here, we are talking about the biological age of the individual at the time of their death. Age information is particularly important to law enforcement officers because it is information that is tracked through public records, such as driver's licenses, and can be helpful in identifying a victim in forensic contexts. Age determination takes two primary forms: age determination based on developmental changes and age determination based on metamorphic changes.

## Age Determination Based on Developmental Changes

There are known rates at which the human body grows and develops. We can use this information to compare a skeleton to the known developmental stages and determine the likely age of that individual. These methods are suitable for aging **juveniles** because their bodies are still undergoing these changes during growth and development. A fully **adult** skeleton, however, cannot be aged using these methods because it is no longer developing.

There are known rates of bone **ossification**—the process of bone mineral solidification and fusion that occurs as the body develops into an adult. Knowing the stages of these ossification processes provides us with useful aging methods. For example, the long bones of the body undergo a particular ossification process known

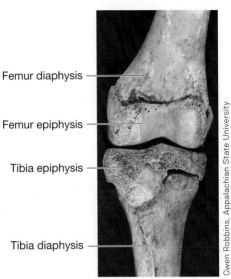

Femur diaphysis
Femur epiphysis
Tibia epiphysis
Tibia diaphysis

Gwen Robbins, Appalachian State University

**FIGURE 7.7 Epiphyseal Fusion**
In the long bones of juveniles, like the femur and tibia seen here, the diaphysis (central shaft) is separate from the epiphyses (ends). These parts grow together and fuse as the child ages. If a biological anthropologist has long bones with unfused ends, she knows she is examining a juvenile. In addition, the bones fuse at known rates, so the extent of fusion can help identify the age of juveniles.

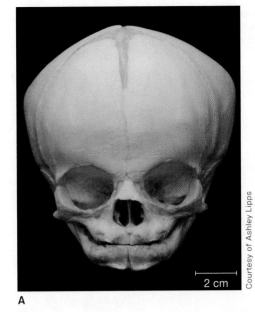

2 cm

Courtesy of Ashley Lipps

A

**FIGURE 7.8 Cranial Suture Closure**
Babies are born with separate cranial bones (A). These individual bones then fuse together over time (B) until they become completely joined (C). If a biological anthropologist recovers a cranium with bones that are not fully fused, this information can be used to determine the age of the individual.

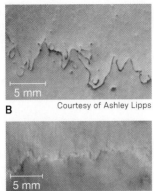

5 mm
Courtesy of Ashley Lipps
B

5 mm
Courtesy of Ashley Lipps
C

**cranial suture closure** the process of ossification where the cranial bones fuse together at the sutures, the extent of which can be used to age a skeleton

**tooth (dental) eruption** the process whereby the deciduous teeth (and later the permanent teeth) grow into the mouth, the extent of which can be used to age juvenile skeletons

as **epiphyseal fusion**. This is the process where the shaft of the bone (**diaphysis**) and the ends of the bone (**epiphyses**) fuse together with age (**FIGURE 7.7**). If a long bone is recovered that has partially fused epiphyses, the extent of fusion can be used to determine age. The more fused the epiphyses, the older the individual. The epiphyses of the various long bones of the body fuse at different ages, with the clavicle (collarbone) fusing last by the early 20s. This means different long bones are suited for determining different ages.

There are also known rates of ossification for the skull (or cranial) bones. Remember, the cranium is actually composed of many flat bones that fuse together as the body grows and develops. The areas where the bones come together and form sutures and the extent of **cranial suture closure** can be used to determine age. In general, if the bones are separate, the individual is very young (**FIGURE 7.8A**). If the bones are fusing but the sutures are very distinct, the individual is older (**FIGURE 7.8B**). If the suture lines are less distinct or almost obliterated, the individual is even older (**FIGURE 7.8C**).

In addition to known rates of bone ossification, there are also known rates of **tooth eruption**—the process whereby the teeth grow into the mouth (**FIGURE 7.9**). The *deciduous teeth* (baby teeth) and *permanent teeth* (adult teeth) come in at different ages as the body develops

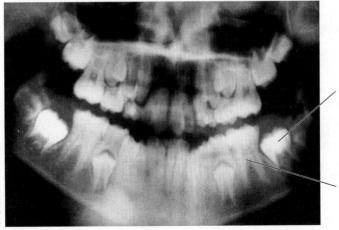

SPL/Science Source

Second permanent molar

First permanent molar

**FIGURE 7.9 Dental Eruption**
Our permanent teeth form in early childhood and replace the deciduous teeth that came before them. The formation of these teeth (and their eruption through the gums) occurs at known ages, so a biological anthropologist can use this information to age juvenile skeletons.

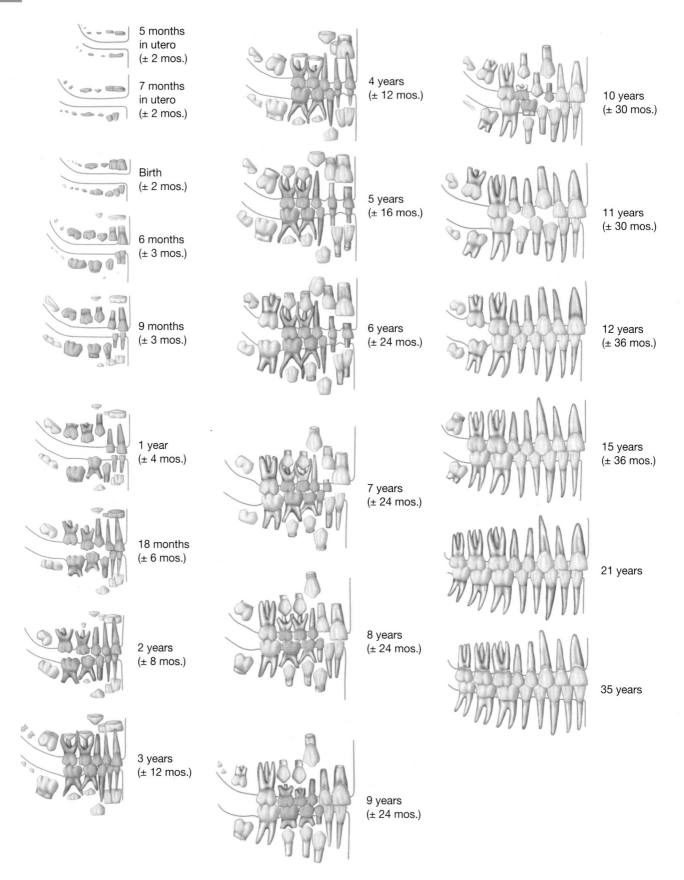

**FIGURE 7.10 Dental Eruption Age Stages**
The deciduous and permanent teeth are formed and erupt through the gum surface at specific ages. Thus, the extent of dental eruption can be used to help determine an individual's age at death.

(FIGURE 7.10). This is something we have all experienced. New parents talk about the period during which their child is *teething*. This is the time when the deciduous teeth are breaking the bone and gum surface and growing in. Most of us are also familiar with the development of the permanent teeth. This process forces the deciduous teeth to fall out to make room for the permanent teeth. Many people remember when they lost their first tooth or have personal photos with missing teeth during their elementary school years. The different teeth erupt at different ages and in a particular order. In general, the middle (or central) incisors are first, and the remaining teeth appear mostly from the front to the back of the mouth. The last teeth to come in are the last or third molars of our permanent dentition, which usually erupt during our late teens or early twenties. We call these the *wisdom teeth* because they come in at a much later age than the other teeth.

## Age Determination Based on Metamorphic or Degenerative Changes

There are also estimated rates at which bone undergoes structural metamorphic changes as we age. Again, we can use these rates of change to help in making age estimations. These methods are suitable for aging adults, as their skeletons and joints begin to undergo degeneration over time. Juvenile skeletons, however, are too young to have accumulated these changes, so these methods are not suitable for aging them.

Most of the metamorphic changes are observed on bone joint surfaces that have little to no movement during life. For example, the degree of age-related metamorphic change can be quantified on the joints at the sternal end of the ribs (where the rib and sternum join), and on the auricular joint surface of the iliac bone (where the iliac bone joins the sacrum). One of the primary areas to observe age-related metamorphic changes is on the pubic bone. Changes occur specifically on the *pubic symphysis* (the joint where the two pelvic bones meet anteriorly along the midline) that can be observed on the symphyseal surface of the pubic bone. Many

age determination methods have been developed from the morphological changes of the pubic symphysis. One of the most recent and best aging methods is called the **Suchey–Brooks method (FIGURE 7.11)**, named after the researchers that developed it. In general, the prevalence of prominent and regular ridges on the symphyseal face decreases with age, the prevalence of rimming and bony nodules on the symphyseal face increases with age, and the symphyseal face becomes more concave with age. These changes occur at differing rates for males and females, so different ranges and charts are used to estimate the age at death of male and female individuals.

Another method for aging adults is analysis of **dental wear (FIGURE 7.12)**. Over time, the chewing surfaces of our teeth wear down from their continual use **(FIGURE 7.13)**. Unlike the bones, the teeth do not undergo remodeling. They are a finite resource, and once they are formed, they cannot be naturally repaired or re-formed. This means we can use the extent of tooth wear as a general or relative age indicator. In general, the more wear on the tooth, the longer and more extensively it has been used. While it cannot tell us an exact age, tooth wear can be used to tell the relative age of an individual. It is important to note that some diets and activities can result in more tooth wear than others, so this aging method is not as precise as some of the other methods. In general, recent human populations have a fairly refined diet that results in little tooth wear. As such, dental wear is not a precise aging method used in forensic anthropology. However, in the case of historic or prehistoric populations, it is often possible to use estimated rates of dental wear for aging.

In general, it is important to remember that when determining the age of a skeleton, more precise estimates can be obtained for juveniles than for adults, particularly when basing the determination on developmental changes in the skeleton. This is because the stages of development are relatively precise and take place over a short period. The stages of wear on the body, however, take place over a long time and can vary within and among individuals and populations depending on external factors, such as diet and activity patterns.

**Suchey–Brooks method** a method of aging adult skeletons that relies on changes to the symphyseal surface of the pubic bone

**dental (tooth) wear** the wearing down of tooth surfaces with continued use, the extent of which can be used to age adult skeletons

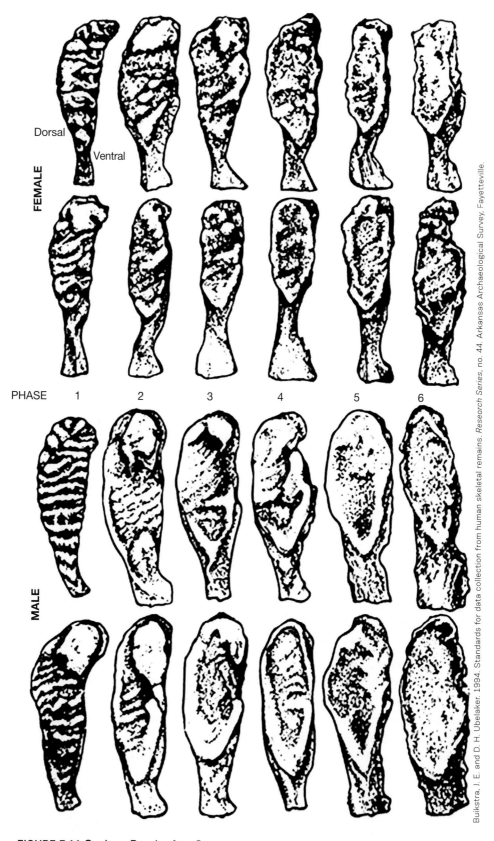

**FIGURE 7.11 Suchey–Brooks Age Stages**
The pubic symphyseal face undergoes changes as we age. Thus, it can be used to help determine an individual's age at death. Note that the age stages differ slightly for females and males.

| Phase | Mean Age at Death, Female (n = 273) | Standard Deviation, Female | 95% Range, Female | Mean Age at Death, Male (n = 739) | Standard Deviation, Male | 95% Range, Male | Description |
|---|---|---|---|---|---|---|---|
| 1 | 19.4 | 2.6 | 15–24 | 18.5 | 2.1 | 15–23 | Symphyseal face has a billowing surface composed of ridges and furrows which includes the pubic tubercle. The horizontal ridges are well-marked. Ventral beveling may be commencing. Although ossific nodules may occur on the upper extremity, a key feature of this phase is the lack of delimitation for either extremity (upper or lower). |
| 2 | 25.0 | 4.9 | 19–40 | 23.4 | 3.6 | 19–34 | Symphyseal face may still show ridge development. Lower and upper extremities show early stages of delimitation, with or without ossific nodules. Ventral rampart may begin formation as extension from either or both extremities. |
| 3 | 30.7 | 8.1 | 21–53 | 28.7 | 6.5 | 21–46 | Symphyseal face shows lower extremity and ventral rampart in process of completion. Fusing ossific nodules may form upper extremity and extend along ventral border. Symphyseal face may either be smooth or retain distinct ridges. Dorsal plateau is complete. No lipping of symphyseal dorsal margin or bony ligamentous outgrowths. |
| 4 | 38.2 | 10.9 | 26–70 | 35.2 | 9.4 | 23–57 | Symphyseal face is generally fine-grained, although remnants of ridge and furrow system may remain. Oval outline usually complete at this stage, though a hiatus may occur in upper aspect of ventral circumference. Pubic tubercle is fully separated from the symphyseal face through definition of upper extremity. Symphyseal face may have a distinct rim. Ventrally, bony ligamentous outgrowths may occur in inferior portion of pubic bone adjacent to symphyseal face. Slight lipping may appear on dorsal border. |
| 5 | 48.1 | 14.6 | 25–83 | 45.6 | 10.4 | 27–66 | Slight depression of the face relative to a completed rim. Moderate lipping is usually found on the dorsal border with prominent ligamentous outgrowths on the ventral border. Little or no rim erosion, though breakdown possible on superior aspect of ventral border. |
| 6 | 60.0 | 12.4 | 42–87 | 61.2 | 12.2 | 34–86 | Symphyseal face shows ongoing depression as rim erodes. Ventral ligamentous attachments are marked. Pubic tubercle may appear as a separate bony knob. Face may be pitted or porous, giving an appearance of disfigurement as the ongoing process of erratic ossification proceeds. Crenelations may occur, with the shape of the face often irregular. |

**FIGURE 7.12 Tooth Wear Age Stages** The surface of the tooth wears down with use, exposing the inner dentin (indicated here in pink). Generally, older individuals have used their teeth for more years and have more tooth wear than younger individuals.

| Age Span | | 17–25 | | | 25–35 | | | 35–45 | | | 45+ |
|---|---|---|---|---|---|---|---|---|---|---|---|
| Tooth | | M1 | M2 | M3 | M1 | M2 | M3 | M1 | M2 | M3 | |
| Wear | or | | | No dentin exposed | | | | | | | More advanced wear |
| Pattern | or | | | | | | | | | | |

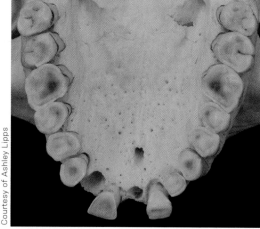

**FIGURE 7.13 Tooth Wear** These teeth are very worn down and belonged to an older individual.

## ESTIMATING STATURE

A person's **stature** (body height) is based in large part on the size of their bones. A person with longer bones will be taller overall, and a person with shorter bones will be shorter overall. For this reason, we can use bone measurements to help us determine a person's stature during life. As with other information, this is useful in forensic cases because height is often tracked in public records, such as on an individual's driver's license.

A number of researchers have developed formulas to estimate stature from bone measurements in both bioarchaeological and forensic contexts. Although some formulas are based on measurement of various bones from the whole skeleton, most researchers use measurements

from long bones. Long bones (particularly those of the arms and legs) are used to estimate stature because their length strongly correlates with overall stature. The forensic anthropologist measures the bone's maximum length using an instrument called an **osteometric board** (**FIGURE 7.14**), but a tape measure can be used if necessary. This measurement is entered into a formula that is dependent on the individual's sex and ancestry. The result is a stature estimate with a range or standard of error (SE) that gives an idea of how much error is possible in the measurement. This means the real stature is probably very close to the resulting number, but not necessarily the exact same number. The measurements for formulas are taken using the metric system and reported in centimeters (cm). To get a value in the English units (U.S. customary units) of inches, you divide stature estimates in centimeters by 2.54 to get inches.

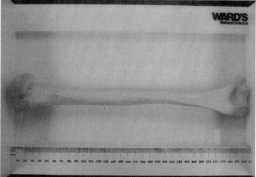

**FIGURE 7.14 Osteometric Board** An osteometric board may be used to measure the maximum length of a long bone for stature estimation.

**stature** an individual's overall body height

**osteometric board** an instrument used to measure bones

You can then divide the inches value by 12 to get a stature estimate in feet.

The formulas used for stature estimates are different for each long bone because the relationship between each bone's length and overall stature varies. In addition, all formulas will vary between males and females because body proportions and overall stature vary slightly by sex. The formulas will also vary for people of different ancestry. Again, as is discussed in greater detail in Lab 8, body sizes and proportions vary slightly between populations from different regions and climates, so this variation must be accounted for by different formulas. The following table shows stature formulas for the major long bones by sex and ancestry.

There are some issues to bear in mind with stature estimation. First, many of the formulas for stature estimation were developed using skeletons from museum collections of people that died in the 1900s (such as the Terry collection at the Smithsonian). There have been gradual changes in body size and height among populations in the last century, and it is unclear if

## EQUATIONS USED TO ESTIMATE STATURE, IN CENTIMETERS, WITH STANDARD ERROR, FROM THE LONG BONES OF VARIOUS GROUPS OF INDIVIDUALS BETWEEN 18 AND 30 YEARS OF AGE[a]

| Males of European Descent | | | | | Males of African Descent | | | | |
|---|---|---|---|---|---|---|---|---|---|
| 3.08 | × | Hum | + | 70.45 | ± 4.05 | 3.26 | × | Hum | + | 62.10 | ± 4.43 |
| 3.78 | × | Rad | + | 79.01 | ± 4.32 | 3.42 | × | Rad | + | 81.56 | ± 4.30 |
| 3.70 | × | Uln | + | 74.05 | ± 4.32 | 3.26 | × | Uln | + | 79.29 | ± 4.42 |
| 2.38 | × | Fem | + | 61.41 | ± 3.27 | 2.11 | × | Fem | + | 70.35 | ± 3.94 |
| 2.68 | × | Fib | + | 71.78 | ± 3.29 | 2.19 | × | Fib | + | 85.65 | ± 4.08 |
| Females of European Descent | | | | | Females of African Descent | | | | |
| 3.36 | × | Hum | + | 57.97 | ± 4.45 | 3.08 | × | Hum | + | 64.67 | ± 4.25 |
| 4.74 | × | Rad | + | 54.93 | ± 4.24 | 2.75 | × | Rad | + | 94.51 | ± 5.05 |
| 4.27 | × | Uln | + | 57.76 | ± 4.30 | 3.31 | × | Uln | + | 75.38 | ± 4.83 |
| 2.47 | × | Fem | + | 54.10 | ± 3.72 | 2.28 | × | Fem | + | 59.76 | ± 3.41 |
| 2.93 | × | Fib | + | 59.61 | ± 3.57 | 2.49 | × | Fib | + | 70.90 | ± 3.80 |
| Males of East Asian Descent | | | | | Males of Mexican Descent | | | | |
| 2.68 | × | Hum | + | 83.19 | ± 4.25 | 2.92 | × | Hum | + | 73.94 | ± 4.24 |
| 3.54 | × | Rad | + | 82.0 | ± 4.60 | 3.55 | × | Rad | + | 80.71 | ± 4.04 |
| 3.48 | × | Uln | + | 77.45 | ± 4.66 | 3.56 | × | Uln | + | 74.56 | ± 4.05 |
| 2.15 | × | Fem | + | 72.57 | ± 3.80 | 2.44 | × | Fem | + | 58.67 | ± 2.99 |
| 2.40 | × | Fib | + | 80.56 | ± 3.24 | 2.50 | × | Fib | + | 75.44 | ± 3.52 |

[a]All bone lengths are maximum lengths (Hum = humerus, Rad = radius, Uln = ulna, Fem = femur, Fib = fibula length, in cm). The tibia is not included because of historical inconsistencies in the measurement and formula for this bone. To estimate the stature of older individuals, subtract 0.06 × (age in years − 30) cm. To estimate cadaveric stature, add 2.5 cm. From Trotter 1970.

the skeletal measurements are accurate for more recent forensic cases. Second, the formulas for the tibia are probably not as precise as the formulas for other bones. The original tibia formulas were developed without including the distal medial malleolus in the tibia measurement. Excluding this area of the bone during measurement can change the accuracy of the measurement.

# IDENTIFYING PATHOLOGY

Bioarchaeologists and forensic anthropologists are also interested in any indicator on an individual's skeleton that is not related to normal variation but is related to disease (**pathology**) or metabolic stress. Further, they must distinguish between antemortem pathology and perimortem pathology. **Antemortem pathology** is pathology that developed at any point prior to an individual's death. **Perimortem pathology** is pathology or trauma that developed around the time of an individual's death and may have contributed to that death. This is a particularly important distinction to make for the forensic anthropologist, as she may be asked to comment on the manner of a victim's death in a legal proceeding. The **manner of death** includes circumstances surrounding death that may have contributed to death, such as traumatic injuries. However, the forensic anthropologist does *not* determine official cause of death. The **cause of death** is a medical determination made by a medical examiner or coroner, often in conjunction with information from the forensic anthropologist. For example, the forensic anthropologist may recognize that the victim's hyoid bone has been broken, indicating likely strangulation. Yet, the official cause of death given by the coroner would be asphyxiation. To properly identify possible contributing factors to the victim's death, the forensic anthropologist must be able to distinguish pathology that occurred earlier in life and did not contribute to death.

## Antemortem Pathology

While antemortem pathology cannot necessarily inform us about the manner of death, it can tell us valuable information about how an individual lived and what their overall health was like during life. For the bioarchaeologist, antemortem pathology tells about the health of one person, and pathology indicators in many individuals in a population can help build a picture of overall stress and lifestyle in the past. For the forensic anthropologist, looking at antemortem pathology can aid in the overall identification of a victim.

In general, there are several categories of antemortem pathology. The first includes pathology related to overall health and metabolic stress. Often, when the body is under nutritional stress, it compensates by slowing down bone growth and focusing metabolic energy elsewhere. When the nutritional stress is over, the bone then begins growing regularly again. Stress indicators are routinely used in the analysis of skeletal remains from bioarchaeological contexts. A classic example of this process is seen in the teeth. If an individual has a period of nutritional stress due to lack of food or severe illness when the teeth are growing during childhood, enamel will stop forming on the tooth crowns for a time. When the period of stress has passed, the enamel-forming process will resume where it ordinarily should be, not where it left off. The

Barry Stark. From Larsen, C. S. 1994. In the wake of Columbus: postcontact Native population biology of the Americas. *Yearbook of Physical Anthropology* 37:109–154. © Wiley-Liss.

**FIGURE 7.15 Dental Enamel Hypoplasia**
These horizontal ridges on the teeth indicate the individual suffered stress (nutritional or health problems) while the tooth was being formed in early childhood. This antemortem pathology reflects health problems in early life.

**pathology** the study of disease, particularly how it changes the body

**antemortem pathology** pathology that developed at any time prior to an individual's death

**perimortem pathology** pathology and trauma that developed around the time of an individual's death and may have contributed to that death

**manner of death** the circumstances surrounding death that may have contributed to death, such as traumatic injuries

**cause of death** the medical determination of the physiological reason for an individual's death

**dental enamel hypoplasia** a gap or horizontal line on a tooth that has less enamel than surrounding areas

**dental caries** areas of the teeth that have undergone demineralization and decay due to acid exposure, also called cavities

**iron-deficiency anemia** a condition caused by a severe lack of iron in the body

result of this is a gap or horizontal line with reduced enamel called a **dental enamel hypoplasia** (FIGURE 7.15). Because we have specific knowledge of when the teeth and enamel are formed, we can use the location of dental enamel hypoplasias to obtain an accurate estimate of the age at which the nutritional or illness-related stress occurred.

Another nutrition-related pathology is the presence of dental caries. **Dental caries**, also called dental cavities, are areas of the teeth that have undergone demineralization and decay due to acid exposure (FIGURE 7.16). The acid is formed naturally by oral bacteria as the mouth begins to break down food to start digestion. However, if the acids are produced in higher quantities (due to what is eaten) or not properly cleaned away through proper dental hygiene, caries can form. The prevalence of dental caries is much higher in populations with an agricultural lifestyle than it is in populations with a foraging lifestyle. This is because an agricultural lifestyle is often based on a diet high in carbohydrates, which results in more acid in the mouth.

In addition to pathology associated with nutrition, there is pathology associated more specifically with disease. For example, **iron-deficiency anemia** is a condition caused by a severe lack of iron in the body. This lack of iron is often due to disease or parasites in the body (and is also potentially related to dietary stress). The primary indicator of this is a type of bone destruction called **porotic hyperostosis** (FIGURE 7.17), which is usually seen on the cranial bones. Porotic hyperostosis results from an expansion of the marrow cavity, which causes the smooth cortex of the flat bones of the cranium to look porous and spongy.

Aside from nutritional and disease-related pathology, there are also pathologies associated with chronic conditions. For example, **osteoarthritis** is common among humans and is a condition where accumulated wear and tear on the joints results in the loss of their cartilage linings. This loss of cartilage causes changes (both bone formation and bone loss) in the underlying bone (FIGURE 7.18). Without healthy cartilage as a cushion between the bones, bone surfaces at a joint end up contacting each other directly. This can result in **eburnation**, an area of bone that is

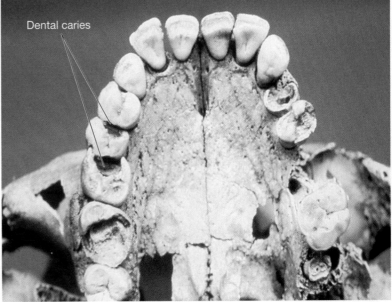

Clark Spencer Larsen

**FIGURE 7.16 Dental Caries**
These areas of tooth decay (also known as cavities) are related to acid levels in the mouth. This antemortem pathology can develop at any time prior to death.

Clark Spencer Larsen

**FIGURE 7.17 Porotic Hyperostosis on the Cranial Vault**
Most commonly found in the cranium, this type of bone destruction results in a spongy bone surface. It indicates iron-deficiency anemia, a type of antemortem pathology.

polished and shiny due to repeated direct contact between bones at the joint. The bone may also respond to dwindling cartilage by forming extra spicules of bone, called **osteophytes**, around the margin of the joint surface. Osteoarthritis is common in highly mobile joints such as the hip, knee, and lower back.

**porotic hyperostosis** a form of bone destruction that usually presents in the cranial bones as porous and spongy bone surfaces, rather than the normally smooth surface

**osteoarthritis** a condition where trauma or accumulated wear and tear on the joints results in loss of their cartilage lining

**eburnation** a polishing of a bone surface caused by repeated direct contact between bones at a joint

**osteophyte** spicule of bone that often forms around the margin of a joint surface when the cartilage at the joint is worn down

Clark Larsen/Mark Griffin

**FIGURE 7.18 Osteoarthritis**
In this form of antemortem pathology, accumulated wear and tear on the joints causes changes in the bone. Note the osteophytes, extra spicules of bone, around the edges of these vertebrae.

## Perimortem Pathology

As with antemortem pathology, there are different types of perimortem pathology. The examination of perimortem pathology in skeletal remains is particularly important in the forensic context. Most perimortem pathology is obviously distinguishable from antemortem pathology because it involves severe, traumatic injuries. For example, **knife wounds** are often indicated by large cuts or nicks in a bone. When a hard blade makes contact with bone tissue, it leaves behind small **cut marks** (indentations). For instance, if an individual has been stabbed repeatedly in the chest, this is likely to leave a series of cut marks on the ribs. The size (length and depth) and shape of the cut marks can indicate the size and type of blade used, and the orientation of the cut marks can indicate the angle of the thrusts.

Another traumatic injury that can be seen in bones is **blunt force trauma**. This is trauma that results from coming in contact with a blunt object, and it can occur through falling or through being hit with an object, such as a

Courtesy of Tiffiny Tung

**FIGURE 7.19 Blunt Force Trauma**
This form of perimortem pathology is indicated by depressions in bone near the point of impact such as the depression and radiating fracture lines seen on the posterior right parietal here. From Monqachayoq sector at Huari Huari in Ayacucho,Peru, ca. AD 1275–1400.

baseball bat. Blunt force trauma is indicated by the presence of a depression in bone at the point of impact (**FIGURE 7.19**). There can also be small bone cracks or fractures that radiate out from the depressed area due to the force of impact.

**Gunshot wounds** (or projectile trauma) can be very obvious in the skeleton. For example, if an individual has been shot, there may be clear points of entry and exit, indicated by holes in the bone. The entry hole is smaller and has more discrete edges than the exit wound, which is larger and has an inward-sloping, beveled edge (when viewed from the outer surface of the bone). The size of the entry wound can be used to determine the maximum possible bullet size, and the orientation of the entry and exit wounds can be used to indicate the trajectory of the shot. Sometimes gunshot wounds are less obvious. If, for example, a victim was shot in the chest, there probably isn't a clear entry or exit hole because the rib cage is not a solid mass

**knife wound** injury caused by a sharp, blade-like instrument, which often leaves telltale nicks or cut marks on bone

**cut mark** indentation left on bone by a sharp instrument, such as a knife or stone tool

**blunt force trauma** injury caused by contact with a blunt object, such as a club, which often causes depressions in the bone that are surrounded by small fractures

**gunshot wound** injury caused by various small arms (gun) fire, which may cause holes or nicks in bone, depending on where the shot enters and exits the body

through which the bullet must pass. The bullet could slip between two ribs and only skim a bone along the edge. This would leave a nick or mark in the bone similar to a cut mark. This nick would have to be examined more closely to distinguish it from a knife-related injury.

Some traumas leave very distinct damage to particular bones. For example, choking or **strangulation** requires that a lot of force be applied to the throat. The small, fragile hyoid bone in the neck is likely to acquire damage as a result of this force. Therefore, an unhealed, fractured hyoid bone is usually indicative of choking or strangulation.

Often, we experience traumatic injuries that do not contribute to death. These injuries must be distinguished from other injuries to understand the manner of death. For example, a person may have suffered a **fracture** in their arm 2 years before dying. This trauma needs to be distinguished from any injuries that may have actually contributed to death. This distinction is based on whether the bone has healed through remodeling **(FIGURE 7.20)**. If the injury is treated well initially, the bone may remodel very cleanly, leaving little evidence of prior fracture. If, however, the injury is not treated well, the bone may heal incorrectly. The two sides of the bone may not line up together correctly, or there may be extra bone formation in the area of the fracture. Either way, if the bone shows signs of remodeling, it indicates the damage occurred long enough before death that the body could begin the healing process.

## ADDITIONAL STEPS OFTEN IN FORENSIC CONTEXTS: DETERMINING ANCESTRY

Often, forensic anthropologists are asked to determine a victim's likely ancestry because this information can aid in the attempt to identify an unknown victim(s). Bioarchaeologists may also be interested in determining ancestry in archaeological populations to help study past migrations or population movements, familial

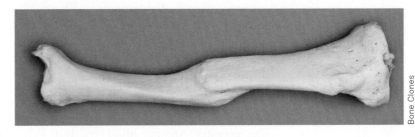

**FIGURE 7.20 Fracture**
When bones experience traumatic injuries, such as fractures, the body will attempt to repair the damage through bone remodeling. If the bone does not repair cleanly, it may leave behind extra bone or offset areas of bone near the injury site.

relationships, and other population trends. As we discuss further in Lab 8 on modern human variation, people from different parts of the world have different biological morphologies that are the combined result of population genetics and human adaptation. Group differences in morphology can also be present in the skeleton. These skeletal differences are superficial, and they have occurred very recently in the deep time of human evolution. Nevertheless, they can often be used to roughly identify a person's regional ancestry.

There are two groups or types of traits that can be used to recognize morphological indicators of ancestry: metric traits and nonmetric traits. **Metric traits** are traits that are measurable on the skeleton, such as the length or breadth of certain bones. Typically dozens of measurements are taken of different skeletal areas, and these measurements are run as part of complex statistical analyses to determine the most likely ancestral group. The use of metric traits is based on the principle that people in different regions will have different sizes, proportions, or degrees of robusticity (again, see Lab 8).

**Nonmetric traits** are traits that are not measurable. Instead, these are traits that one either has or does not have. They are scored as either present or absent, and can be found on the cranial and postcranial skeleton. Different ancestral groups are more likely to have different combinations (or suites) of traits. For example, the shovel-shaped incisor trait

**strangulation** the forcible choking of another individual, which often results in damage to the hyoid bone

**fracture** a break in the bone due to a trauma (or injury)

**metric trait** measurable trait on the skeleton that can be used to estimate ancestry

**nonmetric trait** nonmeasurable trait on the skeleton that can be used to estimate ancestry

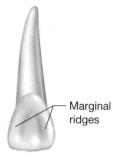

**FIGURE 7.21 Shovel-Shaped Incisors**

Some traits, like shovel-shaped incisors, are more common in some human populations than others. Shovel-shaped incisors have a distinct shovel shape on their back (tongue side) and are more common in some Asian and Native American populations. Anthropologists can study suites of traits like this to try to determine a person's possible ancestry.

is a nonmetric trait **(FIGURE 7.21)**. It refers to a uniquely shaped incisor, in which the lingual (tongue-side) surface of the tooth has a distinct indentation resembling the spade of a shovel. This tooth type is more commonly found in people with Asian or Native American ancestry. Another nonmetric trait is the malar tubercle, which is a bony projection extending from the inferior edge of the zygomatic bone **(FIGURE 7.22)**. This tubercle is pronounced in people of Asian ancestry, but it is usually absent in people of European and African ancestry populations. In addition to these traits, anthropologists may also look for nonmetric variations in the shape of skeletal features. For example, the nasal root (superior nasal margin) is low and rounded in African populations, high and peaked in European populations, and low and peaked in Asian populations (Figure 7.22).

It is important to emphasize that there is individual and within-population variation in both metric and nonmetric traits. This means that within an ancestral group, not everyone will have the exact same metric results or all the same nonmetric features. Further, the determinations of traits that may indicate biological ancestry do not inform us about the cultural or ethnic affiliation that a person identified with during life. Finally, we are dealing with ranges, and the ranges of different populations overlap. For this reason, some anthropologists prefer to emphasize nonmetric traits when possible because they result in less ambiguous identifications. Additionally, anthropologists are always looking at suites of multiple traits. The anthropologist does not make an ancestry determination based only on one trait. She tries to use a combination of metric and nonmetric traits from throughout the body to improve the accuracy of the determination.

## ADDITIONAL STEPS OFTEN IN FORENSIC CONTEXTS: CALCULATING THE POSTMORTEM INTERVAL

The forensic anthropologist is also usually asked to estimate the **postmortem interval** for a victim. This interval refers to the time that has

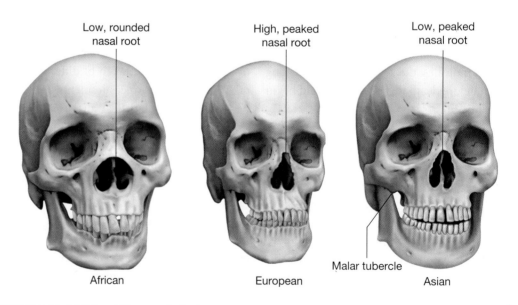

Low, rounded nasal root    High, peaked nasal root    Low, peaked nasal root

African    European    Malar tubercle    Asian

**FIGURE 7.22 Additional Nonmetric Traits**

The malar tubercle is a nonmetric trait used in ancestry determination. This trait is more common in Asian populations than European and African populations. Another nonmetric trait is nasal root shape. In African populations, the nasal root is low and rounded. In European populations, the nasal root is high and peaked. In Asian populations, the nasal root is low and peaked.

**postmortem interval** the time elapsed since an individual died elapsed since death. Generally, as more time elapses, it becomes more difficult to pinpoint the time since death. During the early stages of decomposition, there are regular phases of insect activity, so if insects are present on the body, they can be used to determine postmortem interval. Similarly, soft tissue decays fairly quickly and at known rates, so the degree of soft tissue decay can be used to estimate time since death as well. However, if enough time has passed that there is no longer soft tissue or insect activity on the body, determining the postmortem interval becomes much more challenging. Bones decay too gradually to be used alone for calculating elapsed time intervals.

Calculating the postmortem interval is further complicated by variations in environmental and depositional conditions. If the body has been in an area that is conducive to rapid decay, such as an open and humid environment with a lot of insect activity, it may appear that more time has elapsed because the body will show advanced decomposition. If the body is in a setting that is less conducive to decay, such as being covered in a dry environment, it may appear that less time has elapsed because the body will show less decomposition. The forensic anthropologist will attempt to take these factors into account and provide a rough estimate (range of time) for when the victim died.

# CONCEPT REVIEW QUESTIONS

Name: _____     Section: _____

Course: _____     Date: _____

Answer the following questions in the space provided.

1. Define bioarchaeology.


2. Define forensic anthropology.


3. What is the first step in analyzing skeletal remains in both bioarchaeological and forensic contexts?
   - A. Determine the minimum number of individuals
   - B. Determine the sex of each individual
   - C. Calculate the postmortem interval
   - D. Distinguish between human and animal bone

4. After skeletal remains have been identified as human, what step usually comes next in bioarchaeology and forensic investigations?
   - A. Identify pathology in each individual
   - B. Determine the age at death for each individual
   - C. Determine the minimum number of individuals
   - D. Determine the sex of each individual

5. Describe a method for aging a juvenile skeleton. Be sure to note which bone or bones are necessary for this method.




6. Describe a method for aging an adult skeleton. Be sure to note which bone or bones are necessary for this method.




7. Name one bone that is useful in determining sex.

8. What bone or bones are best suited for stature estimates? Why?




9. Describe the difference between "manner of death" and "cause of death."




10. True or false? Antemortem pathology is pathology that occurs around the time of death and may have contributed to death.

# LAB EXERCISES

Name: _____   Section: _____

Course: _____   Date: _____

## EXERCISE 1   ANIMAL OR HUMAN?

Work with a small group or alone to complete this exercise. Review the skeletal material provided by your instructor (or the image in the lab Appendix) and answer the questions below.

1. Which of the skeletal elements is human?

2. Describe *one* trait that helped you make this distinction:

## EXERCISE 2   MINIMUM NUMBER OF INDIVIDUALS

Work with a small group or alone to complete this exercise. Refer to the skeletal material provided by your instructor (or the mystery assemblage in the lab Appendix) to answer the questions below.

1. List the bones depicted. (Be as specific as possible, including the side of the body that the bone is from, if applicable.)

2. What is the minimum number of individuals in this assemblage?

## EXERCISE 3   AGING

Work with a small group or alone to complete this exercise. Review the skeletal material provided by your instructor (or the images in the text or lab Appendix) to answer the questions below.

1. Examine the X-ray of a juvenile upper and lower jaw in Figure 7.9 and compare it to the dental eruption age stages in Figure 7.10. What is the approximate age of this individual?

2. Examine the skeletal material, which is from a female and shows the symphyseal face of the pubis (see lab Appendix). Compare this to the Suchey–Brooks age stages provided in Figure 7.11 of the text. What is the approximate age of this individual?

**SEXING**

Work with a small group or alone to complete this exercise. Review the skeletal material provided by your instructor (or the images in the lab Appendix) and answer the questions below.

1. Which cranium is female?

2. Describe *two* cranial sexing traits you used to make this determination.

3. Which pelvis is female?

4. Describe *two* pelvic sexing traits you used to make this determination.

**ANCESTRY**

Work with a small group or alone to complete this exercise. Refer to the skeletal material provided by your instructor (or the images in the lab Appendix) to answer the questions below.

1. Which individual has shovel-shaped incisors?

2. Which individual has a malar tubercle?

3. What might these two traits indicate about these individuals' ancestry?

4. Are these two traits alone enough to make an ancestry determination? Why or why not?

## EXERCISE 6 STATURE

Work with a small group or alone to complete this exercise. Review the skeletal material provided by your instructor (or the description below) and answer the question.

1. A forensic anthropologist has determined that a female victim has a maximum femur length of 49.5 cm. The anthropologist also determined the victim is of African ancestry. Using the table of equations to estimate stature from long bones provided in the text, estimate this individual's stature. (Be sure to give the estimation in feet and inches, using the conversion information provided in the text.)

## EXERCISE 7 PATHOLOGY

Work with a small group or alone to complete this exercise. Review the skeletal material provided by your instructor (or the images in the lab Appendix) and answer the questions for each scenario below.

### SCENARIO A

1. What bone is this?

2. What pathology is indicated on this bone?

3. Describe *one* trait you used to make this pathology identification.

4. Is this pathology antemortem or perimortem?

**SCENARIO B**

1. What bone is this?

2. What pathology is indicated on this bone?

3. Describe *one* trait you used to make this pathology identification.

4. Is this pathology antemortem or perimortem?

## EXERCISE 8   TYING IT ALL TOGETHER

Work with a small group or alone to complete this exercise. A collection of skeletal remains has just been unearthed at a crime scene. You have been asked to help law enforcement officials in their investigation of this skeletal material. Refer to the skeletal material provided by your instructor (or the mystery forensic assemblage in the lab Appendix) to answer the questions below.

1. Is any of this skeletal material nonhuman? If so, which bone is nonhuman? Why do you think this?

2. List all of the human skeletal elements, being as specific as possible. What is the minimum number of individuals (MNI) represented?

3. Does any of the skeletal material appear to be juvenile? If so, which bone(s)? Why do you think this?

4. Can any of the skeletal material be used to determine the biological sex of the victim(s)? If so, which bone(s)? What is the sex you determined? What evidence supports that conclusion?

5. Bone I in the assemblage has been measured with an osteometric board. It has a maximum length of 35.7 cm. You have determined the individual is of European ancestry. Based on this information and what you know about this person's sex, what is the estimated stature of this individual? (Be sure to give the estimation in feet and inches.)

6. Based on the materials recovered, can you make any suggestions for additional analyses you might use to further understand the circumstances surrounding the death of the victim(s)?

# CRITICAL THINKING QUESTIONS

On a separate sheet of paper, answer the following questions.

1.  This question may be completed independently or as a group discussion. You have been asked to examine a bioarchaeological assemblage. You have identified the bones and made the following list of the material:

    - 1 left femur with unfused epiphyses
    - 1 right femur with fused epiphyses
    - 2 adult sacrums
    - 1 cranium with extensive tooth wear
    - 1 mandible with some teeth erupted and others unerupted

    What is the minimum number of individuals for this assemblage?

2.  This question may be completed independently or as a group discussion. Why are age estimates for adults less accurate than age estimates for juveniles?

3.  This question may be completed independently or as a group discussion. In Exercise 6, you determined the stature of an individual based on femur measurements. Imagine that you also recovered this individual's right humerus. The maximum length of the humerus is 35.1 cm. What is the individual's estimated stature based on the humerus data? (Again, use the table of equations to estimate stature from long bones provided in the text and be sure to convert your estimate into feet and inches.) Is this consistent with the estimation you made based on the femur measurement? Why or why not?

4.  What is the difference between antemortem pathology and perimortem pathology? Why must a forensic anthropologist be able to distinguish between the two types of pathology?

5.  How are forensic anthropology and bioarchaeology similar? How are they different?

6.  Following the September 11 attacks on the World Trade Center in New York City, numerous forensic anthropologists were called on to help with identifying victims. Using information in your classroom, online, or in books, answer the questions that follow. What types of analysis did the forensic anthropologists conduct in this situation? What impact did this work have on the investigation? What impact did this work have on the broader community (such as the city of New York's medical examiner's office or the field of forensic anthropology in general)?

7.  This question may be completed independently or as a group discussion. Imagine that you are working with a team of bioarchaeologists that have just excavated a medieval cemetery site in Italy. The cemetery has over 200 graves, with all sexes and ages represented in the skeletal sample. You are interested in knowing whether there were gender differences in health among the medieval community. How would you answer this question from the skeletal remains? What analyses would you need to conduct with the skeletons, and what health indicators might you look for in the bones?

8. A team of forensic anthropologists (named Julia and Marco) have identified the following skeletal remains as belonging to the same individual. Both anthropologists have examined the pelvis and cranium for indicators of the victim's biological sex. Julia argues the individual was male, but Marco argues the individual was female. Review the skeletal material depicted here. Why might the anthropologists disagree? Which anthropologist do you think is correct? Provide evidence from the skeletal material to support your conclusion.

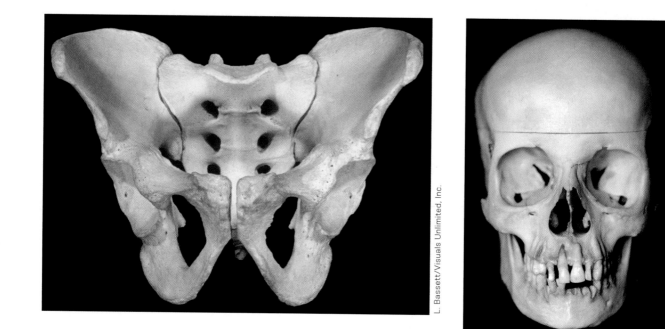

L. Bassett/Visuals Unlimited, Inc.

John Davis/Getty Images

9. This question may be completed independently or as a group discussion. As part of a forensic analysis, you have been asked to determine an individual's ancestry using skeletal indicators. The metric measurements you collect indicate the individual is of European ancestry, but you see several nonmetric traits in the cranium that are typically found in individuals of Asian ancestry. Why might the two methods disagree? Be sure to consider the differences between metric and nonmetric traits as well as other factors that might contribute to individual skeletal variation.

# APPENDIX:
# LAB EXERCISE IMAGES

## Exercise 1 Animal or Human

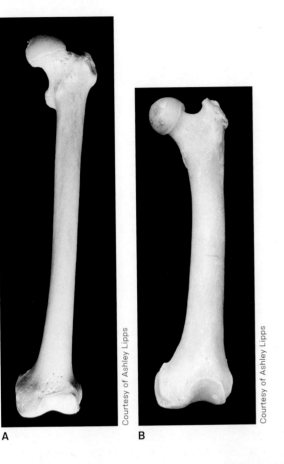

A

B

Courtesy of Ashley Lipps

## Exercise 2 Minimum Number of Individuals

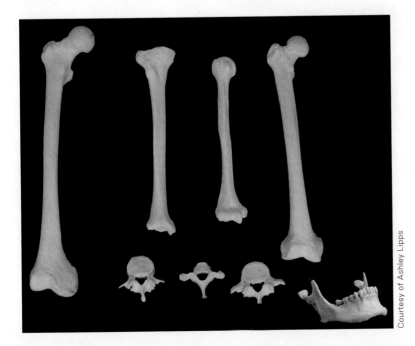

Courtesy of Ashley Lipps

## Exercise 3 Aging

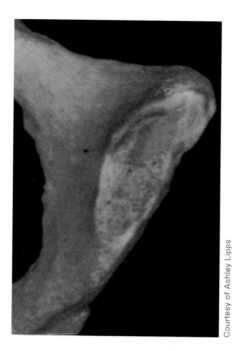

Courtesy of Ashley Lipps

## Exercise 4 Sexing

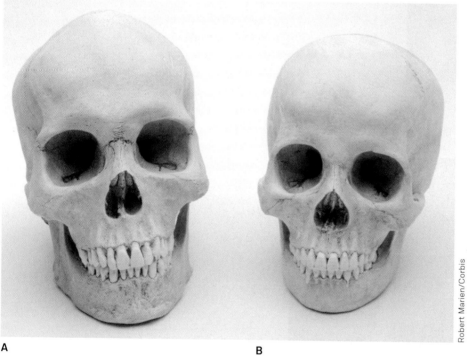

A

B

Robert Marien/Corbis

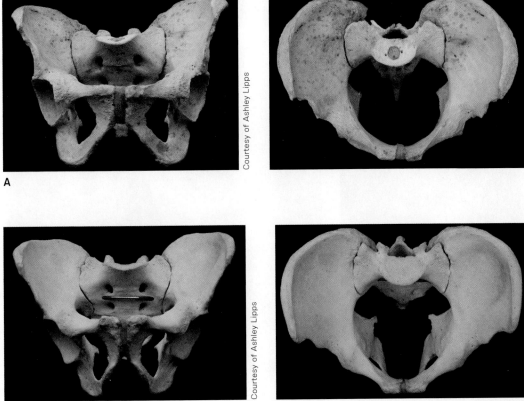

Courtesy of Ashley Lipps

A

Courtesy of Ashley Lipps

B

Courtesy of Ashley Lipps

Courtesy of Ashley Lipps

## Exercise 5 Ancestry

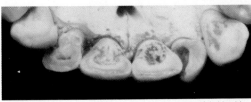

**Individual A**

Courtesy of Ashley Lipps

Donald J. Ortner

**Individual B**

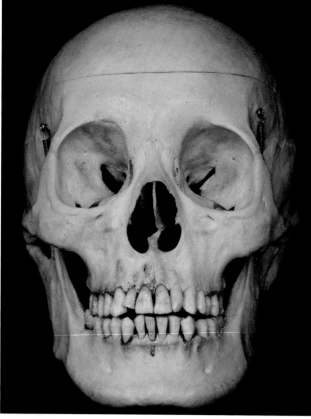

**Individual A**

*Courtesy of Ashley Lipps*

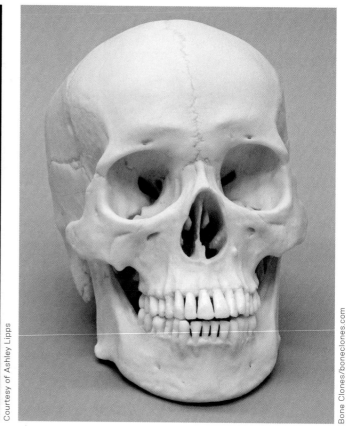

**Individual B**

*Bone Clones/boneclones.com*

## Exercise 7 Pathology

Scenario A: Signs of disease or stress on bone

Scenario B: Signs of disease or stress on bone

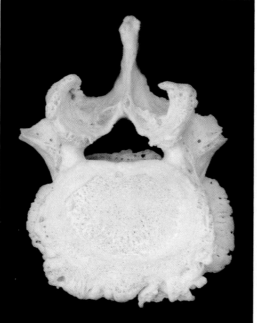

*Courtesy of Ashley Lipps*

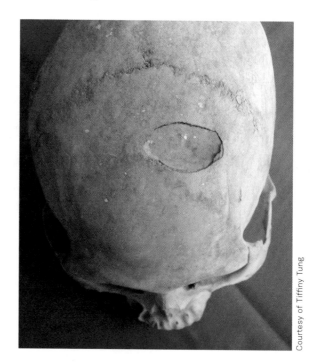

*Courtesy of Tiffiny Tung*

## Exercise 8 Tying It All Together

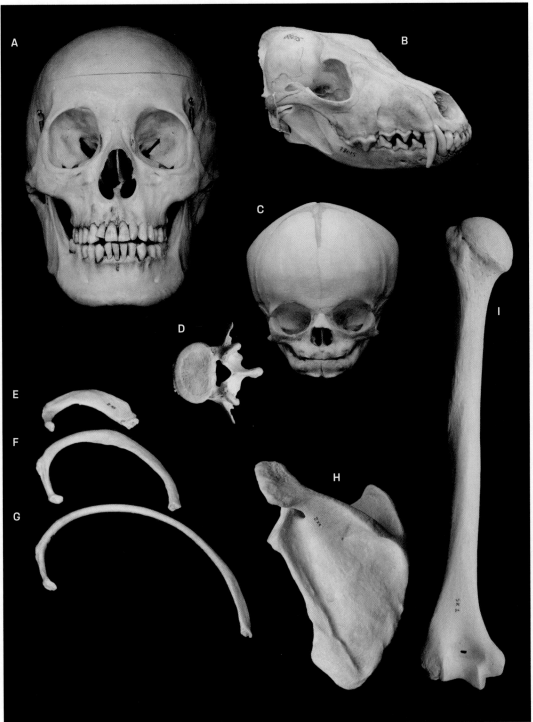

People are not all the same. We have different skin colors, body types, heights, and so on.

## Lab Learning Objectives

By the end of this lab, students should be able to:

- describe the difference between the variation found *within* human populations and the variation *between* human populations and how this relates to issues of race.

- explain the adaptive significance of variation in skin color, altitude adaptations, and climate adaptations.

- use variations, such as ABO blood allele frequencies, to discuss the impact of evolutionary forces on our species.

- discuss the role of cultural practices in shaping human variations, such as adult lactose tolerance and sickle-cell trait frequencies.

# Modern Human Variation

When we look around at a crowd of people, we notice that people appear different. Some people are taller, and others are shorter. Some people have darker hair and skin color, and others have lighter hair and skin color. Some people are lean, and others are stocky. Are these differences significant? Can we group people based on their similarities and differences? If we *can*, are these groupings universal; or do the groups vary depending on what traits we emphasize? If we *cannot* group people based on their similarities and differences, does that mean these physical traits are biologically meaningless? Or, do physical similarities and differences tell us something about the people who carry them? Can we reconstruct the evolutionary history of a group based on this kind of information? This lab examines these issues of modern human variation.

# INTRODUCTION

We begin this lab with a consideration of the topic of race. In this consideration, we specifically explore whether there is a biological basis for race in humans. We then turn to an exploration of other key dimensions of human variation, including skin color, altitude, climate, ABO blood alleles, and lactose tolerance. For each of these dimensions of variation, we focus on the adaptive significance of the variation and what these variations tell us about human population histories. We conclude with a closer examination of the sickle cell trait as an example of the complexity of human variations.

# RACE

Since early naturalists began classifying biological organisms centuries ago, various scientists have attempted to subdivide the human species into distinct racial categories. Historically, biological anthropologists contributed to this work, especially through the use of various skeletal traits for racial affiliation. Much of this research was conducted by Europeans who created hierarchical schemes of human variation that suggested they (Europeans) were superior to other groups of people (non-Europeans). Often, physical traits were linked with personality traits in racial classifications, such that different racial groups were linked with different levels of intelligence, propensities toward violence, and degrees of "savagery." Governments and other ruling bodies often used these racial categories and their associated behavioral traits to justify the subjugation or systematic extermination of certain groups. For example, many colonial powers used the classification research of anthropologists to justify their unfair treatment of colonized, indigenous populations. Today, anthropologists are trying to both better understand human variation and prevent the misuse of their research. With this in mind, we must recognize the history of the discipline and the complications surrounding racial categorization, while simultaneously examining the nuances of human variation and its significance.

Dividing people into distinct racial categories assumes that people from different groups are biologically distinct. For example, in many racial classifications people from Europe are differentiated from people from Africa. It is assumed that there are numerous biological distinctions between these two populations. Traditionally, racial classification was based on obvious physical characteristics, such as skin color, stature, and eye color. These traits were readily observable and seemed to vary between populations. In more recent years, we have been able to analyze underlying genetic data, and this genetic data has presented us with a very different picture of human variation. Comparisons of genetic information show that most of human variation is actually found *within* populations, rather than between populations. For example, in many traditional racial classifications, all people from Africa are treated as one population that is distinct from populations from other continents. However, newly studied genetic data shows us that the greatest variation is actually within this broad, African population **(FIGURE 8.1)**.

This greater degree of within-population variation makes sense in terms of the evolutionary history of our species. First, it is important to note that humans are a very recent species. As we will see in later labs, our species evolved as distinct from other species no more than 200,000 years ago. While this seems like a really long time, it is very little time in terms of evolution. Human populations have not had enough time to accumulate a lot of biological changes, which makes them very genetically similar. Second, humans have a tendency toward mobility and interbreeding. People are not as deterred by mountain ranges and bodies of water as other primates. People move between environments and territories regularly, and they often mate with people

Javic/Wikimedia Commons

DavidDennisPhotos.com/Wikimedia Commons

Jonathan Larsen/Diadem Images/Alamy

**FIGURE 8.1 Human Variation within Groups**
Humans have a lot of variation within groups, such as the wide phenotypic variation seen among African people here.

they find in other areas. This means human populations have not been subject to as much reproductive isolation as many other primate species. Humans have been undergoing gene flow regularly throughout their evolutionary history, helping humans to be more genetically similar to one another.

Our species today certainly has some genetic differences between populations; however, most of our genetic differences are minor variations within populations. We have a great deal of underlying genetic similarity, even across great geographical distances. This suggests that any differences we might see between populations are relatively superficial. They have evolved recently, sometimes only within the last few thousand years, and often reflect recent adaptations to particular environmental or cultural circumstances. Beneath it all, humans are very biologically similar, and we cannot readily divide humans into distinct racial groups. There is no biological basis for these large-scale classifications. However, our superficial variations can be used to better understand the nuances of our ancestry. We can apply our knowledge of evolutionary processes to understand patterns of variation that reflect population movement (the **founder effect**), interbreeding (**gene flow**), and adaptation (**natural selection**). We can move beyond a rigid structure of racial categorization to a

more fluid understanding of evolutionary history and ancestry.

It is crucial to note that while the genetics suggests that there is no biological basis for distinct racial categories, this does not mean racial categories lack cultural significance. Many people self-identify with a particular racial group(s). Race often helps in the forging of group identities and provides a sense of solidarity among people. At the same time, race is still central to issues of discrimination and disenfranchisement around the world. People continue to be mistreated due to their perceived or self-ascribed racial identity. Distinct racial categories misrepresent the complexity of human variation, and genetic evidence suggests human populations are often more similar than different. However, race does exist as a cultural phenomenon and is fundamental to many aspects of human cultural life.

In the context of this exploration of biological anthropology, we take a nuanced (and biologically based) consideration of human variation. As such, we trace the variation of a few key traits. We pay particular attention to what these variations may tell us about the evolutionary history of the populations who carry them.

When we are discussing human variations seen in people today, we are actually reconstructing ancestral histories and adaptations. There has been significant population

**founder effect** a special type of genetic drift that occurs when a subset of a larger population founds the next generation due to substantial population loss or population movement

**gene flow** the exchange of genes between previously isolated populations that begin to interbreed

**natural selection** the theory outlined by Charles Darwin to explain evolution: it argues that some traits are more suited to an organism's particular environmental context and are therefore passed on preferentially into the next generation, and these traits become more common in successive generations, resulting in evolutionary shifts in populations

**clinal distribution** a distribution of trait variations that has a continuous gradation across a geographical area

**melanin** a pigment that helps to give skin its brownish color

movement via colonization and globalization in recent centuries, and it is difficult at present to track the impact of these recent trends. Instead, we focus on the variants people carry from their ancestral population. For example, when thinking about the ancestral variations of people in the United States, we might be considering the variations of indigenous Native Americans, descendants of enslaved Africans, or a wide range of recent immigrant populations from around the world. We must be clear about which *ancestral* group we are studying. Throughout this lab, we will generally be dealing with data and information about indigenous populations. Therefore, when we are talking about variations in American populations, we are discussing Native American populations. When we are discussing variations in African populations, we are discussing indigenous African populations. We are not including recent immigrants and colonial descendants in these populations unless explicitly stated as such.

# SKIN COLOR

Skin color has been widely used as a trait for distinguishing human "races" throughout history. However, the use of this trait to categorize races is very problematic. First, it misrepresents the nature of skin color variation. Using skin color to differentiate distinct races assumes that skin color variation can be neatly divided into distinct groups of color. In reality, skin color has a **clinal distribution**. This means that there is a continuous and progressive gradation of a given trait over a geographic region. In the case of skin color we see that long-term residents of the tropics have the most pigmentation in the skin, while long-term residents of Arctic locations have the least amount of pigmentation in the skin (**FIGURE 8.2**). However, the transition of pigmentation from the tropics to northern parts of the globe is very gradual—if you were to walk across the continents from the equator northward, you would not see sudden changes in skin color from one group to the next.

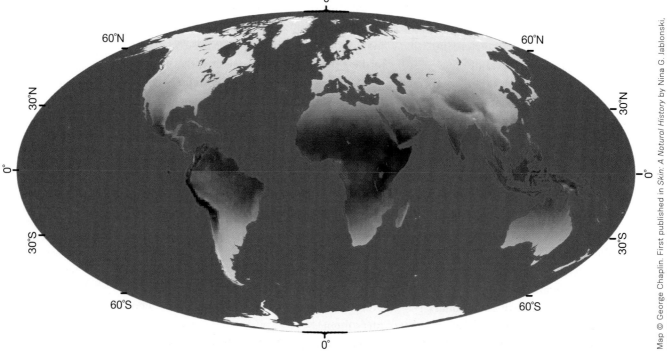

**FIGURE 8.2 Regional Skin Color Variation**
Human skin color varies geographically. Darker skin colors are more common near the equator, and lighter skin colors are more common away from the equator. Remember, although the map seems to show distinct color categories, each of the color bands on the map accounts for a range of skin color variants that have been grouped together to simplify the map.

The second problem with using skin color to differentiate races is that it ignores the adaptive significance of skin color variations. Darker skin color is more common closer to the equator, and lighter skin color is more common further from the equator. This is because darker skin color provides greater protection from damaging ultraviolet (UV) radiation. When we are exposed to the sun, we are also exposed to the sun's UV rays. These rays can have harmful consequences for our bodies, including cell death (such as that experienced in a sunburn) and skin cancer. UV radiation also depletes the folate stored in our bodies. Folate is important for cell division, growth and development, and reproductive functions, such as sperm production. In areas where sun exposure is high throughout the course of the year, such as near the equator, our bodies require more protection from the sun's destructive UV rays. Over countless generations, populations from these areas have adapted by producing more protective **melanin** in their skin. Melanin is a pigment in the skin, and it helps give skin its brownish color. In general, the more melanin that is present in the skin, the darker the skin color. The increased melanin—and corresponding darker skin color—seen in populations near the equator act as a natural shield, blocking some of the sun's UV radiation from penetrating deeply into the body.

This protective function explains why human populations who lived near the equator for many generations evolved dark skin color. However, how do we explain the light skin color found in populations who have lived many generations in nonequatorial areas? While exposure to the sun increases harmful UV exposure, it is also necessary for our well-being. We need some sun exposure to synthesize vitamin D in our bodies. Vitamin D is necessary for many of our bodily functions and is particularly important for good bone health, so it is crucial that we are able to synthesize it regularly. In areas where sun exposure is limited throughout the year, such as in temperate and Arctic areas far from the equator, human populations needed to be able to maximize the benefits of their limited sun exposure and maintain the proper levels of vitamin D. Populations that lived in these areas for generations evolved less melanin and lighter skin color to take in as much UV energy as possible when it was available. This resulted in lighter skin color variants in nonequatorial populations.

The evolution of skin color was a balancing act. Each population needed to adapt by acquiring the appropriate skin color variant to suit its ancestral area. Our earliest ancestors in Africa would have been covered in body hair that protected them from the sun. As human populations in this equatorial area lost their body hair, they needed to have enough melanin to protect themselves from the harmful effects of the sun, while still allowing for vitamin D synthesis. When human populations left Africa and settled in latitudes with less sun exposure, dark skin color was not necessary for protection, and it was more important to possess light skin color to help with vitamin D synthesis. Interestingly, the evolution of lighter skin color appears to have occurred independently in various regions. For example, lighter skin color evolved in Europeans and East Asians separately at different times. This complex evolutionary history contributes to the clinal distribution we see in skin color today. Equatorial and Arctic populations have extreme differences in skin color because of the extreme differences in these climates. Other populations distributed between these regions have adapted by evolving the skin color that is best suited to their particular, intermediate climate.

## ALTITUDE

Humans live all over the world, often in extreme environments. One such extreme environment is found at high altitudes. The further you live above sea level, the more stress is placed on your body. You are exposed to colder temperatures, more intense solar radiation, more wind, and often more difficult terrain. In addition,

**hypoxia** a condition where one cannot take in enough oxygen to meet the body's needs

**acclimatization** a short-term, temporary adjustment the body makes to better suit its current environmental context

**vasodilation** the expansion of the blood vessels near the surface of the body to help heat escape the body

**vasoconstriction** the constriction (narrowing) of the blood vessels near the surface of the body to help maintain heat in the body's core

**adaptation** a trait that has been favored by natural selection and helps a population be better suited to its environmental context

oxygen concentrations in the air continuously decrease the further above sea level you go. This can lead to **hypoxia**. This is a condition where you cannot take in enough oxygen to meet the metabolic needs of your body. In its mildest form, it can result in dizziness, headaches, and nausea. However, prolonged or intense hypoxia at high altitudes has the potential to cause much more serious stress and damage to the heart, lungs, and brain.

In general, there are two primary ways that humans respond to physiological stress. The first method is called **acclimatization**. This refers to short-term, temporary adjustments our bodies make to suit the current environmental context better. For example, a suntan is a short-term acclimatization that builds a layer of protection from UV exposure. Another example is the **vasodilation** we may experience in hot temperatures. This refers to the expansion of the blood vessels near the surface of our bodies to help heat escape the body's core. Alternatively, in cold temperatures, we may experience **vasoconstriction**. This is when the blood vessels near the surface of our bodies constrict to help maintain heat in the body's core. All of these acclimatizations are short-term, helping people adjust to their temporary environmental needs and then reverting back to their normal state.

People visiting high altitudes will undergo certain acclimatizations to help them function better in the extreme environment. For example, you might experience increased respiration in a high-altitude environment, taking in extra air through deeper and more frequent breaths to get the necessary oxygen you require. You might have an increase in lung capacity, so you can take in more air with each breath. You might make extra red blood cells to facilitate the transportation of oxygen through the body. Each of these responses is temporary. They will set in relatively quickly to help you avoid hypoxia, but they are reversible.

This process of acclimatization to high altitude can also help professional athletes train for major events. Often, athletes who regularly live in low altitudes will train in high altitudes for a few weeks or months before a major event. In doing this, the athletes expose their bodies to the extreme altitude and trigger the acclimatization process. When the athletes return to a lower altitude for their events, they will maintain the acclimatizations for a short time before their bodies revert to their prior states. The athletes will now have more efficient respiration and oxygen distribution during their events thanks to the temporary acclimatization to their training environments. Similarly, if an athletic event is taking place at high altitudes, athletes will train in high altitudes before the event to gain the acclimatizations they need to avoid hypoxia during the event.

In addition to temporary acclimatizations, there are also **adaptations**. These are permanent, and they are the result of natural selection acting on traits over many generations. These are often more extreme than acclimatizations. For example, populations that have lived in high altitudes for many generations often have special adaptations to help them in this stressful environment (**FIGURE 8.3**). As with altitude acclimatizations, these adaptations help to maximize the limited supply of oxygen and avoid hypoxia. However, unlike altitude acclimatizations, these traits appear to be inherited and permanent. Classic examples are found in indigenous populations from the Himalayas and the Andes mountain ranges. Tibetans

Courtesy of Cynthia Beall

**FIGURE 8.3 Life in High Altitudes**
People who live in high altitudes, like this farmer in Tibet, have adaptations to maximize their oxygen intake. These adaptations include traits like larger hearts and lungs, which result in a broad chest.

have adaptations in the circulatory system that support higher blood flow and oxygen movement than in low-altitude populations. Andeans have adaptations that allow them to take in more oxygen when breathing, and they have a higher proportion of red blood cells to facilitate oxygen movement through their bodies. It is believed that these two populations may have evolved different adaptations to similar high-altitude environments because of differences in their genetic makeup and because of the length of time the populations have inhabited their respective regions. The Himalayas were settled around 25,000 years ago, and the Andes were settled more recently (around 11,000 years ago). This means the Himalayan populations have had a longer time to adapt to their high-altitude environment and may have developed different traits as a result. In addition, the founding populations in these two regions were different and likely carried different genetic variations to the respective locations. The variations present in the founding populations would have limited the possible trajectories of natural selection and adaptation in the two populations.

## CLIMATE

In addition to adaptations for sun exposure and altitude, humans also have adaptations to different climates. Populations with a long history of living in hot climates have different body proportions than populations with a long history of living in cold climates. The principles associated with these body proportion adaptations were outlined by two different researchers. Carl Bergmann outlined a relationship between overall body size and climate. This relationship is called Bergmann's rule. Joel Allen identified a relationship between limb proportions and temperature called Allen's rule.

**Bergmann's rule** recognizes that as volume increases, surface area increases at a slower rate. Imagine a cube that measures 1 unit in all directions (**FIGURE 8.4**). This cube has a volume of 1 cubic unit and a surface area of

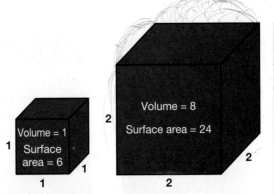

**FIGURE 8.4 Bergmann's Rule**
As volume increases, surface area increases at a slower rate. Notice here we increase the volume of the cube to be eight times larger (from 1 to 8 cubic units). However, the surface area has increased by only four times as much (from 6 to 24 square units). According to Bergmann's rule, a stocky build is a good adaptation for a cold climate. This body type allows for more body mass relative to surface area, and less surface area means less body heat loss.

6 square units. When we increase the size of the cube to measure 2 units in all directions, we find that the larger cube has a volume of 8 cubic units and a surface area of 24 square units (Figure 8.4). This means the volume has increased by eight times, while the surface area has increased by only four times. The volume increases at a faster rate than the surface area. Bergmann's rule applies this scaling principle to body size. It argues that larger, thicker body sizes are well adapted for cold climates because they have more volume relative to surface area. Having less surface area translates to less heat loss, so a large body with less surface area helps conserve body heat in cold temperatures.

**Allen's rule** recognizes that an equiaxed shape (which means having approximately equal dimensions in all directions, like a cube) has less surface area than an elongated shape of the same volume (like a rectangular prism). Imagine an equiaxed cube that measures 2 units in all directions (**FIGURE 8.5**). It has a volume of 8 cubic units and a surface area of 24 square units. Now, imagine an elongated shape that measures $4 \times 1 \times 2$ (Figure 8.5). It also has a volume of 8 cubic units, but its surface area is 28 square units. Both shapes have the same volume, but the elongated form has a larger surface

**Bergmann's rule** based on the principle that volume increases more rapidly than surface area, a large, thick body is well adapted for cold climates because it has less relative surface that would vent vital body heat

**Allen's rule** based on the principle that equiaxed shapes have less surface area than elongated shapes, long limbs are well adapted for hot climates because they have more relative surface to help vent extra body heat

**antigen** (in ABO blood group system) the cell surface marker found on red blood cells that relates to an individual's ABO blood type and triggers antibody reactions to a foreign blood antigen

**lactose** a sugar found in milk

**lactase** a protein required in order to properly digest the lactose in milk

**lactose intolerance** a condition common to all mammals where adults cannot properly digest lactose

**lactose tolerance** an unusual condition in some humans where adults can properly digest lactose

**pastoralism** a lifestyle where raising domesticated herd animals is central to the diet and economy

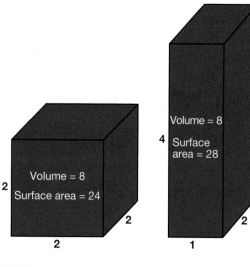

**FIGURE 8.5 Allen's Rule**

An equiaxed shape (left) has less surface area than an elongated shape (right). In this example, both shapes have the same volume, but the elongated shape has more surface area. According to Allen's rule, elongated limbs are well adapted to hot climates. This body type allows for more surface area, and more surface area means more venting of body heat.

area. Allen's rule applies this principle to limb proportions. It suggests that elongated limbs are well adapted for hot climates because they have greater surface area. This increased amount of surface area allows for greater body heat venting in hot temperatures.

# THE ABO BLOOD GROUP

In Lab 3, we introduced the ABO blood group system and discussed the different blood **antigen** alleles involved in blood type. The A allele results in the A antigen, and the B allele gives the B antigen. The O allele produces neither antigen. One allele is inherited from each parent, giving offspring one of six possible genotypes, referred to as *AA, AO, BB, BO, AB,* and *OO*. These genotypes then correspond to different phenotypes.

Interestingly, when we track the distribution of these alleles across indigenous populations worldwide, we find noteworthy patterns. First, the A allele is found more frequently in Europe, parts of Australia, and some far northern areas of North America (**FIGURE 8.6**). The B allele is more frequent in northern and central Eurasia (**FIGURE 8.7**). Lastly, the O allele is very frequent in the Americas and parts of Australia (**FIGURE 8.8**). In fact, in some parts of North and South America, almost 100% of the indigenous population has the O allele.

These blood allele distributions can tell us a lot about the evolutionary history of different populations. Areas with high concentrations of one allele may be the result of the founder effect. Imagine a population that has a relatively even distribution of the blood antigen alleles. A subgroup of this population moves away to settle a new area and found a new population. If the founding subgroup has a disproportionate number of one of the alleles, we will likely see an unusually high frequency of that allele in the descendent population. At the same time, blood antigen allele distributions may also be the result of gene flow. If there are large geographic areas with similar frequencies of an allele, it may suggest the populations in this area were mobile and had a lot of interbreeding.

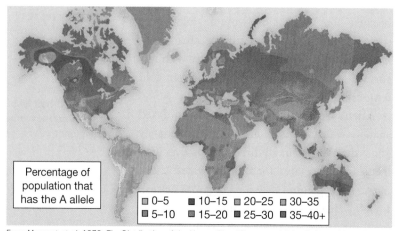

Percentage of population that has the A allele

☐ 0–5 ■ 10–15 ☐ 20–25 ■ 30–35
■ 5–10 ■ 15–20 ■ 25–30 ■ 35–40+

**FIGURE 8.6 Distribution of the A Allele**

Relative distributions of the A allele of the ABO blood group system vary geographically. The A allele is more common in parts of Europe, Australia, and far northern North America.

# LACTOSE TOLERANCE

The human variations discussed so far give us a variety of clues about our evolutionary history. Skin color, altitude, and climate adaptations reflect how natural selection helps to balance the different needs of populations living in different environmental circumstances. Variations in ABO blood allele frequencies reflect issues of genetic drift (the founder effect) and gene flow (interbreeding). In considering these traits, we have emphasized the significance of factors such as population movement and adaptation to natural, environmental conditions. In some cases, however, human variation is more the result of cultural factors than strictly environmental factors. An example of this is lactose tolerance in humans.

Milk contains a sugar called **lactose**. To digest this milk, you need a particular protein called **lactase**. All mammals produce the lactase protein early in life to be able to digest their mother's milk in infancy. As mammals grow and are weaned from their mother's milk, they stop producing lactase; as mature adults, they are no longer able to properly digest lactose. Attempting to consume dairy products containing lactose during adulthood results in a range of digestive discomforts.

Most humans follow this typical mammalian pattern. We are able to digest lactose early in life because we are producing the necessary lactase protein. As we age, we stop producing lactase and lose the ability to digest lactose. We have the condition known as **lactose intolerance**. Despite Western popular culture ideas to the contrary, lactose intolerance is the norm for our species and other mammals. Most humans worldwide are lactose intolerant as adults.

Why, then, are there some exceptions to this rule? When we look at populations around the world, we find that some populations have unusually low frequencies of lactose intolerance (**FIGURE 8.9**). Their adult populations have high **lactose tolerance**, where adults are still producing lactase, making them capable of digesting lactose. Interestingly, the populations with high levels of adult lactose tolerance are primarily descended from northern European and East African groups. These populations have a long history of **pastoralism**. This refers to a lifestyle where raising domesticated herd animals is central to the diet and economy.

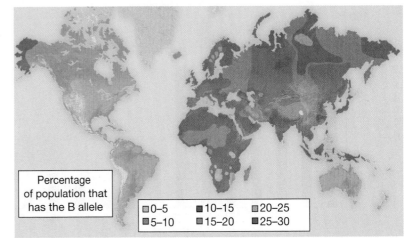

Percentage of population that has the B allele

□ 0–5   ■ 10–15   ■ 20–25
■ 5–10   ■ 15–20   ■ 25–30

From Mourant et al. 1976. *The Distribution of the Human Blood Groups and Other Polymorphisms,* 2nd edition. Map 2. Copyright © Oxford University Press, Inc. By permission of Oxford University Press.

**FIGURE 8.7 Distribution of the B Allele**
Relative distributions of the B allele vary geographically, with the B allele being more common in Central Asia.

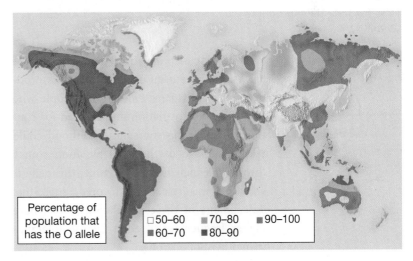

Percentage of population that has the O allele

□ 50–60   ■ 70–80   ■ 90–100
■ 60–70   ■ 80–90

**FIGURE 8.8 Distribution of the O Allele**
Relative distributions of the O allele vary geographically. Notice the O allele is more common in the Americas and parts of Australia.

Animal domestication is very recent, occurring within the last 10,000 years or so, and it is found in various parts of the world, from the Andes Mountains to the grasslands of East Africa. However, not all people practicing pastoralism use their animals for the same purposes. Often, domesticated animals are used as work animals or for their raw materials, such as their meat, hides, and dung. In some cultures, though, there is a history of using the animals specifically for their milk products. In these populations, we see higher frequencies of adult lactose tolerance.

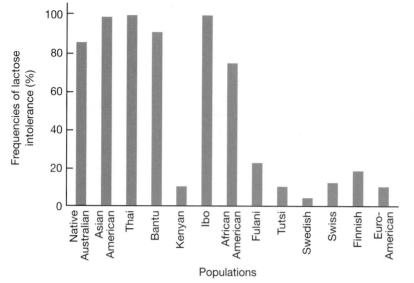

**FIGURE 8.9 Adult Lactose Intolerance Frequency**
Most adult humans are lactose intolerant. Lactose tolerance, which is unusual, is seen in populations with a long history of raising animals for their dairy products (such as some European and African populations).

It seems these populations in parts of Europe and Africa have been using animal milk products for many, many generations. People who had the genetic variation that allowed for continued lactose digestion into adulthood could take advantage of the available food source throughout their lives. Over time, this genetic variation was selectively favored, such that descendants of these populations today have higher frequencies of adult lactose tolerance than other populations.

The lactose tolerance issue has profound implications for the understanding of our evolutionary history. First, it indicates that the evolutionary history of organisms is influenced by their diet and the adaptations that evolve to suit their dietary needs. We will see further examples of this as we trace the connections between diet and dietary adaptations in later labs about primates and our fossil ancestors. Second, today's distribution of human lactose tolerance exemplifies the complex relationship between human culture and biology throughout our evolutionary history. In this case, humans modified their diet through a cultural shift toward pastoralism and the incorporation of dairy products. This new diet created a new environmental context, which then selectively favored the lactose

**sickle-cell trait** a variation of a gene that results from a point mutation and causes misshapen red blood cells

**sickle-cell anemia** a disease that results from the sickle-cell allele

tolerance trait. Through culture, humans have the ability to alter their environment so much that it influences their biological evolution.

## ▶▶▶ EXPLORING FURTHER

**The Sickle-Cell Trait** Often, human variations are the result of balancing complex factors simultaneously, as we saw with skin color. Another classic example of this is seen with the **sickle-cell trait**. The sickle-cell gene causes misshapen red blood cells that take the form of a sickle (**FIGURE 8.10**). These damaged red blood cells cannot properly transport oxygen. People who are heterozygous for the trait (carrying one sickle-cell allele and one normal allele) suffer few effects on their health and reproduction. However, people who are homozygous for the trait (carrying two sickle-cell alleles) have a lot of misshapen red blood cells in their bodies. This impacts oxygen transportation and causes a severe form of anemia called **sickle-cell anemia**. The high numbers of misshapen blood

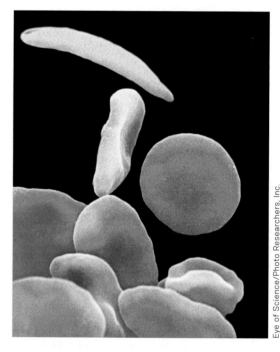

Eye of Science/Photo Researchers, Inc.

**FIGURE 8.10 Sickle-Cell Phenotype**
The sickle-cell gene causes red blood cells to be misshapen. They take a semicircular form, like a sickle, instead of the normal rounded, disk form.

cells in homozygous individuals can also cause blockages in blood vessels that can be fatal. Under most circumstances, a trait with severe, negative consequences, such as the sickle-cell trait, would be weeded out by natural selection. In some populations, however, the sickle-cell trait has been selectively favored despite the obvious disadvantages.

Why has the sickle-cell trait been maintained in these populations? The answer lies in the relationship between the sickle-cell trait and a deadly disease called malaria. Malaria is an infection caused by a parasite that is transmitted via mosquitoes; therefore it is common in tropical areas where mosquito populations are high. The malaria parasite infects red blood cells and can be fatal if untreated. Interestingly, malaria cannot take hold in people who are heterozygous for the sickle-cell trait. Individuals with the sickle-cell trait have red blood cells that are a little smaller than normal cells, so they are not good hosts for the malaria parasite. In populations where the risk of malaria is high, the sickle-cell trait has been maintained (FIGURE 8.11). Individuals with two sickle-cell alleles risk death via sickle-cell anemia, and individuals with two normal alleles risk death with malaria. However, many individuals are heterozygous,

having one sickle-cell allele and one normal allele. These people do not have enough blood cell damage to have sickle-cell anemia, but their blood cells are different enough to protect them from malaria. This is called a **balanced polymorphism** because as natural selection favors the advantageous heterozygous condition, multiple forms of the trait (the sickle-cell and normal alleles) are maintained in balance in the population.

The sickle-cell trait is particularly frequent in some African populations. These populations live in tropical areas that provide a natural habitat for mosquitoes. In addition, these populations have a history of practicing slash-and-burn agriculture, where large areas of land are rapidly cleared to create fields for domesticated crops. This clearing causes extensive damage to the soil and results in large pools of stagnant water. These pools of water are the ideal environment for mosquitoes, which boosts mosquito numbers and exacerbates the risk of malaria. As with the lactose tolerance trait, human cultural practices (slash-and-burn agriculture) modify the environment (mosquito concentration and malaria risk), which then influences selection for particular traits (sickle-cell trait).

**balanced polymorphism** a situation where different alleles for a trait are maintained in balance because natural selection favors the heterozygous condition, where different alleles are needed

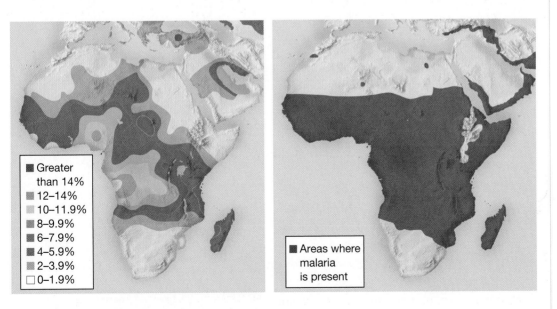

Legend (left map):
- Greater than 14%
- 12–14%
- 10–11.9%
- 8–9.9%
- 6–7.9%
- 4–5.9%
- 2–3.9%
- 0–1.9%

Legend (right map):
- Areas where malaria is present

**FIGURE 8.11 Distributions of Sickle-Cell and Malaria**
The sickle-cell trait is more common in parts of Africa (left) where malaria risk is also high (right). The sickle-cell trait has been selectively favored in these areas and maintained in populations because it provides some protection from malaria.

# CONCEPT REVIEW QUESTIONS

Name: _____     Section: _____

Course: _____     Date: _____

Answer the following questions in the space provided.

1. Which of the following geographical areas is home to people with the darkest skin colors?

   A. Eastern Asia
   B. Central Africa
   C. Northern Europe
   D. Eastern North America

2. True or false? Adaptations are reversible and temporary, while acclimatizations are permanent.

3. Define hypoxia.

4. Why is hypoxia common at high altitudes?

5. According to Bergmann's rule, which trait is advantageous in a cold climate?

   A. Smaller body size
   B. Equiaxed form
   C. Larger body size
   D. Elongated form

6. The B blood antigen allele is most frequent in which region?

   A. South America
   B. Australia
   C. Southern Africa
   D. Central Eurasia

7. Describe the difference between lactose and lactase.

8. True or false? Lactose tolerance is common among adult humans worldwide.

9. Where do we find populations with high frequencies of the sickle-cell trait?

10. Where do we find populations with high exposure to malaria?

# LAB EXERCISES

Name: _____    Section: _____

Course: _____    Date: _____

## EXERCISE 1  SKIN COLOR ACTIVITY 1

Work with a small group or alone to complete this exercise. While exploring a remote area of the world, you have just come across a previously unknown population of people with very light skin color.

1. Where in the world were you most likely exploring?

2. Why would light skin color be advantageous for this population?

3. How might the skin color of this population negatively impact their health if they moved elsewhere?

## EXERCISE 2  SKIN COLOR ACTIVITY 2

Work with a small group or alone to complete this exercise. Recent research has identified a gene (*SLC45A2*) that codes for a protein that impacts melanin production in humans and other animals. There is a mutation in this gene called L374F with two allele variations. The L374 allele correlates with darker pigmentation, and the F374 allele correlates with lighter pigmentation. Researchers collected DNA samples from people in 14 European, Asian, and African populations and identified the frequency of the F374 allele in these groups. Review the data in the chart and answer the questions that follow.

| No. | Population | n (number studied) | Frequency of F374 |
|---|---|---|---|
| 1 | German (Germany) | 241 | 0.965 (96.5%) |
| 2 | French (France) | 98 | 0.893 (89.3%) |
| 3 | Italian (Italy) | 97 | 0.851 (85.1%) |
| 4 | Turk (West Germany) | 200 | 0.615 (61.5%) |
| 5 | Indian (India) | 51 | 0.147 (14.7%) |
| 6 | Bangladeshi (Bangladesh) | 118 | 0.059 (5.9%) |
| 7 | Khalha (Mongolia) | 173 | 0.113 (11.3%) |
| 8 | Buryat (Mongolia) | 143 | 0.115 (11.5%) |
| 9 | Han (China) | 89 | 0.028 (2.8%) |
| 10 | Han (China) | 119 | 0.000 (0%) |
| 11 | Han (China) | 111 | 0.005 (0.5%) |
| 12 | Japanese (Japan) | 87 | 0.000 (0%) |
| 13 | Indonesian (Indonesia) | 105 | 0.005 (0.5%) |
| 14 | African (Germany, Japan) | 17 | 0.000 (0%) |

Modified from Yuasa et al. 2006.

1. In what populations do we see the highest frequencies of the F374 allele?

2. In what populations do we see the lowest frequencies of the F374 allele?

3. The map shows the locations of the populations studied superimposed on Figure 8.2 (showing regional skin color variation). Are these results what you would expect based on the skin color information in the map? Why or why not?

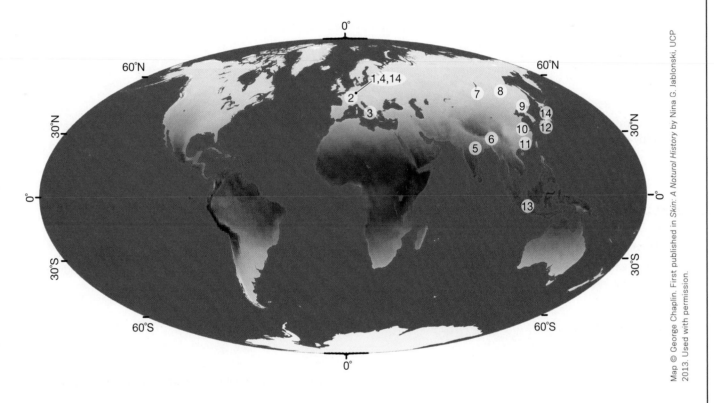

Map © George Chaplin. First published in *Skin: A Natural History* by Nina G. Jablonski, UCP 2013. Used with permission.

4. Why might some light-skinned populations, such as the Japanese, be missing the F374 allele? (*Hint*: Consider the various forces of evolution that may be at play.)

**ALTITUDE**

Work with a small group or alone to complete this exercise. You and your fellow classmates have decided to take a vacation to the Andes Mountains in South America. You plan to spend 2 weeks hiking, camping, and exploring the area.

1. While you are there, you can expect to undergo some acclimatization to this higher altitude environment. Describe *one* of these possible acclimatizations.

2. Why would your body undergo such a change? What benefit or benefits does this acclimatization afford while you are vacationing in higher altitudes?

3. Several weeks after you have returned home from your vacation, can you expect to still have this acclimatization? Why or why not?

4. Also, while you are in the Andes, you notice that local people seem to be better adapted to the altitude conditions than you are. Describe *one* of these possible adaptations.

5. If someone with this adaptation were to come visit you in a lower altitude, would they lose their adaptation? Why or why not?

## EXERCISE 4  CLIMATE

Work with a small group or alone to complete this exercise.

### SCENARIO A

Examine the material provided by your instructor (or the image in the lab Appendix).

1. Is this person adapted for a cold climate or a hot climate?

2. Describe *one* trait that helped you make this determination.

3. Is this trait related to Bergmann's rule or Allen's rule?

### SCENARIO B

Examine the material provided by your instructor (or the image in the lab Appendix).

1. Is this person adapted for a cold climate or a hot climate?

2. Describe *one* trait that helped you make this determination.

3. Is this trait related to Bergmann's rule or Allen's rule?

## EXERCISE 5  ABO BLOOD GROUP

Work with a small group or alone to complete this exercise. Review Figures 8.6, 8.7, and 8.8. Use this information, as well as your understanding of the forces of evolution, to help you answer the following questions.

1. Many populations throughout central Eurasia share high frequencies of the B allele. What does this pattern suggest about the evolutionary history of these populations? Describe the evolutionary force that likely caused this trait distribution.

2. The O allele is unusually frequent in the Americas. What does this pattern suggest about the evolutionary history of these populations? Describe the evolutionary force that likely caused this trait distribution.

## EXERCISE 6  LACTOSE TOLERANCE

Work with a small group or alone to complete this exercise.

1. Describe a population where you would expect to find a low frequency of adult lactose tolerance.

2. Why is adult lactose tolerance infrequent in that population?

3. Describe a population where you would expect to find a high frequency of adult lactose tolerance.

**4.** Why is adult lactose tolerance frequent in that population?

**THE SICKLE-CELL TRAIT ACTIVITY 1**

Work with a small group or alone to complete this exercise. You are conducting a survey about human variation at the bus station. While conducting your survey, you meet a very large student tour group. The tour group has a high number of people who are carriers of the sickle-cell trait.

**1.** Based on this information, what can you suggest about the group's geographic or cultural background? (Consider their economic practices, location in the world, and history.)

**THE SICKLE-CELL TRAIT ACTIVITY 2**

Work with a small group or alone to complete this exercise. Glucose-6-phosphate dehydrogenase deficiency (G6PD deficiency) is an inherited disorder where either the body has less of the G6PD enzyme than normal or the available G6PD is not functioning correctly. This deficiency impacts red blood cell function and may result in anemia (the destruction of red blood cells) when people with the condition have infections, are taking certain medications, or eat certain foods. People with G6PD deficiency may have some protection from malaria because their abnormal red blood cells interfere with the reproduction of the malaria parasite in their bodies.

**1.** Consider the prevalence of G6PD deficiency estimated by the World Health Organization (WHO):

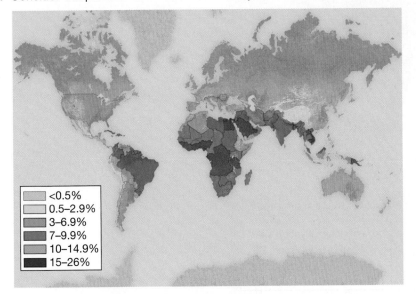

Compare the distribution of G6PD deficiency to the distribution of the sickle-cell trait and malaria (Figure 8.11). What do you notice is similar? What is different?

2. Why might these similarities and differences exist? Be sure to consider the evolutionary context (including the natural environment, cultural practices, and interbreeding).

EXERCISE 9 **VARIATION IN THE *ADH1B* GENE**

Work with a small group or alone to complete this exercise. The *ADH1B* gene is one of the genes that codes for alcohol dehydrogenase (ADH)—an enzyme that helps in the digestion of alcohol. A variant of this gene called the *ADH1B*47His* allele helps metabolize alcohol faster than other versions of the trait, thus reducing the amount of alcohol that saturates the bloodstream. It also causes a negative side effect, where a person's face flushes red when he or she consumes alcohol. This allele is rarely found in African or European populations, but it is very frequent in East Asian populations, where it is often found in more than 50% of the population and may even be found in almost 100% of people in certain populations. These East Asian populations also have a long history of growing rice and making fermented rice beverages over the past 9,000 years. The map shows the frequency of the *ADH1B*47His* allele in East Asia. Sites where evidence of rice cultivation has been found are superimposed on the map.

1. Based on what you know about the evolutionary forces behind human variations, how would you explain the distribution of the *ADH1B*47His* allele? Why do you think this allele is common in East Asian populations? Do you see a relationship between rice cultivation and allele frequency? *Hint*: Consider the benefits and drawbacks of consuming alcoholic beverages and how this might factor into the evolution of the *ADH1B*47His* allele.

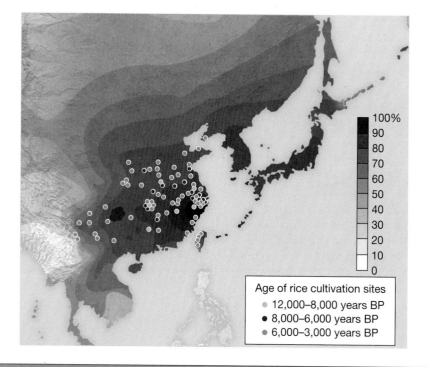

# CRITICAL THINKING QUESTIONS

On a separate sheet of paper, answer the following questions.

1. This question may be completed independently or as a group discussion. Various cultures designate racial categories differently, and they often base these categories on very different traits. For example, some cultures use nose shape as one of the defining traits for a racial group. Other cultures do not use nose shape in defining racial groups, but use hair color instead. What do differences in racial classification such as these suggest about the universality of race and racial groupings?

2. This question may be completed independently or as a group discussion. Review Figure 8.2. Note that skin colors are a little lighter in equatorial parts of the Americas than they are in equatorial Africa. Why might this be the case? (*Hint*: Think about the possible impact of evolutionary forces other than natural selection.)

3. This question may be completed independently or as a group discussion. Skin color has a clinal distribution. This is true for many of our other traits as well. Describe one human trait, other than those discussed here, that you think has a clinal distribution.

4. This question may be completed independently or as a group discussion. In Exercise 3, you considered the adaptations of people living in the Andes Mountains. What other adaptations do you think would be beneficial to indigenous people who live in similar high-altitude environments? Are there any other places in the world where you might expect to find populations with these adaptations to high altitude? (Use material in your classroom, in books, or online to help you.)

5. Bergmann's and Allen's rules apply to many animals, not just humans. Use material in your classroom, online, or in books to locate images of a black-tailed jackrabbit (*Lepus californicus*) and a snowshoe hare (*Lepus americanus*). Based on what you can see in the images, which of these hares is adapted for a cold climate? Which is adapted for a hot climate? What adaptations do they have to suit their respective environments? Do humans living in similar climates share the same adaptations?

6. This question may be completed independently or as a group discussion. Humans are unusual because our cultural practices can actually change our environmental circumstances. We can impact the environment in which natural selection acts on our traits. Describe how this process has played out in the evolution of adult lactose tolerance. Describe how this process has played out in the maintenance of the sickle-cell trait. Can you hypothesize any similar situations where our future evolution may be impacted by cultural practices we have today?

7. So far, we have primarily discussed human adaptations independently of one another. In real life, of course, each person has numerous coexisting ancestral adaptations. Ignore what you know of your family history and consider only your physical traits for the following adaptations: skin color, lactose tolerance, and body shape. Based on these three traits, in what part of the world might your ancestors have originated? Do all three of your traits suggest similar ancestry? Be sure to explain your hypothesized determination using evidence related to all three traits, and be sure to think about all the forces of evolution that might impact your unique history (such as gene flow and the founder effect).

8. In this lab, we considered various human adaptations. It is important to remember that many of these adaptations evolved to suit environmental circumstances of the past, and they may be less helpful (or even maladaptive) in today's world. For example, humans are adapted to store fat in the body for later use. This is very helpful during times when food is limited (such as during extended droughts) because it allows us to live on the fat stores of our body. However, in much of the world today, there is food abundance rather than food scarcity.

In the face of food abundance in many populations today, our ability to store fat becomes maladaptive and contributes to greater obesity and related health problems (type 2 diabetes, heart disease, etc.). One way to measure obesity and other weight categories is called body mass index (BMI). Calculate your own body mass index using this formula:

**[Weight in pounds/(height in inches × height in inches)] × 703 = BMI**

For example, if you are 5 feet 6 inches tall and weigh 120 pounds, your BMI is

**[120/(66 × 66)] × 703 = 19.4**

To answer the following questions, use the BMI database compiled by the World Health Organization: **apps.who.int/bmi/**. The map function on this site is particularly helpful in illustrating regional variations. To get started, select the **Maps** tab. In this exercise, you will use the **Indicator** and **Country** dropdown menus to explore the following questions. What percentage of adults in the United States fall in the same BMI category as you? What is the average total daily calorie intake for a person in the United States [select **DES Total (calories/day)** from the **Indicator** menu]? Looking at the worldwide maps for total daily calorie intake and for the percentage of overweight adults (BMI ≥ 25) in the population, what trends do you notice? Why might there be regional differences in BMI and in calorie intake? What are the implications of these trends for worldwide health now and in the future?

# APPENDIX:
# LAB EXERCISE IMAGES

## Exercise 4 Climate

Scenario A                    Scenario B

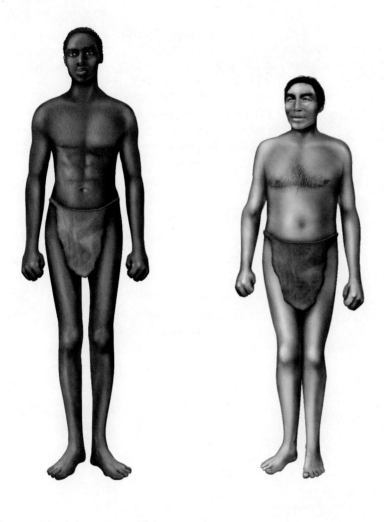

### PART THREE

# PRIMATOLOGY

Because humans are primates, we can learn a lot about our species by studying our other primate relatives.

# LAB 9: CLASSIFICATION

## WHAT TOPICS ARE COVERED IN THIS LAB?

- An introduction to the major levels of classification
- A review of the biological species concept
- An overview of the different types of traits used in classification
- An introduction to the principles of classification

# LAB 10: OVERVIEW OF THE LIVING PRIMATES

## WHAT TOPICS ARE COVERED IN THIS LAB?

- A review of what it means to be a primate
- An introduction to the major groups of primates and their defining characteristics

# LAB 11: PRIMATE BEHAVIOR

## WHAT TOPICS ARE COVERED IN THIS LAB?

- An overview of the different approaches and skills used to study primate behavior
- A consideration of both affiliative and aggressive primate behaviors
- A review of primate ecology and its impact on primate behavior
- A look at primate social organization and sexual behavior
- A discussion of the possibility that nonhuman primates have culture

# LAB 12: COMPARATIVE PRIMATE ANATOMY

## WHAT TOPICS ARE COVERED IN THIS LAB?

- A consideration of the relationship between biology and behavior
- A review of primate dental and digestive adaptations for different diets
- An introduction to skeletal adaptations for the primary forms of primate locomotion
- An overview of sexual dimorphism and its relationship to social organization

LeonP/Shutterstock

Rainbow/iStock/Thinkstock

We categorize supermarket produce to help shoppers find what they want in the store. We classify living organisms to better understand how they relate to one another.

## Lab Learning Objectives

By the end of this lab, students should be able to:

- differentiate biological species and write genus and species names in their scientific format.

- distinguish between homologous and analogous traits, using examples.

- compare the different types of homologies, using examples.

- use cladistics to classify material.

LAB 9

# Classification

Imagine you are standing in the produce section of a supermarket. All around you, the produce is clustered into groups on tables or shelves. The oranges are next to the lemons and the grapefruit on a table; the romaine lettuce and iceberg lettuce are next to each other on a shelf; organic produce is clustered together on a separate table. Why is the produce arranged this way? There are numerous reasons. It helps shoppers to easily identify what they need, and it helps the store managers to keep track of their inventory so they can easily restock shelves when necessary.

Just as the supermarket clusters similar fruits (such as citrus fruits) in one area, the biologist clusters similar organisms into a group. This small group of organisms can also be clustered together with other small groups to make a larger classification cluster of related organisms. Similar to the way the supermarket's categories help shoppers find the produce they want in the store, the biologist's classifications help us to identify the organism we are studying and to understand how it fits into a larger biological picture. Classification allows us to place an organism into the context of its close and distant relatives. This context gives us a better sense of the evolutionary history of the organism, and it allows us to make more accurate and relevant comparisons across groups of organisms. Classification is an essential element of biology and biological anthropology, and it is the focus of this lab.

## INTRODUCTION

This lab begins with a consideration of the different levels of classification and how we distinguish between the most specific levels of classification—the biological species. We then look at the types of traits used to classify organisms. We pay particular attention to traits known as homologies because these are the most helpful when trying to reconstruct the relationships between organisms. We conclude with a look at the approaches to classification used by anthropologists today.

## WHAT ARE THE LEVELS OF CLASSIFICATION?

In the 1700s, a Swedish naturalist named Carl von Linné (also known by his Latinized name, Carolus Linnaeus) assigned all plants and animals two levels of classification: the genus and the species. The **genus** was a more general level of classification, and the **species** was a more specific level of classification. Each type of organism had its own species, and species that were similar shared a common genus. Later, additional levels of classification were added to incorporate broader levels of relationship.

Today, the major levels of classification, based on Linnaeus's system, begin with the species—the most specific classification. Similar species are grouped into the same genus to reflect their relationship to one another. Similar genera (the plural of genus) are then clustered into the same **family**, and similar families are clustered into the same **order**. Related orders are grouped together in the same **class**, and related classes are grouped together in the same **phylum**. This leads to the highest level of classification—the **kingdom**, which is made up of related phyla (plural of phylum). Every known organism belongs to a group at each major level of classification (**FIGURE 9.1**). These groups reflect how the organism relates to other organisms. There are also levels of classification that fall between these major levels. For example, in addition to the order, there can be a suborder. These

additional levels allow for even more specific classifications (see Lab 10 for more information on the classification of living primates).

### What's in a Name?

Each known type of organism has a two-part scientific name (or *binomial*), made up of the genus and species title for the organism. The names often tell us something about the organism. For example, *Homo erectus* means "upright man." The names also follow certain rules, particularly in terms of how they are written. The scientific name is written with the genus name first, followed by the species name. The genus name is always capitalized, the species name is always lowercase, and both words must be italicized (or underlined if they are written by hand).

If you are referring to the same species repeatedly, you can abbreviate the genus name to the first initial, followed by a period. The letter is still capitalized, as it is when the whole genus name is written out completely. This type of abbreviation can only be done if you have already written out the entire genus name earlier in the work. For example, since we have already written *Homo erectus* above, we could now shorten this to *H. erectus*. If we are writing about two genera that start with the same first letter, we then abbreviate the genera to be the first letter (capitalized) and the second letter (lowercase), followed by a period. For example, if we have written an article about *Australopithecus afarensis* and *Ardipithecus ramidus* we can abbreviate these names (after their first usage) to *Au. afarensis* and *Ar. ramidus*.

## THE BIOLOGICAL SPECIES CONCEPT

One of the most fundamental levels of classification is the species, but what is a species? How do we know if two organisms are from the same species or from different species? There is ongoing debate as to the meaning of the word "species," and there are dozens of definitions used by biologists today. It is particularly difficult to define a species in the case of plants or

**genus** (**genera**, plural) the level of classification that includes multiple related species

**species** one of the most specific levels of classification uniting related organisms

**family** the level of classification that includes multiple related genera

**order** the level of classification that includes multiple related families

**class** the level of classification that includes multiple related orders

**phylum** (**phyla**, plural) the level of classification that includes multiple related classes

**kingdom** the highest level of classification, which includes multiple related phyla

| Taxonomic Category | Taxonomic Level | Common Characteristics |
|---|---|---|
| Kingdom | Animalia | Mobile multicellular organisms that consume other organisms for food and develop during an embryo stage. |
| Subkingdom | Eumetazoa | All major animals (except sponges) that contain true tissue layers, organized as germ layers, which develop into organs in humans. |
| Phylum | Chordata | Group of vertebrate and invertebrate animals that have a notochord, which becomes the vertebral column in humans and other primates. |
| Subphylum | Vertebrata | Animals with vertebral columns or backbones (including fish, amphibians, reptiles, birds, and mammals). |
| Superclass | Tetrapoda | Vertebrate animals with four feet or legs, including amphibians, birds, dinosaurs, and mammals. |
| Class | Mammalia | Group of warm-blooded vertebrate animals that produce milk for their young in mammary glands. They have hair or fur and specialized teeth. |
| Subclass | Theria | Group of mammals that produce live young without a shelled egg (including placental and marsupial mammals). |
| Order | Primates | Group of mammals specialized for life in the trees, with large brains, stereoscopic vision, opposable thumbs, and grasping hands and feet. |
| Infraorder | Anthropoidea | Group of primates, including monkeys, apes, and humans. They have, in general, long life cycles and are relatively large-bodied. |
| Superfamily | Hominoidea | Group of anthropoids, including humans, great apes, lesser apes, and humanlike ancestors. They have the largest bodies and brains of all primates. |
| Family | Hominidae | Great apes, humans, and humanlike ancestors. |
| Genus | *Homo* | Group of hominids including modern humans, their direct ancestors, and extinct relatives such as Neanderthals. They are bipedal and have large brains. |
| Species | *sapiens* | Modern and ancestral modern humans. They have culture, use language, and inhabit every continent except Antarctica. |

**FIGURE 9.1 The Classification of Humans**
This chart shows how humans are classified in Linnaeus's taxonomy. Note that we are assigned to a group at each taxonomic level from the kingdom to the species.

**biological species concept** the biological concept that argues two organisms are from the same species if they can produce viable (fertile) offspring

**viable offspring** offspring that are capable of reproduction

**paleospecies** an extinct species that is known through fossil evidence

microorganisms (such as bacteria). In biology, the **biological species concept** is often used to address the issue of delineating and differentiating species. This definition is not universal, but it is the most practical definition used, particularly in the case of vertebrate animals. According to the biological species concept, two organisms are from the same species if they can produce **viable offspring**. Two organisms are from different species if they cannot produce viable offspring. Note that we are talking about *viable* offspring. We would assume that this means *living* offspring. In biology, though, viable offspring must be living *and* be capable of reproduction. So, it is not enough that the two organisms produce a living offspring. The living offspring must also be capable of reproduction to be considered viable.

A classic example will illustrate this point. Horses have 64 chromosomes, and donkeys have 62 chromosomes. When female horses and male donkeys mate, each contributes half of their genetic information. So, their offspring receives 32 horse chromosomes and 31 donkey chromosomes. This chromosomal combination can produce a living offspring—the mule (**FIGURE 9.2**). However, the presence of the unmatched chromosome interferes with the meiosis cell division involved in producing gametes, and all male mules (and most female mules) are infertile. Despite the fact that the mule is alive, it is not considered to be a biologically viable offspring because it cannot reproduce. Therefore, according to the

biological species concept, horses and donkeys are separate species because their offspring are not viable (fertile).

Distinguishing species based on the biological species concept is challenging when we are dealing with extinct organisms. In these situations, we are trying to distinguish **paleospecies**—extinct species. To do this, we are dependent on the fossil record. We cannot place two fossils in a room, encourage them to mate, and see if they produce viable offspring. Instead, we are forced to use physical traits as indicators of the relationship between specimens. These physical traits also reflect behaviors, such as diet and forms of locomotion. So, we can use physical traits to determine if two fossils have both anatomical and behavioral similarities. The more similar the fossils are, the more likely they are to be related. We can also take into account the geographic distribution of the fossils and their dates. If two similar fossil specimens are from the same time period at the same site, they are more likely to be related than two similar fossil specimens that are from different continents and are separated by vast time spans.

## HOMOLOGY VERSUS ANALOGY

What kinds of traits do biological anthropologists consider when they classify organisms?

A          B          C

**FIGURE 9.2 Biological Species Concept**
When female horses (A) and male donkeys (B) mate, they produce mules (C). Even though mules are living offspring, they are not considered "viable" because they are infertile.

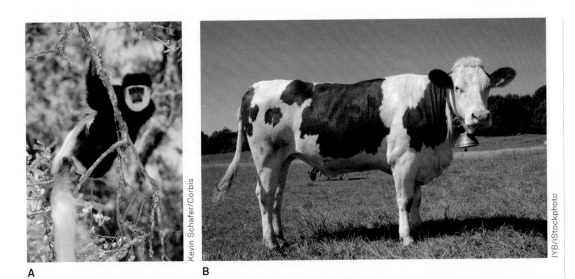

Kevin Schafer/Corbis

JYB/iStockphoto

A                                B

**FIGURE 9.3 Analogous Traits**
Colobus monkeys (A) and cows (B) both have complex digestive systems. However, this similarity is not due to common ancestry. It is the result of similar adaptations to a plant-based diet. Having complex digestive systems is an analogy in these species.

There are generally two types of trait similarities found between biological organisms. They are called homologies and analogies. In both cases, we are dealing with similarities that are shared between organisms. However, shared traits may come about for different reasons, and homologies and analogies are the result of two different processes.

**Analogies** are traits that are similar across organisms due to similar adaptations. These traits are the result of what is called homoplasy. **Homoplasy** refers to the evolutionary development of similar traits in unrelated organisms. This can often result from such circumstances as similarities in diet and environmental conditions. For example, consider the complex stomachs of colobus monkeys and cows (**FIGURE 9.3**). Both colobus monkeys and cows eat a lot of plants, which are difficult to digest and require specialized digestive tracts. The common ancestor of colobus monkeys and cows did not have a complex stomach. The trait evolved separately in the colobus monkey and cow lineages. Thus, the fact that both colobus monkeys and cows have long digestive tracts is the result of similar dietary adaptations, rather than something that was inherited from a common ancestor.

When we classify organisms, we are trying to group them based on their biological relationships to one another. If we simply look for similarities, without considering the underlying reasons for the similarities, we may be misled in our classifications. If we had simply observed that colobus monkeys and cows had similarly complex stomachs, we might have classified them as being more closely related than they really are. This is why biological anthropologists have to distinguish between analogies, which can be misleading, and homologies, which are actually helpful for classification.

**Homologies** are traits that are similar among organisms that share common ancestry because they were passed down from a common ancestor to its descendants. These are traits that reflect real, ancestral relationships between organisms; homologies are much more helpful for classification than misleading analogies. Even so, there are different types of homologies, and some of these homologies may be more helpful than others.

## TYPES OF HOMOLOGY

**Ancestral traits** (or plesiomorphies) are traits that are inherited by two organisms from a relatively distant common ancestor. For example,

**analogy** a trait that is similar across organisms due to similar adaptations

**homoplasy** the evolutionary development of similar traits in unrelated organisms

**homology** a trait that is similar across organisms because the organisms share common ancestry

**ancestral trait** a trait that is shared by two organisms from a relatively distant common ancestor, also called a plesiomorphy

**derived trait** a trait that is a modification of an ancestral form, also called an apomorphy

**shared derived trait** a modified trait that is shared by two or more organisms, also called a synapomorphy

**unique derived trait** a modified trait that is unique to one group, also called an autapomorphy

A

B

**FIGURE 9.4 Ancestral Traits**
Ring-tailed lemurs (A) and humans (B) both have mammary glands. This trait was also shared by their last common ancestor. Having mammary glands is an ancestral trait (type of homology) in these species.

humans and ring-tailed lemurs both have mammary glands **(FIGURE 9.4)**. This is a shared trait that was found in the common ancestor of humans and lemurs. The mammary gland trait is useful in that it supports the idea that humans and ring-tailed lemurs are somehow related. However, this is a trait that is found in all mammals and can be traced to the last common ancestor of this entire group of animals. It is not particularly useful in helping us actually distinguish between humans and ring-tailed lemurs. For this reason, biological anthropologists often focus on the other kinds of homologies, called derived traits.

**Derived traits** (or apomorphies) are traits that are modifications of ancestral forms.

There are two types of derived traits: shared derived traits and unique derived traits. **Shared derived traits** (or synapomorphies) are traits that are modified traits *shared* by two different groups of organisms. For example, apes and Old World monkeys have the same dental formula (number of teeth) **(FIGURE 9.5)**. This is a modification of an ancestral trait, a dental formula that was slightly different. Thus, it is a derived trait. Because it is a modification that is shared between the two organisms, it is a shared derived trait. The second type of derived trait is the unique derived trait. **Unique derived traits** (or autapomorphies) are modified traits *unique* to one group. For example, humans have an unusual pelvis that is very round and bowl-shaped **(FIGURE 9.6)**. This is a modification of an ancestral pelvis that was flatter. Thus, it is a derived trait. Because the modification is unique to humans, it is a unique derived trait.

So far, we have only considered physical (or morphological) characteristics. In reality, researchers today also use genetic analysis to help classify organisms. Anthropologists may examine DNA or amino acid sequences to look for similarities and differences between organisms. As with physical features, genetic similarities are used to infer ancestral relationships. The more similar two organisms' genes are, the more closely related they are assumed to be. In Lab 10, we will see how genetic analysis has impacted the classification of some of the living primates, particularly tarsiers.

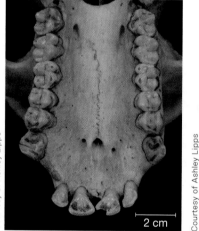

A

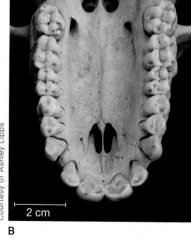

B

**FIGURE 9.5 Shared Derived Traits**
Apes (A) and Old World monkeys (B) both have the same dental formula. This dental formula is a modification of an ancestral form with more teeth, so it is a shared derived trait.

# THE PROCESS OF CLASSIFICATION

As we saw above, people have been interested in classifying organisms for a long time. This classification of life is called **taxonomy**, and it forms the basis for **systematics**—the study of the relationships between organisms. Biological classification today usually falls under the heading of systematics, taking into account the biological relationships between the organisms being classified. In modern systematics, biological anthropologists use two primary approaches to classification.

The first and longest running approach to classification is called **evolutionary systematics**. This approach emphasizes both derived traits and ancestral traits as useful tools in classification. The second and more recent approach to classification is called **cladistics** (or phylogenetic systematics). This approach emphasizes derived traits and deemphasizes ancestral traits. Proponents of this view argue that the more derived traits are more useful in distinguishing groups. Note that both approaches to classification emphasize homologies and avoid misleading analogies. The difference between the approaches is the type of homology emphasized.

Imagine a researcher has just used cladistics to identify the biological relationship between a set of primates. How will she share this classification with others? The easiest way to do this is to create a diagram of the relationships. The diagram used to represent cladistic classifications is called a **cladogram**. A cladogram lists every organism included in the classification at one level (usually in a row along the top). The organisms are then connected by a series of lines. The fewer the lines between two organisms, the more closely related they are.

Let's review an example of a primate cladogram prepared by a hypothetical researcher (**FIGURE 9.7**). The four primates represented are the black-and-white colobus, the red colobus, the chimpanzee, and the human. The two

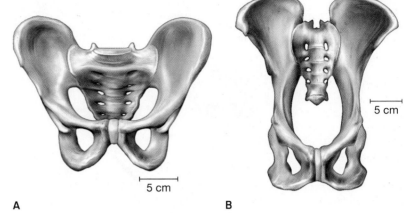

**FIGURE 9.6 Unique Derived Traits**
The human pelvis (A) is a modification of an ancestral form that is unlike the pelvis of other living primates (B). The rounded pelvis is a unique derived trait.

types of colobus connect to each other at point A on the diagram. This point reflects their common ancestor, and it shows that they are more closely related to each other than they are to the other primates in the cladogram. Similarly, the chimpanzee and the human are closely related to each other. They also connect to each other before they connect to any other primates, showing their common ancestry (point B on the diagram). All four primates are distantly related. This is why they all connect at point C to show their common ancestry.

Cladograms like Figure 9.7 are constructed through a process of cladistic analysis that begins with identifying potential homologies. The presence or absence of these traits (or characters) are identified and recorded in a matrix that includes each organism under investigation (see the following table). The data matrix allows researchers to quickly identify if the traits are shared across many organisms (ancestral traits), shared by some organisms (shared derived traits), or unique to one organism (unique derived traits). With this information, researchers can then begin grouping the organisms based on their relationships. In real life, researchers consider so many traits that they use computers to analyze data matrices for patterns.

**taxonomy** the classification of organisms

**systematics** the study of the relationships between organisms

**evolutionary systematics** an approach to classification that emphasizes both derived traits and ancestral traits

**cladistics** an approach to classification that emphasizes derived traits and deemphasizes ancestral traits, also called phylogenetic systematics

**cladogram** a diagram used to represent cladistic classifications, where lines are used to link organisms in different degrees of relationship to one another

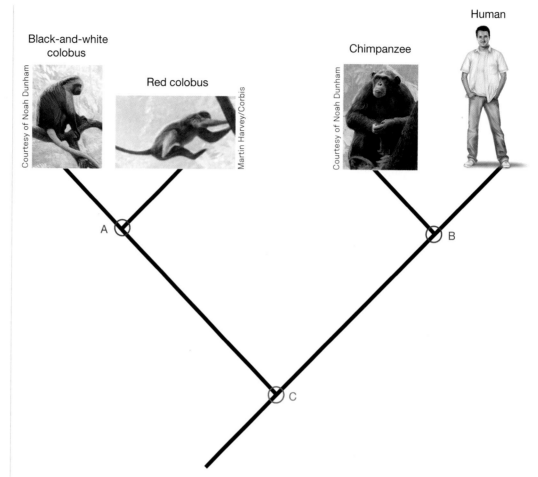

**FIGURE 9.7 Sample Cladogram**
In this cladogram, the black-and-white colobus and the red colobus are closely related and share a common ancestor (point A). The chimpanzee and the human are also closely related and share a common ancestor (point B). Both groups are also related to each other and share a common ancestor (point C).

## SAMPLE DATA MATRIX

| | Narrow Nose | Multicolored Fur | Broad Chest | Fur-covered Body |
|---|---|---|---|---|
| Black-and-white Colobus | Yes | Yes | No | Yes |
| Red Colobus | Yes | Yes | No | Yes |
| Chimpanzee | Yes | No | Yes | Yes |
| Human | Yes | No | Yes | No |

When we return to our sample cladogram, we can see how the traits studied helped to both cluster and distinguish the organisms. All the organisms have a narrow nose. This is an ancestral trait that demonstrates they are all related to each other via a common ancestor.

The black-and-white colobus and the red colobus both have multicolored fur. This is a shared derived trait that indicates these two organisms are more closely related to one another than they are to the other organisms. Similarly, the chimpanzee and the human share a broad chest. This

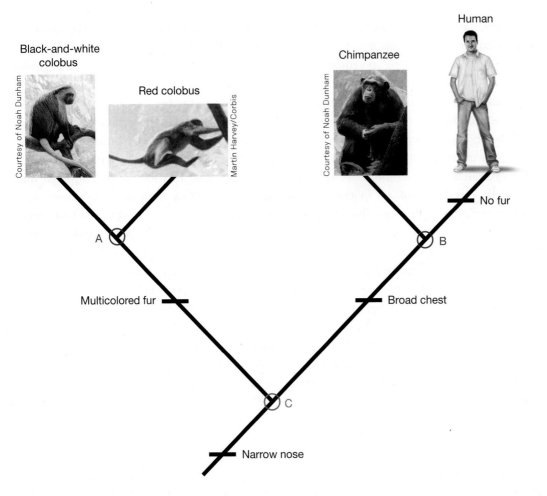

**FIGURE 9.8 Sample Cladogram Showing Traits**
Here, we can see how the researcher used particular traits to cluster and differentiate the organisms in the cladogram.

is a shared derived trait that reflects their close relationship to one another. Last, the human seems to be unusual because it is the only organism without fur all over its body. This is a unique derived trait that distinguishes the human from even its closest relative (the chimpanzee). These traits can be placed on the cladogram to show which organisms have each trait (**FIGURE 9.8**). Each trait is placed below the point that represents the common ancestor of all the different organisms with the trait, which signifies that all organisms above that point possess this trait.

Another type of diagram that can be used to reflect evolutionary relationships is the **phylogram**. This diagram is similar in style and meaning to a cladogram, but it also accounts for the amount of change (which usually correlates with time) through varying branch lengths. For

example, a longer branch is used to indicate a greater amount of change and thus a longer time span since the split between two organisms. Both types of diagrams—cladograms and phylograms—are used by biological anthropologists to show important information about the relationships between organisms. They tell us which species are closely related to one another and how other relationships extend out beyond different pairs of species.

# CONFLICTING CLASSIFICATIONS

Many people assume that classifications are exact, with only one "right answer." However, there is often disagreement about how to classify

**phylogram** a diagram used to represent evolutionary relationships that also accounts for the amount of change (and usually length of time) separating organisms

organisms, particularly when dealing with fossils that cannot be genetically tested or directly observed for interbreeding potential. Some researchers are considered "lumpers" because they tend to group (or lump) organisms into a few, large groups. They emphasize the similarities between organisms and often interpret differences as minor variations within the group. Other researchers are considered "splitters" because they tend to divide (or split) organisms into numerous, smaller groups. They emphasize the differences between organisms and often interpret differences as substantial variations between the behavior, ecology, and adaptation of separate species. These two perspectives on classification often result in two very different interpretations of the same evidence, which is why there is not always agreement on how to classify organisms, particularly fossil species.

At the same time, there are additional points of disagreement and departure in classification schemes. For example, anthropologists may choose different traits to analyze. In our earlier cladogram (Figures 9.7 and 9.8), we chose four traits for analysis, but there were numerous other traits we could have used instead. The traits we use will impact the conclusions we come to. If we had not chosen the broad chest trait, we might not have recognized the relationship between the chimp and the human. Without this connection between the chimp and human, we might have classified the chimp as more closely related to the black-and-white colobus and red colobus because they all have fur.

In some cases, it is difficult to distinguish traits. We often see this in genetic analysis. For example, a researcher has sequenced the DNA from two organisms, and she is now looking for stretches of DNA that are similar and thereby indicate an ancestral relationship between the organisms. This requires her to align the stretches of DNA from both organisms and look for overlap. Because overlap in bases may occur at multiple points (see **FIGURE 9.9**), the anthropologist must make a judgment call and decide which alignment is accurate and shows a meaningful similarity between the DNA. Other anthropologists may make different judgments about where the DNA strands are similar, so they may come to different conclusions about the relationship between the organisms.

In other situations, as we discuss in Lab 15, anthropologists may choose the same traits but interpret them differently. For example, two anthropologists agree that individual A has more robust (dense, heavy) bony facial structures than individual B. The first anthropologist argues that individual A is the male of the species, which explains why he has larger facial structures than individual B, who is interpreted as female. This anthropologist considers the differences in robusticity to be minor, and he interprets the individuals to be from the same species. In contrast, the second anthropologist argues that individual A has a more robust face because it has a diet that requires more chewing and physical exertion than the diet of individual B. This anthropologist thinks the differences in robusticity reflect significant differences in ecology and adaptation, and she interprets the individuals to be from two different species. In this situation, the anthropologists agreed on the traits but came to different conclusions.

It is important to remember that the process of classification is full of choices, and those choices may lead researchers to different conclusions. The overall perspective of the researcher, the traits they use, and how they interpret those traits will all affect the final classifications made by the researcher.

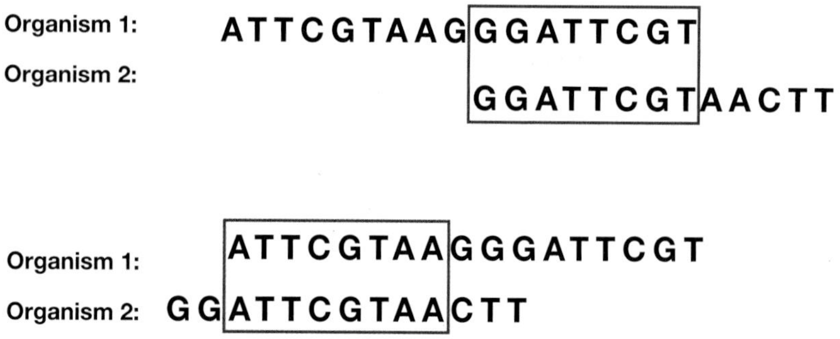

Organism 1: **A T T C G T A A G G G A T T C G T**

Organism 2: **G G A T T C G T A A C T T**

Organism 1: **A T T C G T A A G G G A T T C G T**

Organism 2: **G G A T T C G T A A C T T**

**FIGURE 9.9 Variations in DNA Analysis**
The DNA strands from the two organisms studied appear to be similar at two different places (the red box and the blue box), depending on how the strands are aligned. The anthropologist must judge where the DNA strands actually align and whether the strands are similar due to common ancestry.

# CONCEPT REVIEW QUESTIONS

Name: _____  Section: _____

Course: _____  Date: _____

Answer the following questions in the space provided.

1. List the major levels of classification in order from the most general to the most specific.

2. True or false? In the biological species concept, the phrase "viable offspring" refers to offspring that are alive.

3. True or false? The correct abbreviation for *Pongo pygmaeus* (orangutan) is *P. pygmaeus*.

4. What is the correct abbreviation for *Pan troglodytes* (chimpanzee)?

   A. *P. Troglodytes*
   B. P. troglodytes
   C. *P. troglodytes*
   D. *p. Troglodytes*

5. Beetles and hummingbirds have wings, but these organisms are not related to one another. The fact that they both have wings is an example of:

   A. an analogy.
   B. an ancestral trait.
   C. a unique derived trait.
   D. a shared derived trait.

6. Humans and baboons have noses with nostrils that face downward, but many other primates have noses with nostrils that face out to the sides. Humans and baboons are also more closely related to each other than they are to primates with outward-facing nostrils. Therefore, the fact that both humans and baboons share the downward-facing nostril orientation is an example of:

   A. a unique derived trait.
   B. a shared derived trait.
   C. an analogy.
   D. an ancestral trait.

7. True or false? Cladistics places equal emphasis on ancestral traits and derived traits during classification.

For questions 8–10, refer to the baboon-gorilla-human cladogram.

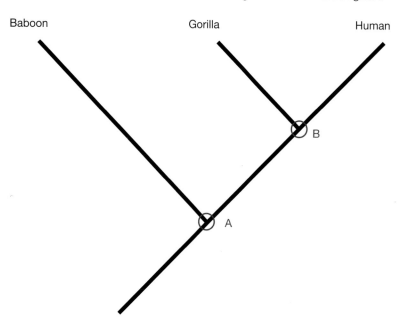

8. In the cladogram, which two primates are most closely related to one another?

9. In the cladogram, what does point A of the diagram represent?

    A. The ancestor of gorillas and humans
    B. The ancestor of humans only
    C. The ancestor of gorillas and baboons
    D. The ancestor of baboons, gorillas, and humans

10. In the cladogram, what does point B of the diagram represent?

    A. The ancestor of gorillas and humans
    B. The ancestor of humans only
    C. The ancestor of gorillas and baboons
    D. The ancestor of baboons, gorillas, and humans

# LAB EXERCISES

Name: _____    Section: _____

Course: _____    Date: _____

## EXERCISE 1   SCIENTIFIC NAMES

Work with a small group or alone to complete this exercise.

For each of the following scientific names, identify what is wrong with the way it is currently written. Then, provide the correct format.

| Scientific Name | What Is Wrong? | Correct Format |
|---|---|---|
| *Homo Sapiens* | | |
| Pan paniscus | | |
| *pan troglodytes* | | |

Complete the following chart by providing the appropriate abbreviation for each of the scientific names.

| Scientific Name | Correct Abbreviation |
|---|---|
| *Homo habilis* | |
| *Gorilla gorilla* | |
| *Hylobates agilis* | |
| *Homo neanderthalensis* | |

Use the chart of abbreviations to answer the following questions:

1. If you were writing about *Homo habilis* and *Homo neanderthalensis* at the same time, would you need to change your abbreviations? Why or why not? If you needed to change them, what would the new abbreviations be?

2. If you were writing about *Hylobates agilis* and *Homo neanderthalensis* at the same time, would you need to change your abbreviations? Why or why not? If you needed to change them, what would the new abbreviations be?

## EXERCISE 2   HOMOLOGOUS STRUCTURES

Work with a small group or alone to complete this exercise.

In this lab, we discussed homologous traits. In addition to these specific traits that reflect common ancestry, there are also general traits (such as the basic organization and layout of body parts) that reflect shared ancestry. These general similarities due to common ancestry are called *homologous structures*. In this exercise, you will examine homologous structures in the limbs of several different animals.

1. Examine the limb specimens provided by your instructor (or the images in the lab Appendix) and complete the chart below.

    » For bone length, indicate whether you think the animal's limb bones are relatively long, short, or intermediate *for its overall body size*. (For example, a kangaroo would be described as having long legs for its body.)

    » For bone robusticity, indicate whether you think the animal's bones are robust (heavy and dense), gracile (slender), or intermediate.

| Animal | Bone Length | Bone Robusticity |
|--------|-------------|------------------|
| Frog   |             |                  |
| Dog    |             |                  |
| Bird   |             |                  |
| Pig    |             |                  |

2. What do you notice is generally similar across all the specimens?

3. What do you notice is generally different across the specimens?

4. How do these similarities and differences relate to the evolutionary relationships between these species?

5. What similarities and differences in adaptation (for example, different locomotor needs or different weight-bearing needs) may also relate to the similarities and differences you see across these specimens?

## EXERCISE 3  TYPES OF HOMOLOGIES

Work with a small group or alone to complete this exercise.

Review the material provided by your instructor (or the image in the lab Appendix) representing different organisms that need to be classified. The first step in classification is identifying useful homologous traits. Examine the objects, and use them to answer the following questions.

1. Describe *one* trait that all the objects have in common (an ancestral trait).

2. Describe *two* traits that some of the objects share but other objects do not (shared derived traits).

3. Describe *one* trait that is particularly unusual, perhaps found in only one object (a unique derived trait).

You may find it useful to complete a data matrix to help you see patterns in the traits. Remember to indicate what your traits are and add more rows as needed for additional objects.

| | Trait 1: _____ | Trait 2: _____ | Trait 3: _____ | Trait 4: _____ |
|---|---|---|---|---|
| Object 1 | | | | |
| Object 2 | | | | |
| Object 3 | | | | |
| Object 4 | | | | |
| Object 5 | | | | |

## EXERCISE 4  INFERRING RELATIONSHIPS FROM TRAITS

Work with a small group or alone to complete this exercise.

The second step of classification is using homologous traits to determine the relationships between organisms. Based on the traits you identified in Exercise 3, it should now be possible to group some of the objects together. Objects that share a derived trait are related to each other, and they should be grouped together. Objects that share *multiple* shared derived traits are really closely related and should be subgroups within larger, related groups.

Draw your groups here:

| EXERCISE 5 | **MAKING A CLADOGRAM** |

Work with a small group or alone to complete this exercise.

The final step in classification is to diagram the relationships you have identified. Using the groups you made in Exercise 4, identify the nested relationships between the objects. Consider which objects are most closely related, and what object or objects are the next most closely related.

Draw the cladogram of these relationships in the space below. Show which objects possess which traits by labeling your cladogram with the traits you used (as in Figure 9.8).

# CRITICAL THINKING QUESTIONS

On a separate sheet of paper, answer the following questions.

1. Use material in your classroom, online, or in books to identify the species, genus, family, order, class, phylum, and kingdom for humans. Be sure to check in at least two different sources. Do your sources agree on all of these levels of classification? Why might there be some disagreement about how we (or any other species) are classified?

2. This question may be completed independently or as a group discussion. Humans have 46 chromosomes, and chimpanzees have 48 chromosomes. Based on what you know about the mating of donkeys and mules, what do you think would happen if a human and chimpanzee mated? Would they produce a living offspring (a "human-zee")? Would they produce a viable offspring in the biological sense? Would humans and chimpanzees no longer be considered separate species?

3. This question may be completed independently or as a group discussion. In Exercise 2, you examined animal hind limbs as examples of homologous structures. What other body structures do you think these animals share due to their common ancestry (homologies)?

4. For the following traits, identify whether you think the trait is an analogy or a homology and why.

   A. Dolphins and sharks both have fins.
   B. Horses and zebras have hooves.
   C. Turtles and snails have shells.
   D. Some snakes and spiders have venom.
   E. Crabs and lobsters have claws.

   Now, use material in your classroom, online, or in books to verify your answers about whether the traits are due to similar adaptation or common ancestry. Why is it important to distinguish between analogies and homologies when we classify organisms?

5. This question may be completed independently or as a group discussion. Today, classification research incorporates more and more genetic data. Why might this genetic information sometimes reinforce previous classification schemes? Why might the genetic data sometimes force us to rethink previous classification schemes? What data do you think researchers should use to make the most accurate classifications?

6. This question may be completed independently or as a group discussion. In Exercises 3, 4, and 5, you classified buttons representing different organisms. Repeat these exercises using the blocks below.

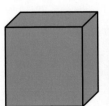 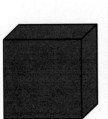 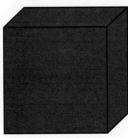  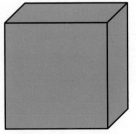

7. This question may be completed independently or as a group discussion. Review your work from Exercises 3, 4, and 5 (or your work from Question 6 above). How do you think a lumper would approach the classification of the objects? How do you think a splitter would approach the classification of the objects? What would be similar and different in the results of the two perspectives? (*Hint*: Does each object need to be considered a separate species?)

# APPENDIX:
# LAB EXERCISE IMAGES

## Exercise 2 Homologous Structures

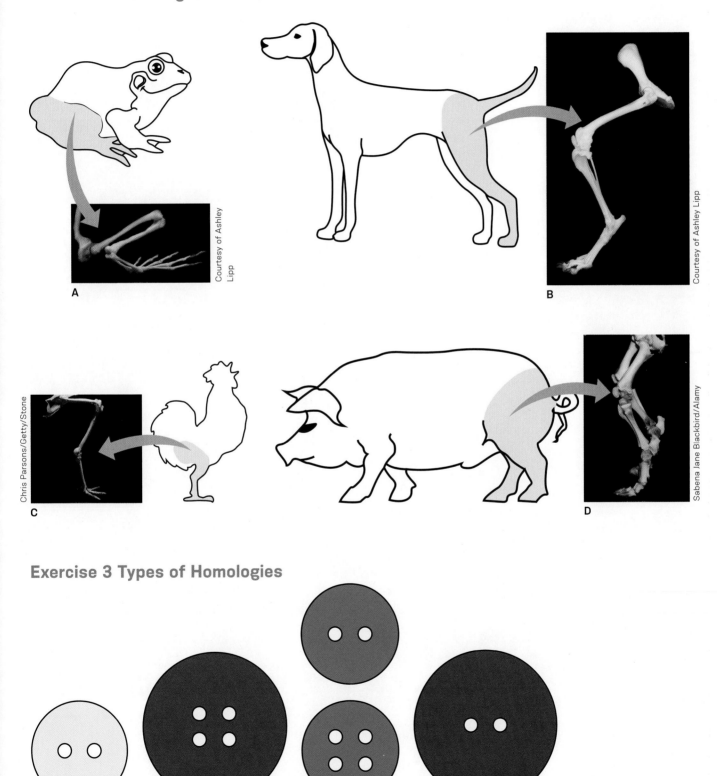

Courtesy of Ashley Lipp

A

Courtesy of Ashley Lipp

B

Chris Parsons/Getty/Stone

C

Sabena Jane Blackbird/Alamy

D

## Exercise 3 Types of Homologies

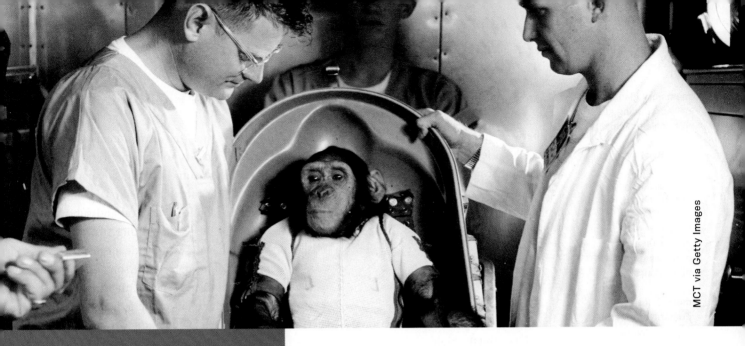

MCT via Getty Images

Ham, the chimpanzee seen here, was one of several chimpanzees sent into space in the early 1960s.

## Lab Learning Objectives

By the end of this lab, students should be able to:

• describe the key features that differentiate primates from other mammals.

• recognize and describe the defining features of the major primate groups.

• classify primates based on their defining features.

LAB 10

# Overview of the Living Primates

In late January 1961, a 4-year-old chimpanzee named Ham was put into space aboard a rocket. Ham was brought from his birthplace in western Africa to Holloman Air Force Base in New Mexico to participate in early rocket tests for space travel. Although it was short, Ham's flight was similar to later ones taken by the first human astronauts. After the flight, data were collected about Ham's health. This information was invaluable to further pursuits of manned missions to space, and Ham was eventually retired to the Washington Zoo (and later, the North Carolina Zoological Park). Why send a chimpanzee to space before attempting to send a human? Test animals were common on rocket missions in the United States and the former Soviet Union prior to Ham's flight. The earliest efforts also sent mice, and later rocket tests often used dogs or monkeys. However, to really test the viability and safety of human space travel, it was believed that chimpanzees made the best test subjects. Chimpanzees are our closest living biological relatives, so they were thought to be good models for what might happen to humans in similar space flight conditions.

Today, there is significant debate about the use of nonhuman primates in experimental research, and strict guidelines exist for these practices.

**mammary gland** a milk-producing gland in female mammals

**terrestrial** living on the ground

**arboreal** living in trees

**nocturnal** active primarily during the night hours

**diurnal** active primarily during the daylight hours

**uniparous** producing one offspring at a time

**opposable digit** a finger or toe capable of being positioned opposite the other digits (fingers or toes), which allows for the ability to grasp objects

**forward-facing eyes** eyes that are positioned at the front of the face and point directly ahead

No matter where one stands in the debate, there is no denying the great biological similarity between humans and chimpanzees. In addition to the features we share as primates, we share numerous shared derived traits as great apes. In this lab, we explore the living primates to help us situate humans in the appropriate biological context.

## INTRODUCTION

In this lab, we explore the living primates to better understand the biological context of our own human species. We begin with a look at what distinguishes primates from other mammals. We then discuss some of the debates regarding primate classification. Finally, we review each of the major groups of primates and their defining characteristics.

## WHAT IS A PRIMATE?

Primates are an order of mammals. There are hundreds of known nonhuman primate species today, although some are critically endangered (see Lab 11 for more information). Nonhuman primates are found in tropical and subtropical areas around the world (**FIGURE 10.1**). Humans, of course, have a worldwide distribution. As mammals, all primates share some mammalian traits, such as the presence of **mammary glands**, fur, the development of the fetus in the womb, and giving birth to live young. The primates also share several anatomical and behavioral traits that differentiate them from other mammals.

We will begin with behavioral similarities. While a few primate species are **terrestrial** and live on the ground, most primates are **arboreal**, spending the majority of their time in trees. This means many primates live in densely forested

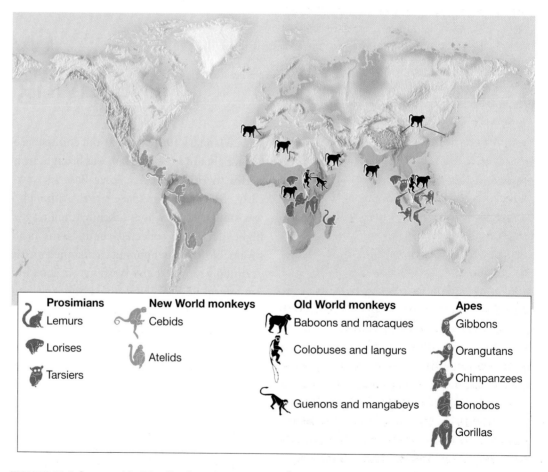

**FIGURE 10.1 Geographic Distribution of the Living, Nonhuman Primates**
Today, the nonhuman primates primarily inhabit tropical and subtropical forests.

environments. Primates tend to have generalized diets. They eat a range of foods, rather than eating just meat or just plants. Because of this, primates have a generalized dentition with four different types of teeth that are each suited to a variety of biting and chewing tasks (see Lab 6 for more information). However, within the range of possible food sources, individual primate species focus on particular resources more than others, so they will have some minor differences in their dentition and other anatomy (see Lab 12 for more information). While a few primates are **nocturnal** (active primarily at night), most primates tend to be **diurnal**, meaning they are active in the daytime.

Most primates are relatively social, spending much of their time in groups made up of multiple individuals. Even the primates that do not eat together usually socialize and sleep together. Most primates are **uniparous**, meaning they give birth to one offspring at a time, and primate offspring tend to take longer than other mammals to reach reproductive age. Because of this, primates are limited in the number of offspring they can have in a lifetime. This means most primates, especially females, invest a lot of time and energy into caring for and raising their offspring.

In addition to these behavioral similarities, primates also share important anatomical similarities. Primates usually have relatively **opposable** thumbs and big toes that can be placed opposite the other fingers and toes. This gives primates the ability to grasp objects and tree branches (**FIGURE 10.2**). Primates have a sensitive sense of touch, particularly in the tactile pads on the tips of their fingers and toes; primate hands and feet also usually have nails instead of the claws seen in many other mammals. In addition to an enhanced sense of touch, primates usually have an enhanced sense of vision. Primates have **forward-facing eyes** that provide better depth perception because the fields of vision from each eye overlap in the center (**FIGURE 10.3**). They have more bone around their eyes than other mammals. Most primates also have color vision. These traits—depth perception, structural eye support, and color vision—all provide primates a better sense of

vision than many other mammals. There has been a trade-off between the senses, such that primates tend to emphasize seeing and touching over smelling and hearing. While primates have many traits to help improve their sight, they have shorter snouts and are less sensitive to smells than many other mammals (**FIGURE 10.4**).

Primates also have larger brains relative to their body size than many other mammals. If we compare a primate and a nonprimate mammal of approximately the same body size, the primate will probably have a larger brain. However, not all sections of the primate brain are enlarged. For example, the areas of the brain associated with the sense of smell (the olfactory bulbs) are much smaller in primates than in many other mammals, which correlates with primates' reduced sense of smell.

**FIGURE 10.2 Grasping Hands**
Primates have opposable thumbs that give them the ability to grasp things, such as tree branches and food.

**FIGURE 10.3 Forward-facing Eyes**
Primates have forward-facing eyes. This makes the fields of vision from both eyes overlap, giving primates enhanced depth perception.

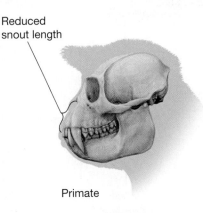

Reduced snout length

Primate

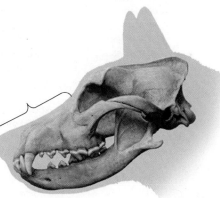

Dog

**FIGURE 10.4 Reduced Snout**
Compared to many other mammals (such as dogs), primates have less reliance on their sense of smell. Accordingly, primates have shorter snouts than many other mammals.

# PRIMATE TAXONOMY

As discussed in Lab 9, there are often debates surrounding classification. Experts may identify or emphasize different traits, which can lead to totally different classification schemes. In biological anthropology, there has been a significant amount of debate surrounding how best to classify the primates. We will be using the approach that is increasingly common in biological anthropology, which takes into account physical characteristics as well as genetic similarity.

The primate order is divided into the suborders Strepsirhini (the strepsirhines) and Haplorhini (the haplorhines) **(FIGURE 10.5)**.

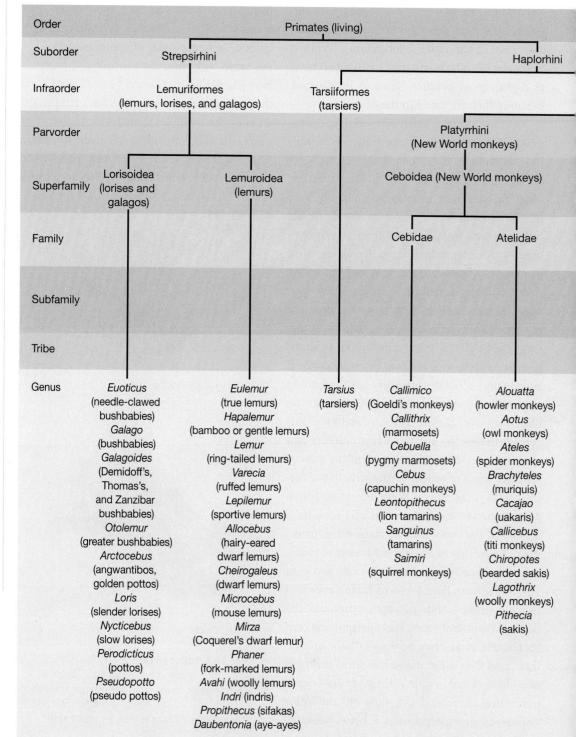

**FIGURE 10.5 Primate Taxonomy**

This classification provides an overview of the relationships among living primates. It has gained support from growing knowledge about living primate DNA.

The strepsirhine group includes the lemurs (Lemuroidea) and lorises (Lorisoidea), and the haplorhine group includes the tarsiers (Tarsiiformes) and the anthropoids (Anthropoidea). While there has been some debate about whether the tarsiers should be included with the lemurs and lorises, current research suggests tarsiers are more closely related to anthropoids than they are to lemurs or lorises; this taxonomy reflects this relationship. The Anthropoidea infraorder includes all of the monkeys and apes. The New World monkeys are differentiated in their own parvorder: the Platyrrhini. These monkeys then further break down into the Ceboidea superfamily and the Cebidae and Atelidae families. The Old World

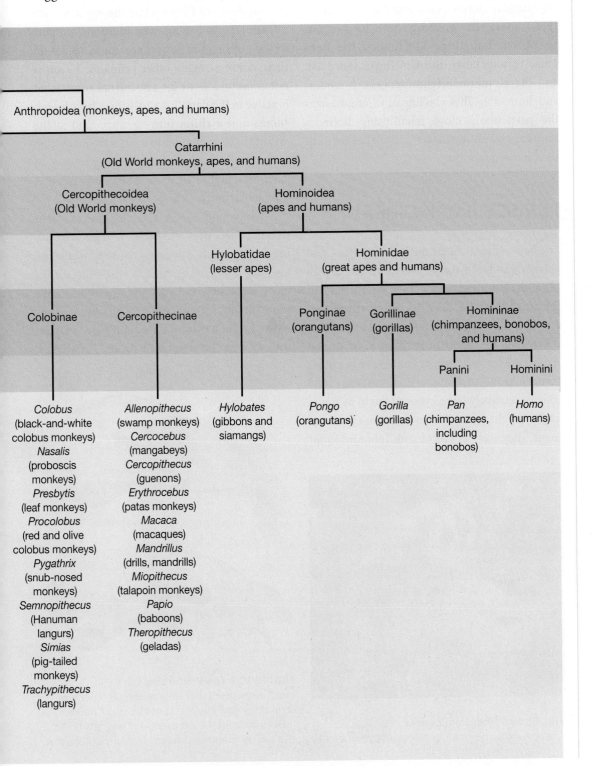

monkeys and the apes are placed in the Catar-rhini parvorder. This further differentiates into the superfamilies Cercopithecoidea (Old World monkeys) and Hominoidea (apes). The Old World monkeys are classified into two subfamilies: the Colobinae (colobines) and the Cercopithecinae (cercopithecines). The apes are classified into two families: the Hylobatidae (lesser apes) and the Hominidae (great apes). The great apes are further differentiated into three subfamilies: the Ponginae (orangutans), the Gorillinae (gorillas), and the Homininae (chimpanzees, bonobos, and humans). This classification emphasizes the particularly close relationship between humans and chimpanzees and places them in the same subfamily.

## LORISES (LORISOIDEA)

The Lorisoidea includes the lorises, pottos, and galagos (or bushbabies). Here, we discuss all these primate species together as "lorises," in the broad sense, because they are closely related and classified together. Lorises are small primates that are found in Africa and Southeast Asia. Unlike most primates, lorises are nocturnal **(FIGURE 10.6)**. Because of this, they tend to have relatively large eyes to take in as much ambient light as possible in their dark environment. They also have more rods (photoreceptor

cells in the retina) in their eyes that help improve their vision in low-light environments. They have an unusual bony eye structure called a **postorbital bar** that provides more structural support than is found in most mammals but is less supportive than the full enclosure seen in many other primates **(FIGURE 10.7)**. The postorbital bar is a bar of bone that is lateral to the eye but does not fully enclose the eye in a bony pocket. Despite having some additional support in their eye region, lorises are not as reliant on their vision as many other primates. Vision is not as useful a sense for a nocturnal animal that is active in the dark. Instead, lorises have longer snouts and a **rhinarium**—a damp pad at the end of the nose, similar to what is found in a cat or dog—which gives them a stronger sense of smell (see Figure 10.10 for a similar snout and nose in a lemur).

Lorises tend to eat a lot of insects, often stalking their prey very slowly before pouncing. They usually eat alone, but they will come together to socialize and sleep. Some lorises move very slowly on all fours. Others move more rapidly, leaping through the trees. Lorises have a mix of nails and claws, and they often use their claws to help groom their fur. They have a

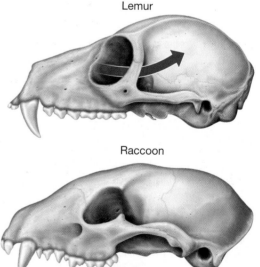

**FIGURE 10.7 The Postorbital Bar**
Most mammals (such as raccoons) have very little bony eye support. Lorises and lemurs have postorbital bars posterior and lateral to their eyes. However, their orbits are still hollow.

Martin Harvey/Getty Images

**FIGURE 10.6 Nocturnal Lorises**
The lorises tend to be nocturnal (active at night).

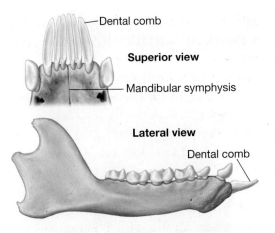

Dental comb

**Superior view**

Mandibular symphysis

**Lateral view**

Dental comb

**FIGURE 10.8 The Loris and Lemur Mandible**
Lorises and lemurs have dental combs formed by the elongation and protrusion of their lower incisors and canines. They also have unfused mandibles attached by cartilage at the mandibular symphysis.

2.1.3.3 dental formula and a special type of tooth structure called a **dental comb** (FIGURE 10.8). The dental comb is made of lower incisors and canines that project out from the face. These teeth are elongated and slender, and they are positioned very closely together. This makes the teeth resemble the tines on a comb. Lorises use the dental comb primarily for feeding (to help scrape at tree bark and extract tree gums), but the dental comb is also helpful for grooming (much like brushing a comb through your hair). Lorises also have an **unfused mandible**, meaning their mandible is made of two separate bones that are attached by cartilage at the midline (called the **mandibular symphysis**).

It appears to be a single bone, but in reality it is not. This unfused mandible is common in mammals, both primate and nonprimate.

# LEMURS (LEMUROIDEA)

Lemurs are closely related to lorises, and they share many traits in common. Lemurs are a very diverse group of primates (FIGURE 10.9). Restricted to Madagascar, they adapted to a wide variety of environmental contexts on the island, resulting in an extensive diversity of species. Some lemurs are very similar to lorises. They are small, nocturnal, and eat a lot of insects. Other lemurs are more unusual. For example, some species are medium-sized animals with a diurnal lifestyle and a diet of more leaves and fruit. Lemurs also form a wide range of social groups. Some species are similar to lorises and are only limitedly social. Other species, such as ring-tailed lemurs, are very social and live in large groups of many individuals. They also have very different forms of locomotion depending on their environmental contexts. Most lemurs are arboreal, and they either move on all fours or leap through the trees. A few species, again, such as the ring-tailed lemur, are more terrestrial and spend a lot of time on all fours on the ground.

Despite this great diversity in the lemur group, all lemurs share some key traits with lorises. They have postorbital bars, but they are often less reliant on vision than monkeys and apes. This is

**postorbital bar** a bar of bone that sits lateral to the eye but does not fully enclose the eye in a bony pocket

**rhinarium** a damp pad at the end of the nose

**dental comb** a tooth structure made of elongated and closely situated lower incisors and canines that project out from the front of the face

**unfused mandible** a mandible (jawbone) that is made of two separate bones that are attached by cartilage along the midline

**mandibular symphysis** the area where the two sides of the mandible are attached by cartilage in an unfused mandible

A

B

**FIGURE 10.9 Lemur Diversity**
Although found only on the island of Madagascar, modern lemurs are a diverse group of species, including ring-tailed lemurs (A) and aye-ayes (B).

Robert Ross/Getty Images

**FIGURE 10.10 The Lemur Snout and Nose**
Unlike many other primates, the lemurs and lorises are still somewhat dependent on their sense of smell and have longer snouts than other primates. They also have a wet nose (called a rhinarium), seen here in a black-and-white ruffed lemur, that resembles the nose of a dog or cat.

Cheryl Ravelo/Reuters/Corbis

**FIGURE 10.11 Tarsiers**
Because they are nocturnal, tarsiers have very large eyes. They also have very long legs and feet to help them leap through the trees.

especially true of the nocturnal lemur species. Lemurs tend to be more dependent on smell and have long snouts and a rhinarium (similar to lorises) (**FIGURE 10.10**). Most lemurs have a 2.1.3.3 dental formula, although some species have fewer teeth, such as the unusual aye-aye with an upper dentition of 1.0.1.3 and lower dentition of 1.0.0.3. Lemurs have dental combs in their lower dentition, and they have unfused mandibles. They also have a mix of claws and nails. All of these similarities between lemurs and lorises reflect their close relationship.

## TARSIERS (TARSIIFORMES)

Tarsiers are small primates that live in Southeast Asia (**FIGURE 10.11**). Tarsiers share a few traits in common with lemurs and lorises. They are generally small and eat primarily insects. They are nocturnal, and they live in small social groups. They leap through the trees, similar to galagos and some lemurs. They also have a mix of claws and nails. However, tarsiers also share traits with the anthropoid primates. For example, they have more enclosed bony orbits, instead of a postorbital bar, and they lack the dental comb seen in lemurs and lorises. Like

anthropoids, tarsiers have a shorter snout and a dry nose instead of a wet rhinarium. They also have a more anthropoid-like inner ear structure. Tarsiers also share more genetic similarity with anthropoids than with lemurs and lorises. Because of these similarities, tarsiers are classified as being more closely related to anthropoids.

Tarsiers also have some unusual traits that set them apart from all other primates. First, they have a unique dental formula. Their upper dentition is 2.1.3.3, as in lorises and most lemurs. However, their lower dentition is 1.1.3.3, unlike what is seen in lorises and lemurs. Second, tarsiers have remarkably large eyes. While many lorises have enlarged eyes to aid their nocturnal lifestyle, tarsiers have a more extreme adaptation for their nocturnal activity pattern. The eyes of a tarsier are so large that they dominate its face, and a single tarsier eye is larger than its entire brain. In addition to their exaggerated eyes, tarsiers also have highly mobile necks. They can turn their heads almost 180° in each direction, which gives them the ability to rotate their heads almost 360°. Tarsiers also

have incredibly long legs and feet. In fact, the origin of the name "tarsier" is related to their very large tarsal (foot) bones. They also have unusual lower leg bones, in which the tibia and fibula are fused together. These leg and foot features help tarsiers leap through the trees (see Lab 12 for more information on locomotor adaptations).

# ANTHROPOIDS (ANTHROPOIDEA)

The remaining primate species (the monkeys and apes) are all anthropoids. The anthropoid primates are generally larger than the lemurs, lorises, and tarsiers. They also tend to have bigger brains for their body size. Almost all anthropoids are diurnal and rely more on their vision than their sense of smell. They lack the olfactory adaptations of the longer snout and rhinarium of lemurs and lorises. Instead, anthropoids have several traits related to their enhanced sight. They usually have color vision, and they have full bony enclosures for their eyes **(FIGURE 10.12)**. They also have eyes that are closer together in the front of the face, providing even more overlap between the fields of vision.

## New World Primates (Platyrrhini) versus Old World Primates (Catarrhini)

The anthropoid group is subdivided into the New World primates (platyrrhines) and the Old World primates (catarrhines). The New World primates are the monkeys that inhabit the Americas (or **New World**). The Old World primates are the monkeys and apes that inhabit Africa and Asia (the **Old World**). These two groups can be distinguished by a few key traits. First, the New World monkeys have broad noses, with nostrils that face out to the sides and a wide **septum** (the soft tissue between the nostrils). In contrast, the Old World monkeys and apes have narrower noses, with nostrils that face downward and a narrow septum **(FIGURE 10.13)**. Their names highlight this distinction. Platyrrhini is from the Greek for "broad-nosed," and Catarrhini is

from the Greek for "hook-nosed." The second key difference between these primate groups is their dentition. New World monkeys tend to have three premolars in each quadrant of their mouth, while the Old World monkeys and apes have two.

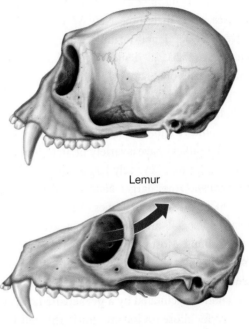

**FIGURE 10.12 Fully Enclosed Bony Orbits**
Whereas lemurs and lorises have postorbital bars, anthropoids such as gibbons have full bony enclosures for their eyes. Therefore, anthropoids' orbits are less open than those of lemurs and lorises.

**New World** the name traditionally assigned to the American continents (North and South America)

**Old World** the name traditionally assigned to the majority of the non-American continents, specifically Africa, Asia, and Europe

**septum** the soft tissue between the nostrils

**FIGURE 10.13 New World Primates versus Old World Primates**
New World monkeys (platyrrhines) have broad noses with nostrils that are far apart and face outward. Old World monkeys and apes (catarrhines) have narrow noses with nostrils that are close together and face downward.

**prehensile tail** a tail with the ability to grasp tree branches and act like a fifth limb

# NEW WORLD MONKEYS (CEBOIDEA)

The New World monkeys live in the forests of Central and South America. As noted above, they have the platyrrhine nose structure and three premolars in each quadrant of their mouths. The number of molars differs between species, such that some New World monkeys have a 2.1.3.3 dental formula while other species have a 2.1.3.2 dental formula. There are many species of New World monkeys, and they vary considerably. Most are arboreal and diurnal. However, one genus—comprised of the owl monkeys (*Aotus*)—is nocturnal. The New World monkeys have a variety of diets. Some of the smaller monkeys rely largely on insects or tree gums. Other, larger New World monkeys rely more on fruits or leaves. They tend to be relatively social, and some species live in very large groups. Most of the New World monkeys move through the trees on all fours, but some New World monkeys have a special form of locomotion facilitated by a **prehensile tail** (see Lab 12 for more on locomotion). This tail has the ability to wrap around and grasp things, such as tree branches, so it can be used as a fifth limb (**FIGURE 10.14**). In contrast, none of the Old World monkeys have a prehensile tail.

Capuchin monkeys are perhaps the most famous of the New World monkeys (**FIGURE 10.15**). They regularly appear in television shows and films as pets. They are also trained as service animals, similar to service dogs, to help disabled people. Howler monkeys are also well-known for their incredibly loud, "howling," vocalizations (**FIGURE 10.16**). Some

Dietmar Nill/naturepl.com

**FIGURE 10.15 Capuchin Monkeys**
Well-known for their appearances in television shows and films as pets, capuchins are sometimes trained as service animals to help disabled people.

Kevin Schafer/Corbis

**FIGURE 10.14 Prehensile Tails**
Some New World monkeys (such as the woolly spider monkeys seen here) have prehensile tails that can grab onto tree branches and be used like fifth limbs.

David Tipling/Getty Images

**FIGURE 10.16 Howler Monkeys**
One of the loudest animals on Earth is the howler monkey. These New World monkeys make howling vocalizations to mark and defend their territories and females.

Charles Krebs/zefa/Corbis

**FIGURE 10.17 Tamarins**
Tamarins (such as the lion tamarin seen here) are very unusual New World monkeys. They are very small, often give birth to twins, and often live in unusual social groups with more adult males than adult females.

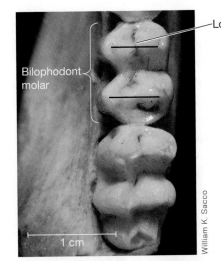

Bilophodont molar

Loph (ridge)

1 cm

William K. Sacco

**FIGURE 10.18 Bilophodont Molars**
All Old World monkeys have unusual molars where the cusps are organized into two parallel ridges. These teeth are called bilophodont molars.

**bilophodont molar**
a molar with four cusps arranged in two parallel ridges (or lophs)

**ischial callosity** a roughened patch of skin located in the ischial area (on the rump)

of the most unusual New World monkeys are the tamarins and marmosets (**FIGURE 10.17**). These are the smallest New World monkeys, and they tend to eat a lot of tree gums and insects. They typically give birth to twins, which is rare among primates, and they sometimes live in a highly unusual *polyandrous* social group with more adult males than adult females (see Lab 11).

# OLD WORLD MONKEYS (CERCOPITHECOIDEA)

The remaining primates (the Old World monkeys and the apes) are catarrhines. They all have the catarrhine nose structure, as well as two premolars in each quadrant of their mouth (giving a dental formula of 2.1.2.3). The Old World monkeys (also called cercopithecoids) live in various habitats in Africa and Asia. In general, Old World monkeys are diurnal, usually live in large social groups, and move on all fours (whether they are arboreal or terrestrial). They also have unique molars, called **bilophodont molars** (**FIGURE 10.18**).

These molar teeth have four cusps that are arranged in two parallel ridges (or lophs), hence *bi-loph-o-dont* ("two-ridged teeth"). Old World monkeys also have special patches of roughened skin on their rears, called **ischial callosities** (**FIGURE 10.19**). Ischial refers to the area of the pelvis that one sits on, and callosity refers to the callous-like, roughened skin. There are two subgroups of Old World monkeys: the colobines and the cercopithecines.

Courtesy of Joan Silk

**FIGURE 10.19 Ischial Callosities**
All Old World monkeys have special rough patches of skin on their rears, called ischial callosities.

**cheek pouch** a pouch in the cheek and neck area that can expand to store food

## Colobines (Colobinae)

The colobine group includes monkeys such as the langur and the colobus monkey. Most colobines, such as the proboscis monkey (**FIGURE 10.20**), live in Asia, but a few species are found in Africa, such as the black-and-white colobus (**FIGURE 10.21**). The monkeys of the colobine group tend to be medium-sized and have long tails. They are usually arboreal and eat a lot of leaves. Many colobines also have special adaptations for their leaf-eating diet, such as complex stomachs (see Lab 12 for more information).

Gavriel Jecan/Corbis

**FIGURE 10.20 Proboscis Monkeys**
The proboscis monkeys are Asian colobines with unusually long noses.

Kevin Schafer/Corbis

**FIGURE 10.21 Colobus Monkeys**
Colobus monkeys, such as the black-and-white colobus seen here, are among the colobines that live in Africa.

Tom Brakefield/Corbis

**FIGURE 10.22 Olive Baboons**
Many of the cercopithecines are baboon species that live in Africa (such as the olive baboons seen here).

## Cercopithecines (Cercopithecinae)

The cercopithecine group includes monkeys that are often larger than the colobines, such as the baboons and macaques. The cercopithecines are usually found in Africa, such as the olive baboon (**FIGURE 10.22**), but some species live in Asia. Many of the cercopithecines are terrestrial and have relatively short tails. However, some cercopithecines are arboreal and have long tails like colobines. Cercopithecines tend to have a more diverse diet with more fruit than that of the leaf-eating colobines. They also have special **cheek pouches** that allow them to store food, comparable to some rodents. These cheek pouches help cercopithecines collect a lot of food in a short time and store it for later.

## APES (HOMINOIDEA)

Humans are apes and have a worldwide distribution, but the other apes are restricted to central Africa and Southeast Asia. The apes (or hominoids) are catarrhines, like the Old World monkeys, so they have several catarrhine traits in common with the cercopithecoids. They have two premolars in each quadrant of their mouth (and a dental formula of 2.1.2.3). If you examine your own teeth in the mirror, you will discover you have this same dental formula because you are an ape. However, if you do not have your wisdom teeth, you will be missing the third molars found in most humans. Although some people have had their last molars removed (or have molars that never came in), as a species we tend to maintain the 2.1.2.3 dental formula of all apes and Old World monkeys. In addition to the catarrhine dentition, apes also have the catarrhine nose structure. Again, you can observe this on your own nose. Your nostrils face downward, are positioned relatively close together, and are separated by a narrow septum.

While apes share some traits with Old World monkeys, they also have numerous traits that differentiate them from their close relatives. All apes have a special type of molar called the **Y-5 molar** in the lower dentition (**FIGURE 10.23**). Remember, Old World monkeys have bilophodont molars with four cusps arranged in two rows. In apes, the lower molars each have five cusps that are positioned such that a pronounced Y-shaped groove forms between them. The upper molars are slightly different and tend to have four cusps without the Y-shaped groove. In addition to these unusual molars, apes also have flatter (more **orthognathic**) faces, while other primates have more projecting (**prognathic**) faces. Compared to other primates, apes also tend to have larger brains for their body size.

The apes are diurnal and usually live in heavily forested areas, where they spend at least some of their time in the trees. In fact, all apes retain adaptations for swinging through the trees. We see this in their long arms and long, curved fingers (see Lab 12 for more information on locomotor adaptations). However, for some of the larger apes, such as gorillas, a more terrestrial lifestyle is necessary. One of the most defining ape characteristics that distinguishes them from other primates is their lack of a tail. Remember, most primates have a tail. The fact that all apes (including humans) are tailless is an important shared derived trait that highlights their close evolutionary relationship. The apes are divided into two families: the lesser apes (Hylobatidae) and greater apes (Hominidae).

## Gibbons and Siamangs (Hylobatidae)

The gibbons and siamangs are also called the lesser apes, and they are classified together in the hylobatid family (see Figure 10.5). There are numerous species of gibbons and one species of siamang living in the forests of Southeast Asia (**FIGURE 10.24**). They are diurnal, eat a lot of fruit, and live in small social groups.

**Y-5 molar** a molar in the lower dentition that has five cusps positioned such that a pronounced Y-shaped groove forms between the cusps

**orthognathic** having a flat face

**prognathic** having a projecting or protruding face

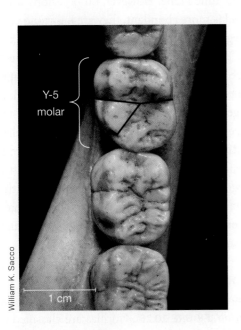

**FIGURE 10.23 Y-5 Molars**
All apes have special molars in their lower dentition. These molars have five cusps that are arranged such that a Y-shaped groove is present between the cusps. These teeth are called Y-5 molars.

**FIGURE 10.24 Gibbons**
The lesser apes include gibbons (such as the one seen here) and siamangs. They are smaller than the other apes, which is why they are called "lesser."

**gracile** having nonrobust, thin, light musculature and bone

**robust** having thick, dense, heavy musculature and bone

**dish-shaped face** a somewhat concave face formed by a sloping upper face and protruding lower face

Both males and females help to defend their territory through complex vocalizations, often referred to as songs. In some species, the males

Cyril Ruoso/JH Editorial/Minden Pictures/Corbis

**FIGURE 10.25 Orangutans**
Orangutans are large-bodied apes that live only on the islands of Borneo and Sumatra in Southeast Asia.

and females also share parenting responsibilities and help take care of offspring.

The lesser apes primarily move around by swinging through the trees, more so than any other type of primate. They have smaller, more **gracile** bodies than the other apes, and even longer arms and longer, more curved fingers to help with this locomotion (see Lab 12 for more information on locomotor adaptations). In addition, their thumbs are very short, so they do not interfere with the apes' rapid arboreal swinging, and they have strong shoulders with a lot of mobility.

## Orangutans (Ponginae)

Orangutans (*Pongo pygmaeus*) are great apes found exclusively on the islands of Borneo and Sumatra (**FIGURE 10.25**). Orangutans are classified in the family Hominidae and subfamily Ponginae (see Figure 10.5). Orangutans are known for their unusual orange fur and for the extreme size difference between the males and females, or *sexual dimorphism* (see Lab 11). They move through their dense forest habitats using a form of slow climbing. They are diurnal and eat a lot of fruit, and they spend most of their time alone. However, on occasions when food is more abundant, they are known to congregate temporarily.

The orangutan cranium is relatively **robust**. The orbits are large, particularly from the superior to inferior edge, and they sit relatively close together in the face. The upper portion of the face angles in slightly, creating what is called a **dish-shaped face**. When seen in profile, the orangutan face appears to be shaped like the edge of a dish (or plate). In addition to this unusual facial structure, orangutans also have lateral incisors that are considerably smaller than their medial incisors.

## Gorillas (Gorillinae)

Another type of great ape is the gorilla, *Gorilla gorilla* (**FIGURE 10.26**). Gorillas are classified in the same hominid family with orangutans, but they are placed in a separate subfamily (Gorillinae) (see Figure 10.5). Gorillas live in forests in equatorial Africa. Some gorillas live in highlands, while others live in lowlands; thus, they

Gallo Images/Corbis

**FIGURE 10.26 Gorillas**
Gorillas are large-bodied apes that inhabit equatorial forests in Africa, where they eat a lot of leaves.

have some minor differences in their lifestyles and features. In general, gorillas (especially the males) are very large; they are actually the largest of the primates. Since they are so large, they are more terrestrial than many of the other apes. There are significant differences between male and female gorillas, including the trademark silver fur color seen on the backs of adult males but not females (see Lab 11 for more on sexual dimorphism). Gorillas are diurnal and live in relatively large social groups. They also eat a lot of leaves, far more than any other ape. The gorilla cranium is very robust. This robusticity mostly relates to their heavy plant diet and the extensive chewing required with this lifestyle (see Lab 12 for more information on dietary adaptations).

## Chimpanzees and Bonobos (Panini)

Chimpanzees and bonobos are also great apes in the Hominidae family. They are the closest living relatives of humans, and they are classified with humans in the Homininae subfamily to reflect this. Within the hominine subfamily, both chimpanzees and bonobos belong to the tribe Panini and the genus *Pan*, indicating their particularly close relationship to one another (see Figure 10.5). Chimpanzees are classified as *Pan troglodytes*, and bonobos are classified as *Pan paniscus* (**FIGURE 10.27** and **FIGURE 10.28**, respectively).

Both chimpanzees and bonobos live in equatorial Africa, but the chimpanzee is found in several areas (including parts of western equatorial Africa) while the bonobo is limited to a particular area of the Democratic Republic of Congo. The two species are separated by the Congo River (known in the past as the Zaire River), and they are not found in overlapping areas. Chimpanzees often live in territories shared by gorillas, but gorillas do not live in the area where bonobos are found.

Chimpanzees and bonobos are smaller than the other great apes but larger than the lesser apes. They are diurnal and spend some of their time in the trees and some time on the ground. Both species eat a wide variety of foods, including fruit, leaves, nuts, insects, and small

**FIGURE 10.27 Chimpanzees**
One of the most well-known apes, chimpanzees live in equatorial African forests. Sometimes their territories overlap with gorilla ranges.

**FIGURE 10.28 Bonobos**
Found only in a particular area of the Democratic Republic of Congo, the bonobos are a little more arboreal and have longer, leaner bodies than chimpanzees.

animals. Their crania are relatively robust but not nearly as robust as those of gorillas. They live in large social groups, and there are some differences between adult males and females in the species (see Lab 11).

There are some important physical and behavioral differences between bonobos and chimpanzees that help distinguish them as different species. Bonobos tend to have longer, leaner bodies than chimpanzees. They are also a little more arboreal than chimps. The major differences between the two species relate to their level of aggression and their sexual activities. Chimpanzees tend to be more violent and have fewer sexual interactions. In contrast, bonobos tend to be less violent and have frequent (often nonreproductive) sexual interactions.

## Humans (Hominini)

Humans (*Homo sapiens*) are apes too! As described above, humans are classified in the same hominine subfamily with chimpanzees and bonobos. Humans are then separated from these other species in the tribe Hominini (see Figure 10.5). Compared to other primates, humans have larger brains for their body size, flatter (more orthognathic) faces, and smaller relative tooth sizes. They have generalized diets, limited sexual dimorphism, and numerous adaptations for walking on two legs. Because many of the labs in this text are devoted to humans, we will not discuss them at length here. We do, however, want to highlight that humans are apes that fit within the broader context of living primate groups.

Name: _____     Section: _____

Course: _____     Date: _____

Answer the following questions in the space provided.

1. List *three* traits found in primates that distinguish them from other mammals.

2. True or false? According to the primate taxonomy provided in this lab, lemurs are more closely related to tarsiers than they are to lorises.

3. Lorises
   A. rely heavily on their vision.
   B. have large bodies.
   C. eat a diet of mostly leaves.
   D. are nocturnal.

4. What is the only place on Earth where you can find lemurs living in the wild?

5. Describe *one* trait that tarsiers share with lorises and lemurs. Describe *one* trait that tarsiers share with the anthropoids.

6. Describe *one* trait that distinguishes the platyrrhines and catarrhines. (Be sure to describe how the trait varies between the two groups.)

7. Which of the following traits is found in some New World monkeys and none of the Old World monkeys?
   A. Arboreal lifestyle
   B. Diet emphasizing fruit
   C. Prehensile tail
   D. Ischial callosities

8. I live in the forests of central Africa. I am arboreal and have a long tail. I have bilophodont molars, and I have a diet that includes a lot of leaves. Which type of primate am I?
   A. Ape
   B. Colobine
   C. New World monkey
   D. Cercopithecine

9. List *two* traits that are found in apes but not in other primates.


10. I live in the forests of Southeast Asia. I am arboreal and swing through the trees. I have Y-5 molars, and I eat a lot of fruit. I live in small social groups, where males and females work together to defend the territory and raise offspring. What type of primate am I?

    A. Orangutan
    B. Gorilla
    C. Bonobo
    D. Gibbon

# LAB EXERCISES

Name: _____    Section: _____

Course: _____    Date: _____

## EXERCISE 1  DISTINGUISHING MAMMALS AND PRIMATES

Work with a small group or alone to complete this exercise. Use the mystery mammals provided by your instructor (or depicted in the lab Appendix) to complete the chart below. Identify whether the mystery mammal is a primate and list *one* trait that helped you make this identification.

|  | Primate (Yes or No)? | Trait |
|---|---|---|
| Mystery Mammal A |  |  |
| Mystery Mammal B |  |  |

## EXERCISE 2  LORISES AND LEMURS

Work with a small group or alone to complete this exercise.

### PART A

Use the primate material provided by your instructor (or depicted in the lab Appendix) to complete the chart below. Identify whether the primate is nocturnal or diurnal and list *one* trait that helped you make this determination.

|  | Nocturnal or Diurnal? | Trait |
|---|---|---|
| Primate A |  |  |
| Primate B |  |  |

### PART B

Use the primate crania provided by your instructor (or depicted in the lab Appendix) to complete the chart below. Identify whether the primate is a lemur or an anthropoid and list *one* trait that helped you decide this.

|  | Lemur or Anthropoid? | Trait |
|---|---|---|
| Primate A |  |  |
| Primate B |  |  |

EXERCISE 3  **TARSIERS**

Work with a small group or alone to complete this exercise. Review the material provided by your instructor (or depicted in the lab Appendix).

1. Tarsiers have an unusual mix of anatomical features. Describe *one* anatomical trait that is unique to tarsiers.

2. Are tarsiers more closely related to lemurs and lorises or to monkeys and apes? Describe *three* anatomical traits that can be used as evidence to support your answer.

EXERCISE 4  **NEW WORLD MONKEYS VERSUS OLD WORLD MONKEYS**

Work with a small group or alone to complete this exercise. Use the monkey crania provided by your instructor (or depicted in the lab Appendix) to answer the following questions:

1. Which of these monkeys is a New World monkey?

2. Which of these monkeys is an Old World monkey?

3. Describe *two* traits you used to make these identifications. (Be sure to describe how each trait varied in the two monkeys.)

**EXERCISE 5** **OLD WORLD MONKEYS VERSUS APES**

Work with a small group or alone to complete this exercise.

**PART A**

Use the primate material provided by your instructor (or depicted in the lab Appendix) to complete the chart below. Identify whether the primate is an Old World monkey or ape and list *one* trait that helped you decide this.

|  | Old World Monkey or Ape? | Trait |
|---|---|---|
| Primate A |  |  |
| Primate B |  |  |

**PART B**

Use the primate crania provided by your instructor (or the lower premolar and molar teeth depicted in the lab Appendix) to complete the chart below. Identify whether the primate is an Old World monkey or ape and list *one* trait that helped you decide this.

|  | Old World Monkey or Ape? | Trait |
|---|---|---|
| Primate A |  |  |
| Primate B |  |  |

# CRITICAL THINKING QUESTIONS

On a separate sheet of paper, answer the following questions.

1. This question may be completed independently or as a group discussion. Use material in your classroom, online, or in books to find images and descriptions of two nonprimate mammals (such as dogs, horses, dolphins, or raccoons). What traits do these animals share in common with primates? What important primate traits do they lack?

2. The National Primate Research Center at the University of Wisconsin-Madison has assembled taxonomical information about living primates into "primate factsheets" on the following website: http://pin.primate.wisc.edu/factsheets. Visit this website and choose one primate factsheet. For this primate species (or genus), describe its geographic distribution and a few anatomical and behavioral traits. Then, identify its larger taxonomic group (loris, lemur, tarsier, New World monkey, Old World monkey, or ape). Finally, describe how its geographic distribution and traits justify its classification as a member of this taxonomic group.

3. In this lab we reviewed a lot of different primate groups and the traits that distinguish these groups. To help you make comparisons across these primate groups and understand larger trends in primate traits, complete the following Living Primate Chart.

## LIVING PRIMATE CHART

| Primate Group | Anatomical Traits | Diet | Locomotion | Other |
|---|---|---|---|---|
| Lorises | | | | |
| Lemurs | | | | |
| Tarsiers | | | | |
| New World Monkeys | | | | |
| Old World Monkeys | | | | |
| Gibbons and Siamangs | | | | |
| Orangutans | | | | |
| Gorillas | | | | |
| Chimpanzees and Bonobos | | | | |

# APPENDIX:
# LAB EXERCISE IMAGES

## Exercise 1 Distinguishing Mammals and Primates

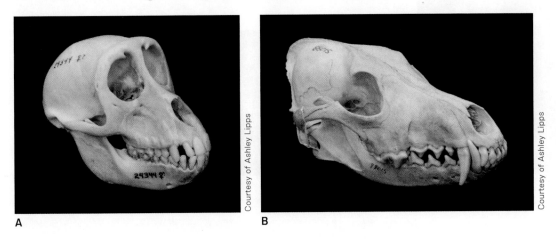

A

Courtesy of Ashley Lipps

B

Courtesy of Ashley Lipps

## Exercise 2 Lorises and Lemurs

Part A

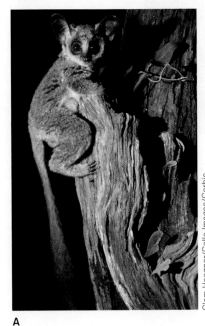

A

Clem Haagner/Gallo Images/Corbis

B

DLILLC/Corbis

Part B

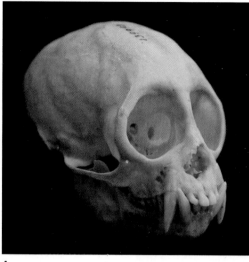

A

Courtesy of Ashley Lipps

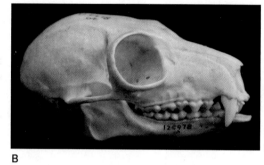

B

Courtesy of Ashley Lipps

Note: These crania are shown at the same scale.

## Exercise 3 Tarsiers

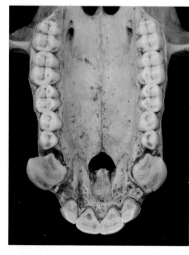

Frans Lanting/Corbis

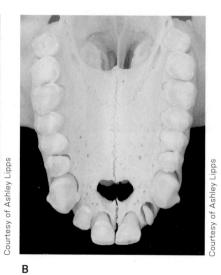

E. R. Degginger

## Exercise 4 New World Monkeys versus Old World Monkeys

A

Courtesy of Ashley Lipps

B

Courtesy of Ashley Lipps

# Exercise 5 Old World Monkeys versus Apes

Part A

apple2499/shutterstock

**A**

raliand/Shutterstock

**B**

Part B

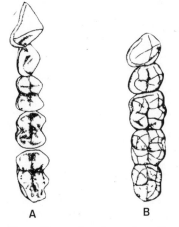

**A**       **B**

Note: These drawings show the lower premolars and molars from two mystery primates.

*Sunset Boulevard/Corbis*

*Ignacio Palacios/Lonely Planet Images/Getty Images*

Gorillas are often portrayed as aggressive and beastly, along the lines of the exaggerated King Kong character. In reality, however, gorillas are usually peaceful and calm.

## Lab Learning Objectives

By the end of this lab, students should be able to:

- describe the differences between laboratory and field primate studies.

- make observations of primate behavior, collecting both quantitative and qualitative data.

- discuss how primate ecology impacts primate social life.

- differentiate between the forms of primate social organization.

- describe examples of "cultural" behaviors in nonhuman primates.

LAB **11**

# Primate Behavior

With the release of the film *King Kong* in 1933, gorillas stormed the popular imagination as aggressive and frightening beasts. In the most famous scene of the film, an oversized gorilla-like creature kidnaps a woman and climbs the Empire State Building of New York City with the woman in tow. The great marauding beast is then brought down by biplanes firing a rain of bullets. For many people this was the first popular and iconic image of gorillas, and it has been reinforced by contemporary media representations, including militant gorillas in the Planet of the Apes franchise and a kidnapping gorilla in the Donkey Kong video game series. Yet the true nature of gorillas is far from this fictionalized exaggeration.

Through the fieldwork of Dian Fossey and other primatologists beginning in the late 1960s, we have gained a much clearer understanding of gorilla behavior. Gorillas do engage in some aggressive and violent behaviors, particularly when their infants are threatened or when a new male assumes control of a group, but this violence is relatively uncommon. Instead, they are among the gentlest nonhuman primates. Gorillas spend most of their time eating leafy vegetation and resting. They regularly engage in soft vocalizations that symbolize their contentment and social bonds, and they form strong attachments to other members of their social group, particularly infants.

**captive primate study** research conducted with primates in captivity (in laboratories or zoos)

**field primate study** research conducted with primates in their wild habitat

The realities of primate behavior are often very different from our fictitious imaginings. The raging King Kong character that kidnaps women is very unlike the real male gorilla who sits contentedly with his offspring during an afternoon period of rest in the African forests. As biological anthropologists, it is important that we move beyond popular stereotypes and try to understand the true behaviors of our various primate relatives. This provides the context necessary to understand our own behaviors, and how we are similar to and different from other primates.

## INTRODUCTION

In this lab, we explore the behavior of living primates to better understand our own biological context. We begin with a look at how researchers actually study primates in captivity and in the wild. We then outline typical affiliative and aggressive primate behaviors. We also consider the various forms of social organization found in primates, as well as how food availability impacts social groups. We discuss primate

sexual behavior, with a particular look at the unusual practices of bonobos, and we review some of the possible practices among nonhuman primates that resemble human culture. We conclude with a consideration of the complexity of primate field research in the face of rapidly declining primate population sizes and growing primate species endangerment.

## STUDYING PRIMATES

There are generally two different contexts for conducting primate research: captive contexts and field contexts. Each research context has benefits and drawbacks, and each is more or less suitable for different research topics. A **captive primate study** is a research program that is conducted with primates in captivity (in laboratories or zoos). These contexts provide a controlled environment. The researcher can often work with a primate or group of primates for their whole lives, and the researcher can carefully select primates of the appropriate age and sex to study. In captive contexts, researchers can also expose nonhuman primates to human-like tasks and skills to test their capability for human-like thought processing and behavior. For these reasons, captive studies are often used to assess such things as nonhuman primate language capacity and problem-solving skills.

Captive contexts are not well suited to research more "natural" behaviors that occur in the wild, such as group interactions, resource use, territory defense, and primate health. For research along these lines, primatologists turn to field studies (**FIGURE 11.1**). A **field primate study** is a research program conducted with primates in their wild habitat. Field studies are conducted in less controlled environments than captive studies. The researcher may have trouble locating and observing primates that travel often or live at high levels of the forest canopy. The researcher may also have little choice about the age and sex of the available primates for study. For example, a primatologist may set out to research the interactions between infants and their mothers in the wild and then is unable to

**FIGURE 11.1 Primate Field Studies**
In order to understand how nonhuman primates behave in the wild, primatologists conduct primate field studies.

Courtesy of Dawn Kitchen

find any infants in the study area. While the lack of control can make field studies challenging, these contexts are well suited to investigations of wild primate behaviors. Researchers can observe primate social interactions, food-gathering processes, territory defense, vocalization patterns, and any other behaviors in wild, natural settings. Of course, even in the wild, nonhuman primates are impacted by encroaching human populations (see later in this lab) and the presence of the human researchers themselves. However, field studies are the closest we can get to a "natural" nonhuman primate context.

Whether conducting primate research in the captive context or in the field context, the primatologist must consider two things: (1) Will the data collected be qualitative or quantitative? (2) Will observations be made of a primate group or an individual? Answers to these questions will often depend on the primatologist's hypotheses (or research questions), and how the primatologist answers these two questions will dramatically impact how the work is conducted. **Qualitative data** is data that is more descriptive and centers on the *qualities* that are observed (such as appearance and smell). This kind of data often provides rich detail and additional contextual information. For example, observing a primate and describing the details of its appearance and all its behaviors would be qualitative data. The details of the behavior may not be readily comparable to other primates, but the details can be helpful in providing more contextual information for making interpretations. Qualitative data is helpful for research that is descriptive, such as reporting previously unknown behavior.

In contrast, **quantitative data** is more focused and clearly measurable. It is more about the measurable *quantities* observed (such as the number of instances of a behavior). This kind of data often provides information that is good for making comparisons. For instance, observing a primate and noting when and how many times the primate performs specific behaviors (such as grooming or vocalizing) would be quantitative data. Tracking how many times a primate vocalizes within a time period

can be easily compared to similar patterns in other primates. Quantitative data is helpful for research that emphasizes comparisons, such as contrasting the behavior patterns of males and females or of young and old primates. In many instances, researchers use a combination of qualitative and quantitative data. For example, a primatologist that is researching vocalization patterns between mothers and their infants may collect qualitative data about the vocalizations that describe the sounds and corresponding gestures or body language that are made. The primatologist might also collect quantitative data about how often the mothers and infants vocalize at certain times of day or under certain circumstances.

In addition to deciding whether quantitative data, qualitative data, or a combination of both will be used, the primatologist must also consider whether to observe a group of primates or focus on individual primates. As with the type of data collected, there are benefits and drawbacks to each option. When primatologists observe the behavior of multiple primates simultaneously, they are conducting a **group observation**. These observations allow researchers to collect data about how primates interact with one another, such as how they share food, have sex, build social bonds, and communicate. However, it is often difficult to observe numerous primates at one time, so a single researcher is likely to miss some behaviors and individual variations that occur outside the line of sight. Instead, the primatologist could choose to do a **focused observation** and focus attention on the behaviors of a single individual at a time. These observations allow researchers to collect data about individual behavioral variations, such as unusual practices seen in a particular primate. These observations are also useful for observing behaviors that may be more private and conducted alone, such as giving birth or collecting food. However, when researchers are focusing on one primate, they may miss some of the broader social context and important social interactions of a larger group. As with the choice between qualitative and quantitative data, primatologists often use a combination of

**qualitative data**
descriptive data about the qualities that are observed

**quantitative data**
focused and clearly measurable data

**group observation**
the observation of many individuals simultaneously

**focused observation**
the observation of a single individual at a time

**affiliative behavior** behavior that is generally cooperative

**grooming** the removal of foreign objects (such as insects or plant parts) from another primate's fur

**affiliative communication** verbal or nonverbal communication that reinforces social relationships.

**vocalization** a verbal communication

**aggressive behavior** behavior that challenges, threatens, or harms others

**threat display** an action (such as flashing the teeth) that seeks to threaten others from a distance

group and focused observations. For example, if researchers want to study chimpanzee diet, they would probably conduct group observations of chimpanzees congregating together and eating leaves. However, the researchers would also probably want to observe chimpanzees collecting and eating other resources, such as ants. This would require more focused observations because chimpanzees tend to collect these resources independently, rather than in large groups.

## AFFILIATIVE BEHAVIOR

What types of behaviors do primates practice? In general, primatologists tend to characterize primate social behavior as one of two types: affiliative behavior and aggressive behavior. **Affiliative behavior** is behavior that is generally cooperative. It reinforces social bonds and affiliations. The most common form of affiliative behavior in primates is **grooming** (**FIGURE 11.2**). Primates often pick through each other's fur and remove insects or plant parts. Sometimes they eat the removed materials, such as the insects.

Grooming generally promotes good health and hygiene by keeping the fur clean and free of pests. In addition, grooming is a soothing behavior that relaxes the primate being groomed and reinforces social bonds. Often lower-ranking individuals will groom higher-ranking individuals as a sign of submission, and males and females will groom each other to reinforce mating relationships. Humans also engage in grooming behavior to promote social bonds. Parents often make a ritual or game out of bath time and hair brushing. This relaxes the children and strengthens their bonds with their parents. Similarly, adults often find themselves relaxed by the experience of having their hair washed at the salon and are more open to conversation with the hair stylist afterward.

In addition to grooming, primates also engage in a range of **affiliative communications**. These communications reinforce social relationships and may be verbal or nonverbal. Nonverbal communications often take the form of embracing gestures, such as the grooming hand clasp seen in some chimpanzees. This is a combination of typical grooming behavior and hand-holding. The action communicates social connectedness and bonding. Verbal communications usually take the form of **vocalizations**. These are particular sounds that communicate different types of information. Many primates, such as gorillas, have particular vocalizations that indicate contentment and satisfaction. These sounds are made when individuals are relaxed, and they reinforce the general sense of social connection between the primates involved.

## AGGRESSIVE BEHAVIOR

The second category of primate behavior is **aggressive behavior**. This behavior is anything that challenges, threatens, or harms the primates involved. The most common types of aggressive primate behaviors are threats. Direct violence is dangerous, and any primates directly involved or in close proximity can be injured. Therefore, most primates try to avoid fighting and use **threat displays** instead. These are

John Giustina/Corbis

**FIGURE 11.2 Chimpanzee Grooming**
Primates, such as these chimpanzees, often engage in grooming as a way to strengthen social bonds and maintain good hygiene. This is an example of an affiliative behavior.

actions that highlight the actor's strength from a distance. They are meant to threaten potential enemies and scare them into submission before violence breaks out. Threat displays take a variety of forms. One of the most common is the **threat yawn**, which is an opening of the mouth that displays the teeth (FIGURE 11.3). It is called a yawn because it involves wide opening of the mouth, not because it is a motion triggered by being tired. This display allows the yawner to warn others that a fight would expose them to the dangers of the yawner's very large teeth. Many primates engage in threat yawns or similar displays of teeth, such as flipping the upper lip to expose the top teeth. Other threats can take a variety of forms, including stomping up and down, thrashing tree branches, or banging fists on the ground. In all of these cases the loud noise and violent body movements are meant to herald the potential for further violence.

Not all aggressive encounters end with just threats. Many primate species regularly engage in direct violence. This is particularly true when males are fighting one another for access to females or territory. Chimpanzees are perhaps

**FIGURE 11.3 Baboon Threat Yawn**
Primates, such as this baboon, often use threat displays to warn off enemies. The threat yawn seen here is a common example of this type of aggressive behavior.

the most violent primates in the wild. They often engage in violent attacks. These attacks are usually perpetrated by adult males against other adult males and females; however, adult females also attack other adult females with some frequency. In addition, adults of both sexes are known to attack adolescents and juveniles. But in general, males attack more often than females. The most violent chimpanzee attacks are usually directed at outsider chimps from nearby groups. Chimpanzee males have even been known to patrol the boundaries of their territory and attack stray chimps found near their borders. Violent attacks often involve biting, scratching, and beating, and they can result in serious injury and death.

In some primates, aggressive behavior includes a practice known as **infanticide**. This refers to killing infants or young members of the species. Unlike the infanticide occasionally seen in humans where a person kills his or her own children, infanticide in nonhuman primates usually involves killing the offspring of another individual. In most of these cases, the infanticide seems to be related to the reproductive potential of the infant's mother. When a nonhuman primate is breast-feeding, she is less fertile and less likely to become pregnant. (Note that in human primates breast-feeding does not necessarily suppress fertility in the same way.) When a male takes over a group that includes females who are breast-feeding their offspring, the male is likely to kill the existing offspring. The male did not sire these infants because he is new to the group and has not had sex with the females. As long as the females are breast-feeding, they will not produce any offspring with the new male. Therefore, the male kills the present infants, and the females become capable of producing his offspring. We also see infanticide when a new female with an infant migrates into an existing group. Again, the male or males of the group know the infant is not their own, and it is killed to allow the incoming female to mate with the male or males of the group. The practice of infanticide may have been selected for because it increases the reproductive success of the perpetrators.

**threat yawn** an opening of the mouth that displays the teeth in a threatening manner

**infanticide** the killing of infants or young members of the species

Males who kill infants that are not their own are able to mate with the newly lactating mothers and pass on their genes more frequently.

## PRIMATE ECOLOGY

Primates lead complicated social lives, and as with most animals, their social life is impacted to some extent by their environmental circumstances. Understanding these relationships falls under the heading of **primate ecology**. This refers to the study of the relationship between primates and their environments. Primate ecology research has shown that primate group structure in particular is impacted by food availability and the risk of predator attacks.

In situations where food is scarce, there are not enough resources to support large primate groups. For example, primates that hunt insects as their primary food source tend to live in smaller groups because insects are scarce. One stick insect or beetle will not feed a large group. Even a tree full of many insects will still not provide enough food for a large group to regularly eat together. Similarly, primates that eat a lot of fruit may live in smaller groups, depending on the availability of fruit in their area. While we often assume that a tropical forest is full of fruit trees that provide food year-round, in reality fruit trees can be scattered throughout the forest and bear fruit infrequently. In these situations, we also see primates living in small groups. Occasionally, we see primates take another approach to dealing with sparse resources. Some primates, such as chimpanzees, will spend most of their time in a large group but will separate into smaller groups when they pursue food that is sparsely distributed in their territory. This is called a **fission–fusion** structure. The group fissions into smaller subgroups when they seek sparsely distributed foods, and they fuse back together when they seek other foods or sleep at night.

In contrast to the small social groups we usually find when food is sparse, primates often form much larger social groups when their food is abundant. For example, many primates that emphasize leaves and plants in their diets follow this pattern. These primates tend to live in forests or grasslands where plant food is abundant, so they can form large groups that eat and live together. Even primates that do not normally live in large groups may congregate into large groups when food is temporarily abundant. For example, adult orangutans usually spend their time alone because the fruit they eat is very sparsely distributed in their environment and does not normally support multiple adults at one time. Sometimes, however, there is a temporary abundance of fruit in a particular tree or location. In these instances, many adults from the extended area will congregate into a much larger social group for as long as the food lasts.

In addition to resource distribution, primate group size is also impacted by predation risk. If there is a high risk of attack from predators in an area, a larger social group is favored because it provides extra eyes and ears to warn of danger. It also decreases the chance that a particular individual will be killed. If you live in a group of 3 and are attacked by a predator, there is a 1 in 3 chance you will be the one killed. If you live in a group of 30 and are attacked by a predator, there is now only a 1 in 30 chance you will be the one killed. This is important because most primates have numerous predators to fear in their habitats, including big cats, birds of prey, large reptiles, and sometimes other primates.

Similar to other animals, primates must always strike a balance between having a large enough group to protect against predation and a small enough group that everyone has access to food. For some primates, resource availability will be more important, especially if predation risk is low. For other primates, predation risk will be more important, especially if food is abundant.

## PRIMATE SOCIAL ORGANIZATION

Within most primate social groups, especially those that are larger, there is a complex **social hierarchy**. As in our own societies, some individuals will have a higher status than other individuals. Often this status is inherited, and an infant is born into a higher or lower status based on the rank of its mother or father. These hierarchies are important because they impact a primate's access to food and mating partners. Generally, individuals of higher status have better access to food and mates, while individuals of lower status have less access to food and mates. Primate social hierarchies are not completely set in stone. There is usually some room for changing one's social status.

Often, forming **coalitions** facilitates negotiating the social hierarchy within large, complex social groups. Multiple individuals work together in a coalition against others outside the coalition. For example, the individuals in a coalition may work together to overthrow others and assume their status, or they may work together to maintain their own social status and prevent being overthrown by others. Perhaps the most well-known coalitions are those formed by male chimpanzees. These coalitions involve complex social relationships. They may be temporary and fluid, depending on individual needs at a given time, or they may be long-lasting alliances. The coalitions are often reinforced through affiliative behavior, such as grooming and sharing food.

Primates are very social animals, and primate social groups can take a variety of forms. Sometimes group structure will vary from one species to the next, and sometimes primates from the same species may have very different group structures due to differences in their local food availability and predation risk. Here, we will describe the six types of primate social organization: solitary, monogamy, polyandry, single-male polygyny, multimale polygyny, and bachelor groups. For each type of social organization, we will describe the general pattern and provide examples of primates who practice this pattern in the wild.

## Solitary

A **solitary** social structure is one where adults spend most of their time alone (**FIGURE 11.4**). Adult females (and their offspring) occupy

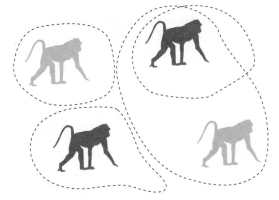

**FIGURE 11.4 Solitary Social Organization**
In solitary primates, each adult female (red) and her offspring occupy a separate territory (dashed lines). An adult male (blue) occupies a territory that overlaps with the territory of one or more females. There may also be free-ranging adults.

separate, individual territories. An adult male will occupy a territory that overlaps with female territories, giving him access to the females as mating partners. There may also be free-ranging adults that do not occupy a specific territory. These free-ranging adults may have less access to food and mates than adults in specific territories. When studying primates with a solitary social structure, a researcher is unlikely to see multiple adults together in the wild. However, even though adults in these social groups spend a lot of time alone, they are not asocial. They often engage in social behavior and interactions, particularly if they temporarily congregate into larger groups when food is more abundant. The solitary social structure is seen in orangutans, as well as in some lemurs and lorises.

## Monogamy

**Monogamy** refers to a social group composed of one adult male, one adult female, and their offspring (**FIGURE 11.5**). This mated pair lives together, sometimes for most of their reproductive lives. They often work together to raise their offspring and defend their territory against outsiders. Some lemurs and many tarsiers practice monogamy. In addition, some of the New World monkeys, especially several types of marmosets, live in monogamous groups. Among the apes, the gibbons and siamangs (the lesser apes) have a monogamous social structure as well.

**coalition** a group of multiple primates that work together against other members of their group

**solitary** a form of social organization where adults spend most of their time alone; adult females (and their offspring) occupy separate territories, and an adult male occupies a territory that overlaps with that of several females

**monogamy** a form of social organization where one adult male, one adult female, and their offspring live together

**polyandry** a form of social organization where one adult female, multiple adult males, and their offspring live together

**polygyny** a form of social organization where there are multiple adult females for each male

**single-male polygyny** a form of social organization where one adult male, multiple adult females, and their offspring live together

**multimale polygyny** a form of social organization where multiple adult males, multiple adult females, and their offspring live together

**FIGURE 11.5 Monogamous Social Organization**
In monogamous primates, an adult female (red), an adult male (blue), and their offspring occupy a territory together. Their territory is separate from the territories of other adult pairs.

## Polyandry

*Poly* means "multiple," and *andry* refers to males. **Polyandry** is a particularly rare form of social organization where one adult female, multiple adult males, and their offspring live together (**FIGURE 11.6**). This form of social organization is seen only in some New World monkeys, especially the tamarins. These primates are very small and often give birth to twins. Having an additional male in the group allows for each offspring to be looked after by an adult while leaving one adult unencumbered and able to feed or defend as needed. If the additional adults were females, there would be the potential for additional twins,

which would further burden the social group. So, instead, there are additional males who can contribute to raising the offspring without burdening the group with more infants. All males will copulate with the female, so at any time a male will not know if he is taking care of his own offspring.

## Polygyny

Here, *poly* means "multiple," and *gyny* refers to females. **Polygyny** is a type of social organization where there are multiple females for each male. This can take two forms. The first form is **single-male polygyny**, where one male, multiple females, and their offspring live together (**FIGURE 11.7**). This social group is seen in some New World monkeys, such as the howler monkey. It is also seen in some Old World monkeys, such as gelada baboons and colobus monkeys. Among the apes, many gorillas live in single-male polygynous groups.

The second form of polygyny is **multimale polygyny**, where multiple males, multiple females, and their offspring live together (**FIGURE 11.8**). This type of polygyny is seen in ring-tailed lemurs and some New World monkeys, such as the squirrel monkey. Many Old World monkeys, such as savanna baboons and most macaques, also practice it. Among the apes, both the bonobos and the chimpanzees live in multimale polygynous groups.

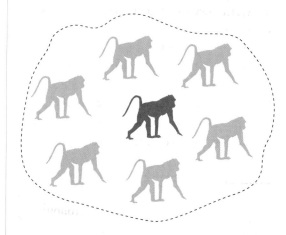

**FIGURE 11.6 Polyandrous Social Organization**
In polyandrous primates, an adult female (red), multiple adult males (blue), and their offspring occupy a territory together.

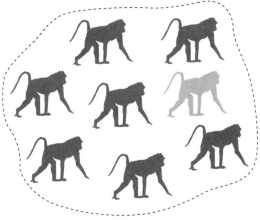

**FIGURE 11.7 Single-male Polygynous Social Organization**
In single-male polygynous primates, a single adult male (blue), multiple adult females (red), and their offspring occupy a territory together.

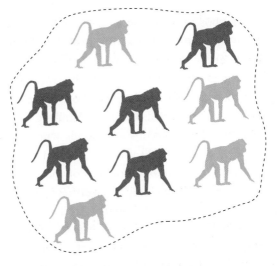

**FIGURE 11.8 Multimale Polygynous Social Organization**
In multimale polygynous primates, multiple adult males (blue), multiple adult females (red), and their offspring occupy a territory together.

## Bachelor (All-Male) Groups

In solitary and single-male polygnous species, such as gorillas, one male is paired with numerous females. However, in these species, a relatively equal number of males and females exist across the entire population. This means many of the males of the species are living without a group of females. These males often form social groups together, called **bachelor groups** (FIGURE 11.9). These all-male groups often roam the landscape because they do not yet control a territory or a group of females. When an opportunity arises to take over a territory or group of females from a reigning male leader, males from the bachelor group may work together to fight off the current leader and gain control.

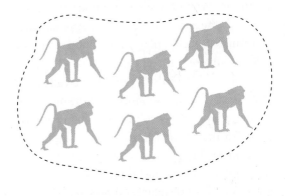

**FIGURE 11.9 Bachelor Groups**
In some primates, males who do not have a territory or a group of females will live together in all-male groups.

# PRIMATE SEXUAL BEHAVIOR

To fully understand primate behavior, we must consider primate sexual and reproductive practices. Male and female primates often have different strategies. For most male primates, emphasis is placed on getting access to females for mating. This is often accomplished through competition, and it may be related to a male's status within the social hierarchy and the strength of his male coalition. For most female primates, emphasis is placed on getting access to resources for supporting offspring. This is also impacted by competition, and it may be related to a female's status in the social hierarchy. In both instances, primates are competing with other primates of the same sex. Males compete with males for female mating partners; females compete with females for resources.

Competition and reproductive behavior can impact primate anatomy. Many primates, particularly the Old World monkeys, have special coloring that indicates from a distance if one is facing a male or female of the species. Males sometimes even have brightly colored fur around their genitals, which calls further attention to their maleness. As we discuss further in Lab 12, male primates may also be larger than their female counterparts and have larger canine teeth. All of these traits indicate to competitors that they are facing another male, and they facilitate aggressive competition for mates.

In some primates, such as chimpanzees and savanna baboons, female anatomy is also impacted by competition and sexual behavior. In these species, females have extreme swelling in their genital region around the time of ovulation. This is called **estrus swelling** because it is timed with the female estrus (or fertility) cycle. A female's estrus swelling indicates to everyone in the group that she is ovulating and sexually receptive. Primates with pronounced estrus swelling tend to live in large, multimale polygynous groups where males will compete over access to females in estrus. Conversely, pronounced estrus swelling is not seen in social groups where male access to female mates is

**bachelor group** an all-male social group where multiple adult males live together, without females or offspring

**estrus swelling** the swelling of the female genital region around the time of ovulation

**alarm call** a vocalization that indicates a particular threat

more guaranteed, such as in single-male polygynous groups or monogamous groups. Thus, female estrus swelling relates to male–male competition.

For almost all primates, reproduction is a central component of social life, and sexual interactions emphasize reproduction. This is true for most animals, so it is not unusual that primates also follow this reproduction-centered pattern. In fact, one thing that makes humans different is that we break with this typical pattern and regularly engage in sexual activities that are nonreproductive. We are not alone in this, however. There are a few other nonhuman primates that also engage in nonreproductive sexual activities.

For example, the bonobos participate in a wide range of sexual behaviors. Bonobo sexual encounters cross age groups and can involve adults and even juveniles. They have male–female sex in numerous positions, including ventral–ventral mating where both parties face each other (which is extremely rare in animals). Bonobos also engage in male–male genital stimulation and female–female genital stimulation, and they are known to practice self-stimulation. This diversity of sexual behavior distinguishes the bonobos from all other primates, apart from humans. This begs the question, why do the bonobos behave this way?

Bonobos seem to use sexual activities as a relatively standard affiliative behavior. Similar to grooming, it is used to reinforce social bonds and avoid escalating tensions. This may help to explain why the combinations of sexual partners are so varied. If everyone in the group is forming relationships and bonds with one another, everyone will use sexual interactions as part of this bonding process. Bonobo social groups tend to be close-knit with few violent attacks. This is in stark contrast to their close relatives—the chimpanzees—whose social groups are marked by limited sexual interactions, competing male coalitions, and considerably more violence.

## PRIMATE COMMUNICATION AND CULTURE

We previously discussed how primates use some forms of vocalizations to reinforce social bonds. Primate vocalizations may serve other purposes, as well. For example, many primates use vocalizations as a way to mark their territory and warn off intruders. In gibbons a paired male and female make particular sounds, similar to a duet song. When the song is sung, it warns others to stay away from their territory. Similarly, howler monkeys in Central and South America engage in regular vocalizations (reminiscent of howls) that mark their territory and inform intruders of their presence **(FIGURE 11.10)**. Many primates also have specific **alarm calls**. These are vocalizations that indicate a particular threat. When these vocalizations are made, it sounds the alarm that danger is approaching. A primate species may have different alarm calls for different threats, such as one for lions and another for birds of prey. These calls usually elicit different responses from the members of the group, with each response being appropriate to the specific threat. For example, the reaction to the lion call may be very different from the reaction to the bird call because avoiding these predators requires different behaviors. Interestingly, primate species that regularly live side by side often understand the alarm calls of

David Tipling/Getty Images

**FIGURE 11.10 Howler Monkey Vocalization**
Howler monkeys use loud, howling vocalizations to mark their territorial boundaries.

their neighboring primate species. This allows multiple species to form something similar to a "neighborhood watch," where the alarm sounded by one individual sparks a response in all of the local primates.

In addition to complicated forms of communication, many nonhuman primates have behavioral practices somewhat reminiscent of those of our own cultures. Human culture is unique to our species and perhaps some of our most closely related fossil relatives (see Lab 16). Human culture is a multifaceted phenomenon that encompasses our beliefs, practices, languages, and all other learned aspects of our social lives. In contrast, **nonhuman primate culture** is defined more simply as group-specific, learned behavior. When we refer to culture in nonhuman primates, we do not mean to suggest that these primates have culture on a scale anywhere near what is seen in humans. Instead, we are highlighting some of the similarities between human and nonhuman primate behaviors. For example, in both cases we find that cultural behaviors vary from one local group to another. Also, in both human and nonhuman primates, culture is centered on learned behavior, rather than natural or innate behavior.

In nonhuman primates, culture can take a variety of forms. Research traditionally emphasizes the wide range of tool use seen among the great apes. For example, orangutans select twigs, remove the leaves, and use the modified sticks to extract insects and honey from holes in trees. Chimpanzees also shape twigs into tools they use to extract ants and termites from trees and insect mounds **(FIGURE 11.11)**. Several chimpanzee groups also use particular methods of cracking nuts to access the edible meat inside the shells. Some of these groups use wood hammers and anvils while other groups use rocks instead. Research has also begun to track cultural behavior in monkeys. For example, capuchin monkeys (New World monkeys) follow a list of steps to harvest and extract the meat from clams. And similar to chimpanzees, the capuchins also use rocks to crack seeds or nuts and use sticks to extract insects from trees.

William Wallauer/JGI/www.janegoodall.org

**FIGURE 11.11 Chimpanzee Insect Fishing**
Many chimpanzees form twigs into tools with which they can collect insects. This skill must be learned, and juveniles may spend years observing and practicing before they master the skill.

In addition, Japanese macaques (Old World monkeys) have been observed washing food to remove undesirable sand particles.

In all of these examples, the primates are learning the behavior through an extended process of observing others and practicing on their own. Often it will take years to learn the behavior, and some individuals will never master the technique. This is particularly true with tool use in which a raw material must be carefully selected and then modified. For example, in making an insect fishing tool, a twig of the appropriate size and strength must be chosen and the leaves removed before it is ready for use.

A final category of nonhuman primate culture includes social hunting practices **(FIGURE 11.12)**. While chimpanzees are most famous for their hunting, similar practices are seen in capuchin monkeys (New World monkeys) and some baboons (Old World monkeys). The primates work together in the hunt, often by herding prey toward an ambush. While adult males are usually the hunters, they share

**nonhuman primate culture** group-specific, learned behavior in nonhuman primates

Ian C. Gilby

**FIGURE 11.12 Chimpanzee Hunting**
Chimpanzees often hunt other animals, such as monkeys. The hunt requires cooperation, and the distribution of the meat is based in part on social status and affiliations. In this way, hunting plays an important social role in chimpanzee life.

the meat with females and juveniles of the group. This meat distribution is often based on social status and affiliations. The choreography involved in the hunt must be learned, and the strategy and preferred meat vary between groups. At the same time, the meat obtained in hunts is usually only a small dietary supplement, making the hunt at least as important socially as nutritionally.

### ▶▶▶ EXPLORING FURTHER

**Primate Conservation** To conduct primate field studies, there must be primate populations living in the wild. Unfortunately, finding substantial populations of nonhuman primates is becoming increasingly difficult, especially for particular species. For example, bonobos, chimpanzees, gorillas, and orangutans are all endangered or critically endangered. Almost all gibbons and the siamang are endangered as well. We are facing a great loss of diversity as these and other primate populations decline and face extinction. In addition, the surviv-

ing primate groups are smaller and often hide deeper in the forest. This makes it more difficult to locate, count, study, and conserve these fractured primate populations.

What is causing nonhuman primate population decline? There are a number of factors involved, and any combination of them may be present at any particular location. The two most significant factors are habitat loss and hunting. Many nonhuman primates live in tropical forests that are increasingly under threat of deforestation. To support themselves and their families, many of the humans in these areas cut down the forest to make room for villages and farmland. As the forests shrink, fewer habitats are available for forest-dwelling nonhuman primates. In addition, as global climate change continues, forests will shrink more and more. This will exacerbate the already troubling situation and lead to even further habitat loss. Similar circumstances of habitat loss are at play in some nonforested environments, which will impact nonhuman primates living in these locations as well.

The second factor contributing to nonhuman primate population decline is hunting. Humans often hunt nonhuman primates. The juveniles are collected and sold in the illegal pet trade, and adults that defend their juveniles are killed in the process. Some nonhuman primates are killed and eaten by local people desperately in need of food or sold to international markets. Still others are accidentally caught and fatally injured in snares and traps meant for other animals living in their habitats.

What is being done to conserve nonhuman primates? In most of the countries where these problems occur, laws already exist banning some of these practices. For example, in many countries it is illegal to keep an endangered primate as a pet. However, the laws are not always strongly enforced. In many parts of the world where nonhuman primates are at risk, the humans are facing numerous challenges themselves. These may be war-torn countries where individuals are simply trying to survive and support their families. There often is not enough money and infrastructure to fully enforce the existing conservation laws.

In addition to law enforcement, efforts have also focused on establishing protected habitats (parklands and preserves) where nonhuman primates can live. Again, maintaining enough park personnel and equipping them to properly enforce the laws and restrictions of the park can be challenging. There are also efforts to form rehabilitation areas where primates rescued from the illegal pet trade can be rehabilitated and eventually released back into the wild. Of course this requires financial and personnel support for the rehabilitation facility, as well as habitats where primates can be successfully released.

In support of nonhuman primate conservation efforts, many primatologists advocate more outreach with local human populations. Primatologists often give presentations to local groups or hire local workers to help with their research. In doing this, they are spreading knowledge about and interest in the nonhuman primates of the area. Primatologists also sometimes advocate providing local populations with economic opportunities, such as employment in ecotourism, that decrease their reliance on deforestation and hunting, particularly in protected parkland.

Field primate studies are an important component in our efforts to understand who we are as a species. These research projects help us to understand how primates negotiate social status, obtain and distribute food, and work together to defend territories or mates. By learning about these behaviors in other primates, we may also learn more about similar behaviors in our ancestral species and ourselves. The world of primate field research today is complex. Primatologists face numerous research challenges, especially as it becomes harder to find primate populations to study. In addition, primatologists face ethical challenges as they attempt to balance the conservation needs of nonhuman primates with the survival needs of humans in the same areas. Undoubtedly these challenges will continue into the future, and primatologists will continue to tackle them to gain more knowledge about us and our primate relatives.

# CONCEPT REVIEW QUESTIONS

Name: _____     Section: _____

Course: _____     Date: _____

Answer the following questions in the space provided.

1. True or false? Research conducted with primates in a zoo would be considered a field primate study.

2. True or false? Quantitative data refer to easily measurable information that facilitates comparisons.

3. You are observing two juvenile chimpanzees. When they first meet, they embrace. They then begin tickling each other and wrestling mildly. Would you characterize this behavior as affiliative or aggressive?

4. True or false? When food is sparsely distributed, primates tend to live in smaller groups.

5. I am an adult female primate. I live in a territory with my offspring. My territory is separate from those of other females, so I don't see them often. An adult male has a territory that overlaps with mine, but we hardly ever spend time together. What type of social organization do I participate in?

   A. Polygynous
   B. Monogamous
   C. Solitary
   D. Polyandrous

6. I am an adult female primate. I live in a territory with two adult males and our offspring. What type of social organization do I have?

   A. Solitary
   B. Polyandrous
   C. Monogamous
   D. Polygynous

7. True or false? While most male primates emphasize getting access to resources for their offspring, most female primates emphasize getting access to mates for reproduction.

8. Compared to chimpanzees, bonobos have:

   A. a wider range of sexual practices.
   B. more violent behavior.
   C. a higher degree of male–male competition.
   D. less social bonding between individuals.

9. Define nonhuman primate culture.

10. Describe *one* of the threats to wild primate populations today.

# LAB EXERCISES

Name: _____    Section: _____

Course: _____    Date: _____

## EXERCISE 1  CAPTIVE AND FIELD STUDIES

Work with a small group or alone to complete this exercise. Review the research topics described below. For each topic, identify whether you think it is best studied in captivity or in the field and the reason(s) for your choice.

### SCENARIO A

Do chimpanzees have the ability to learn and use language? This research project will attempt to teach chimpanzees how to use sign language. They will be taught a certain number of signs and then evaluated on their ability to use the signs in innovative combinations and settings.

1. Is this topic best studied in a captive or field study?

2. Why?

### SCENARIO B

Do capuchin monkeys use meat sharing to reinforce social bonds? This research project will observe how capuchin monkeys distribute meat from hunts. Data will be collected about who obtains meat, how much they receive, and in what order they receive their shares.

1. Is this topic best studied in a captive or field study?

2. Why?

### SCENARIO C

Do bonobos use sexual encounters to avoid or mediate conflict? This research project will observe bonobo sexual behavior. Particular attention will be paid to situations when sexual encounters occur around the time of social conflicts. Data will be collected about the type of sexual act and degree of conflict, who is involved, and the length of time elapsed between the sexual behavior and the conflict.

1. Is this topic best studied in a captive or field study?

2. Why?

**EXERCISE 2**   **OBSERVING PRIMATES**

The following two pages provide observation forms for qualitative and quantitative data collection. Use these forms to observe human primates around your classroom or nonhuman primates at a local zoo or online via zoo cams.

## QUALITATIVE PRIMATE OBSERVATION FORM

Date: _____          Start time: _____          End time: _____

Location: _____

Weather: _____

Primate species: _____

Check one:    Group observation ☐          Focused observation ☐

Number of adult males: _____    Number of adult females: _____    Number of juveniles: _____

**Description of study primate(s):** Describe each primate, including its size, coloring, and unusual features. If you are studying a group, assign each primate a code, such as F1 for female 1, F2 for female 2, and J1 for juvenile 1. Then use the codes to streamline your note taking.

_____

_____

_____

**Observations:** Choose a time interval, such as every 2 minutes. Record your choice below. Then after each time interval, describe the behaviors you observe in that instant.

**Length of time interval:** _____

**Time interval 1:** _____

_____

_____

**Time interval 2:** _____

_____

_____

**Time interval 3:** _____

_____

_____

**Time interval 4:** _____

_____

_____

## QUANTITATIVE PRIMATE OBSERVATION FORM

**Date:** _____          **Start time:** _____          **End time:** _____

**Location:** _____

**Weather:** _____

**Primate species:** _____

**Check one:**     Group observation ☐          Focused observation ☐

**Number of adult males:** _____     **Number of adult females:** _____     **Number of juveniles:** _____

**Description of study primate(s):** Describe each primate, including its size, coloring, and unusual features. If you are studying a group, assign each primate a code, such as F1 for female 1, F2 for female 2, and J1 for juvenile 1. Then use the codes to streamline your note taking.

_____

_____

_____

**Observations:** Choose a time interval, such as every 2 minutes. Record your choice below. Then after each time interval, write the primate's code in the appropriate box in the chart if it is practicing that behavior in that instant.

**Length of time interval:** _____

| Behavior | Interval 1 | Interval 2 | Interval 3 | Interval 4 |
|---|---|---|---|---|
| Grooming or Scratching | | | | |
| Playing | | | | |
| Affiliative Vocalization | | | | |
| Threat Display | | | | |
| Violence | | | | |
| Aggressive Vocalization | | | | |
| Food Collecting | | | | |
| Eating | | | | |
| Food Sharing | | | | |
| Tool Use | | | | |
| Courtship or Soliciting Sex | | | | |
| Sex | | | | |
| Sleeping | | | | |
| Caring for Juvenile | | | | |
| Moving or Locomotion | | | | |
| Other (Please Describe) | | | | |

## EXERCISE 3   AFFILIATIVE VERSUS AGGRESSIVE BEHAVIOR

Work with a small group or alone to complete this exercise.

### PART A

Examine the primate behavior depicted in the image provided by your instructor or in the lab Appendix.

1. Do you think this is affiliative behavior or aggressive behavior?

2. Why?

### PART B

Examine the primate behavior depicted in the image provided by your instructor or in the lab Appendix.

1. Do you think this is affiliative behavior or aggressive behavior?

2. Why?

### PART C

Consider your own experiences with human behavior.

1. How are human affiliative and aggressive behaviors similar to what is seen in nonhuman primates? Provide specific examples.

2. How are human affiliative and aggressive behaviors different from what is seen in nonhuman primates? Provide specific examples.

## EXERCISE 4   PRIMATE ECOLOGY AND GROUP SIZE

Work with a small group or alone to complete this exercise. Match each of the mystery primates below to the description of their corresponding environment.

**Primate 1** _____
The majority of my diet consists of fruit, and I live in a monogamous social group.

**Primate 2** _____
I eat mostly insects (such as beetles and moths) that I hunt at night. I am mostly solitary.

**Primate 3** _____
I eat a range of foods, including a lot of grass and flowers. I live in a polygynous group.

**A. Tropical Forest (Southeast Asia)**
Trees are everywhere in this habitat, but fruit trees produce fruit sporadically and are sparsely distributed throughout the forest.

**B. Highlands (Ethiopia)**
Large fields are tucked among rocky hillsides and steep slopes. These fields contain a range of grasses, herbs, and small plants.

**C. Savanna Woodland (Southern Africa)**
Pockets of wooded areas are interspersed in an open, grassy landscape. The wooded areas offer a variety of trees and shrubs that appeal to a range of insects, birds, and small mammals.

## EXERCISE 5   PRIMATE SOCIAL ORGANIZATION

Work with a small group or alone to complete the following exercise.

### PART A

Examine the primate group depicted in the image provided by your instructor or in the lab Appendix.

1. What type of social group do you think this is?

2. Why?

### PART B

Examine the primate group depicted in the image provided by your instructor or in the lab Appendix.

1. What type of social group do you think this is?

2. Why?

## EXERCISE 6  NONHUMAN PRIMATE CULTURE

Work with a small group or alone to complete this exercise.

Research has found that chimpanzees in one area make spears to help them hunt bushbabies (African lorises). The chimps locate a tree trunk in which the bushbabies live. They then select a tree branch, trim off the leaves and side branches, and trim the end of the branch to form a sharpened tip. The chimps thrust these branches, like spears, into the tree to try to stab bushbabies (see the lab Appendix for associated images).

1. Is this an example of nonhuman primate culture?

2. Why or why not?

# CRITICAL THINKING QUESTIONS

On a separate sheet of paper, answer the following questions.

1. In Exercise 2, you completed observations of primates. Based on your experience, write a brief reflection. What behaviors were common? Would these behaviors be common in other primates? Did you see anything unusual or surprising? How might your experience be different if you were researching nonhuman primates in the field? Did you prefer collecting quantitative data or qualitative data? Why? What did you learn by doing this assignment?

2. This question may be completed independently or as a group discussion. In this lab, we reviewed different examples of affiliative behavior and aggressive behavior in primates. To help you make comparisons and understand the similarities and differences between these behaviors, complete the Primate Behavior Chart on the following page. Describe two examples of affiliative behavior and two examples of aggressive behavior. For each example, be sure to specify the primate or primates involved. Use material in your classroom, online, or in books and films to help you if necessary.

3. This question may be completed independently or as a group discussion. We also reviewed the different types of primate social groups. To help you make comparisons and understand the similarities and differences between these groups, complete the Primate Social Organization Chart. For each type of social group, be sure to describe the group's members (proportions of adult males, adult females, and offspring) and specify a primate or primates with this social group.

4. This question may be completed independently or as a group discussion. We also reviewed different examples of nonhuman primate culture. To help you make comparisons and understand the general pattern of these behaviors, complete the Nonhuman Primate Culture Chart. Describe three examples of nonhuman primate culture. Try to include examples from apes and monkeys. For each example, be sure to specify the primate involved. Use material in your classroom, online, or in books and films to help you if necessary.

5. As discussed in this lab, nonhuman primate conservation is a growing concern, particularly as many primate populations are rapidly declining. Locate a recent news article (from the last 5 years) about the conservation of a primate. You can use an article about an ape species (such as those discussed in this lab) or a non-ape species. Popular news sources could include magazines (such as *Discover*, *Scientific American*, and *National Geographic*) or newspapers (such as the *New York Times* or *San Francisco Chronicle*). Read the article and answer the following questions. What primate is being discussed? Why does it need to be conserved (what is negatively impacting its population)? How is this primate being conserved (what is being done to try to protect this primate from further population decline)?

## PRIMATE BEHAVIOR CHART

|  | Example | Primate(s) |
|---|---|---|
| Affiliative Behavior 1 |  |  |
| Affiliative Behavior 2 |  |  |
| Aggressive Behavior 1 |  |  |
| Aggressive Behavior 2 |  |  |

## PRIMATE SOCIAL ORGANIZATION CHART

|  | Description | Primate(s) |
|---|---|---|
| Solitary |  |  |
| Monogamy |  |  |
| Polyandry |  |  |
| Single-male Polygyny |  |  |
| Multimale Polygyny |  |  |

## NONHUMAN PRIMATE CULTURE CHART

| Example | Primate(s) |
|---|---|
|  |  |
|  |  |
|  |  |

# APPENDIX: LAB EXERCISE IMAGES

## Exercise 3 Affiliative versus Aggressive Behavior

Part A

Courtesy of Joan Silk

Part B

K. G. Preston-Mafham/Premaphotos Wildlife

## Exercise 5 Primate Social Organization

Part A

Andrew Plumptre/Getty Images

Part B

Matthias Kabel/Wikimedia Commons

# Exercise 6 Nonhuman Primate Culture

2.54 cm

Clark S. Larsen

Ryne A. Palombit, Anthropology Dept., Rutgers University

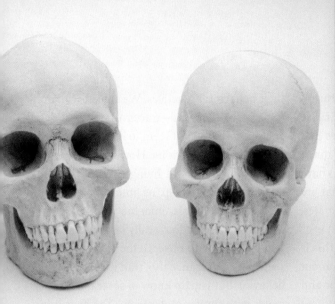

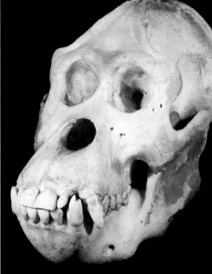

Although there are slight differences between human males and females, in other primates such as orangutans the differences between males and females can be extreme.

# LAB 12

///////////////////////////////////////////////////////////////////////////////////////////////

# Comparative Primate Anatomy

## Lab Learning Objectives

By the end of this lab, students should be able to:

- define the four major primate diets, as well as their corresponding adaptations and sample primates.

- define the major types of primate locomotion, as well as their corresponding adaptations and sample primates.

- identify males and females of a primate species using their physical features.

- identify the social organization of a primate group based on its degree of sexual dimorphism.

Human males and females look physically different. While these biological differences begin to manifest early in life, they become even more pronounced in puberty. For example, females generally grow tall and gain body fat during adolescence. Meanwhile, males grow even taller, gain more muscle mass, and gain more body and facial hair than females during adolescence. These physical differences are most obvious when we see a typical adult human male and female standing next to each other. Men are usually slightly larger and more robust, while women are usually slightly smaller and more gracile. While this is a generalization and many individuals show variation in physical morphology, these general differences in skeletal size and robusticity between males and females often enable forensic anthropologists to identify the probable sex of a victim.

Physical differences between the sexes are often even more pronounced in nonhuman primates. Many nonhuman primates follow the general patterns seen in humans, with males being larger and more robust than females. In addition, the sexes of some species may have differences in tooth size, coloration, or other features. For example, adult male gorillas are considerably larger and have more robust features than female gorillas.

Adult male gorillas also have silver-gray fur on their backs that is not seen in female gorillas. The differences between orangutan males and females are also extreme. Besides being much larger than females, adult male orangutans have additional fat pads around their faces that are not seen in females. Why would some primates, such as gorillas and orangutans, have such pronounced differences between the sexes? This is one of the issues we address in this lab about the relationship between primate behavior and anatomy.

## INTRODUCTION

In this lab, we discuss the relationship between primate behavior and anatomy. This information helps us to identify patterns that we can use to interpret the fossil record and better understand our evolutionary history. We begin with a look at the major types of primate diets and their corresponding anatomical adaptations. We then consider the major forms of primate locomotion and the anatomical traits that correspond with each type of locomotion. We conclude with a discussion of the physical, biological differences between males and females of a species and what these differences can tell us about the primates' social organization.

## PRIMATE BEHAVIOR AND ANATOMY

Some anatomical traits are better suited to a specific behavior than others. Therefore, if a population practices the same behavior for many generations, we find that particular anatomical traits are selectively favored and become more prevalent in the population. Biological anthropologists identify particular anatomical adaptations that correspond to particular primate behaviors. They then use these patterns as an analogy for interpreting the fossil record.

When we study extinct fossil species, we do not have the opportunity to directly observe the behavior of the animals or ask them about their behavioral practices. We are left with only their fossil remains—traces of their skeletal anatomy. This would seem to limit our research to anatomical questions. However, we can use what we know about living primate anatomy and behavior to help us interpret the fossil record. For example, imagine you have found a fossil species that has really large molar teeth. You are unable to observe the fossil species to see what significance this trait may have for its behavior, but you do know of several living primates with similar molar teeth. You have information about the behavior of these primates because they have been observed in the present day. This research has shown that primates with molars of this type tend to have a diet that requires a lot of chewing, such as a plant-based diet (see more on dietary adaptations below). Even though you cannot travel to the past and observe the fossil species actually eating these foods, you can hypothesize that its large molars served this purpose because there is a strong pattern of association between large molars and plant eating in living primates today. You have used a pattern of behavior and anatomy seen in living primates to interpret your fossil data. In this lab, we discuss the three most important patterns of behavior and anatomy: those related to diet, locomotion, and social organization.

## DIET AND DIETARY ADAPTATIONS

One of the most important patterns of behavior and anatomy is the relationship between diet and dietary adaptations. Some foods are more difficult to digest than others, so they will require special adaptations to facilitate digestion. Primates with different diets often have different tooth forms and digestive tracts. This is particularly useful when interpreting the fossil record because many dietary adaptations are found in teeth, and teeth are the best preserved and most common element found in the fossil record. In addition, some foods provide small bursts of energy, while others provide slow-burning energy. Because of this, primates with different diets often have different body sizes, depending on the energy available from their food.

Most primates eat a wide range of foods, including things such as fruits, leaves, insects, and even meat. However, each primate will tend to emphasize some types of food over others. For example, orangutans eat fruit, leaves, honey, and insects. Of these various foods, fruit makes up the majority of the diet, with leaves, honey, and insects serving as supplements. A primate has anatomical adaptations that suit its dietary emphasis. For example, orangutans have adaptations for fruit-eating, as opposed to leaf-eating or insect-eating, because fruit is their dietary emphasis. Among the primates, there are four different dietary emphases: insectivory, gummivory, folivory, and frugivory.

## Insectivory

**Insectivory** is a diet that emphasizes insects, such as beetles and moths. These foods provide small packets of energy. A large-bodied primate would need to eat massive quantities of insects to obtain enough energy to support its size. This is not feasible. Thus, insectivorous primates tend to have small bodies that can survive more efficiently on these small packets of energy. Insects have exoskeletons: skeletons on the outside of their bodies, rather than the inside. To get to the squishy food inside an insect, a primate must first break through the exoskeleton. Insectivores have teeth with very pointy cusps that help crunch through the hard exteriors of insects (**FIGURE 12.1**). Once an insect has been

broken into smaller pieces through chewing, it is swallowed and sent down the digestive tract. Insects are very easy to digest, so the digestive tracts of insectivores are simple and short. Many of the lorises and tarsiers are insectivorous, as are some of the marmosets (New World monkeys).

## Gummivory

**Gummivory** is a diet that emphasizes tree gums (or sap). In many trees, sap oozes out of the bark of the stem or trunk. Think of the maple tree sap that humans collect and turn into maple syrup and maple sugar candy. Some nonhuman primates also eat tree sap. Similar to insects, tree gums provide small bursts of energy, so gummivorous primates tend to be small-bodied. However, gums do not provide necessary proteins, so many gummivores supplement their diet with insects. Tree gums are trapped inside the tree bark, and the bark must be gnawed to expedite the release of gums. Gummivorous lemurs and lorises often have *dental combs* (**FIGURE 12.2**) that help to scrape tree bark and encourage gum seepage. Gums are easy to digest, like insects, so gummivorous primates also have relatively simple and short digestive tracts. In addition to some lemurs and lorises, many marmosets (New World monkeys) are gummivorous.

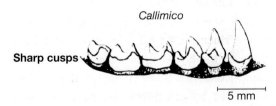

*Callimico*

Sharp cusps

5 mm

**FIGURE 12.1 Insectivore Dentition**
Insectivorous primates have teeth with sharp cusps to help crunch through insect exoskeletons.

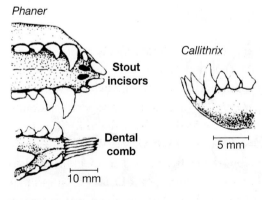

*Phaner*

Stout incisors

*Callithrix*

Dental comb

10 mm

5 mm

**FIGURE 12.2 Gummivore Dentition**
Gummivorous primates often have a special tooth structure, called a dental comb, formed by the elongation and protrusion of the lower incisors and canines.

**folivory** a diet that emphasizes leaves (foliage) and other plant parts

**sagittal crest** a ridge of bone along the midline of the cranium that allows for the attachment of extra-large chewing muscles

**frugivory** a diet that emphasizes fruit

## Folivory

**Folivory** is a diet that emphasizes leaves (foliage) and other plant parts, such as stems. Plants, particularly leaves, can be very difficult to digest because they are often very fibrous. Before they can be swallowed, plants often require extensive chewing to break them apart. We encounter this with plants in our diet. When we eat celery, it requires a lot of extra chewing to break through the long plant fibers. Similarly, when we eat a raw spinach salad, we have to chew the leaves to break them up into pieces we can swallow. Because their diet emphasizes chewing rather than biting, many folivorous primates have large molars and smaller incisors (**FIGURE 12.3**). Their molars also have special shearing crests. When folivorous primates chew, the shearing crests of their top molars work with the shearing crests of their bottom molars to shred fibrous plant material, like a pair of scissors. These primates also tend to have large mandibles and jaw muscles to help with chewing. Large jaw muscles sometimes require extra areas of bone for muscle attachment. For example, folivorous gorillas have a **sagittal crest**: an extra ridge of bone along the midline of the cranium that allows for the attachment of powerful jaw muscles (see Figure 5.8).

Even after leafy material has been shredded in the mouth, it still requires extensive digestion to maximize the extraction of available nutrients. Because of this, folivorous primates often have special adaptations in their digestive tracts. Many leaf-eating primates have elongated intestines that help digest plant material. The folivorous colobus monkeys (Old World monkeys) even have special stomachs (similar to cow stomachs) that contain bacteria to help break down the leaves. Leaves provide limited, slow-burning energy, and leaf-eating requires a longer digestive tract. Thus, folivorous primates tend to have larger bodies. The classic example of this is the folivorous gorilla, the largest living primate. Other folivorous primates include colobines, such as the langur and black-and-white colobus (leaf-eating Old World monkeys), as well as the howler monkey (New World monkeys).

## Frugivory

**Frugivory** is a diet emphasizing fruit. Fruit is relatively easy to digest and provides an intermediate amount of energy. Frugivorous primates tend to have medium-sized bodies and relatively simple digestive tracts. To properly crush fruit, frugivores have molars with low, rounded cusps that act similar to juicers to squeeze the fruit and help reduce it to pulp (**FIGURE 12.4**). Chewing fruit is much easier than chewing leaves, so the molars of a frugivore are

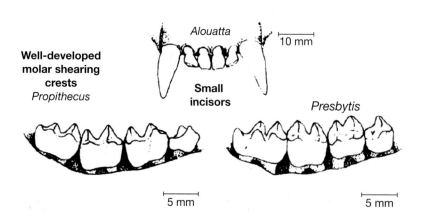

**FIGURE 12.3 Folivore Dentition**
Folivorous primates have small incisors and large, shearing molars to help shred leafy material.

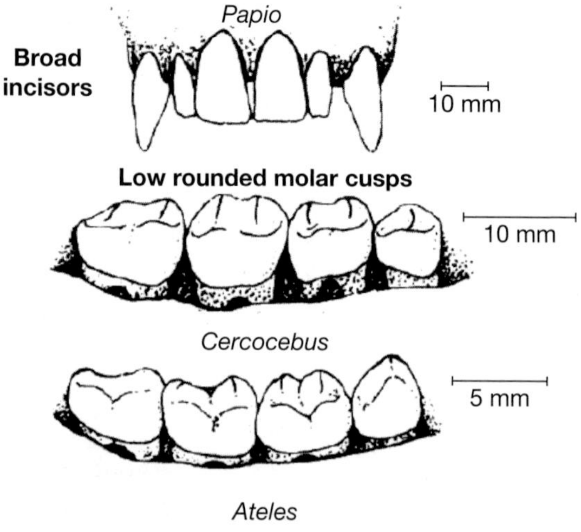

**FIGURE 12.4 Frugivore Dentition**
Frugivorous primates have large incisors and low, rounded molars to help them bite into and chew fruits.

not as large as the molars of a folivore. At the same time, biting is more important to a frugivore than it is to a folivore. While a folivore can fold and wad leaves into the mouth, a frugivore often has to take bites of fruit before it can be chewed and digested. This biting emphasis results in wider incisors in frugivores than folivores. Most primates are frugivorous, including some lemurs and lorises, most New World monkeys, numerous cercopithecines (a group of Old World monkeys), and many of the non-human apes, such as gibbons and orangutans.

# LOCOMOTION AND LOCOMOTOR ADAPTATIONS

Another important pattern of primate behavior and anatomy is the relationship between locomotion and locomotor adaptations. The term **locomotion** refers to an animal's form of movement—how they travel from one place to another. There are different forms of locomotion, and each form of locomotion requires different things of the body. For example, some locomotor strategies may rely more on the arms (**forelimbs**) while other strategies rely more on the legs (**hind limbs**). Because the areas of the body are used differently in each locomotor approach, the anatomical adaptations for each form of locomotion will vary as well.

## Vertical Clinging and Leaping

One of the more unusual forms of primate locomotion is called **vertical clinging and leaping**. In this form of locomotion, the body is oriented vertically and movement occurs by leaping from tree to tree. The primate begins by clinging upright to a tree trunk (or similar surface). It then pushes off the tree with its legs and leaps through the air. It lands on another nearby tree in an upright clinging position. In vertical clinging and leaping, the legs do most of the work—both leaping and absorbing some of the shock of landing. Thus, vertical clingers and leapers have very long legs and feet **(FIGURE 12.5)**. This form of locomotion is unusual and practiced only by some lemurs and

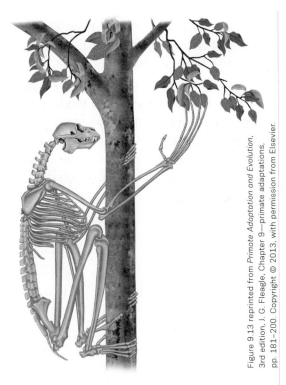

Figure 9.13 reprinted from *Primate Adaptation and Evolution*, 3rd edition, J. G. Fleagle, Chapter 9—primate adaptations, pp. 181–200. Copyright © 2013, with permission from Elsevier.

**FIGURE 12.5 Vertical Clinger and Leaper Skeleton**
Vertical clingers and leapers have very long legs and feet to help them leap from one tree to the next.

lorises, as well as the tarsiers. The adaptations are perhaps most extreme in tarsiers, whose ankles are so elongated the primates have been named for their dramatic foot (tarsal) bones. Tarsiers also have unusual tibia and fibula bones that are fused together at the distal end, providing more support and shock absorption.

## Suspensory (Brachiation, Semibrachiation)

Some primates practice forms of **suspensory locomotion**, meaning they hang (or suspend) below tree branches. There are two types of suspensory locomotion: brachiation and semibrachiation. **Brachiation** refers to a form of suspensory locomotion where movement occurs through arm-over-arm swinging. This form of locomotion is very similar to the movements humans make to cross the monkey bars on a playground. In brachiation, movement is dependent on the arms, so brachiators

**locomotion** an animal's form of movement in traveling from one place to another

**forelimb** the upper or front limb (commonly called the arm)

**hind limb** the lower or back limb (commonly called the leg)

**vertical clinging and leaping** a form of locomotion where the body is oriented vertically and movement occurs by leaping from tree to tree

**suspensory locomotion** a form of locomotion where the body is suspended (or hanging) below tree branches

**brachiation** a form of suspensory locomotion where movement occurs through arm-over-arm swinging

**semibrachiation** a form of suspensory locomotion where movement occurs through the use of the arms and a specially adapted prehensile tail, which can grasp tree branches

have very long arms (**FIGURE 12.6**). They also have long, curved fingers to help the body hang from tree branches. Brachiators need to have mobile shoulder joints to have full range of motion in their arms, so these primates have scapulas positioned on the posterior surface of the rib cage rather than on the lateral surfaces. This frees up some of their shoulder area and allows for more mobility. Brachiators, such as the gibbon, also have mobile wrists that allow the hand to stay in place holding a

tree branch while the arm and body rotate in different directions. Finally, most brachiating primates have broad chests and short lumbar areas that improve stability and decrease movement in the trunk while they suspend from tree branches.

Interestingly, humans have many of these features. When we relax our hands, we find that our normal hand position is slightly curved. In addition, our scapulas are positioned on the back of our rib cage and allow for a full 360° rotation in our arms. Humans have these features because in our evolutionary past our ancestors were brachiators, and we have maintained some of those adaptations. In fact, all apes have adaptations for brachiation, because the last common ancestor of all apes was probably a brachiator. Today, the only apes that regularly practice brachiation are the gibbons and siamangs (the lesser apes), and true brachiation is not seen in any of the non-ape primates. So, in reality, those monkey bars on the playground should probably be called "lesser ape bars."

The second type of suspensory locomotion is called **semibrachiation**. This is a form of suspensory locomotion where movement occurs through the use of the arms and tail. It is similar to brachiation because it involves hanging from tree branches, but it is not true brachiation because it does not involve arm-over-arm swinging. Semibrachiation requires a *prehensile tail* (**FIGURE 12.7**). This type of tail has the ability to grasp, so it can act as an additional hand. In fact, semibrachiators can hang from a tree branch using only their tail and keep their arms free for feeding and other activities. Because semibrachiators do not practice arm-over-arm swinging they do not have the skeletal adaptations seen in true brachiators, such as highly mobile shoulder joints. Instead, the semibrachiator skeleton resembles that of a quadrupedal primate with the addition of a prehensile tail (compare Figures 12.7 and 12.8). Semibrachiation is only seen in some of the New World monkeys, such as the howler monkeys, the spider monkeys, the woolly monkeys, and the capuchin monkeys.

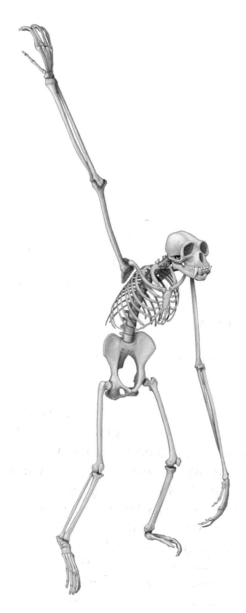

**FIGURE 12.6 Brachiator Skeleton**
Brachiators have long arms and long, curved fingers. In addition, their scapulas are positioned on the back of their rib cage, and they have mobile shoulder joints.

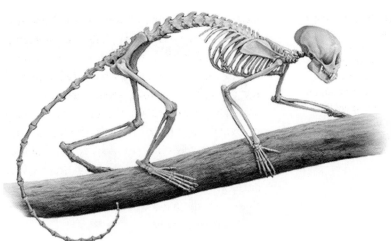

**FIGURE 12.8 Arboreal Quadruped Skeleton**
Arboreal quadrupeds have long tails to help them balance. They also sometimes have legs that are slightly longer than their arms to help them jump between tree branches.

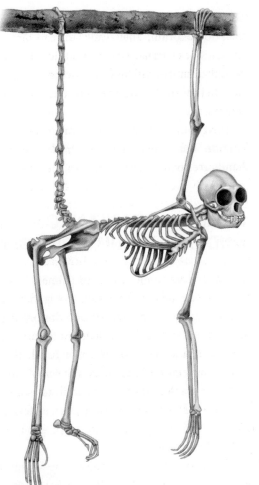

**FIGURE 12.7 Semibrachiator Skeleton**
Semibrachiators have prehensile tails that can grasp onto tree branches and act like fifth limbs.

## Quadrupedalism (Arboreal and Terrestrial, and Knuckle-walking)

The most common form of primate locomotion is **quadrupedalism**. *Quad* means "four," and *pedal* refers to feet (think of pedals for your feet on a bicycle). Quadrupedalism refers to locomotion that uses all four limbs (or is "four-footed"). There are two major types of quadrupedalism in primates: arboreal quadrupedalism and terrestrial quadrupedalism. **Arboreal quadrupedalism** is quadrupedalism that is practiced in the trees. Arboreal quadrupeds walk and run along the horizontal surfaces of tree branches and jump from branch to branch. While arboreal quadrupeds frequently

use both their arms and their legs, their legs may be slightly longer to facilitate leaping between tree branches **(FIGURE 12.8)**. An arboreal quadruped's hands and feet are prehensile and have relatively long fingers and toes to help hold on to tree branches. They also usually have a long tail to help with balance. Arboreal quadrupeds have narrow chests with scapulas positioned laterally on the rib cage. This is similar to the trunk of many other quadrupedal animals. Most primates are arboreal quadrupeds, including some lemurs, most New World monkeys, and the colobines (arboreal Old World monkeys).

The other type of quadrupedalism in primates is **terrestrial quadrupedalism**. This refers to quadrupedalism that is practiced on the ground. Terrestrial quadrupeds walk and run along the surface of the ground. This form of locomotion uses the arms and legs relatively equally. Unlike in arboreal quadrupedalism, leaping is rare in terrestrial quadrupedalism, so a terrestrial quadruped's arms and legs are more similar in length **(FIGURE 12.9)**. Compared to an arboreal quadruped, a terrestrial quadruped has shorter and more robust hands and feet, which are well suited for bearing weight and supporting the body on the ground. Terrestrial quadrupeds do not need long tails for

**quadrupedalism** a form of locomotion that uses all four limbs

**arboreal quadrupedalism** a form of quadrupedal locomotion that is practiced in the trees

**terrestrial quadrupedalism** a form of quadrupedal locomotion that is practiced on the ground

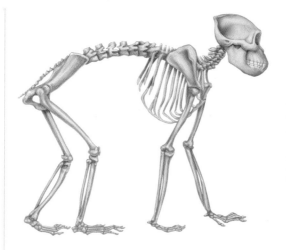

**FIGURE 12.9 Terrestrial Quadruped Skeleton**
Terrestrial quadrupeds have short tails and
arms and legs of relatively equal length.

balance, so they have much shorter tails than
arboreal quadrupeds. The trunk of a terrestrial
quadruped is very similar to that of an arboreal
quadruped, with a narrow chest and scapulas
positioned laterally on the rib cage. Terrestrial
quadrupedalism is less common than
arboreal quadrupedalism and is mostly
found in the cercopithecines (terrestrial
Old World monkeys).

There is one type of quadrupedalism that is particularly rare. It is called
**knuckle-walking**, and it is seen only in
the gorillas, chimpanzees, and bonobos. This is a form of terrestrial quadrupedalism that involves walking on the
knuckles of the hands (**FIGURE 12.10**).
Chimpanzees, bonobos, and gorillas are
unusual because they maintain adaptations for brachiation, but they spend a lot
of their time on the ground. This forces
these apes into a locomotion compro-
mise. They must balance their ancestral
brachiation traits with their current terrestrial quadrupedal behaviors. Unlike
other terrestrial quadrupeds, these apes
do not have arms and legs of similar
length or short fingers. Their brachiator
arms are much longer than their legs,
so their chests are elevated high off the
ground when their hands are on the
ground (**FIGURE 12.11**). Because they do

Keenan Ward/Corbis

**FIGURE 12.10
Knuckle-walking**
When they knuckle-walk,
primates such as gorillas
walk on the dorsal (back)
surface of the middle phalanges of all four fingers.
Their knuckles support the
weight of their upper body.

not have the short fingers optimal for terrestrial locomotion, they walk instead on the
dorsal (back) surfaces of the middle phalanges
of their hands, with their knuckles supporting their weight. Their fingers naturally curl
toward their palms while they knuckle-walk
because they have the curved fingers of a brachiator. The phalanges (finger bones) of their
hands are robust to help support their weight.

## SOCIAL ORGANIZATION AND SEXUAL DIMORPHISM

The third important pattern of primate behavior and anatomy is the relationship between
social organization and sexual dimorphism.
*Di* means "two," and *morph* refers to form. So,
**sexual dimorphism** refers to physical differences between the male form and female form
within a species. This often manifests as larger
overall body size in adult males than females

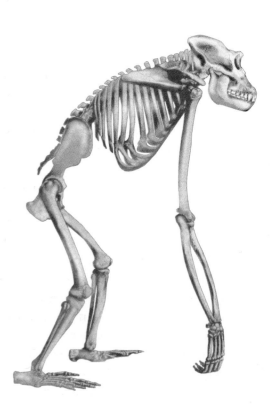

**FIGURE 12.11 Knuckle-walker Skeleton**
Knuckle-walkers have the long arms and
curved hands of a brachiator. They also have
robust finger bones.

Steffen Foerster/Shutterstock

**FIGURE 12.12 Sexual Dimorphism in Body Size**
Some primates such as baboons have pronounced sexual dimorphism in body size, where males are much larger than females.

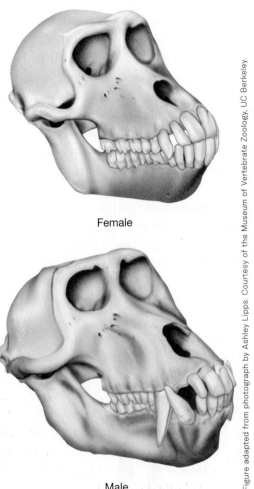

Female

Male

Figure adapted from photograph by Ashley Lipps. Courtesy of the Museum of Vertebrate Zoology, UC Berkeley.

**FIGURE 12.13 Sexual Dimorphism in the Cranium and Dentition**
Some primates have pronounced sexual dimorphism in their crania and dentition, where males have more robust cranial features and larger canine teeth than females. These crania are shown at the same scale.

(FIGURE 12.12) as well as larger canine teeth and more robust cranial features in adult males than their female counterparts (FIGURE 12.13). Humans have only slight sexual dimorphism, particularly when compared to other primates. Human males tend to be a little larger and more robust than females, and size differences are used by forensic anthropologists to help sex skeletons (see Lab 7 for more information). However, as we asked at the start of this lab, why do some primates have more pronounced sexual dimorphism than others?

Degrees of sexual dimorphism relate to degrees of male–male competition. Primate species with more male–male competition also have more pronounced sexual dimorphism. In contrast, primates with less male–male competition have less sexual dimorphism. To understand why this relationship exists, we must consider why sexual dimorphism may have evolved. It is important to recognize that sexual dimorphism is the result of an increase and exaggeration of male size. It is not that female body types are smaller versions of male types. Rather, male body types are enlarged versions of female types. These enlarged traits are selectively favored because they improve reproductive success. Bigger, more robust males outreproduce their smaller, more gracile male competitors. Their enlarged size and features may help them to win direct competitions with smaller males,

so they are able to maintain access to females for reproduction. Furthermore, a male with enlarged traits may be able to maintain access to females by simply threatening males at a distance and avoiding direct competition entirely. In either case, the exaggerated traits of robust males are passed on preferentially to the next generation. Over time, we end up with populations with extreme differences in male and female body types.

Because sexual dimorphism relates to male–male competition, it also relates to social organization. Some types of primate social organization have more intense male–male

**knuckle-walking** a form of terrestrial quadrupedalism that involves walking on the knuckles of the hands

**sexual dimorphism** the physical differences between mature males and females of a species

competition than others. Therefore, in some types of social groups, we are likely to see more pronounced sexual dimorphism than others. In monogamous social groups, male–male competition is limited. Most adult males will be partnered with an adult female and be successfully reproducing. The males do not need to compete for mating partners. We see the least amount of sexual dimorphism in these monogamous groups (**FIGURE 12.14**).

In single-male polygynous groups (and some solitary groups), male–male competition is extremely high. One adult male will have access to a group of females. This leaves many adult males wandering around without sexual partners. These unpartnered males will regularly challenge a male with females and attempt to take over his group or territory. In addition, there is little to limit the intensity of the competition. At the end of the day, the males competing with one another live separately and do not need to maintain a social relationship. Competition in these circumstances can be particularly violent. Consequently, sexual dimorphism is extremely pronounced in single-male groups (Figure 12.14).

Finally, in multimale polygynous groups, male–male competition is relatively high. An adult male will have access to multiple females within his group, but access to mates may be hindered by the position of a male in the social hierarchy. Higher status males will have access to better or more mating partners of the right age and fertility. Thus, competition exists between males trying to improve their social status and their consequent access to females. In contrast to the single-male polygynous group, there is however a limit to the competition within a multimale group. At the end of the day, these males do often continue to live together and maintain social relationships. This usually prevents the competition from becoming particularly violent. As a result, sexual dimorphism in multimale polygynous groups is pronounced but not as extreme as in single-male groups (Figure 12.14). By understanding the relationship between sexual dimorphism and social organization, a biological anthropologist can use the degree of sexual dimorphism present in a population to hypothesize about and infer the likely social organization of a group (just as they can use dietary adaptations to infer diet and locomotor adaptations to infer mode of locomotion).

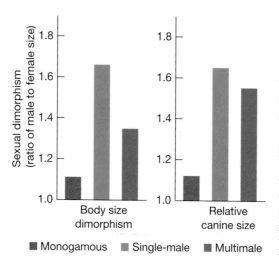

**FIGURE 12.14 Sexual Dimorphism and Social Organization**
The degree of sexual dimorphism in a primate species relates to their social organization. Primates in monogamous groups have little male–male competition and very little sexual dimorphism (near a value of 1.0, which represents no dimorphism). Primates in single-male groups have intense male–male competition and the highest levels of sexual dimorphism. Primates in multimale groups have relatively high male–male competition and relatively high sexual dimorphism.

# CONCEPT REVIEW QUESTIONS

Name: _____    Section: _____

Course: _____    Date: _____

Answer the following questions in the space provided.

1. I have molars with pointy cusps and a simple digestive system. What type of diet do I have?
   A. Insectivorous
   B. Gummivorous
   C. Frugivorous
   D. Folivorous

2. True or false? A gummivorous primate is likely to have a large body size.

3. I have molars with shearing crests and a complex stomach. What type of diet do I have?
   A. Frugivorous
   B. Insectivorous
   C. Folivorous
   D. Gummivorous

4. Define brachiation.

5. Semibrachiation is made possible by the presence of what trait?

6. True or false? An arboreal quadruped moves on all fours on the ground.

7. I have arms and legs of similar length, robust hands and feet, and a short tail. What type of locomotion do I practice?
   A. Terrestrial quadrupedalism
   B. Brachiation
   C. Arboreal quadrupedalism
   D. Vertical clinging and leaping

8. I have long arms, a mobile shoulder, and very robust finger bones. What type of locomotion do I practice?
   A. Brachiation
   B. Arboreal quadrupedalism
   C. Vertical clinging and leaping
   D. Knuckle-walking

9. Describe *one* sexually dimorphic trait in primates. Be sure to note how the trait appears in females and in males.

10. True or false? A single-male polygynous group is likely to have more pronounced sexual dimorphism than a monogamous group.

# LAB EXERCISES

Name: _____   Section: _____

Course: _____   Date: _____

## EXERCISE 1   DIET AND DIETARY ADAPTATIONS 1

Work with a small group or alone to complete this exercise. Refer to the mystery primate dentitions provided by your instructor (or those depicted in the lab Appendix) to complete the chart below. Describe the incisors, molars, and muscle attachment on the mandible of each mystery primate. Using this trait information, also determine the likely diet of each mystery primate, and name an example of one primate that has this diet.

|  | Mystery Primate A | Mystery Primate B | Mystery Primate C | Mystery Primate D |
|---|---|---|---|---|
| Incisors |  |  |  |  |
| Molars |  |  |  |  |
| Mandible Size and Muscle Attachment |  |  |  |  |
| Diet |  |  |  |  |
| Example Primate |  |  |  |  |

## EXERCISE 2   DIET AND DIETARY ADAPTATIONS 2

Work with a small group or alone to complete this exercise.
    Review the primate descriptions below. For each primate, describe the primate's likely body size and digestive tract.

1. Primate A is an insectivore that eats a lot of moths, stick insects, and grasshoppers. These foods provide small packets of energy that are easy to digest.

    » Body size:

    » Digestive tract:

2. Primate B is a frugivore that eats a lot of berries, figs, and other tree fruits. These foods provide intermediate packets of energy that are relatively easy to digest.

    » Body size:

    » Digestive tract:

3. Primate C is a gummivore that eats a lot of tree sap. This food provides small packets of energy that are easily digested.

    » Body size:

    » Digestive tract:

4. Primate D is a folivore that eats a wide variety of leaves, stems, and young plant shoots. This food provides limited, slow-burning energy and is difficult to digest.

    » Body size:

    » Digestive tract:

## EXERCISE 3   LOCOMOTION AND LOCOMOTOR ADAPTATIONS 1

Work with a small group or alone to complete this exercise. Use the mystery primate skeletons provided by your instructor (or those depicted in the lab Appendix) to complete the chart below. Describe the scapula position, body and limb proportions (arm and leg length, size of chest, etc.), and tail of each mystery primate. Using this trait information, also determine the likely form of locomotion of each mystery primate, and name an example of one primate that has this form of locomotion.

|  | Mystery Primate A | Mystery Primate B |
|---|---|---|
| Scapula Position |  |  |
| Body and Limb Proportions |  |  |
| Tail |  |  |
| Locomotion |  |  |
| Example Primate |  |  |

## EXERCISE 4   LOCOMOTION AND LOCOMOTOR ADAPTATIONS 2

Work with a small group or alone to complete this exercise. Use the mystery primate skeletons provided by your instructor (or those depicted in the lab Appendix) to complete the chart below. Describe the scapula position, body and limb proportions (arm and leg length, size of chest, etc.), and tail of each mystery primate. Using this trait information, also determine the likely form of locomotion of each mystery primate, and name an example of one primate that has this form of locomotion.

|  | Mystery Primate A | Mystery Primate B | Mystery Primate C |
|---|---|---|---|
| Scapula Position |  |  |  |
| Body and Limb Proportions |  |  |  |
| Tail |  |  |  |
| Locomotion |  |  |  |
| Example Primate |  |  |  |

## EXERCISE 5   SEXUAL DIMORPHISM

Work with a small group or alone to complete this exercise. Examine the mystery primates provided by your instructor (or those depicted in the lab Appendix). These represent adult individuals from the same species.

1. Which mystery primate is female?


2. Which mystery primate is male?

3. Describe *two* traits you used to make this distinction.

EXERCISE 6 **SOCIAL ORGANIZATION AND SEXUAL DIMORPHISM**

Work with a small group or alone to complete this exercise. Examine the mystery primate species provided by your instructor (or those depicted in the lab Appendix). These represent an adult male and an adult female from two mystery primate species, A and B.

1. Which mystery primate species has a single-male polygynous group?

2. Which mystery primate species has a multimale polygynous group?

3. Describe *one* trait you used to make this distinction.

# CRITICAL THINKING QUESTIONS

On a separate sheet of paper, answer the following questions.

1. This question may be completed independently or as a group discussion. Imagine a biological anthropologist 10,000 years in the future is examining our fossil remains. The anthropologist notices that humans have broad incisors and molars with rounded cusps. What diet would these traits indicate? Would this be accurate? Why might humans have these traits, as opposed to the specialized teeth we see with other primate diets?

2. This question may be completed independently or as a group discussion. What adaptations for brachiation do you have in your body today? Why do humans have these adaptations? What adaptations for brachiation are you missing? Why do you lack some of the brachiator adaptations seen in gibbons?

3. This question may be completed independently or as a group discussion. Consider the degree of sexual dimorphism in humans. What does this suggest about our social organization in the present? Many of our fossil relatives have more sexual dimorphism than we do; what does this suggest about our ancestral social organization?

4. This question may be completed independently or as a group discussion. You come across a primate living in the grassy highlands of eastern Africa. It has arms and legs that are relatively equal in length and a short tail. It has small incisors and large, bilophodont molars. This primate is female, but males of her species have much larger bodies and canine teeth than females. Males also have extra fur around their chests and heads that is not seen in females. What is the likely diet of this primate? Give one trait that supports your determination. What is the likely form of locomotion of this primate? Give one trait that supports your determination. What is the likely social organization of this primate? Give one trait that supports your determination.

5. In this lab, we reviewed primate diets and dietary adaptations, as well as forms of locomotion and locomotor adaptations. To help you make comparisons and understand the general pattern of these behaviors, complete the two charts that follow. In the Primate Diet Chart, describe the adaptations associated with each diet and a sample primate that has this diet. Similarly, in the Primate Locomotion Chart, describe the adaptations associated with each form of locomotion and a sample primate that practices this locomotion.

## PRIMATE DIET CHART

|  | Adaptations | Primate(s) |
| --- | --- | --- |
| Insectivory |  |  |
| Gummivory |  |  |
| Frugivory |  |  |
| Folivory |  |  |

Name: _____  Date: _____

## PRIMATE LOCOMOTION CHART

| | Adaptations | Primate(s) |
|---|---|---|
| Vertical Clinging and Leaping | | |
| Brachiation | | |
| Semibrachiation | | |
| Arboreal Quadrupedalism | | |
| Terrestrial Quadrupedalism | | |
| Knuckle-walking | | |

# APPENDIX:
# LAB EXERCISE IMAGES

## Exercise 1 Diet and Dietary Adaptations 1

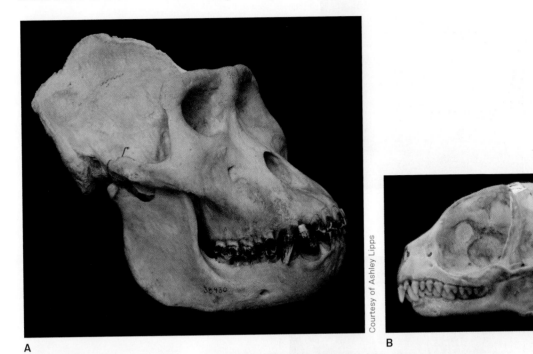

A

Courtesy of Ashley Lipps

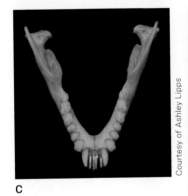

Courtesy of Ashley Lipps

B

Courtesy of Ashley Lipps

C

Courtesy of Ashley Lipps

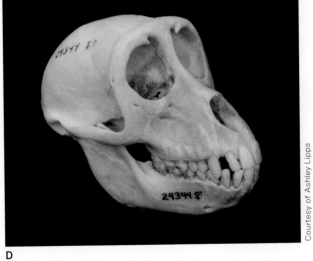

Courtesy of Ashley Lipps

D

## Exercise 3 Locomotion and Locomotor Adaptations 1

Courtesy of Ashley Lipps

A

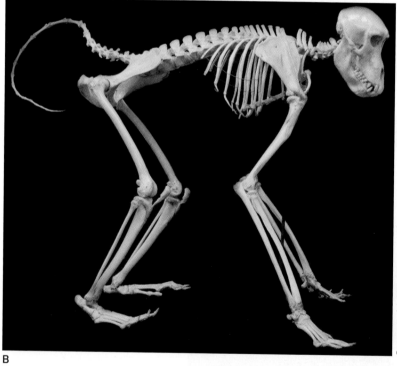

Courtesy of Ashley Lipps

B

# Exercise 4 Locomotion and Locomotor Adaptations 2

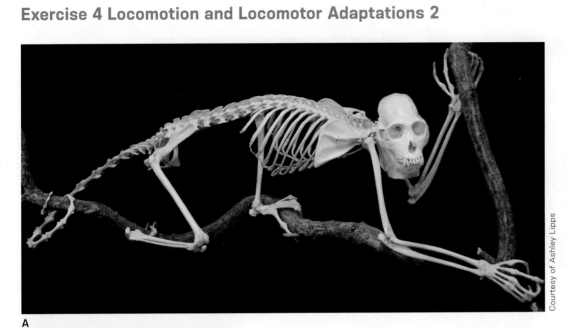

Courtesy of Ashley Lipps

**A**

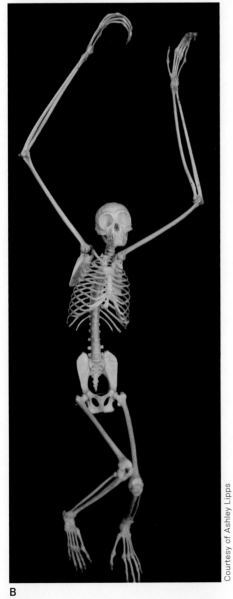

Courtesy of Ashley Lipps

**B**

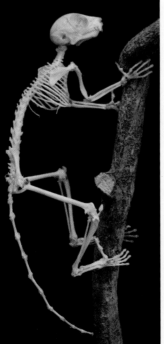

Courtesy of Ashley Lipps

**C**

## Exercise 5 Sexual Dimorphism

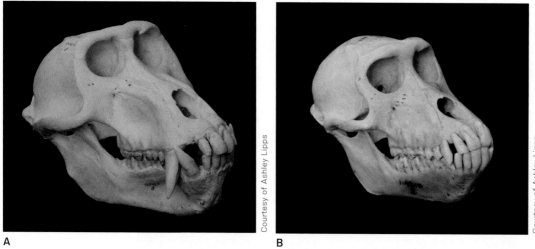

Courtesy of Ashley Lipps

A

B

Courtesy of Ashley Lipps

Note: These crania are shown at the same scale.

# Exercise 6 Social Organization and Sexual Dimorphism

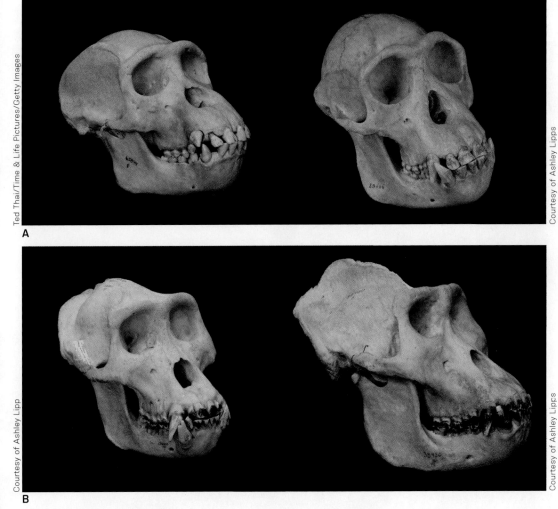

Ted Thai/Time & Life Pictures/Getty Images

Courtesy of Ashley Lipps

A

Courtesy of Ashley Lipp

Courtesy of Ashley Lipps

B

Note: The crania in A are shown at the same scale, and the crania in B are shown at the same scale.

### PART FOUR

# PALEOANTHROPOLOGY

For decades, paleoanthropologists such as Mary and Louis Leakey, seen here in the mid-1900s, have looked for fossilized remains that tell us how our ancestors may have looked and behaved. This information helps us to better understand human evolutionary history since our split from the other apes.

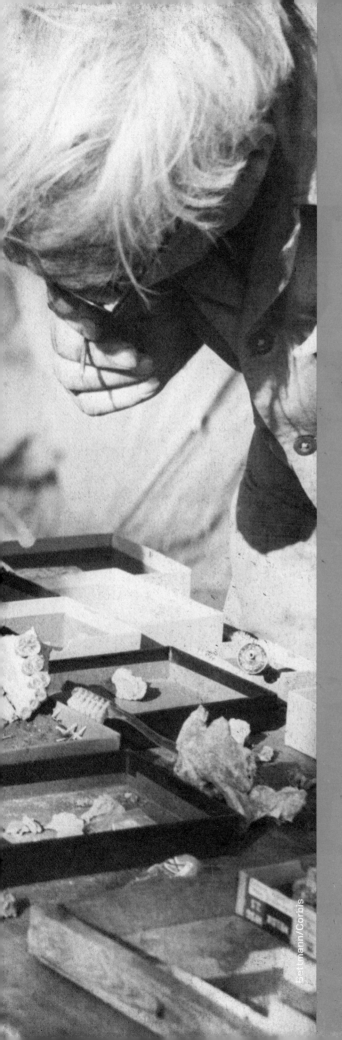

Bettmann/Corbis

# LAB 13: PRIMATE EVOLUTION

## WHAT TOPICS ARE COVERED IN THIS LAB?

- An introduction to the process of fossilization
- An overview of mammalian evolution
- A review of the major fossil finds in primate evolution
- An introduction to the methods used to date fossil sites

# LAB 14: IDENTIFYING THE HUMAN LINEAGE

## WHAT TOPICS ARE COVERED IN THIS LAB?

- A critical review of different approaches to identifying the human lineage
- An introduction to bipedalism and its associated skeletal adaptations
- A look at our earliest possible ancestors since our split from the chimpanzees

# LAB 15: THE AUSTRALOPITHECINES AND EARLY MEMBERS OF THE GENUS *HOMO*

## WHAT TOPICS ARE COVERED IN THIS LAB?

- An overview of the major fossil *Australopithecus* species
- A comparison of the different australopithecines
- An overview of the first species in the *Homo* genus, and a look at the debate surrounding their classification

# LAB 16: LATER MEMBERS OF THE GENUS *HOMO*

## WHAT TOPICS ARE COVERED IN THIS LAB?

- An overview of the later species in the *Homo* genus
- A review of the migration of our ancestors out of Africa
- A comparison of alternate explanations about the origin and spread of our species
- A consideration of the relationship between Neanderthals and humans

Publiphoto/Science Source

Based on evidence of a large crater in Mexico, we know that an asteroid crashed to Earth around 66 mya. This led to the extinction of many of the dinosaurs, but small, nocturnal mammals alive at this time survived and became the diverse group of animals we know today.

## Lab Learning Objectives

By the end of this lab, students should be able to:

- describe the major changes throughout mammalian evolution.

- describe at least one fossil primate for every major group of living primates, including a description of the temporal and spatial distribution, main features, and relationship of the fossil to living primates.

- identify the key trends in primate evolution and place these trends in chronological order.

LAB 13

# Primate Evolution

Imagine Earth 66 million years ago (mya)—it is the Mesozoic era, the Age of Reptiles. Flowering plants are proliferating, and reptiles, including dinosaurs, live throughout the world. For the past 200 million years, a group of small animals has lived side by side with their more famous dinosaur contemporaries. These overlooked animals are generally small, covered in fur, and have specialized teeth. They are nocturnal mammals and come out at night to eat primarily insects. They are less subject to predation at night, so their nocturnal lifestyle is helping them to survive in the dinosaur-dominated landscape. However, they are by no means thriving. Reptiles occupy most of Earth's habitats, and they are stiff competition for the small, nocturnal mammals.

At around this time, something unexpected happens. A large asteroid crashes into Earth, leaving a 180-kilometer-wide crater near the Yucatán peninsula of Mexico. The crash causes massive clouds of dust that block sunlight for months (or possibly years) and triggers a dramatic drop in temperatures. Many organisms are ill adapted to these new environmental conditions, and 50% of the world's animal families (including many of the dinosaurs) go extinct. In contrast, the small nocturnal mammals begin to flourish. As the dinosaurs go extinct and vacate various habitats, the smaller mammals move in. Once in a new habitat, they adapt to their current environmental circumstances, undergoing rapid diversification.

Some become well suited to tree dwelling, while others are more suited to open deserts. Others become better suited for life in water, and still others become suited to life in the air. This formerly struggling group of mammals quickly becomes a diverse and successful class of organisms. The Age of Reptiles is over, and the Age of Mammals begins.

## INTRODUCTION

In this lab, we discuss the important fossil species and major trends of primate evolution. This information helps us place our own evolutionary history into a broader chronological context. We begin with an introduction to the process of fossilization. We then briefly consider the major trends in mammalian evolution. Next, we examine primate evolution more specifically. We review the key fossil species associated with the major groups of living primates. We conclude with a discussion of the complexities of dating fossil sites.

## WHAT IS A FOSSIL?

**Fossils** are the traces or remains of an organism preserved in rock. In some cases, fossils are preserved impressions left by organisms, such as their footprints or tracks. In other cases, fossils are formed as the organic materials of an organism decay and are slowly replaced by minerals from the surrounding environment. Any organic material can become a fossil, but fossils that are of interest to paleoanthropologists are usually formed from bones and teeth. It is important to remember that fossils are basically rocks. For this reason, they often lack organic material and DNA. Although some remains are partly fossilized and do contain small pockets of DNA, this is uncommon. Trace amounts of DNA are more likely to be found in remains that have fossilized more recently (see Lab 16 for an example).

Not all organisms become fossilized when they die. The remains of an organism will undergo the **fossilization** process only under very specific conditions (**FIGURE 13.1**). The organic material must decay slowly to be successfully replaced by surrounding minerals. Conditions that speed up decay are not good for fossilization. For example, if an organism dies and is left exposed to weather or predators, decomposition will occur more rapidly. Similarly, if an organism dies in an oxygen-rich environment with abundant bacteria, its remains will decay quickly. In these situations of rapid decomposition, fossilization is unlikely. At the same time, soil and geological conditions are big factors in the fossilization process. If the surrounding soil is too acidic or has too much groundwater, organic material will dissolve too quickly for fossilization to take place. In addition, if there is too much geological pressure or activity, the bones and teeth may be deformed so much that the fossil is greatly distorted or not formed at all.

There are several key biases in the fossil record that we must always take into account. First, the distribution of fossils is not uniform across time and space. As we discussed, fossilization requires specific environmental conditions. In many parts of the world, at many different times, the environment has not been conducive to fossilization. This causes big gaps in the fossil record. For example, we have virtually no fossil record for the time period when the last common ancestors of humans and the other great apes were alive. These ancestral African species would have lived in rainforests where conditions do not readily allow for fossilization. Similarly, even in time periods where we have extensive fossil data from one area, we might not have any fossil data from a nearby area. For example, we have a lot of fossil material from our ancestors from eastern and southern Africa but virtually none from western and northern Africa. Our ancestors probably lived throughout the vast continent, but ideal conditions for fossilization at that time are found only in the eastern and southern areas.

The issue of fossil distribution is further complicated by continental drift. In the past, all of the land on Earth was concentrated in one very

**fossil** the rock-like traces or remains of an organism

**fossilization** the process of fossil formation that occurs under certain conditions

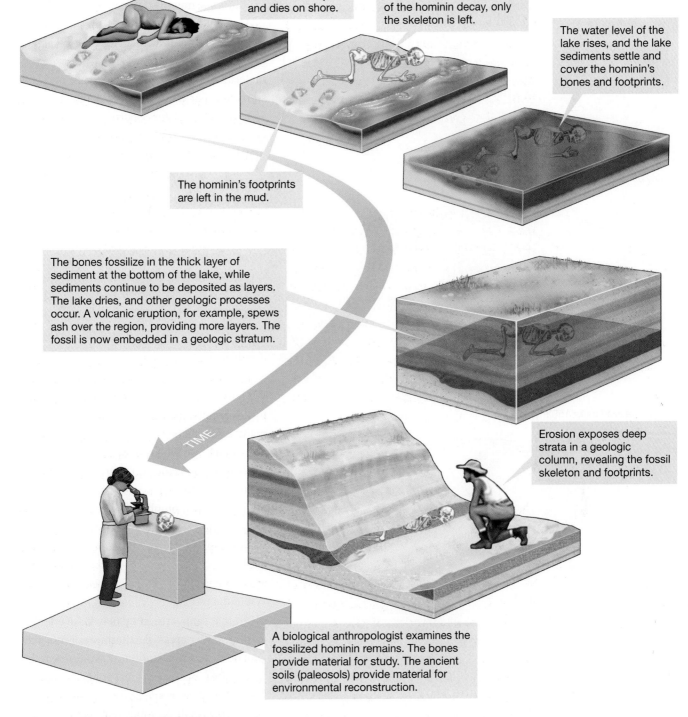

A hominin collapses and dies on shore.

After the soft-tissue remains of the hominin decay, only the skeleton is left.

The water level of the lake rises, and the lake sediments settle and cover the hominin's bones and footprints.

The hominin's footprints are left in the mud.

The bones fossilize in the thick layer of sediment at the bottom of the lake, while sediments continue to be deposited as layers. The lake dries, and other geologic processes occur. A volcanic eruption, for example, spews ash over the region, providing more layers. The fossil is now embedded in a geologic stratum.

TIME

Erosion exposes deep strata in a geologic column, revealing the fossil skeleton and footprints.

A biological anthropologist examines the fossilized hominin remains. The bones provide material for study. The ancient soils (paleosols) provide material for environmental reconstruction.

**FIGURE 13.1 The Process of Fossilization**
Only a handful of organisms become fossils when they die. Fossilization requires specific environmental conditions and processes.

large landmass (**FIGURE 13.2**). This then broke up into separate pieces (continents) that begin shifting apart. This process of shifting is known as **continental drift**, and it continues today. As the continental plates drift, the movement causes earthquakes and other geological events. At different times in the past, the continents we know today were in very different places. These former locations, along with larger variations in climate, allowed for very different primate

**continental drift**
the shifting of the continents that is caused by the movement of Earth's continental plates

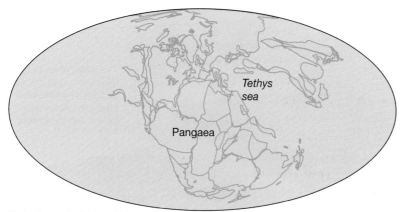

Early Jurassic (about 200 mya)

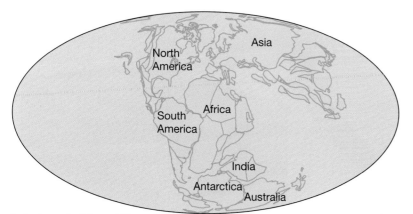

Late Jurassic (about 150 mya)

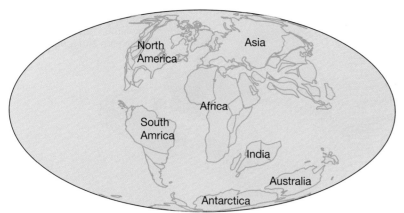

Late Cretaceous (about 70 mya)

**FIGURE 13.2 Continental Drift**
Throughout Earth's history, the continental plates have shifted. In the past, the continents we know today were in very different locations around the world.

distributions in the past than we see today. For example, around 50 mya, similar early primate species were distributed throughout North America and Europe. At that time, the two continents were connected and shared similar environments, so primate species could easily move between regions and live in either area.

In addition to these issues affecting fossil distribution, we must also take into account the fact that even if fossils are formed, they are not necessarily well preserved. Later geological activity, such as earthquakes, may shift or destroy fossil materials. This can lead to more gaps in the fossil record. For example, one site may have a lot of fossil material for a particular time period, but it may have nothing for the period immediately after. Events that occurred after fossilization may have randomly destroyed some of the fossils but not others. Of course, geological events that occurred after fossilization may also help paleoanthropologists today. For example, Olduvai Gorge is a well-researched location in Tanzania with fossil remains from many of our ancestral species. Erosion and other geological forces in the area in more recent years (postfossilization) have created a gorge that has exposed lower levels of sediment and improved access to deeply buried fossils.

Lastly, we as researchers bias the fossil record. We tend to look in a limited number of places for fossil remains. Part of the reason is because many researchers have found remains in these areas before, so we know the area is conducive to fossilization. However, part of the decision about where to look is also based on our own preferences, our emphasis on certain time periods or regions, or current events in the region. For example, researchers interested in a particular species may return to the same regions where others have located the species in the past. While the researcher is likely to find more fossils in that same area, they may be overlooking fossils in other areas. Furthermore, a researcher may be forced to abandon or avoid research in certain areas because of local political conflict or war. The choices made about where to look for fossils may result in some areas being overstudied while others are left completely untouched.

## BEFORE THE PRIMATES

Earth's history is divided into different time spans. The smaller chunks of time are the *epochs*. Numerous epochs form *periods*, which form *eras*; multiple eras then form an *eon*. Each of these divisions is given a name, and increasing detail is provided for more recent times. This time scale is used by geologists, biological anthropologists, and other scientists to help organize the history of Earth and its living creatures.

Although numerous plants, fish, insects, and amphibians flourished in the Paleozoic (545 to 245 mya), the Mesozoic (245 to 66 mya) is the more famous era in Earth's history (**FIGURE 13.3**). Often referred to as the Age of Reptiles, the Mesozoic is known for the proliferation of reptiles, such as dinosaurs. During this same time, however, we also see the very first mammals around 220 mya. These mammals were small, rodent-like animals that were usually nocturnal. As discussed at the beginning of this lab, a large asteroid crashed to Earth and altered environmental conditions around 66 mya. Many of the Earth's animals, including many of the dinosaurs, went extinct as a result.

**FIGURE 13.3 Major Events in the Evolution of Life**
Many early plants, fish, insects, and amphibians lived in the Paleozoic era (the Cambrian through Permian periods). The Mesozoic era (the Triassic through Cretaceous periods) was the Age of Reptiles when dinosaurs flourished and early mammals first appeared on Earth. Our recent evolution as primates and humans occurred in the Cenozoic era (the Paleocene through Holocene epochs).

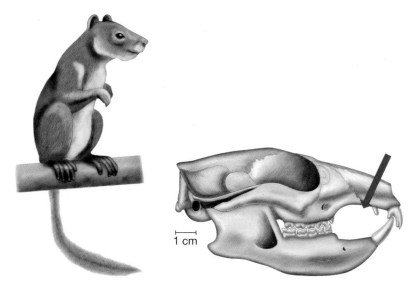

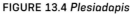
1 cm

**FIGURE 13.4 *Plesiadapis***
Early plesiadapiforms, such as *Plesiadapis*, would probably have been more rodent-like than many modern primates. They had long snouts and specialized front teeth separated from their back teeth by a toothless gap (arrow).

This marked the end of the Mesozoic and the beginning of the Cenozoic (66 mya to present).

During the Cenozoic era, the mammals thrived and proliferated. They moved into the habitats vacated by the dinosaurs and other extinct animals, and they quickly diversified into new environments. Most of the major mammal groups that we know today were formed as a result, such as bats, rodents, horses, and whales. The mammals were so successful in the Cenozoic that the era is often called the Age of Mammals. During this time, when mammals as a whole were rapidly diversifying, the first primates appeared on Earth.

## PRIMATE EVOLUTION

There is a lot of debate about what were the very first primates. During the Paleocene epoch (66 to 56 mya) a group of diverse primate-like mammals lived in North America, Europe, and Asia. These mammals are called **plesiadapiforms**. These species were initially interpreted as the first primates because they share some features in common with primates, such as generalized molar teeth. The later plesiadapiforms often share additional traits with primates, such as long fingers and short palms. However, many researchers have pointed out that despite some

similarities, the plesiadapiforms lack several important primate features. For example, many plesiadapiforms do not have bony eye orbit structures, nails, grasping hands and feet, or a large brain for their body size—all characteristic traits of primates. In addition, plesiadapiforms, such as the genus *Plesiadapis*, often have an elongated snout with specialized front teeth separated from their other teeth by a toothless gap (**FIGURE 13.4**).

### The Early Lemurs and Lorises

While the earliest primates are not clearly identifiable in the fossil record, by the Eocene (56 to 34 mya), we see numerous fossil species in North America and Europe that have clear, defining primate features. These fossils, known as the **adapiforms**, are generally small to medium in size (similar to modern lemurs). The adapiforms, such as the genus *Adapis*, have forward-facing eyes, postorbital bars, grasping hands and feet, nails instead of claws, and larger brains than other mammals (**FIGURE 13.5**). Although some adapiforms have large eyes that suggest nocturnal behavior, most adapiforms have relatively small eyes and appear to have been diurnal. Their **postcranial** traits (those below the head) indicate likely arboreal locomotion, such as climbing and leaping. Many researchers believe the adapiforms are related to living lemurs or lorises. However, the adapiforms lack some key lemur and loris traits (such as the dental comb), so their relationship is unclear.

**plesiadapiform** one of a group of diverse primate-like mammals that lived over 56 mya and may be among the first primates

**adapiform** one of a group of early primates that lived between 56 and 34 mya

**postcranial** relating to the bones below or behind the head

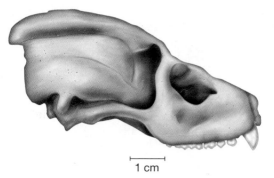
1 cm

**FIGURE 13.5 *Adapis***
Adapiforms, such as the *Adapis* specimen seen here, had forward-facing eyes, postorbital bars, and relatively large brains for their body size. Many adapiforms had small eyes, suggesting a diurnal lifestyle.

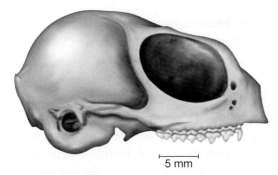

**FIGURE 13.6 *Shoshonius***
Omomyoids, such as the *Shoshonius* specimen seen here, had forward-facing eyes, postorbital bars, and relatively large brains for their body size. Many omomyoids have large eyes, suggesting a nocturnal lifestyle. They also have shorter snouts than adapiforms.

## The Early Tarsiers

During the Eocene (56 to 34 mya), we also see another group of primates, known as the **omomyoids**, throughout North America and Eurasia. Similar to the adapiforms, the omomyoids are definite primates with forward-facing eyes, postorbital bars, grasping hands and feet, nails instead of claws, and large brains. However, compared to adapiforms, omomyoids (such as the genus *Shoshonius*) have shorter snouts and smaller bodies **(FIGURE 13.6)**. The teeth of different species indicate various diets, including frugivory and insectivory. Omomyoids tend to have very large eyes, indicating nocturnal behavior. They also have some postcranial indicators for a leaping form of locomotion. Some researchers consider the omomyoids to be related to modern lorises, but other researchers consider them to be more closely related to tarsiers. As with the adapiforms, the omomyoids lack some of the key traits seen in modern lorises (such as the dental comb) or in modern tarsiers (such as some of the special leaping adaptations), so their relationship remains unclear.

## The Early Anthropoids

It is unclear whether anthropoids evolved from adapiforms, omomyoids, or another primate group. What is apparent is that near the end of the Eocene, we begin to see primates with true anthropoid traits. For example, the genus *Eosimias* dates to around 42 mya in China. It includes some of the smallest known primate species (living or extinct), with dental and postcranial traits that suggest it is an anthropoid. The classification and significance of *Eosimias* and its Eocene relatives are debated. Some researchers believe it is the earliest anthropoid because of its anthropoid-like traits, such as a New World monkey-like dental formula and foot adaptations for arboreal quadrupedalism. Other researchers argue it is more closely related to nonanthropoids because of such features as its insectivorous diet and incredibly small body size (individuals were estimated to weigh less than half a pound).

Toward the end of the Eocene and during the Oligocene (34 to 23 mya), numerous anthropoids are known. Many of these anthropoid species can be found in the Fayum region of Egypt. Today this area is a desert, but in the early Oligocene it was a forested swampland and home to countless species of plants and animals, including numerous anthropoids. Perhaps the most well-known of these anthropoids is *Aegyptopithecus*, with one known species, *Aegyptopithecus zeuxis* **(FIGURE 13.7)**. Dating to around 30 mya, *Aegyptopithecus* has several general

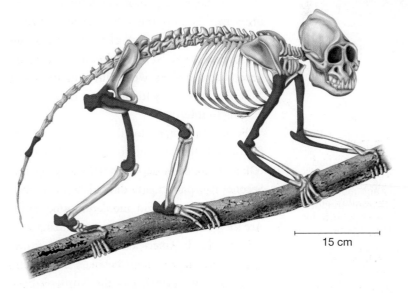

**FIGURE 13.7 *Aegyptopithecus***
Parts of the *Aegyptopithecus* cranium and some postcranial bones (shown in red) have been recovered. This skeletal evidence suggests that *Aegyptopithecus* was an early anthropoid with full bony enclosure of the eye orbits and a fused mandible. In addition, it had a 2.1.2.3 dental formula and large brain for its body, similar to modern catarrhines.

anthropoid traits, such as full bony enclosure of the orbit and a fused mandible. It also has numerous specifically catarrhine-like traits. For example, it has a 2.1.2.3 dental formula and a larger brain than earlier fossil primates. It has a body size similar to that of many living monkeys and postcranial traits that suggest it was an arboreal quadruped. Its dental traits indicate a frugivorous diet, although it also has a sagittal crest and corresponding large chewing muscles. It also appears to have been sexually dimorphic, possibly indicating some form of polygynous social organization. This combination of traits suggests that *Aegyptopithecus* was probably an early catarrhine anthropoid.

### The Early New World Monkeys

While catarrhines probably evolved from *Aegyptopithecus* or something similar in the Old World, the evolution of the New World primate lineage is less clear. The oldest known South American primate is called *Branisella* **(FIGURE 13.8)**. This primate is found in Bolivia and dates to around 26 mya (late Oligocene). It shares several dental traits with living New World monkeys, such as the presence of three premolars in each mouth quadrant. Its teeth also indicate a frugivorous or folivorous diet. *Branisella* is certainly the earliest known platyrrhine to date, but numerous Miocene (23 to 5.3 mya) New World monkeys have been discovered as well. Unfortunately, the New World monkey fossil record is very challenging to interpret.

First, while many fossil species have been discovered, the primate fossil record of Central and South America is relatively sparse. Second, it is particularly difficult to determine where the New World monkeys came from. Are they descended from Eocene primates that lived in North America? If so, why are there no known primate fossils between the Eocene (56 to 34 mya) primates of the North and the late Oligocene to Miocene (26 to 5.3 mya) primates of the South? Alternatively, are the New World primates descended from an anthropoid from the Old World? If this is the case, how did the primate get from Africa to South America

when the continents were already separated by the Atlantic Ocean? Unfortunately, these questions remain unanswered.

### The Early Old World Monkeys

Returning to the Old World, remember that the catarrhines probably evolved from something along the lines of *Aegyptopithecus*. Early catarrhines would have then split into the two distinct groups we recognize today: the Old World monkeys and the apes. The oldest genus in the distinct Old World monkey lineage is *Victoriapithecus*, with one known fossil species, *Victoriapithecus macinnesi* **(FIGURE 13.9)**. Although *Victoriapithecus* first appears in Africa around 19 mya (early Miocene), it is primarily known from a site in Kenya that dates to around 15 mya (middle Miocene). *Victoriapithecus* has the bilophodont molars found in modern Old World monkeys, and it generally has a mix of colobine-like and cercopithecine-like features. It has wide incisors and low molar cusps, suggesting a frugivorous diet. However, it also has a sagittal crest, suggesting prominent chewing muscles and a dietary emphasis on hard fruits (rather than soft fruits). The postcrania indicate at least some adaptations for terrestrial quadrupedalism.

Low, rounded cusps

2 mm

**FIGURE 13.8**
***Branisella***

The earliest known platyrrhine is *Branisella*. It had three premolars in each mouth quadrant and low, rounded molar cusps that indicate a possibly frugivorous diet.

Takai et al. 1996. New specimens of the oldest fossil platyrrhine, *Branisella boliviana*, from Salla, Bolivia. *American Journal of Physical Anthropology* 99:301–314. Copyright © 1996, Wiley-Liss, Inc.

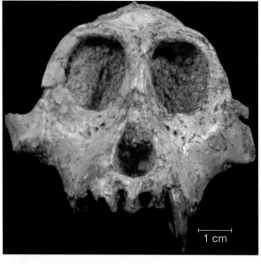

Southern Illinois University/AP Photo

1 cm

**FIGURE 13.9 *Victoriapithecus***
One of the earliest members of the distinct Old World monkey lineage, *Victoriapithecus* had bilophodont molars and dental adaptations for a frugivorous diet.

After the split from apes, Old World monkeys evolved into the distinct groups we recognize today—the colobines and cercopithecines. The exact nature and timing of this split is unclear, but numerous fossils of each group appear throughout Africa and Asia at the end of the Miocene (23 to 5.3 mya). Early on, these fossils often have an unusual mix of traits, such as colobine-like folivory adaptations paired with a more cercopithecine-like terrestrial lifestyle. Within the Pliocene (5.3 to 2.6 mya) and Pleistocene (2.6 mya to 10,000 years ago), the fossil species became more similar to the distinct Old World monkey groups seen today. These more recent fossils often resemble living Old World monkeys so much that they are assigned to the same genus as their living counterparts, such as *Macaca* (living macaques and their extinct relatives) and *Colobus* (living colobus monkeys and their extinct relatives).

## The Early Apes

Similar to the Old World monkeys, the apes probably evolved from an early catarrhine, such as *Aegyptopithecus*. As they split from Old World monkeys, early apes would have likely evolved specific ape traits, such as Y-5 molars, suspensory adaptations, and the lack of a tail. Perhaps the best-known early ape is the genus *Proconsul* (FIGURE 13.10). It was found in Africa from 22 to 17 mya (early Miocene). It has dental traits that suggest a frugivorous diet, and its postcranial traits indicate it was probably an arboreal quadruped. Although it is an early fossil that still shares many features with earlier Oligocene (34 to 23 mya) catarrhines, it has some important ape-like traits. For example, it is tailless, has a large brain for its body size, and has Y-5 molars. The exact relationship of *Proconsul* to living apes is unclear, but it is likely that living apes evolved from a common ancestor similar to *Proconsul*.

By 13 mya (middle Miocene), the apes had become a diverse group of species distributed throughout much of Europe and Asia. In contrast, the fossil record for Africa at this time is quite limited. This gap in the African fossil record probably exists because the apes were

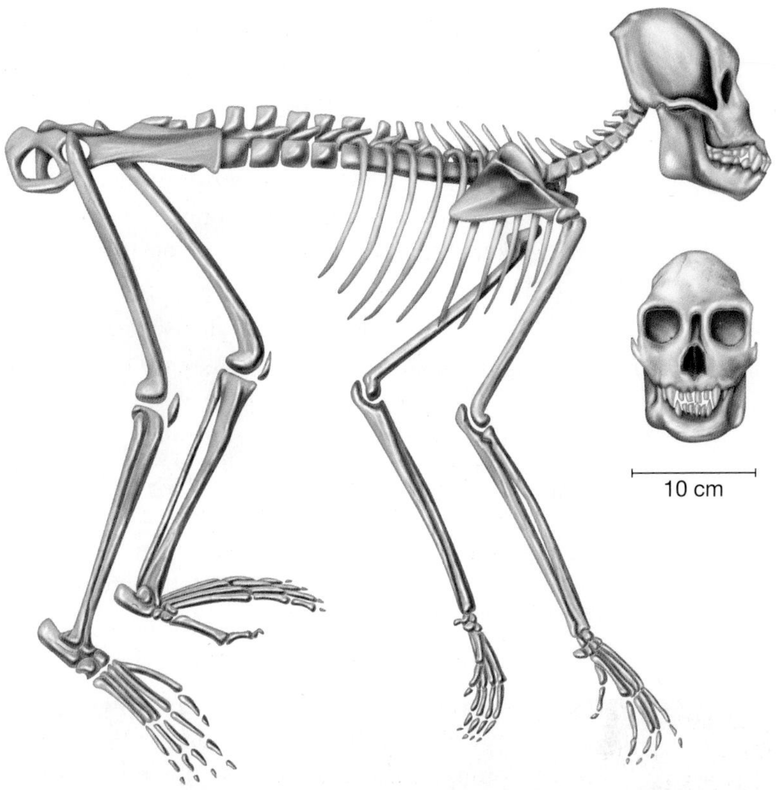

**FIGURE 13.10 *Proconsul***
One of the earliest apes, *Proconsul* had Y-5 molars and was tailless. However, it was not a brachiator. Note that the bones shown in blue have actually been recovered, while the other bones are reconstructions based on available information.

living in areas that were not conducive to fossilization (as discussed above). Among the European apes, we find the genus *Dryopithecus* (FIGURE 13.11). Apes of this genus lived around 12 to 8 mya (late Miocene) and had ape-like canines and Y-5 molars. Both their brain and body size were comparable to that of a modern chimpanzee, and they may have had some adaptations for suspensory locomotion (such as long arms). Around 8 to 7 mya (late Miocene) in Europe, we also find the genus *Oreopithecus* (FIGURE 13.12). This fossil ape was closely related to similar forms that lived a little earlier in Africa. It had teeth with tall cusps for folivory and a medium body size. It also had long, mobile arms suited for suspensory locomotion. Both *Dryopithecus* and *Oreopithecus* are related to living apes, but neither of them appears to be

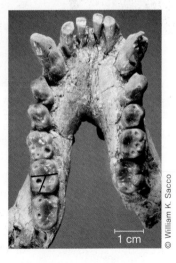

© William K. Sacco

**FIGURE 13.11 *Dryopithecus***
*Dryopithecus*, an early European ape, had Y-5 molars (shown here), a relatively large brain for its body size, and possibly some adaptations for brachiation.

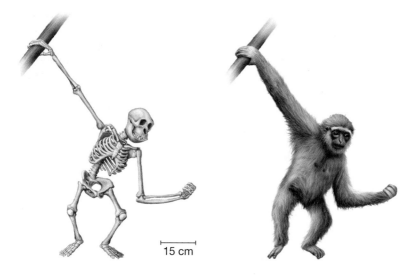

15 cm

**FIGURE 13.12 *Oreopithecus***
*Oreopithecus*, an early European ape, had dental adaptations for folivory and long, mobile arms for brachiation.

**FIGURE 13.13 *Gigantopithecus***
*Gigantopithecus*, an early Asian ape, was incredibly large and had large molars and mandibles for a diet that emphasized chewing. Some research suggests they may have eaten a lot of bamboo.

in the direct lineage of a particular modern ape species. It is perhaps more helpful to think of them as branches in the bushy ape family tree that did not survive to the present day.

Around the same time in Asia, we also find numerous ape species. The genus *Khoratpithecus* lived in Thailand around 9 to 6 mya (late Miocene). It had broad incisors and other dental traits that indicate a frugivorous diet and

a close relationship to modern orangutans. At 8 mya in Asia, we also find the largest primates that ever lived. Some of these huge primates are estimated to have weighed as much as 300 kg (or 660 lb) and have been aptly classified to the genus *Gigantopithecus* (**FIGURE 13.13**). *Gigantopithecus* had thick enamel on its teeth, similar to many other fossil apes. It also had very large molars and mandibles, suggesting a diet requiring a lot of chewing. Some research has suggested that *Gigantopithecus* may have eaten a lot of bamboo. Perhaps the most interesting thing about *Gigantopithecus* is that it lived in parts of Asia until as recently as 100 thousand years ago (kya). This means it lived side by side with *Homo erectus*, an early member of our genus. While *Khoratpithecus* is probably a close relative of living orangutans, *Gigantopithecus* is a more distant relative of living great apes with several unique specializations.

The evolutionary history of the primate order is difficult to interpret. For some time periods we have many fossil primate species, even more than we have today, and in other time periods we have very few fossil species. As we discussed earlier, these patterns of fossil distribution may be the result of past environmental conditions, circumstances of preservation, or researcher bias. There may also have been times when primates thrived and diversified and other times when primates struggled and dwindled. These gaps in the fossil record leave us with unanswered questions about primate evolution. Further complicating matters, we may recognize that a fossil group is generally related to a living primate but may not be able to decipher the details of this relationship. Fossil primates are not exact copies of living species. They often have their own unique combinations of traits and adaptations. The fossil record does not allow us to draw neat lines that connect extinct and living primates like highways connecting cities on a road map. Instead, we often find a complicated web of overlapping lineages, dead ends, and unclear relationships. As we will see in the remaining labs, the same is true of our unique human evolutionary history after our split from the other apes.

# ►►► EXPLORING FURTHER

**Dating Fossil Sites** While the fossil record is difficult to interpret, we are somewhat aided by being able to place fossils in their temporal context. By providing good temporal estimates for when these species were alive, we can better understand their likely relationships and evolutionary histories. How do we come up with these dates? There are generally two types of dating: relative dating and chronometric dating.

**Relative dating** is any dating method that provides the age of something relative to something else—as in X is older than Y. For example, one would say the American Civil War happened before (is older than) World War II, or the Great Pyramid of Giza is older than the Empire State Building. Relative dating methods for fossils are usually based on the law of superposition. Over time, sediment and rock build up in layers (or strata) on the earth's surface. Similar to the layers in a layer cake, the bottom layers are formed first and the top layers form after. The **law of superposition** uses this principle to argue that material from lower (deeper) geological layers must be older than material from higher (shallower) geological layers (FIGURE 13.14).

One of the most common relative dating methods is comparative stratigraphy. **Stratigraphy** is the study of the deposition of layers (or strata). **Comparative stratigraphy** assumes that things found in the same strata will be from the same time period because they were deposited together. This can help us to get a sense of the relative age of materials at a site. Following the law of superposition, all materials found in the lowest layer will be older than all the materials found in the highest layer. This method can also be used to get a relative age for materials at different sites. Often, the same geological events leave similar strata at different sites. For example, a large volcanic explosion may leave a similar layer of ash at multiple sites in a region. Using comparative stratigraphy, we can argue that materials found in the ash layer at one site should be the same age as materials found in the same ash layer at another site. This method is useful in that it gives us a rough estimate for how old or young things are in relation to one another. It can also be used along with other dating methods to get even more accurate data. For instance, a particular material in a layer may be able to be dated by another method. This age could then be assigned to that particular material, all other materials in that layer at the site, and materials found in the same layer at other sites. However, stratigraphy can be very difficult to interpret. An earthquake may shift strata, a rodent may burrow through layers and mix up the materials, or a human may plow layers together to prepare for planting or building. Numerous events could disturb the strata and lead to misinterpretation.

**relative dating** any dating method that provides the age of something relative to something else, rather than as a numerical age

**law of superposition** a principle that argues material from lower geological layers must be older than material from higher geological layers

**stratigraphy** the study of the deposition of geological and cultural layers (or strata)

**comparative stratigraphy** a relative dating method based on the assumption that things found in the same strata (or layer) will be from the same time period because they were deposited together

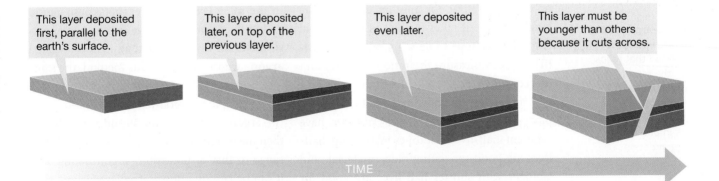

This layer deposited first, parallel to the earth's surface.

This layer deposited later, on top of the previous layer.

This layer deposited even later.

This layer must be younger than others because it cuts across.

TIME

**FIGURE 13.14 The Law of Superposition**
According to the law of superposition, material from lower geological layers must be older than material from upper geological layers because lower layers were deposited first.

**chronometric dating (absolute dating)** any dating method that provides a numerical age estimate for the dated material

**radiometric dating** any dating method that uses the principles of radioactive isotope decay to determine numerical age

**isotope** a variation of a chemical element based on the number of neutrons in its nucleus

**half-life** the length of time it takes for one-half of an amount of a radioactive isotope to decay

**radiocarbon dating** a radiometric dating method that relies on carbon-14, an isotope with a half-life of 5,730 years

**potassium–argon dating** a radiometric dating method that relies on radioactive potassium isotopes with a half-life of about 1.3 billion years

**argon–argon dating** a radiometric dating method that relies on the ratio of two argon isotopes, used for material from similar time periods as in potassium–argon dating

The other main type of dating is called **chronometric dating**. As opposed to simply indicating if something is older or younger, chronometric dating methods provide a numerical age estimate for the material involved. For example, one would say the American Civil War started in 1861 and World War II started in 1939, or the Great Pyramid was built about 4,500 years ago and the Empire State Building was built about 85 years ago. Because these methods give a numerical age, they are sometimes called **absolute dating** methods. This is misleading, though, because it suggests that we are absolutely certain of the precise age assigned. In reality, we are not completely certain, and we often get age ranges instead of one precise date.

There are two kinds of chronometric dating methods: radiometric dating and nonradiometric dating. **Radiometric dating** is any dating method that uses principles of radioactive isotope decay to determine numerical age. **Isotopes** are variations of an element that differ in the number of neutrons in the nucleus. For example, carbon has three isotopes that have different numbers of neutrons. Carbon-12 has six neutrons and six protons (a total mass number of 12), carbon-13 has seven neutrons and six protons (a total of 13), and carbon-14 has eight neutrons and six protons (a total of 14). While many isotopes are stable and remain unchanged indefinitely, other isotopes are radioactive and decay over time. These radioactive isotopes decay until they become a stable isotope for the same element or a stable isotope for another element. The length of time it takes for half of the original amount of isotope to decay is called the **half-life**. We can measure the ratio of the amount of radioactive isotope to its stable counterpart and determine how many half-lives have passed. Importantly, different isotopes have different half-lives. Isotopes with long half-lives are good for dating older material, and isotopes with shorter half-lives are good for dating more recent material.

The most famous radiometric dating method is **radiocarbon dating**. This method relies on the radioactive isotope carbon-14. Carbon is found in all living organisms and in the atmosphere. When organisms are alive, the ratio of radioactive carbon (carbon-14) to stable carbon (carbon-12) is constant. When organisms die, however, the carbon-14 decays to nitrogen-14. Radiocarbon dating requires organic material, such as bone, shell, or wood. It is a particularly useful method because it provides a date for the actual material, rather than the surrounding rocks or soil. It also tells us when the organism died, as opposed to when the surrounding geological layer was formed. However, the half-life for radiocarbon decay is 5,730 years. Therefore, the radiocarbon method is well suited for recent material from between about 2 and 50 kya, but it is not useful for older material.

A similar radiometric dating method depends on radioactive potassium isotopes. This method, called **potassium–argon dating**, measures the decay of potassium-40 to argon-40 in volcanic rocks. The half-life for this decay is very long: 1.3 billion years. This means it is not good for material from less than 200 kya, but it can be used for anything older than this, even for material from as far back as the formation of Earth (4.5 billion years ago). Potassium–argon dating gives an age for volcanic rocks, which is useful because many of the strata associated with primate evolution contain volcanic rocks. As we saw with comparative stratigraphy, the date for volcanic rocks in a layer can then be assigned to the fossil material found in the same layer. However, potassium–argon dating does not give an age for the actual fossil material. Another related method is called **argon–argon dating**. In this method, the sample is irradiated to convert the potassium-39 in the sample to argon-39, and the ratio of the two argon isotopes, argon-39 and argon-40, are then measured. This method has a similar date range to that of potassium–argon dating, and it can be run on a much smaller volcanic rock sample.

**Nonradiometric dating** methods are chronometric techniques that are not based on radioactive isotope decay. **Paleomagnetic dating** is a nonradiometric technique that is based on changes in the magnetism of the planet. Throughout Earth's history, the magnetic poles have shifted back and forth, with magnetic north becoming magnetic south and vice versa. When rocks are formed, their metal particles arrange themselves in relation to the direction of Earth's magnetic field at the time. If we examine the rocks from a geological layer, we can determine what the polarity was at that time. The dates of these shifts have been documented using other methods, such as potassium–argon dating, so we can determine the time interval during which the rock was likely formed. Paleomagnetic dating is useful for material from about 750 kya (when the last major polarity shift occurred) to 200 mya (the extent of our polarity mapping to date). Again, this method can be used to date the rocks from a site, but it cannot be used to directly date the actual fossil remains.

Each dating method has its advantages and disadvantages. Paleoanthropologists must understand what materials are available for dating and roughly how old the material may be before they choose a dating method. If they have organic material that is roughly a few thousand years old, they would be likely to pursue radiocarbon dating. If, however, they have volcanic rock that is roughly a few million years old, they would be more likely to pursue potassium–argon dating. The limitations associated with each dating method make choosing the right one a complicated process. In addition, we often find ourselves in situations where we cannot date the layer we would prefer. For example, we may have fossil remains in one layer that are not associated with the right kinds of organic materials or rocks for dating. We may have to date material from the layers above and below our fossil layer. Using the law of superposition in combination with our chronometric methods, we can determine a date range for the fossil layer. If the layer below the fossils dates to 1.5 mya and the layer above the fossils dates to 1.0 mya, we know the fossil species lived between 1.5 and 1.0 mya. Dating fossil contexts is complex, and the timing of events in our evolutionary history can sometimes be vague. However, our methods are constantly being refined, and our dates are regularly reevaluated and adjusted based on new information.

**nonradiometric dating** any chronometric dating method that is not based on the principles of radioactive isotope decay

**paleomagnetic dating** a nonradiometric dating method based on changes in Earth's magnetic polarity

# CONCEPT REVIEW QUESTIONS

Name: _____    Section: _____

Course: _____    Date: _____

Answer the following questions in the space provided.

1. Define fossil.

2. True or false? Researchers agree that plesiadapiforms were the first primates.

3. Compared to adapiforms, omomyoids:

    A. are usually more nocturnal.
    B. have longer snouts.
    C. are usually larger.
    D. have more enclosed bony orbits.

4. Describe *one* trait found in *Aegyptopithecus* that suggests it was an early catarrhine.

5. I lived in Africa around 15 mya. I had bilophodont molars and a frugivorous diet. I had some adaptations for terrestrial quadrupedalism. What fossil primate am I?

    A. *Aegyptopithecus*
    B. *Khoratpithecus*
    C. *Dryopithecus*
    D. *Victoriapithecus*

6. *Proconsul* lived in Africa around 20 mya. It had Y-5 molars and a frugivorous diet. It also had some adaptations for arboreal quadrupedalism and was tailless. What living primate group is its closest living relative?

    A. Tarsiers
    B. Old World monkeys
    C. Apes
    D. New World monkeys

7. What is the genus assigned to the largest primate that ever lived?

8. True or false? Relative dating provides a more precise age than chronometric dating.

9. True or false? According to the law of superposition, deeper geological layers are older than layers near the surface.

10. What type of material would you need to conduct radiocarbon dating?

# LAB EXERCISES

Name: _____     Section: _____

Course: _____     Date: _____

Answer the following questions in the space provided.

*Note*: When completing these exercises, it may be useful to refer back to Labs 10–12 for information about living primates.

## EXERCISE 1   PLESIADAPIFORMS

Work in a small group or alone to complete this exercise.

In 2002, researchers reported the discovery of a partial skeleton from the fossil *Carpolestes*. It lived in North America around 56 mya. It was about the size of a mouse and had a pronounced snout. It also had grasping hands and feet and a mix of nails and claws. It did not have a postorbital bar. This fossil genus has been classified as a plesiadapiform. (See lab Appendix for image.)

1. Describe *one* feature that it shares in common with other plesiadapiforms, such as *Plesiadapis*.

2. Describe *one* feature that makes it different from most other plesiadapiforms.

3. Do you think this new find forces us to reconsider the relationship between plesiadapiforms and primates? Why or why not?

## EXERCISE 2   ADAPIFORMS AND OMOMYOIDS

Work in a small group or alone to complete this exercise. Use the fossil descriptions here and material provided by your instructor (or in the lab Appendix) to answer the questions that follow.

Mystery fossil genus A lived in North America in the mid-Eocene. Its teeth had shearing crests, indicating a folivorous diet.

Mystery fossil genus B lived in North America in the early Eocene. Its teeth suggest it was insectivorous.

1. Which of these mystery fossils is an adapiform?

2. Which of these mystery fossils is an omomyoid?

3. Describe *two* traits you used to make these identifications. (Be sure to describe how each trait varied in the two mystery fossils.)

## EXERCISE 3    *DARWINIUS*

Work in a small group or alone to complete this exercise.

A new fossil called *Darwinius* was discovered in Germany. It lived around 47 mya. It had a small brain, short snout, and postorbital bar. Its diet probably included a lot of fruit and leaves. It did not have a dental comb. It had nails instead of claws and was probably an arboreal quadruped. Researchers disagree about whether the fossil is more similar to living haplorhines (tarsiers, monkeys, and apes) or more similar to strepsirhines (lemurs and lorises). (See lab Appendix for image.)

1. Describe *two* features that the fossil shares in common with living haplorhines.

2. Describe *two* features that the fossil shares in common with living strepsirhines.

## EXERCISE 4    FOSSIL NEW WORLD AND OLD WORLD MONKEYS

Work in a small group or alone to complete this exercise. Use the fossil descriptions here and material provided by your instructor (or in the lab Appendix) to answer the questions that follow.

Mystery fossil genus A has been dated to the late Pliocene and early Pleistocene. It had two premolars in each mouth quadrant and bilophodont molars. Its canines were sexually dimorphic, and males had slightly larger and longer crania than females. Its postcranial traits indicate it was a terrestrial quadruped, and its overall body size was considerably larger than its living primate relatives.

Mystery fossil genus B has been dated to the early Miocene. It had three premolars in each mouth quadrant and sexually dimorphic canines. Its teeth indicate a frugivorous diet. It had a medium body size similar to its living primate relatives.

1. Which of these mystery fossils is a fossil Old World monkey?

2. Which of these mystery fossils is a fossil New World monkey?

3. Describe *two* traits you used to make these identifications. (Be sure to describe how each trait varied in the two mystery fossils.)

## EXERCISE 5  *THEROPITHECUS*

Work in a small group or alone to complete this exercise.

*Theropithecus* lived in Africa at the end of the Pliocene and the early Pleistocene. It had two premolars in each mouth quadrant and bilophodont molars. Its teeth indicate an unusual diet that emphasized grasses. It had larger canines and a much larger body size than its living primate relatives. Its postcranial traits suggest it was a well-adapted terrestrial quadruped. (See lab Appendix for image.)

1. Based on this information, do you think this fossil has more in common with living colobines or cercopithecines?


2. Describe *one* trait you used to make this identification.



## EXERCISE 6  *SIVAPITHECUS*

Work in a small group or alone to complete this exercise.

*Sivapithecus* lived in Asia 12–8 mya. It had a 2.1.2.3 dental formula and adaptations for chewing hard food such as seeds and nuts. It had very few postcranial adaptations for suspensory locomotion, but it did have long fingers. It also had tall orbits that sat close together.

1. Based on this description and the material provided by your instructor (or depicted in the lab Appendix), is *Sivapithecus* more similar to living Asian great apes or African great apes?


2. Describe *two* traits you used to make this distinction.

## EXERCISE 7    DATING METHODS

Work in a small group or alone to complete this exercise. Use the stratigraphy drawing provided to answer the questions that follow.

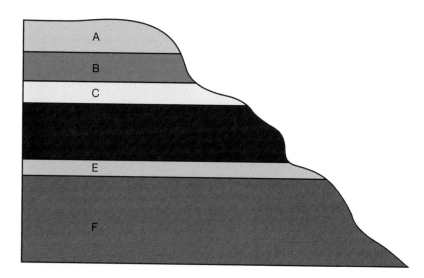

1. Which layer is the oldest?

2. Which layer is the youngest (most recent)?

3. In layer B, you find an unfossilized bone. What chronometric dating method could you use to date this layer? For what date range would this method be appropriate?

4. In layer D, you find a fossilized bone. Layer C and layer E are made of volcanic rock. Based on what is available at the site, what strategy will you use to determine a chronometric date for layer D? (Be sure to specify the exact dating method or methods used and the corresponding applicable age ranges.)

# CRITICAL THINKING QUESTIONS

On a separate sheet of paper, answer the following questions.

1. This question may be completed independently or as a group exercise. As we discussed, plesiadapiforms were initially interpreted as being the first primates. They were then interpreted as being outside the direct primate lineage because they lacked many of the key traits that define the primate order. This debate continues today. Based on what you know about the defining traits found in most living primates, describe four traits you think should be found in the earliest primates. What advantages would these traits have provided the first primates? Are any of these traits found in plesiadapiforms? (Use material in your classroom, online, or in books to help you if necessary.)

2. This question may be completed independently or as a group exercise. Below are descriptions for five mystery fossil primates. Use the information provided to determine which mystery fossil primate is an adapiform, an omomyoid, a New World monkey, an Old World monkey, or an ape.

   **Mystery fossil primate A** lived in the early to middle Miocene in South America. It had an enclosed bony orbit, three premolars in each mouth quadrant, and dentition suggesting a frugivorous and folivorous diet. Its postcrania indicate it was a quadruped.

   **Mystery fossil primate B** lived in the early Eocene in North America. It had an unfused mandible, long snout, and small forward-facing orbits. It had sexually dimorphic canines and teeth that suggest a frugivorous diet. Its postcrania indicate some leaping behaviors.

   **Mystery fossil primate C** lived in the late Miocene and Pliocene in Africa. It had two premolars in each mouth quadrant, bilophodont molars, and dental adaptations for folivory. Its postcrania suggest it practiced a combination of arboreal and terrestrial quadrupedalism.

   **Mystery fossil primate D** lived in the middle Miocene in Europe. It had two premolars in each mouth quadrant. It had a flexible wrist, a broad chest, and short fingers. It is likely that its scapulas were positioned on the back of its rib cage.

   **Mystery fossil primate E** lived in the middle and late Eocene in Europe. It had a postorbital bar, very large orbits, and a short snout. Its dentition suggests an insectivorous diet, and its postcrania indicate it did a lot of leaping.

3. This question may be completed independently or as a group exercise. Based on your knowledge of living and fossil primates, what traits do you think define the anthropoid group? What traits define the catarrhine group? What traits define the ape group?

4. In this lab, we reviewed important fossil primates related to each of the major living primate groups. To help you make comparisons across groups and understand the general patterns of primate evolution, complete the Fossil Primate Chart on the following pages. For each fossil primate, provide its date and location, its important anatomical traits, its behavior (such as diet and locomotion), and its most closely related living primate group.

5. In this lab, we also reviewed several important dating methods used by paleoanthropologists. To help you make comparisons between these methods, complete the Dating Methods Chart on the following pages. For each dating method, identify whether the method is a relative or chronometric method, the material needed for analysis, and the approximate date range covered by the method.

## FOSSIL PRIMATE CHART (PART ONE)

| Fossil Group or Species | Dates and Locations | Anatomical Traits | Behavior | Relationship to Living Primates |
|---|---|---|---|---|
| Plesiadapiform (*Plesiadapis*) | | | | |
| Adapiform (*Adapis*) | | | | |
| Omomyoid (*Shoshonius*) | | | | |
| *Aegyptopithecus* | | | | |
| *Branisella* | | | | |

**FOSSIL PRIMATE CHART (PART TWO)**

| Fossil Group or Species | Dates and Locations | Anatomical Traits | Behavior | Relationship to Living Primates |
|---|---|---|---|---|
| Victoriapithecus | | | | |
| Proconsul | | | | |
| Dryopithecus | | | | |
| Oreopithecus | | | | |
| Khoratpithecus | | | | |
| Gigantopithecus | | | | |

## DATING METHODS CHART

| Dating Method | Relative or Chronometric? | Material Needed | Date Range |
|---|---|---|---|
| Comparative Stratigraphy | | | |
| Radiocarbon | | | |
| Potassium–Argon and Argon–Argon | | | |
| Paleomagnetism | | | |

# APPENDIX: LAB EXERCISE IMAGES

## Exercise 1 Plesiadapiforms

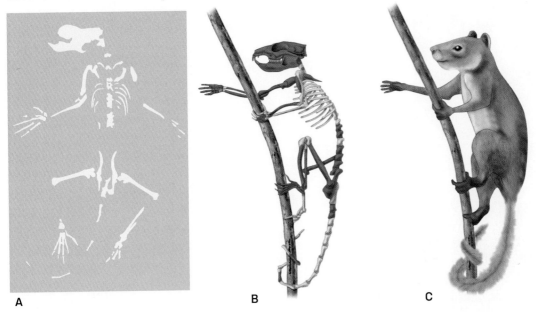

A    B    C

*Carpolestes*
This fossil skeleton of *Carpolestes* was discovered in North America in 2002: (A) drawing of fossil remains recovered, (B) reconstruction of skeleton with recovered material in red, and (C) reconstruction of specimen.

## Exercise 2 Adapiforms and Omomyoids

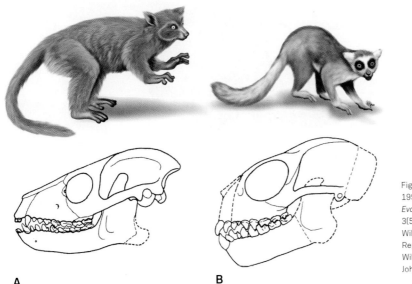

A    B

Figure 3 from Rose, Kenneth D. 1994. The earliest primates. *Evolutionary Anthropology* 3(5):159–173. Copyright © 1994 Wiley-Liss, Inc., A Wiley Company. Reprinted with permission of Wiley-Liss, Inc., a subsidiary of John Wiley & Sons, Inc.

## Exercise 3 *Darwinius*

Shaun Curry/AFP/Getty Images

**Darwinius**
The fossil *Darwinius* was found in Germany.

## Exercise 4 Fossil New World and Old World Monkeys

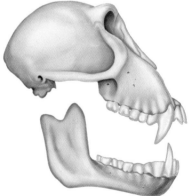

A

B

## Exercise 5 *Theropithecus*

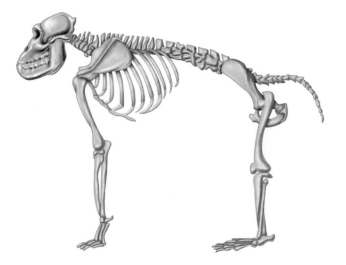

*Theropithecus*

## Exercise 6 *Sivapithecus*

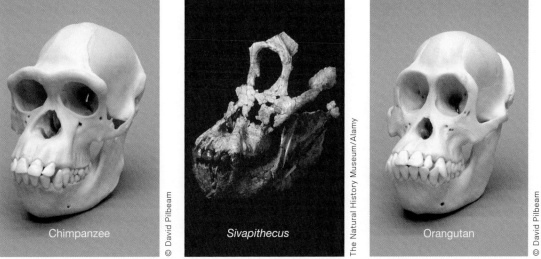

Chimpanzee

*Sivapithecus*

Orangutan

© David Pilbeam

The Natural History Museum/Alamy

© David Pilbeam

*Sivapithecus*
*Sivapithecus* (center) is compared to a modern chimpanzee (left) and a modern orangutan (right).

In Laetoli, Tanzania, paleoanthropologists uncover tracks made around 3.5 mya as numerous animals, including our extinct relatives, traversed an open grassland covered by a layer of damp ash. When the ash hardened, it preserved the tracks of the animals that had walked through the area.

John Reader/Science Source

## Lab Learning Objectives

By the end of this lab, students should be able to:

- differentiate between the three types of bipedalism, using examples.

- describe the major skeletal adaptations for bipedalism, as well as the advantages afforded by each of these adaptations.

- describe the savanna hypothesis and how pre-australopithecine fossils challenge this hypothesis.

LAB 14

# Identifying the Human Lineage

It is a warm day 3.5 million years ago in Laetoli, Tanzania. The dry season is coming to an end in the open savanna grassland. The rhinoceroses, rabbits, antelopes, and birds that have lived here for months are wandering the landscape. Other animals, such as horses and baboons, are starting to venture into the area in anticipation of the coming rains.

A recent volcanic explosion has covered the land with a layer of ash. As it starts to rain, the ash layer becomes damp and muddy; the animals crossing the savanna leave tracks in the damp ash. These tracks will soon harden and preserve the overlapping paths taken by antelopes, elephants, cats, pigs, horses, and other animals. Among these animals, there is a small group of apes. A large ape and a small ape leave a trail of parallel tracks in the ash. A second small ape leaves a trail that overlaps and partially obscures the tracks of the large ape.

Over 3 million years later (in 1978), a team of paleoanthropologists uncovers these tracks. The anthropologists soon realize that the tracks made by the group of apes are remarkable. They resemble human footprints and indicate that these apes practiced an unusual form of locomotion—they walked on two legs. Although they are now extinct, these walking apes were among the earliest members of our human lineage.

## INTRODUCTION

In this lab, we discuss how paleoanthropologists identify fossil species in the human lineage. This information helps us to understand our unique evolutionary history since our split from the other apes. We begin with a reflection on the utilization of brain size and tool use as hallmarks of species in our lineage. We then discuss how bipedalism may be the key component of our lineage. We introduce the three types of bipedalism, and we discuss the major skeletal adaptations for bipedalism. For each adaptation, we specifically consider the advantage afforded by this trait. We conclude with a discussion of why our ancestors may have become bipedal and how recent research is challenging our long-standing assumptions about the evolutionary shift to bipedalism.

## HOW DO WE KNOW IF A FOSSIL SPECIES IS PART OF OUR HUMAN LINEAGE?

Over the years, several different traits have been used as the hallmark indicator that a fossil species is part of the human lineage. For example, large *brain size* was long considered to be the defining characteristic of humanness. However, most researchers today recognize that emphasis on brain size is problematic for several reasons. First, brain tissue does not fossilize, so researchers are forced to work with indirect indicators. For example, we have difficulty determining the exact size of the brain, and we work instead with measurements of a fossil species' **cranial capacity** (the amount of space available in the cranium for a brain) to estimate brain size. In addition, we can use indentations and ridges on the inside of the cranium to estimate the size of different brain regions, but these estimates are often imprecise and do not tell us about brain organization. Second, having a large brain is not actually unique to humans. Numerous animals, such as elephants, have brains that are larger than ours, as brain size is generally proportional to

body size. Moreover, although we have large brains relative to our body size, this is also not unique. Other animals (such as mice) have brains that are even larger for their body size than we do. Therefore, it is not enough to say that humans (and our extinct relatives) are special because we have large brains, rather it is a matter of what our brains do—how they are organized and function—which is often difficult to assess in fossil species. Finally, as we will see in the coming labs, an increase in brain size to the modern human range is relatively recent in our evolutionary history; if we used brain size as the defining characteristic for our lineage, we would miss several million years of our history. For all of these reasons, large brain size may not be a good indicator of membership in our lineage.

Another popular trait that has been used to distinguish our lineage is *tool use*. Like brain size, this too is problematic. First, this approach has traditionally emphasized stone tools because they preserve well and are visible in the fossil record. However, this emphasis downplays the potential significance of tools made from less durable materials, such as plants, and may inadvertently exclude from our lineage numerous species that used plant-based tools. Second, as discussed in Lab 11, research has demonstrated widespread tool use in nonhuman apes and some monkeys. This suggests that tool use is not limited to humans and our closely related ancestors. Rather, it is a more common behavior of primates in general. For these reasons, tool use may not be a unique characteristic of our lineage.

In light of the problems associated with these traits, a different characteristic needs to be used to identify members of our lineage. The best characteristic for this purpose is **bipedalism**. Here, *bi* means "two," and *pedal* refers to feet. Thus, bipedalism is a form of two-footed locomotion where movement occurs primarily through the use of the hind limbs (legs). It is an unusual form of locomotion among primates, and as we will see in the coming labs, it appears very early in our evolutionary history.

**cranial capacity** the amount of space available in the cranium for the brain

**bipedalism** a form of two-footed locomotion where movement occurs primarily through the use of the legs

# TYPES OF BIPEDALISM

Although bipedalism defines our lineage, it is not restricted to our species. In fact, many primates practice some sort of bipedalism. What distinguishes us is that we practice a particular kind of bipedalism, called obligate bipedalism. There are two other kinds of bipedalism, called occasional bipedalism and habitual bipedalism. To fully understand our own bipedalism, we must understand all three types of bipedalism seen in primates.

**Occasional bipedalism** is bipedal locomotion that is practiced sometimes (or occasionally). Occasional bipeds rely on a different form of locomotion as their primary means of movement, and they often fall back on bipedalism under certain circumstances. For example, nonhuman apes will sometimes move bipedally on the ground when they are using their hands to carry things (**FIGURE 14.1**). In these situations, the hands cannot be used in locomotion because they are otherwise occupied, so the primate uses only its legs and moves bipedally. Because the primate rarely practices bipedalism, it has few, if any, anatomical adaptations for bipedalism. Instead, it is anatomically adapted for its primary form of nonbipedal locomotion. Chimpanzees and bonobos are good examples of this. Although they occasionally move bipedally, they are not really adapted for bipedalism. Rather, they are anatomically adapted for their primary form of locomotion: knuckle-walking (see Lab 12 for more information).

**Habitual bipedalism** is bipedal locomotion that is practiced regularly (or habitually). Habitual bipeds may also rely on a different form of locomotion, but they use bipedalism and their other locomotion strategy more equally. For example, many of the early members of our lineage practiced habitual bipedalism. The australopithecines that produced the Laetoli footprints discussed at the beginning of this lab are classic examples of habitual bipeds (see Lab 15 for more examples). They were still somewhat arboreal and spent a lot of time climbing in trees. On the ground, however, they often practiced bipedalism. These species used bipedalism more often than an occasional biped, but they also maintained and used other forms of locomotion. Habitual bipeds have a mix of locomotor adaptations. They are bipedal enough that they have some selectively favored bipedal adaptations. However, they also use an alternate form of locomotion (such as arboreal climbing) enough that they have some selectively favored adaptations for that form of locomotion as well.

**Obligate bipedalism** is bipedal locomotion that is practiced all the time. Obligate bipeds are obliged to move around bipedally. Unlike occasional or habitual bipeds, obligate bipeds have no other realistic locomotor option. Humans today are obligate bipeds, as were all of our ancestors since *Homo erectus* about 1.8 mya (million years ago) and perhaps even *Homo habilis* about 2.5 mya (see Labs 15 and 16 for more information). We can cover short distances by crawling on all fours, and we can climb trees and practice arm-over-arm

Frans Lanting Studio/Alamy

**FIGURE 14.1 Occasional Bipedalism**
Nonhuman apes sometimes walk short distances bipedally while they carry things in their hands.

**occasional bipedalism** bipedal locomotion that is practiced sometimes (or occasionally)

**habitual bipedalism** bipedal locomotion that is practiced regularly (or habitually)

**obligate bipedalism** bipedal locomotion that is practiced all the time

**foramen magnum**
the large hole at the base of the cranium that allows the brain to connect to the spinal cord

**mastoid process**
the bony projection located posterior to the ear that allows for the attachment of neck muscles

swinging. However, we cannot do these things comfortably for any length of time without special training and practice. Once we reach a certain age and body size, we are anatomically obliged to walk on two legs. While we maintain a few adaptations for other forms of locomotion, such as the suspensory traits shared by all apes, most of our locomotor adaptations are for bipedalism. Our bodies are more suited for bipedal locomotion than any other alternative.

When we analyze the fossil record, we examine the physical traits of a fossil species. We then use the data to make hypotheses and interpretations about the behavior of the species. Thus, when we are trying to identify if a fossil species was a member of our lineage, we look for anatomical traits for bipedal locomotion. Bipedal anatomical traits indicate that a species was at least habitually bipedal, practicing bipedalism frequently enough that natural selection favored traits that facilitated this locomotion. These habitual bipeds are more

bipedal than members of nonhuman primate lineages and therefore belong in our human lineage.

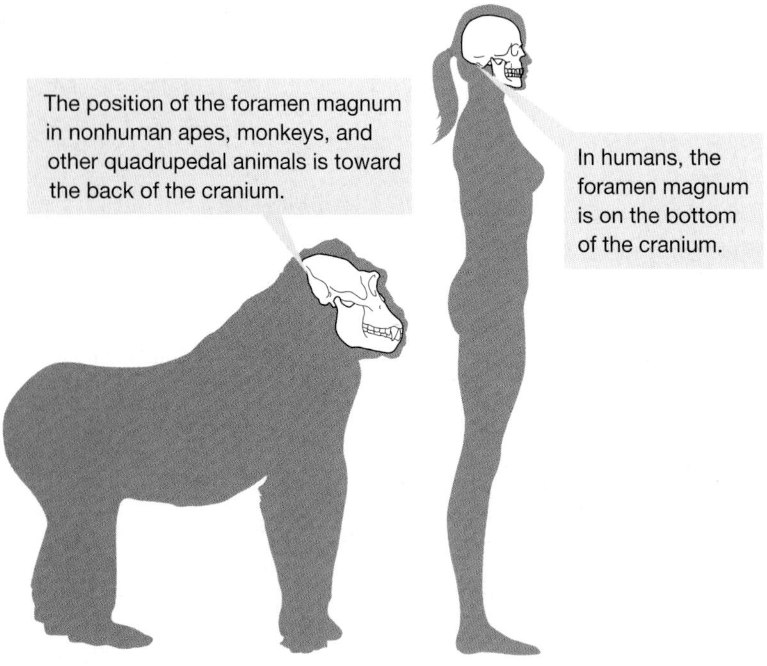

## BIPEDAL ADAPTATIONS

There are numerous adaptations for bipedalism that can be seen in our skeletons (and therefore also seen in the fossilized skeletons of our ancestors). We discuss the major bipedal adaptations and the advantages they afford, working our way from the head to the toes. There are two important bipedal adaptations found in the cranium. The first is the position of the foramen magnum. As discussed in Lab 6, the **foramen magnum** is the large hole at the base of the cranium that allows the brain to connect to the spinal cord. In a quadruped, the foramen magnum is positioned more posteriorly (toward the back of the cranium) **(FIGURE 14.2)**. This allows the vertebral column to remain parallel to the ground while extending outward from the braincase. In a biped, the body is oriented more upright, and the vertebral column is perpendicular to the ground (rather than parallel). Thus, the *foramen magnum of a biped is positioned more anteriorly* (toward the front of the cranium) *and inferiorly* (on the underside of the cranium) (Figure 14.2). This helps to center the head over the upright vertebral column. If a biped had a more posteriorly positioned foramen magnum, its normal relaxed head orientation would be tilted slightly upward because its upright vertebral column would extend down from the back of its skull. This would require the biped to constantly use its neck muscles to pull its head down to look forward. Instead, a biped has the anteriorly and inferiorly positioned foramen magnum, which centers the head over the upright vertebral column. The normal, relaxed head position of a biped has the eyes facing forward, and neck muscles are not overworked to orient the head correctly.

The other cranial trait associated with bipedalism is the mastoid process. As discussed in Lab 6, the **mastoid process** is a triangular bony

The position of the foramen magnum in nonhuman apes, monkeys, and other quadrupedal animals is toward the back of the cranium.

In humans, the foramen magnum is on the bottom of the cranium.

**FIGURE 14.2 Position of the Foramen Magnum**
The foramen magnum (hole at the base of the cranium for the brain to connect to the spinal cord) is positioned differently in a quadruped and a biped.

projection at the base of the cranium behind each ear, and it is an area for neck muscle attachment. Bipeds have *larger mastoid processes* than quadrupeds **(FIGURE 14.3)**. This reflects a difference in their neck muscles. In bipeds, the head is centered over the body, and there is a lot of potential for anterior, posterior, and lateral head movement. Because of this, we have numerous, relatively large neck muscles that help to move our head and hold it in place. The mastoid processes are areas of muscle attachment for several of these neck muscles, and they are large in bipeds to accommodate these muscles. In contrast, a quadruped has less head mobility, particularly in the posterior direction. The muscles that attach to their mastoid processes are smaller, so the mastoid processes themselves are also smaller.

Moving down the body, the next major bipedal adaptation is found in the **vertebral column**. Bipeds have an *S-shaped vertebral column* with curves in the thoracic and lumbar areas **(FIGURE 14.4)**. In the thoracic region, the vertebral column curves back, creating a convex dorsal (or posterior) surface. In the lumbar region, the vertebral column curves forward, creating a convex ventral (or anterior) surface. When looking at the right side of the body, these two curves resemble the two curves of an *S*. In nonbipeds, the vertebral column is straighter, with only a single curve that gradually forms a long, convex dorsal surface. The presence of the lower lumbar curve in bipeds helps to shift the upper body weight forward and center it over the pelvis and lower body. In addition, bipeds have *large lumbar vertebrae*. These vertebrae support the weight of all the body parts above them, so they often have large vertebral bodies to accommodate this function.

The pelvis of bipeds is also specially adapted for bipedalism and has an unusual bowl shape **(FIGURE 14.5)**. The *bowl-shaped pelvis* is largely the result of differences in the two **ilia (ilium**, singular). In a biped, the ilia are short and broad, and they are positioned more laterally in the pelvis. This shape is related to differences in the leg muscles of bipeds. While we are all probably familiar with the gluteus maximus muscle of the buttocks, we are probably less familiar with two related muscles: the gluteus minimus and the gluteus medius. These muscles attach to the ilium on one end and the femur on the other. In quadrupeds, these muscles straighten the thigh, acting as powerful extensors for quadrupedal locomotion. In bipeds, these muscles perform a very different function. When we walk, we only have one foot on the ground at a time. This foot and leg need help to remain steady and balanced during walking. In bipeds, the gluteus medius and minimus serve to stabilize the pelvis when all of the weight of the body is on the balancing leg. Because these muscles serve a different function in bipeds than quadrupeds, they have a different shape and position. In turn, the biped pelvis is shaped differently to accommodate these unusual gluteal muscles. Overall, the bowl-shaped pelvis and corresponding gluteal muscles help us to maintain a stable and

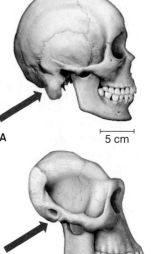

A

5 cm

B

5 cm

**FIGURE 14.3 Size of Mastoid Processes** The mastoid processes of a biped (A) are larger than the mastoid processes of a quadruped (B) due to differences in the size of the neck muscles that attach at these points.

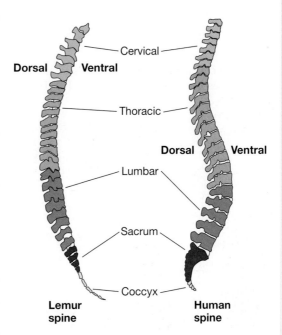

Cervical

Dorsal    Ventral

Thoracic

Dorsal    Ventral

Lumbar

Sacrum

Coccyx

**Lemur spine**    **Human spine**

**FIGURE 14.4 The Vertebral Column** In most primates (such as the lemur shown here) the vertebral column forms one gradual curve down its length from the head to the sacrum. In bipeds, the vertebral column curves back in the upper chest and curves toward the front at the lower back. This gives the bipedal vertebral column an S-shape.

**vertebral column** the row of bones that form the backbone

**ilium (ilia,** plural) the large, blade-like area of each os coxa (hip bone)

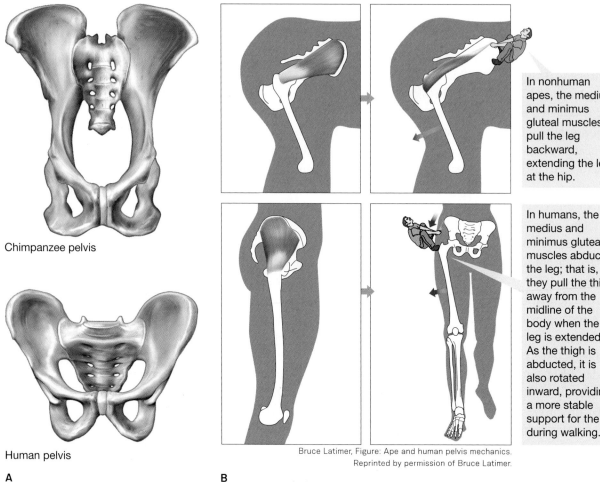

Chimpanzee pelvis

Human pelvis

**A**

**B**

In nonhuman apes, the medius and minimus gluteal muscles pull the leg backward, extending the leg at the hip.

In humans, the medius and minimus gluteal muscles abduct the leg; that is, they pull the thigh away from the midline of the body when the leg is extended. As the thigh is abducted, it is also rotated inward, providing a more stable support for the hip during walking.

Bruce Latimer, Figure: Ape and human pelvis mechanics. Reprinted by permission of Bruce Latimer.

**FIGURE 14.5 The Pelvis**
The bipedal pelvis is shorter, broader, and more bowl-shaped than the pelvis of a quadruped (A). This is the result of differences in the muscles that attach to the pelvis (B). These pelvises are shown at the same scale.

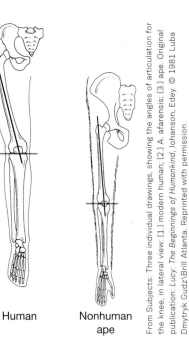

From Subjects: Three individual drawings, showing the angles of articulation for the knee, in lateral view: (1.) modern human; (2.) A. afarensis; (3.) ape. Original publication: *Lucy: The Beginnings of Humankind*, Johanson, Edey. © 1981 Luba Dmytryk Gudz\Brill Atlanta. Reprinted with permission.

**FIGURE 14.6 The Femur**
Bipeds have femurs that angle in toward the midline of the body and center the knees under the body. The other apes have straight femurs and knees positioned more toward the lateral sides of their bodies.

Human        Nonhuman ape

efficient bipedal gait (rather than a teetering gait that wobbles from side to side). In addition to the more significant muscle-attachment function, the bowl-shaped pelvis also helps support our intestines and other organs when our bodies are positioned upright.

Bipeds also have different overall body proportions. In Lab 12, we often found that the largest primate body parts were also the parts used most for their form of locomotion. For example, a leaping tarsier has incredibly long legs and feet to help with jumping, but a brachiating gibbon has incredibly long arms and hands to help with swinging. Bipeds follow this same pattern. Compared to our other living ape relatives, we have much *longer legs* **(FIGURE 14.6)**. This is largely the result of our elongated femurs, tibias, and fibulas.

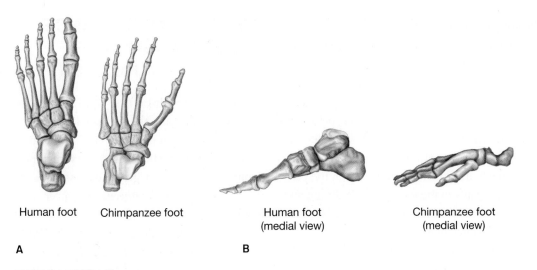

Human foot    Chimpanzee foot        Human foot              Chimpanzee foot
                                       (medial view)           (medial view)

A                                  B

**FIGURE 14.7 The Foot**
Bipeds have short toes and a nondivergent hallux (big toe), but other primates have long toes and a divergent hallux (A). Bipeds also have a longitudinal arch in their feet, whereas other primates have flatter feet (B). These feet are shown at the same scale.

In addition to being longer, the biped **femur** also has an unusual angled position (Figure 14.6). In most primates, the femur extends relatively straight from the pelvis to the knee. This keeps the knee toward the lateral side of the body. In contrast, bipeds have an *angled femur* that extends down and medially (inward) from the femur to the knee. This centers the knees (and lower legs) under the body and near the midline, which improves our balance and walking efficiency. As we move forward, our body follows a central path, rather than wobbling from side to side. In addition, when we briefly balance on one foot each time we take a step, the lower leg is closer to our midline and more stable.

In bipeds, the two feet support the entire weight of the body and are the only areas to make contact with the ground while moving. Therefore, they are incredibly important and have several key adaptations. First, bipeds have *short toes* (**FIGURE 14.7**). Unlike other primates, we do not use our toes for grasping. Instead, we use our toes for support while standing and to help push off when we step forward. Our toes are much shorter than the toes of other primates for these reasons. Interestingly, our big toe (the **hallux**) is larger than our other toes, which is the opposite of what is seen in most primates. Our relatively enlarged hallux helps

with bearing weight and transmitting force as we take steps. Second, bipeds have a *nondivergent hallux* that is in line (parallel) with the other toes (Figure 14.7). Again, since we do not use our feet for grasping, we do not need the opposable hallux seen in other primates. Instead, our hallux is lined up with the other toes to provide better balance and pushing off ability. Third, the biped foot has a *longitudinal arch* that extends down the length of the foot from the base of the toes to the heel (Figure 14.7). This arch helps with shock absorption as we walk, and it helps to direct our body weight and energy to create a smooth push off while stepping forward.

## WHY DID BIPEDALISM EVOLVE?

Bipedalism is a unique and central component of our lineage. As such, researchers have often asked why bipedalism evolved. What happened in our evolutionary history that led to our unusual locomotion? Numerous explanations have been put forward and have gained varying amounts of support in the scholarly community. Perhaps the most famous of these explanations is the savanna hypothesis. This explanation was supported by Raymond Dart, an early paleoanthropologist who first

**femur** the bone that forms the thigh of each leg

**hallux** the biggest and most medial of the toes on each foot

**savanna hypothesis**
an explanation for the evolution of bipedalism that argues bipedalism was selectively favored as open grassland environments expanded throughout Africa in the past

**savanna environment**
open grassland interspersed with pockets of trees

identified *Australopithecus africanus* (see Lab 15 for more information on this species). The **savanna hypothesis** argues that bipedalism was selectively favored as open grassland environments expanded throughout Africa. Around 8–5 mya, Earth was experiencing a period of dramatic cooling. Some of Earth's water became trapped in glaciers at the poles, and conditions were much drier than they had been in the past. In Africa, many of the forested areas shrank and were replaced by **savanna environments**—open grasslands interspersed with pockets of trees. The shift to savanna environments was further facilitated by geological activity in eastern Africa. Large tectonic plates were splitting apart (or rifting), causing landscape changes that contributed to more dramatic differences between wet and dry seasons. These seasonal changes, combined with overall drying, encouraged the expansion of grassland habitats in the region. According to the savanna hypothesis, bipedalism evolved as a favorable adaptation that facilitated life in these grasslands, where earlier forms of arboreal locomotion would be less helpful. The savanna hypothesis was supported by researchers for many years, but since the 1990s, paleoanthropologists have discovered numerous fossils of the earliest members of our human lineage, which challenge the validity of this explanation. Many of these earliest species may not have lived in savanna grasslands at all. Thus, alternate hypotheses for the evolution of bipedalism, such as the provisioning hypothesis, must be considered as well. The provisioning hypothesis, first proposed by biological anthropologist Owen Lovejoy, argues that bipedalism evolved in early humans that were monogamous, specifically to allow male human fathers to provision food and resources to human female partners; this would ensure the survival of their offspring and secure mating access to mothers. The provisioning of females required males to have free hands for carrying food, so bipedalism is argued to have evolved to facilitate this. However, the validity of this hypothesis has also been challenged, particularly as it depends on the social structure (specifically monogamous pair bonding) of early humans, which is not clearly known.

# THE FIRST APPEARANCE OF BIPEDALISM: PRE-AUSTRALOPITHECINES

When did bipedalism first appear, and by extension when did the human lineage first diverge from that of the other apes? For almost a hundred years, we believed the first members of our lineage were a group of fossil species in the genus *Australopithecus*. However, four new fossil species (classified in three different genera) have been identified since the 1990s that possess the bipedal adaptations unique to members of our lineage. These species lived between 7 and 4.4 mya, which predates the famous *Australopithecus* species, so they are called the pre-australopithecines. The pre-australopithecine species have a mix of adaptations for bipedalism and arboreal climbing, showing that the evolution of bipedalism was probably gradual and occurred in a mosaic fashion, with different bipedal adaptations evolving separately over time instead of simultaneously.

The first of the pre-australopithecine species is *Sahelanthropus tchadensis*. It lived around 7 to 6 mya (late Miocene) in the modern central African country of Chad. This location is particularly unusual because it is over 1,000 miles from the more well-known fossil sites of East Africa. Known largely from the remains of one fossil cranium, nicknamed Toumaï, this species has a pronounced brow ridge and a small cranial capacity (around 350 cubic centimeters), similar to living nonhuman apes **(FIGURE 14.8)**. However, it is argued that its foramen magnum is positioned more anteriorly, indicating more human-like bipedal locomotion. *Sahelanthropus* also has a relatively smaller, less prognathic face than nonhuman apes. This mixture of facial and bipedal traits, as well as the early date for *Sahelanthropus*, suggest it may have been the earliest member of our unique lineage or a common ancestor of humans and other apes, such as chimpanzees.

The second pre-australopithecine is *Orrorin tugenensis*. This species was found in the Tugen Hills of Kenya (eastern Africa) and dates to around 6 mya. While its teeth are more similar

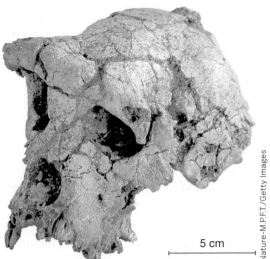

Nature-M.P.F.T./Getty Images

**FIGURE 14.8** *Sahelanthropus tchadensis*
The species *Sahelanthropus tchadensis* is primarily known from this fossil cranium (nicknamed Toumaï). The foramen magnum of this specimen appears to be positioned more anteriorly, suggesting it used bipedal locomotion.

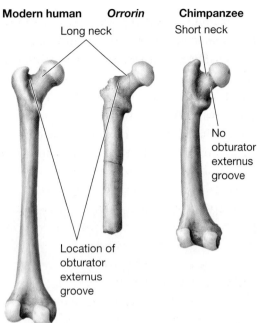

**FIGURE 14.9** *Orrorin tugenensis*
The femur of *Orrorin tugenensis* has the obturator externus groove present in bipedal humans and absent in quadrupedal chimpanzees. This suggests *Orrorin* was a biped.

to those of nonhuman apes than humans, it appears to have had adaptations for bipedalism. Although the available fossil fragments cannot be used to identify if their femurs were angled, the available proximal ends of a few *Orrorin* femurs have bipedal traits **(FIGURE 14.9)**. The femurs have long necks as well as a groove for the obturator externus muscle, which helps to stabilize and rotate the leg. Both of these features are seen in modern bipedal humans but not in modern chimpanzees. This suggests *Orrorin* was likely another early bipedal member of our lineage.

The last two pre-australopithecines have both been classified as members of the *Ardipithecus* genus. Both species were found in the Middle Awash region of Ethiopia (eastern Africa). *Ardipithecus kadabba* is the older of the two species, living around 5.5 mya (latest Miocene). The teeth of this species appear to have some modern human-like features and some chimpanzee-like features, and its early date makes it a contender as a possible ancestor of humans and chimps **(FIGURE 14.10)**. The other species, *Ardipithecus ramidus*, is more recent, living around 4.4 mya (early Pliocene). More is known about this *Ardipithecus* species because fossilized remains of

© Tim D. White

**FIGURE 14.10** *Ardipithecus kadabba*
*Ardipithecus kadabba* (right) had a honing canine similar to what is seen in chimpanzees today (left). This honing upper canine is naturally sharpened by rubbing against the lower premolar when the mouth is opened and closed.

at least 35 individuals have been recovered. The most famous of these is the partial skeleton of a single individual, nicknamed Ardi. *Ardipithecus ramidus* had a small cranial capacity and short stature (around 4 feet tall)

**(FIGURE 14.11A).** It had very long arms and fingers, but other upper limb features indicate it probably practiced more arboreal climbing than suspensory locomotion. It also had bipedal adaptations, such as a shorter and wider pelvis. Its foot is particularly interesting because it has a mixture of locomotor adaptations **(FIGURE 14.11B).** The toes are

long, and the hallux is divergent, suggesting the feet were still frequently used for arboreal grasping. However, the feet also show clear signs they were used for pushing off in bipedal walking.

As a group, the pre-australopithecine species share two important things in common. First, the pre-australopithecines are habitual bipeds with a mix of adaptations for bipedalism and arboreal locomotion. This means they practiced arboreal locomotion, but they also practiced bipedalism frequently enough that bipedal adaptations were selectively favored as well. Second, based on analyses of animal (and sometimes plant) remains from pre-australopithecine sites, we know they lived in forested environments. When taken together, these features of pre-australopithecine life directly challenge the long-standing savanna hypothesis. The pre-australopithecines were bipedal in the forest, so the evolution of bipedalism was not the result of living in open savanna grasslands. Rather, bipedalism must have evolved for a different reason.

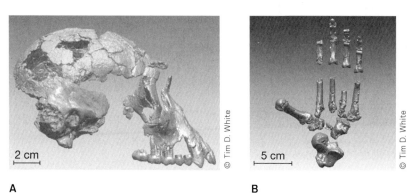

2 cm

5 cm

© Tim D. White

A

B

**FIGURE 14.11** *Ardipithecus ramidus*
*Ardipithecus ramidus* had a small cranial capacity (A) and a mix of bipedal and arboreal traits, such as the adaptations for grasping and bipedal walking seen in its foot (B).

# CONCEPT REVIEW QUESTIONS

Name: _____  Section: _____

Course: _____  Date: _____

Answer the following questions in the space provided.

1. True or false? We know a lot about the brains of our extinct relatives because their brain tissue is regularly preserved through fossilization.

2. True or false? Tool use is unique to members of our own human lineage.

3. The kind of bipedalism practiced by a living chimpanzee is called:

   A. random bipedalism.
   B. habitual bipedalism.
   C. occasional bipedalism.
   D. obligate bipedalism.

4. True or false? In a biped, the foramen magnum is positioned more anteriorly at the base of the skull.

5. The human S-shaped vertebral column is formed by two curves. Describe where these two curves are located.

6. How is the human pelvis different from the pelvis of a nonbipedal primate?

7. Describe the bipedal adaptations that can be found in the femur.

8. What is the savanna hypothesis?

9. The pre-australopithecines lived around:

   A. 8 mya to 5 mya.
   B. 7 mya to 4.4 mya.
   C. 6 mya to 3 mya.
   D. 9 mya to 6.5 mya.

10. Which of the following adaptations for bipedalism is *not* known to be present in the available pre-australopithecine fossils?

    A. S-shaped vertebral column

    B. Anteriorly positioned foramen magnum

    C. Obturator externus muscle groove on femur neck

    D. Short, broad pelvis

# LAB EXERCISES

Name: _____  Section: _____

Course: _____  Date: _____

## EXERCISE 1  BIPEDAL ADAPTATIONS OF THE CRANIUM

Work in a small group or alone to complete this exercise.

### PART A

Examine the skeletal material provided by your instructor (or depicted in the lab Appendix).

1. Which mystery primate is a biped?

2. Describe *one* adaptation seen *in this primate's cranium* that indicates it practices this locomotion.

3. How does this adaptation help the primate to move bipedally?

### PART B

Examine the skeletal material provided by your instructor (or depicted in the lab Appendix).

1. Which mystery primate is a biped?

2. Describe *one* adaptation seen *in this primate's cranium* that indicates it practices this locomotion.

3. How does this adaptation help the primate to move bipedally?

## EXERCISE 2  BIPEDAL ADAPTATIONS OF THE VERTEBRAL COLUMN

Work in a small group or alone to complete this exercise. Examine the skeletal material provided by your instructor (or depicted in the lab Appendix).

1. Which mystery primate is a biped?

2. Describe *two* adaptations seen *in this primate's vertebral column* that indicate it practices this locomotion.

3. How do these adaptations help the primate to move bipedally?

## EXERCISE 3    BIPEDAL ADAPTATIONS OF THE PELVIS

Work in a small group or alone to complete this exercise. Examine the skeletal material provided by your instructor (or depicted in the lab Appendix).

1. Which mystery primate is a biped?

2. Describe *two* adaptations seen *in this primate's pelvis* that indicate it practices this locomotion.

3. How do these adaptations help the primate to move bipedally?

## EXERCISE 4    BIPEDAL ADAPTATIONS OF THE FEMUR

Work in a small group or alone to complete this exercise. Examine the skeletal material provided by your instructor (or depicted in the lab Appendix).

1. Which mystery primate is a biped?

2. Describe *one* adaptation seen *in this primate's femur* that indicates it practices this locomotion.

3. How does this adaptation help the primate to move bipedally?

## EXERCISE 5    BIPEDAL ADAPTATIONS OF THE FOOT

Work in a small group or alone to complete this exercise. Examine the skeletal material provided by your instructor (or depicted in the lab Appendix).

1. Which mystery primate is a biped?

2. Describe *two* adaptations seen *in this primate's foot* that indicate it practices this locomotion.

3. How do these adaptations help the primate to move bipedally?

## EXERCISE 6 THE PRE-AUSTRALOPITHECINES

Work in a small group or alone to complete this exercise.

### PART A

Match each of the pre-australopithecines described below to its corresponding description.

*Sahelanthropus tchadensis* _____

*Orrorin tugenensis* _____

*Ardipithecus ramidus* _____

**1.** I lived about 6 mya in eastern Africa. My femurs had long necks with grooves for my obturator externus muscles.

**2.** I lived about 7–6 mya in central Africa. I had a small cranial capacity, large brow ridge, and anteriorly positioned foramen magnum.

**3.** I lived about 4.4 mya in eastern Africa. I had long arms and fingers and a relatively short, broad pelvis.

### PART B

Examine the material provided by your instructor (or depicted in the lab Appendix). What adaptations for bipedalism are seen in this *Ardipithecus ramidus* pelvis?

### PART C

The pre-australopithecine fossils are especially significant because they challenge some of the long-standing explanations of our evolutionary history. Describe *two* reasons the pre-australopithecines force us to rethink the savanna hypothesis in particular. (*Hint*: Think about the anatomical traits of the pre-australopithecines and the environmental and temporal context in which they lived.)

**THE EVOLUTION OF BIPEDALISM**

Work in a small group or alone to complete this exercise.

In this lab, we considered the savanna hypothesis and provisioning hypothesis as different explanations for the evolution of bipedalism. Other explanations for the shift to bipedalism exist as well. For example, an alternate explanation focuses on the issue of thermoregulation. According to the thermoregulation hypothesis, bipedalism was selectively favored because it helped our ancestors to stay cool in their warm environment.

Your instructor has provided you with a lamp (representing the sun) and a doll (representing one of our extinct relatives). Using these tools, follow the steps below to further explore the thermoregulation hypothesis.

**STEP 1**  Position the lamp so it is above the doll and facing directly downward (as if the sun were directly overhead).

**STEP 2**  Position the doll so that it is on all fours under the lamp, similar to a baboon wandering the open savanna. Note the amount of sun exposure the doll receives in this position.

**STEP 3**  Position the doll so that it is standing on two legs under the lamp, similar to a human wandering the open savanna. Note the amount of sun exposure the doll receives in this position.

**STEP 4**  Answer the following discussion questions:

1. In which position did the doll have the least sun exposure?

2. Why might having less sun exposure be an advantage in a warm environment?

3. In which position do you think the doll has the most exposure to wind and air circulation?

4. Why might having more exposure to the wind be an advantage in a warm environment?

5. Based on this test, do you think the thermoregulation hypothesis might provide a valid explanation for the evolution of bipedalism? Is it challenged by the pre-australopithecine finds?

# CRITICAL THINKING QUESTIONS

On a separate sheet of paper, answer the following questions.

1.  This question may be completed independently or as a group exercise. Describe the three different types of bipedalism. For each one, be sure to discuss the frequency of bipedal locomotion, describe the extent of bipedal adaptations, provide at least one sample primate who practices this type of bipedalism, and describe why the sample primate uses this form of bipedalism.

2.  Although bipedalism is unusual, humans are not the only living bipeds. For example, some flightless birds are also bipedal. Identify a living nonprimate animal that is also a biped. Then, compare its bipedalism to our bipedalism. Try to consider how it moves and some of its possible adaptations (such as limb length). Use material in your classroom, online, or in books to help you if necessary.

3.  This question may be completed independently or as a group exercise. A paleoanthropologist has uncovered a fossilized pelvis in Africa. She has sent you the drawing below and wants your opinion. Was this individual bipedal? Provide two traits that support your interpretation.

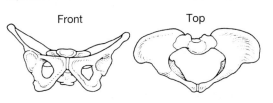

Front    Top

4.  This question may be completed independently or as a group exercise. At the start of this lab, we discussed the footprints discovered at Laetoli in Tanzania. These footprints have been interpreted as belonging to our relatives because they show bipedal adaptations. Examine the picture of one of these footprints below. Describe two of the bipedal adaptations visible here.

J. Reader/Science Source

5.  This question may be completed independently or as a group exercise. In some cases, our bipedal adaptations have changed areas of our bodies so much that it is difficult (if not impossible) for these areas to perform other functions. For example, our pelvis provides the areas of muscle attachment we need, but its unusual shape makes human childbirth more difficult. The foot is another area that reflects the impact of bipedal specialization. What foot traits and corresponding functions seen in other primates have been lost in our feet? Why would we have lost helpful features such as this?

6. This question may be completed independently or as a group exercise. In this lab, we have discussed the savanna hypothesis and how pre-australopithecines challenge this explanation of the evolution of bipedalism. If the savanna environment was not the factor favoring bipedalism, what was? Describe some of the advantages of bipedalism (be sure to think about what life would have been like for our ancestors millions of years ago when bipedalism evolved, including their risk of predation, food availability, etc.). Are there any disadvantages to bipedalism? If so, what are they? Taking into account the possible advantages and disadvantages, why do you think bipedalism might have evolved?

7. In this lab, we reviewed several important adaptations for bipedalism. To help you make comparisons between these adaptations, complete the following Bipedal Adaptations Chart. For each skeletal element, describe the features you would expect to find in a bipedal primate and in a nonbipedal primate.

## BIPEDAL ADAPTATIONS CHART

|  | Bipedal Primate | Nonbipedal Primate |
|---|---|---|
| Cranium |  |  |
| Vertebral Column |  |  |
| Pelvis |  |  |
| Legs |  |  |
| Feet |  |  |

# APPENDIX:
# LAB EXERCISE IMAGES

## Exercise 1 Bipedal Adaptations of the Cranium

1. Part A

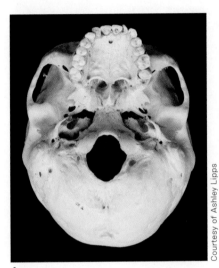

A

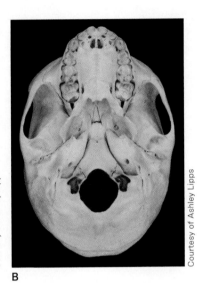

B

2. Part B

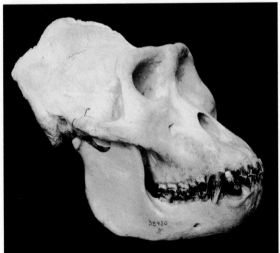

A

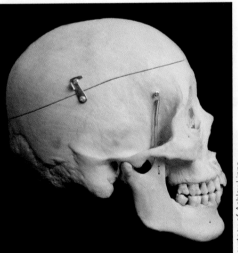

B

## Exercise 2 Bipedal Adaptations of the Vertebral Column

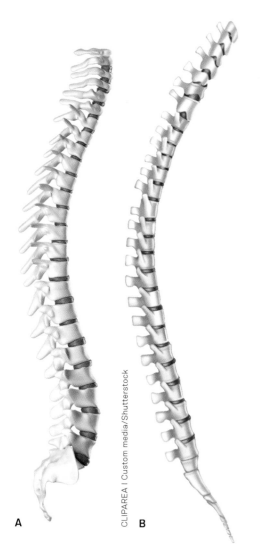

CLIPAREA | Custom media/Shutterstock

A          B

## Exercise 3 Bipedal Adaptations of the Pelvis

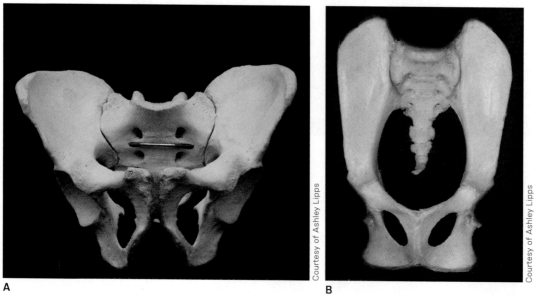

Courtesy of Ashley Lipps

Courtesy of Ashley Lipps

A                              B

## Exercise 4 Bipedal Adaptations of the Femur

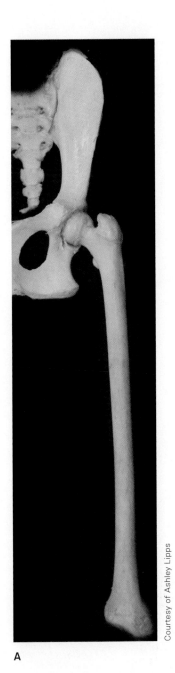

Courtesy of Ashley Lipps

A

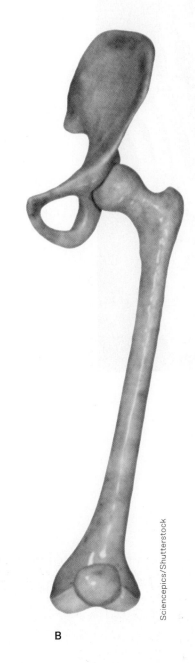

Sciencepics/Shutterstock

B

## Exercise 5 Bipedal Adaptations of the Foot

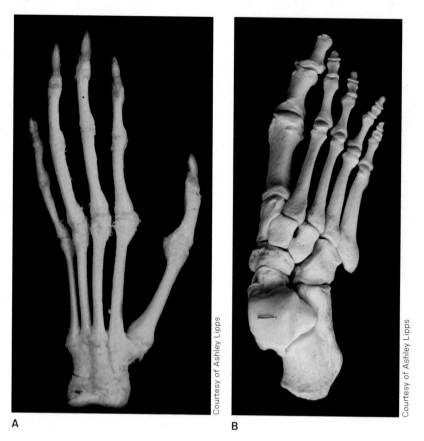

A

B

Courtesy of Ashley Lipps

## Exercise 6 The Pre-Australopithecines

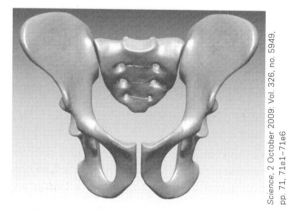

Science, 2 October 2009: Vol. 326, no. 5949, pp. 71. 71e1–71e6

Bettmann/CORBIS

© 1985 David L. Brill, www.humanoriginsphotos.com

## Lab Learning Objectives

By the end of this lab, students should be able to:

- describe the key australopithecine species, including their distributions and defining characteristics.

- compare and distinguish among the various australopithecines.

- discuss why some researchers classify the robust australopithecines in their own genus.

- describe the first species of our genus, including its distribution and defining characteristics.

- compare and distinguish between australopithecines and members of the *Homo* genus.

LAB 15

# The Australopithecines and Early Members of the Genus *Homo*

It is a late November day in 1974, and Donald Johanson's field season has been underway for several weeks. He is a paleoanthropologist helping lead a team of researchers in Hadar, Ethiopia. As on most other days, Johanson wakes up and enjoys his morning coffee just after dawn. It is already a balmy 80°F, and it will reach 110°F by lunchtime. He is a little edgy and anxious to get to work. Johanson agrees to show a colleague named Tom Gray a part of the research area with which Tom is less familiar. After a bumpy ride in their Land Rover, the two men work in the area for a couple hours. They are about to return to camp (before the heat of the day becomes too intense) when they spot fossil fragments scattered along an exposed slope of land. They quickly recognize parts of bones from an arm, skull, pelvis, and leg. The fragments seem to be laid out in order, as if they belong to a single individual, and they have telltale traits that suggest the individual was a member of the human lineage.

The two men are incredibly excited and begin jumping up and down, shouting and embracing. They return to camp and immediately share the news with the rest of the research team. The whole camp celebrates with music and dancing. They listen to the Beatles song "Lucy in the Sky with Diamonds" over and over again. After their initial excitement, the researchers spend the next 3 weeks returning to the site every day. They slowly uncover the fossilized remains first spotted by Johanson and Gray so that the discovery and its significance can be better understood. They call the individual Lucy, after the Beatles song that figured prominently in their celebration. Today, Lucy is one of the most well-known fossils ever reported, but over 3 million years ago, she was just one among many members of the species *Australopithecus afarensis*.

## INTRODUCTION

In this lab, we continue our exploration of our fossil relatives. We introduce the most important australopithecine species and their defining characteristics. We have hundreds of australopithecine

fossils, from as many as nine species. The species vary mostly in size and robusticity. Some researchers argue that the differences between the early australopithecines and later robust forms are so great that the robust forms should be in their own genus called *Paranthropus*. For simplicity, we will refer to the robust species as *Australopithecus*, but we keep the *Paranthropus* name in parentheses because some researchers use this genus name instead. We pay particular attention to the different types of australopithecines in both East and South Africa, as well as the significant differences that evolve over time in the later, more robust forms. We then introduce the earliest member of our own genus, *Homo*, and its defining characteristics. We conclude with a discussion of how the first *Homo* species differs from the australopithecines and why some scholars think there may have been two early *Homo* species, instead of just one. Perhaps the most significant finding from fossil discoveries in recent years is that throughout the evolutionary history of our lineage, there were periods when several different human ancestors were alive at the same time. Since there are many evolutionary branches at different points in time, it makes it difficult to identify clear ancestor–descendant relationships for all the species in our lineage.

## THE AUSTRALOPITHECINES (4 MYA–1 MYA)

The members of the *Australopithecus* genus, commonly referred to as the australopithecines, were a group of our ancestors that lived between about 4 and 1 mya (million years ago), during the early Pliocene to early Pleistocene, at numerous sites in eastern and southern Africa **(FIGURE 15.1)**. All of these species were habitual bipeds, with a mixture of bipedal and arboreal adaptations. They varied mostly in size and robusticity, with some species that were smaller and more gracile and other species that were larger and more robust. As a group, the australopithecines generally had much smaller cranial capacities and body sizes than modern humans, with small canines, large premolars, and large

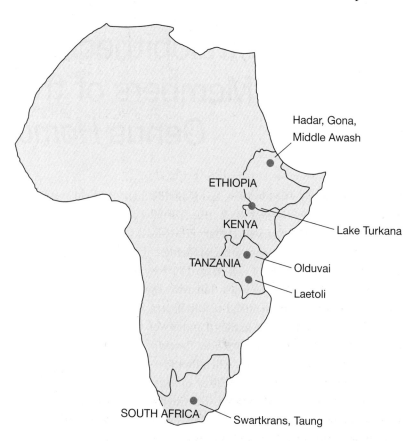

**FIGURE 15.1 The Distribution of Australopithecines and Early *Homo***
Australopithecines (and paranthropines) and early members of the *Homo* genus have been recovered from several major fossil sites in East and South Africa.

molars. The later australopithecines (sometimes placed in their own genus, *Paranthropus*) have notably larger faces, jaws, and teeth.

## Australopithecus anamensis

The earliest australopithecine is *Australopithecus anamensis* (FIGURE 15.2). This species lived around 4.0 mya (early Pliocene) in eastern Africa. *Australopithecus anamensis* individuals had a number of primitive ape-like traits such as very large canines, parallel upper tooth rows, and asymmetrical lower premolars with outer cusps that were much larger than the inner cusps. Postcranial remains of this species indicate it was a habitual biped with some adaptations for walking on two feet. There are enough similarities between *Au. anamensis* and earlier *Ardipithecus* specimens to suggest they might be directly related in an ancestor–descendant relationship. In addition, the combination of ancestral, ape-like traits and more derived, australopithecine-like traits seen in *Au. anamensis* has been interpreted as evidence that *Au. anamensis* was the first australopithecine and may have been ancestral to the later australopithecine species.

## Australopithecus afarensis

Another early australopithecine is *Australopithecus afarensis*, which lived 3.6 to 3.0 mya (late Pliocene) in eastern Africa. Members of this species had relatively small **cranial capacities** (around 350–500 cubic centimeters or cc) similar to living, nonhuman apes (FIGURE 15.3). In many other features, they appear to have been intermediate between a living chimpanzee and living human. For example, their faces were more **prognathic** (protruding) than a human face but flatter than a chimpanzee face, and their canine teeth were larger than human canines but smaller than chimpanzee canines. *Australopithecus afarensis* has many similarities to *Au. anamensis*, suggesting they share a direct ancestor–descendant relationship. However, in some features *Au. afarensis* appears less primitive than *Au. anamensis*. For example, the cusps of its lower premolars are relatively equal in size, and the upper tooth rows have an arched

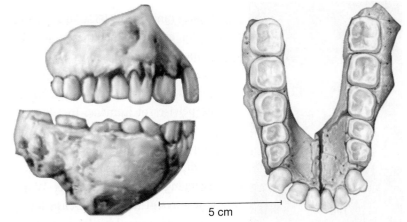

**FIGURE 15.2** *Australopithecus anamensis*
*Australopithecus anamensis* had parallel tooth rows with large canines and asymmetrical premolars, with outer cusps that were larger than the corresponding inner cusps.

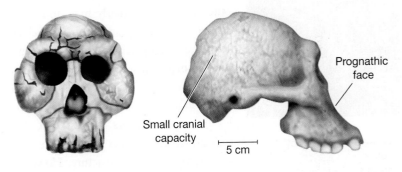

Prognathic face

Small cranial capacity

**FIGURE 15.3** *Australopithecus afarensis*
*Australopithecus afarensis* had a small cranial capacity and a more prognathic face than humans today.

shape like in humans as opposed to the parallel rows seen in *Au. anamensis* and nonhuman apes. *Australopithecus afarensis* also seems to have had a broader diet than *Au. anamensis*, whose diet more closely resembles that of modern chimpanzees living in savanna habitats. Researchers who conducted carbon isotope analysis that examines chemical traces in fossil teeth have found evidence that *Au. afarensis* had a very broad diet that probably incorporated a wider range of plants than the diet of living chimpanzees or *Au. anamensis*.

*Australopithecus afarensis* is the best known australopithecine, represented by dozens of individuals. The most famous specimen of *Au. afarensis*, nicknamed Lucy, was introduced at the start of this lab. The remains of Lucy and other *Au. afarensis* individuals tell us a lot about

**cranial capacity** the amount of space available in the cranium for the brain

**prognathic** having a projecting or protruding face

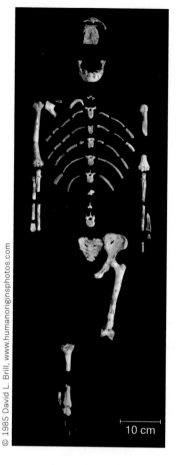

10 cm

**FIGURE 15.4 The Lucy Skeleton**

The *Australopithecus afarensis* specimen nicknamed Lucy provides valuable information about the postcrania of this species. For example, we can tell the species had angled femurs and somewhat short and broad pelvises.

**sexual dimorphism**
the physical differences between mature males and females of a species

their postcranial traits **(FIGURE 15.4)**. We know, for example, that these australopithecines had angled femurs. They also had pelvises (or pelves) that were short and broad, although not as bowl-shaped as the pelvises of humans. In addition, the Laetoli footprints (discussed in Lab 14) that were left by members of this species indicate *Au. afarensis* had slightly divergent big toes and arched feet. While these features of the *Au. afarensis* lower body indicate it was bipedal, features of its upper body (such as its long forearms and curved fingers) indicate it also had adaptations for arboreal locomotion.

Interestingly, Lucy is estimated to have been small (around 3.5 ft or 1 m tall), but other fossils, particularly male individuals, are estimated to have been as much as 1.5 or 2 ft taller than Lucy. The level of **sexual dimorphism** found in many regions of the *Au. afarensis* skeleton is similar to that seen in living chimpanzees and gorillas. Some researchers suggest that this indicates *Au. afarensis* might have had a polygynous social structure. However, *Au. afarensis* had smaller canines similar to those in pre-australopithecines like *Ardipithecus*, suggesting they experienced less male–male competition than living apes with polygynous social structures. Because of complex and potentially contradictory evidence like this, it is often difficult for researchers to determine the social organization of our extinct relatives.

### Australopithecus africanus

*Australopithecus africanus* was first identified by Raymond Dart in the 1920s, making it the first australopithecine species discovered. Members of this species lived around 3.0 to 2.0 mya (late Pliocene) in southern Africa. Compared with the earlier *Au. afarensis* species, *Au. africanus* had a slightly larger cranial capacity (around 450–550 cc), slightly smaller incisors and canines, slightly larger premolars and molars, and a slightly flatter face **(FIGURE 15.5)**. Despite these differences, however, carbon isotope evidence suggests *Au. africanus* had a diverse diet

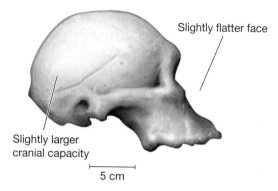

Slightly flatter face

Slightly larger cranial capacity

5 cm

**FIGURE 15.5** *Australopithecus africanus*
Compared to *Australopithecus afarensis*, *Australopithecus africanus* had a slightly larger cranial capacity, slightly smaller front teeth, and a slightly flatter face.

similar to that of *Au. afarensis*. The postcranial traits of *Au. africanus* (such as a short, broad pelvis and long arms) show a mix of bipedal and arboreal adaptations similar to that seen in *Au. afarensis*. Furthermore, the two species seem to have had similar body sizes and degrees of sexual dimorphism.

### Australopithecus garhi

Around the same time that *Au. africanus* was living in southern Africa 2.5 mya (latest Pliocene), *Australopithecus garhi* was living in eastern Africa. Like the other australopithecines, *Au. garhi* had a small cranial capacity (around 450 cc) and a prognathic face. It also had a small sagittal crest **(FIGURE 15.6)**. In contrast to earlier australopithecines, *Au. garhi* had larger canine, premolar, and molar teeth. Based on the evidence available, *Au. garhi* seems to have had longer legs than the earlier australopithecines, potentially indicating a more bipedal lifestyle with less use of arboreal locomotion, but more postcranial evidence is needed before definitive interpretations can be made. The anatomical features seen in *Au. garhi* and its date of 2.5 mya have led some researchers to suggest this species was ancestral to the early *Homo* species that followed.

Perhaps the most interesting feature of *Au. garhi* is its suggested behavior. Recent evidence from Ethiopia indicates that *Au. garhi* might have produced and used the first stone tools. Animal bones with cut marks have been found at an *Au. garhi* site in the Middle Awash region of Ethiopia. These cut marks could only have been made by stone tools, and they suggest that *Au. garhi* was using stone tools to butcher animals. Stone tools recovered from another site in the Gona area of Ethiopia date to around 2.5 mya, the time when *Au. garhi* occupied the area. However, the tools were not found at the same site as the *Au. garhi* fossils. It was previously believed that stone tool production was limited to members of our genus (*Homo*), so these finds are revolutionizing our understanding of tool use in the human lineage.

## Australopithecus (Paranthropus) aethiopicus

Around 2.5 mya (early Pleistocene), the same time that *Au. africanus* was in southern Africa and *Au. garhi* was in eastern Africa, a new australopithecine named *Australopithecus aethiopicus* appeared in eastern Africa. While the cranial capacity (around 410 cc) of *Au. aethiopicus* was similar to that of the earlier australopithecines, several of its cranial features were very different. *Australopithecus aethiopicus* is the earliest *robust* australopithecine form known, and it shows the classic cranial and dental traits seen in robust australopithecines **(FIGURE 15.7)**. It had smaller front teeth but larger premolars and molars than gracile australopithecines. It also had a large sagittal crest, a large mandible, and large zygomatic arches that made its face seem wide and flared **(FIGURE 15.8)**. As with all robust australopithecines, these enlarged features indicate *Au. aethiopicus* had a diet that required heavy chewing. However, it is not clear whether or not this early robust form evolved into the later robust *Australopithecus boisei* and *Australopithecus robustus* species.

## Australopithecus (Paranthropus) boisei

Between 2.3 and 1.2 mya (Pleistocene), another robust australopithecine named *Australopithecus boisei* lived in eastern Africa. It had a slightly larger cranial capacity (around 510 cc) than *Au. aethiopicus*, and its cranial and dental features suggest a specialized, heavy chewing diet **(FIGURE 15.9)**. Among the robust australopithecines, *Au. boisei* was particularly robust and had the largest molars. It was long assumed that

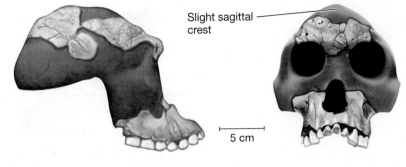

Slight sagittal crest

5 cm

**FIGURE 15.6 *Australopithecus garhi***
*Australopithecus garhi* had a small cranial capacity, a slight sagittal crest, and a relatively prognathic face.

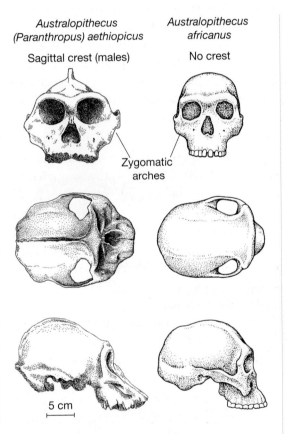

*Australopithecus (Paranthropus) aethiopicus*
Sagittal crest (males)

*Australopithecus africanus*
No crest

Zygomatic arches

5 cm

**FIGURE 15.7 Robust versus Gracile Australopithecines**
The robust australopithecines (or paranthropines), such as *Australopithecus (Paranthropus) aethiopicus*, generally have larger, more robust features (particularly in their crania and teeth) than the gracile australopithecines, such as *Australopithecus africanus*.

robust australopithecines like *Au. boisei* were primarily eating small, hard foods such as nuts and seeds because their cranial and dental traits seemed well suited for grinding these kinds of resources. However, carbon isotope studies suggest some robust australopithecines may

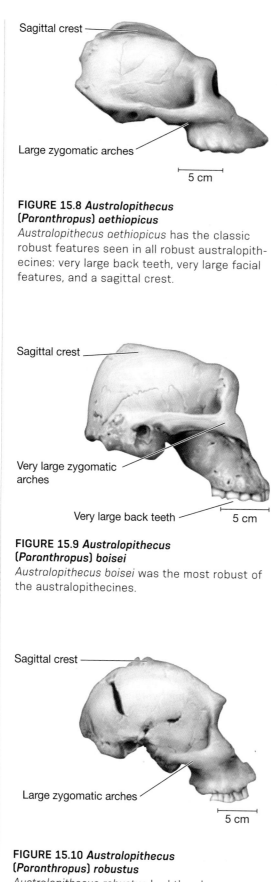

**FIGURE 15.8 *Australopithecus (Paranthropus) aethiopicus***
*Australopithecus aethiopicus* has the classic robust features seen in all robust australopithecines: very large back teeth, very large facial features, and a sagittal crest.

**FIGURE 15.9 *Australopithecus (Paranthropus) boisei***
*Australopithecus boisei* was the most robust of the australopithecines.

**FIGURE 15.10 *Australopithecus (Paranthropus) robustus***
*Australopithecus robustus* had the classic robust features seen in all the robust australopithecines.

have had a broader diet, more similar to those of earlier australopithecines, than previously expected. Interestingly, carbon isotope analysis indicates *Au. boisei* differed from these other australopithecines and had a diet that more narrowly focused on sedges and grasses.

### *Australopithecus (Paranthropus) robustus*

Named for its telltale robusticity, *Australopithecus robustus* lived in southern Africa around 2.0 to 1.5 mya (late Pleistocene) and was contemporaneous with *Au. boisei* in East Africa. It had a small cranial capacity of around 410–530 cc **(FIGURE 15.10)**. Like the other robust australopithecines, *Au. robustus* had traits adapted for heavy chewing, such as large molars, large zygomatic arches, and large sagittal crests. However, as mentioned above, carbon isotope studies indicate *Au. robustus* had a broader diet than *Au. boisei*. The potentially contradictory information gained from the analysis of cranial traits and isotopes suggests that diets and dietary adaptations were probably complex and variable in our ancient ancestors.

## THE NEWEST AUSTRALOPITHECINE: *AUSTRALOPITHECUS SEDIBA*

In 2010, researchers reported the discovery of a new australopithecine species called *Australopithecus sediba* **(FIGURE 15.11)**. Found in southern Africa, this species dates to around 2.0 mya (middle Pleistocene). Although it was a contemporary of *Au. robustus*, its cranial features were more similar to those of *Au. africanus*. For example, *Au. sediba* had a small cranial capacity (around 420 cc), small overall body size, and long arms for arboreal locomotion. Interestingly, while many features suggest that *Au. sediba* may have descended from *Au. africanus*, *Au. sediba* also shares several features in common with members of our own *Homo* genus. For example, *Au. sediba* had smaller teeth,

Photo by Brett Eloff, courtesy of Lee Berger and the University of Witwatersrand. From Berger et al. April 2010. *Australopithechus sediba*: A new species of *Homo*-like australopith from South Africa. *Science* 328(5975):195–204.

**FIGURE 15.11 *Australopithecus sediba***
*Australopithecus sediba* was found in South Africa. It is relatively gracile and has a combination of australopithecine-like traits and *Homo*-like traits.

mandibles, and zygomatic arches than most australopithecines. It also had a broad pelvis very similar to that seen in early members of the *Homo* genus. Ongoing research will help to further illuminate this new australopithecine species and clarify its relationship to other australopithecines and members of our own *Homo* genus.

## THE *HOMO* GENUS

From 2.5 to 1.8 mya (early Pleistocene), a very different type of species lived side by side with the robust australopithecines in eastern and southern Africa. This species, called *Homo habilis*, was the first member of our own genus. Unlike the large teeth, jaws, and face characteristic of the robust australopithecines, *H. habilis* had a much smaller chewing complex and a larger brain size **(FIGURE 15.12)**.

The name *Homo habilis*, meaning "handy man," is the result of its discovery with associated stone tools. At the time, tool use was believed to be limited to our genus, and *H. habilis* was

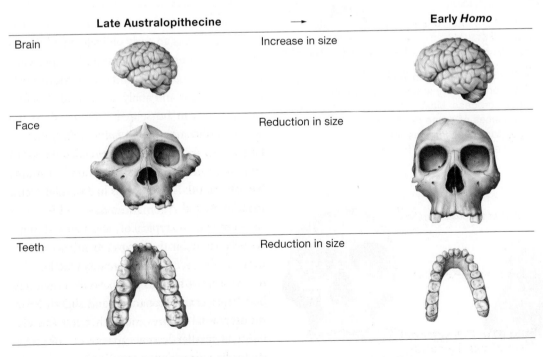

**FIGURE 15.12 Robust Australopithecines (Paranthropines) versus Early *Homo***
The robust australopithecines and early members of the *Homo* genus coexisted in Africa but had very different traits.

Oldowan technology
this earliest stone tool technology is characterized by chopper and flake tools

**chopper** a large, heavy stone tool with a sharp edge where small pieces of rock have been removed

**flake** a small piece of rock that has been removed from a larger rock and can be used as is or further modified into a specialized tool

**direct percussion** the process of stone tool production where two rocks are hit directly together in order to break off flakes

thought to have been the first stone tool user. As we discussed above, the finding of stone tools in the Gona area that date to 2.5 mya suggests that *Australopithecus garhi* may also be one of the first stone tool users.

The earliest stone tools are considered to be part of the **Oldowan technology (FIGURE 15.13)**. This technology was named after the Olduvai Gorge site in eastern Africa where stone tools like this were first found. These tools generally take two forms: choppers and flakes. **Choppers**

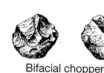
Bifacial chopper

Hammer stone

Discoid

Flake scraper

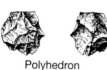
Polyhedron

Flake

5 cm

Heavy-duty (core) scraper

**FIGURE 15.13 Oldowan Tools**
Oldowan tools are made using a relatively simple process. Most Oldowan tools are flakes (the pieces of stone removed) or choppers (the stone that remains after flakes have been removed). Scale bar is for choppers on left only.

are large, heavy tools that have a sharp edge where smaller bits of rock have been broken off. The smaller bits of rock that are removed from choppers are called **flakes**. The size and weight of choppers make them well suited to chopping tasks, such as chopping up the long bones of animals to extract the marrow inside. In contrast, the smaller flakes have delicate, sharp surfaces that are well suited to fine cutting tasks, such as cutting animal meat off the bone. Producing these tools involves a relatively simple process of **direct percussion** (where two stones are hit directly together to break off flakes). The tools are generalized, so they can be used for a variety of tasks, and they vary considerably in size, shape, and raw material. However, if a small-brained australopithecine like *Au. garhi* made these tools, it suggests that tool use may not be as unique a behavior as was previously thought (see Lab 14 for more information about brain size, tool use, and the human lineage).

### *Homo habilis*

Like the australopithecines, *Homo habilis* was probably a habitual biped with a short stature, relatively long arms, and hands suitable for climbing. However, some researchers question the limb proportion estimates for *Homo habilis* and argue it was an early obligate biped due to its lack of an opposable hallux and the presence of a longitudinal arch in its foot. More postcranial remains and analysis are needed before this debate can be settled. Compared to the australopithecines, *Homo habilis* had a slightly larger cranial capacity (averaging about 650 cc) and more gracile cranial and dental features **(FIGURE 15.14)**. *Homo habilis* had smaller teeth, mandibles, and zygomatic arches, and it lacked the sagittal crests typical of robust australopithecines. Based on the recovered fossil material for early *Homo*, it seems there was a fair amount of variation within this group. Some individuals had larger cranial capacities and slightly more robust cranial features and teeth. Other individuals had smaller cranial capacities (more similar to the australopithecines) and more gracile cranial features and teeth. Some researchers believe this variation reflects minor differences

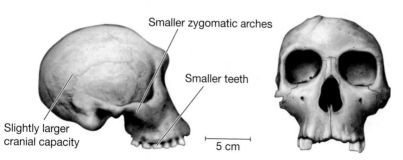
Smaller zygomatic arches
Smaller teeth
Slightly larger cranial capacity
5 cm

**FIGURE 15.14 *Homo habilis***
*Homo habilis* had a slightly larger cranial capacity than the australopithecines, and it had more gracile cranial features.

due to sexual dimorphism (with the robust individuals being male and the more gracile individuals being female). These researchers classify all of the individuals into the same single species, *Homo habilis*. Other researchers argue the differences are more significant and warrant separation of the group into two distinct species—*Homo habilis* (the smaller individuals) and *Homo rudolfensis* (the larger individuals). In 2012, researchers reported evidence from Koobi Fora, Kenya, that has further bolstered the latter view. These new Koobi Fora specimens are anatomically similar to the larger individuals classified as *H. rudolfensis,* but they are much smaller, indicating that large size alone is not responsible for the distinctive features of *H. rudolfensis*. This suggests that there are two distinct clusters of early *Homo* fossils that reflect two distinct species.

The anatomical traits seen in *Homo habilis* suggest it had a more diversified diet, particularly compared to the diet of the late australopithecines. This dietary diversity is confirmed by carbon isotope evidence that shows early *Homo* individuals incorporated a wider range of plants into their diet than

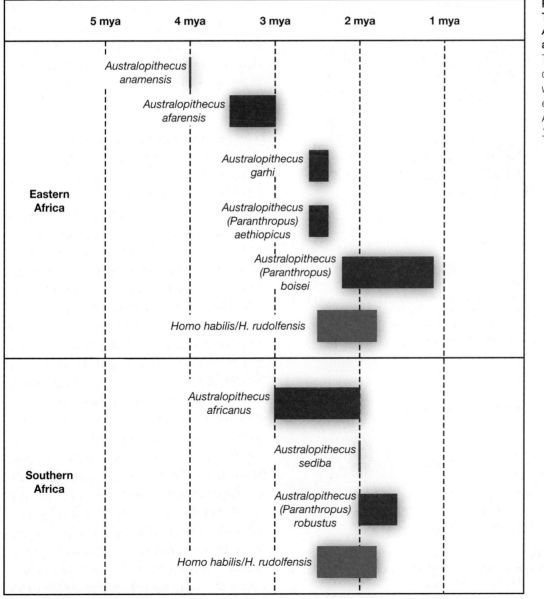

**FIGURE 15.15**
**Time Line of *Australopithecus* and Early *Homo***
The fossil species discussed in this lab were distributed in eastern and southern Africa between 4 and 1 million years ago.

the more grass-focused *Au. boisei* individuals. While robust forms like *Au. boisei* were very well adapted for chewing abrasive grassy diets during the grassland expansion across East Africa starting 3 mya, early *Homo* was perhaps better adapted for a flexible diet that accommodated fluctuating climates and landscapes. While we do not know precisely what all our early human ancestors were eating, it is clear which dietary adaptations were ultimately more successful: those for a more generalized diet, which modern humans possess today.

These earliest members of our genus *Homo* mark the beginning of a shift toward more human-like traits, particularly bigger brains and smaller faces, and the use of stone tools. This shift becomes even more dramatic in the next species in the *Homo* lineage, *Homo erectus*, which is discussed in Lab 16.

# CONCEPT REVIEW QUESTIONS

Name: _____     Section: _____

Course: _____     Date: _____

Answer the following questions in the space provided.

1. As a group, the australopithecines lived around
   A. 4 mya to 1 mya.
   B. 7 mya to 4.4 mya.
   C. 2.5 mya to 1 mya.
   D. 4 mya to 2.5 mya.

2. The fossil individual nicknamed Lucy was
   A. a typical robust australopithecine.
   B. a habitual biped.
   C. unusually tall.
   D. alive around 2 mya.

3. Name *two* East African australopithecines.

4. Name *two* South African australopithecines.

5. The oldest australopithecine is
   A. *Australopithecus afarensis.*
   B. *Australopithecus garhi.*
   C. *Australopithecus africanus.*
   D. *Australopithecus anamensis.*

6. True or false? Some researchers argue the robust australopithecines should be classified in a separate genus called *Paranthropus.*

7. I lived around 2.5 mya in eastern Africa. I had a small cranial capacity (around 410 cc), large molars, large zygomatic arches, and a sagittal crest. What species am I?
   A. *Australopithecus afarensis*
   B. *Australopithecus* (*Paranthropus*) *aethiopicus*
   C. *Homo habilis*
   D. *Australopithecus garhi*

8. Describe the *two* tool forms associated with the Oldowan tool industry.

9. Based on evidence from Gona, Ethiopia, who may be the first stone tool user?

   A. *Homo habilis*
   B. *Australopithecus africanus*
   C. *Australopithecus garhi*
   D. *Australopithecus (Paranthropus) boisei*

10. Describe *one* feature that decreases in size between the australopithecines and early members of the *Homo* genus.

# LAB EXERCISES

Name: _____     Section: _____

Course: _____     Date: _____

## EXERCISE 1  AUSTRALOPITHECINE VARIATION 1

Work in a small group or alone to complete this exercise. Refer to the casts provided by your instructor (or the pictures in the lab Appendix) to answer the following questions.

1. Which of these mystery australopithecines is a later, more robust form?

2. Describe *two* anatomical traits you used to make this determination. (Be sure to describe how each trait varied in the two fossils.)

## EXERCISE 2  AUSTRALOPITHECINE VARIATION 2

Work in a small group or alone to complete this exercise. Review the casts provided by your instructor (or the pictures in the lab Appendix) and answer the following questions.

1. Which of these mystery fossils is *Australopithecus robustus*?

2. Which of these mystery fossils is *Australopithecus boisei*?

3. Describe *one* trait you used to make these identifications. (Be sure to describe how the trait varied in the two fossils.)

## EXERCISE 3  AUSTRALOPITHECINE BIPEDALISM

Work in a small group or alone to complete this exercise. Review the casts provided by your instructor (or the picture in the lab Appendix) and answer the following questions.

1. Describe *two* postcranial traits that indicate *Au. afarensis* was adapted for bipedalism.

2. Compare the Lucy (*Au. afarensis*) postcrania to the human (*Homo sapiens*) postcrania depicted in Figure 5.11 (Lab 5). Describe *two* postcranial traits that differ between these species.

3. What does this suggest about the kind of bipedalism practiced by *Au. afarensis*?

## EXERCISE 4   *AUSTRALOPITHECUS* VERSUS *HOMO*

Work in a small group or alone to complete this exercise. Use the casts provided by your instructor (or the pictures in the lab Appendix) to answer the following questions.

1. Describe *two* traits that differ between these fossils. (Be sure to describe how each trait appears in the two fossils.)

2. Based on this information, which of these fossils is an australopithecine?

3. Based on this information, which of these fossils is a member of the *Homo* genus?

## EXERCISE 5   THE EARLY MEMBERS OF THE GENUS *HOMO*

Work in a small group or alone to complete this exercise. Refer to the casts provided by your instructor (or the pictures in the lab Appendix) to answer the following questions.

1. Describe *two* traits that differ between these fossils. (Be sure to describe how each trait appears in the two fossils.)

2. Do *you* believe these differences are the result of sexual dimorphism or different adaptations? Why?

## EXERCISE 6   STONE TOOL TECHNOLOGY

Work in a small group or alone to complete this exercise. Review the casts provided by your instructor (or the pictures in the lab Appendix) and answer the following questions.

1. What type of tool form is this?

2. Describe the features of this tool that led you to identify it as this tool form.

3. What tool technology does it belong to?

4. Name *one* fossil species that may have made this stone tool.

# CRITICAL THINKING QUESTIONS

On a separate sheet of paper, answer the following questions.

1. This question may be completed independently or as a group exercise. Biological anthropologists disagree about the best way to classify the robust australopithecines. Describe the *two* approaches to classifying these species. Which classification do *you* support? Why? (Be sure to support your decision with specific evidence.)

2. This question may be completed independently or as a group exercise. The *Australopithecus sediba* finds demonstrate that evolution is mosaic, meaning that species often have a combination of ancestral and new traits. How would this fossil material be interpreted if only the arm bones were found? How would this fossil material be interpreted if only the pelvis were found? Based on this example, what problems do paleoanthropologists face when trying to interpret the fragmentary fossil record?

3. This question may be completed independently or as a group exercise. During a period of almost a million years, *Australopithecus boisei* and *Homo habilis* lived in the same region of East Africa. If these species shared a habitat, how did they not outcompete one another? (*Hint*: Think about their possible ecologies and adaptations.)

4. This question may be completed independently or as a group exercise. In this lab we discussed the earliest known stone tools. Do you think this was the first time our extinct relatives used tools? Why might older tools not be preserved in the fossil record? For comparison, describe three tools from your own life (a cell phone, a pencil, a plastic fork, etc.). Do you think these tools will be preserved 2.5 million years from today?

5. In this lab we reviewed a lot of different fossil species and their defining characteristics. To help you make comparisons across these species and understand larger trends in our evolutionary history, complete the following Australopithecine and Early *Homo* Chart.

## AUSTRALOPITHECINE AND EARLY *HOMO* CHART (PART ONE)

| Fossil | Dates and Location | Cranial Traits | Postcranial Traits | Suggested Behavior |
|---|---|---|---|---|
| *Australopithecus anamensis* | | | | |
| *Australopithecus afarensis* | | | | |
| *Australopithecus africanus* | | | | |
| *Australopithecus garhi* | | | | |
| *Australopithecus (Paranthropus) aethiopicus* | | | | |
| *Australopithecus (Paranthropus) boisei* | | | | |

## AUSTRALOPITHECINE AND EARLY *HOMO* CHART (PART TWO)

| Fossil | Dates and Location | Cranial Traits | Postcranial Traits | Suggested Behavior |
|---|---|---|---|---|
| *Australopithecus (Paranthropus) robustus* | | | | |
| *Australopithecus sediba* | | | | |
| *Homo habilis* (including *H. rudolfensis*) | | | | |

# APPENDIX:
# LAB EXERCISE IMAGES

## Exercise 1 Australopithecine Variation 1

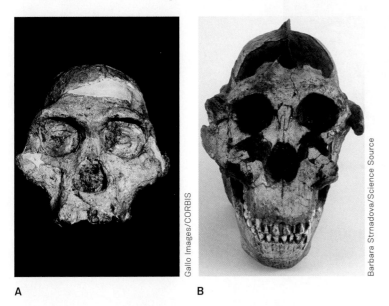

A

B

Gallo Images/CORBIS

Barbara Strnadova/Science Source

## Exercise 2 Australopithecine Variation 2

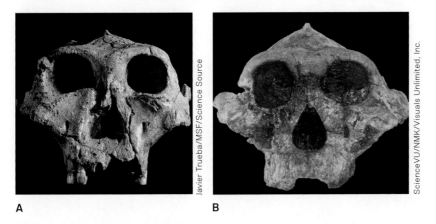

A

B

Javier Trueba/MSF/Science Source

ScienceVU/NMK/Visuals Unlimited, Inc.

## Exercise 3 Australopithecine Bipedalism

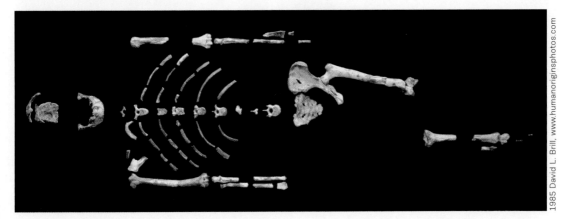

1985 David L. Brill, www.humanoriginsphotos.com

## Exercise 4 *Australopithecus* versus *Homo*

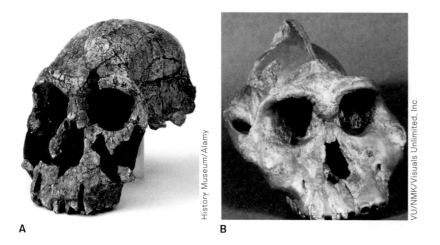

A

B

## Exercise 5 The Early Members of the Genus *Homo*

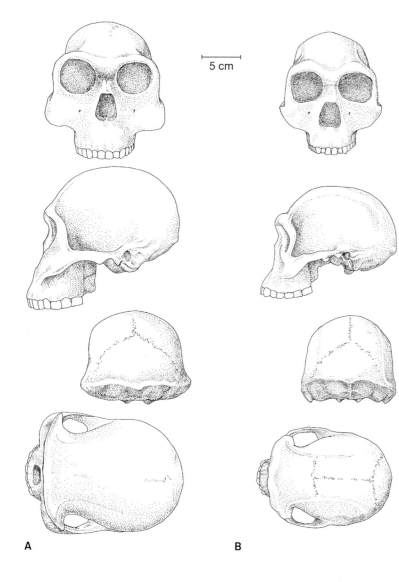

5 cm

A                                    B

## Exercise 6 Stone Tool Technology

Side view 1          Top view          Side view 2

Pete Bostrum/Lithic Casting Lab

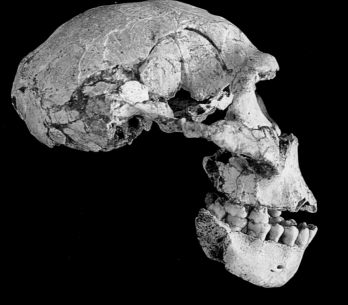

David Lordkipanidze et al. 18 October 2013. A complete skull from Dmanisi, Georgia, and the evolutionary biology of early *Homo*. *Science* 342(6156):326–331. Copyright © 2013 AAAS.

## Lab Learning Objectives

By the end of this lab, students should be able to:

- describe the later species of our genus, including their distribution and defining characteristics.

- describe the variation seen in *Homo erectus* fossils, particularly in specimens from Africa and Asia.

- discuss the relationship between humans and Neanderthals, based on current evidence.

- compare and distinguish between the major stone tool technologies.

- describe the explanations for the origin and spread of humans.

LAB 16

# Later Members of the Genus *Homo*

Around 1.75 mya (million years ago) in Eurasia, the world was changing. Fifty miles southwest of what is now the city of Tbilisi (the capital of the Republic of Georgia), the land held an array of environmental zones including a river valley, meadows, and grasslands. This place (now called Dmanisi) was home to a variety of animals such as deer, rodents, wild dogs, and rhinoceroses. It was also home to a group of our relatives called *Homo erectus*. Only 500,000 years after the species originated in Africa, it had expanded to another continent. How was *Homo erectus* able to make this extraordinary migration?

This Dmanisi population had an interesting mix of traits that reflected the transition from more ancestral, early *Homo* traits to more derived, later *Homo* traits. The small cranial capacity (600–775 cubic centimeters or cc), small body size, and primitive shoulder anatomy suggest they were related to *Homo habilis* in Africa. However, the shape of the mandible and cranium more closely resembled a newer species in Africa, called *Homo erectus*. They also had *H. erectus*-like lower limbs with long, angled femurs; arched feet; and nondivergent big toes. Their legs were more specialized for bipedalism than the earlier *Homo habilis*, and their gait was more efficient. The Dmanisi population also used Oldowan tools. Although they

**orthognathic** having a flat face

did not travel great distances to acquire special rocks for their tools, they did select the best locally available materials. They produced choppers and flakes that helped them take better advantage of meat resources, which were probably obtained through intensive scavenging. This meat was part of a diverse diet that also included a range of plant and fruit resources.

The Dmanisi group is significant because their fossil remains show us an important transition in our evolutionary history. In addition to the physical changes that took place at this time, a remarkable cultural change occurred as well. For over 5 million years, our ancestors lived only in Africa, but around 1.8 mya they began to move out and settle other parts of the world. The Dmanisi population was among the first of our relatives to make this move out of Africa.

## INTRODUCTION

In this lab, we conclude our exploration of our fossil relatives. We introduce the most important later *Homo* species and their defining physical

and cultural characteristics. We also consider the geographic distribution and coexistence of several of these species. We pay particular attention to the coexistence of humans and Neanderthals and what current evidence tells us about their relationship. In addition, we discuss the major explanations for the origin and spread of our own species.

## LATER MEMBERS OF THE GENUS *HOMO*

The later members of the genus *Homo* share some key traits that distinguish them from early species, such as *Homo habilis*. The later *Homo* species had larger cranial capacities, more **orthognathic** (or flatter) faces, and smaller teeth. Their postcrania were more similar to those of modern humans, and unlike our earlier relatives, these later *Homo* species were obligate bipeds. These species had wider geographic distributions than earlier species, and they lived in places outside of Africa **(FIGURE 16.1)**. They also had more complicated culture and technology than earlier species.

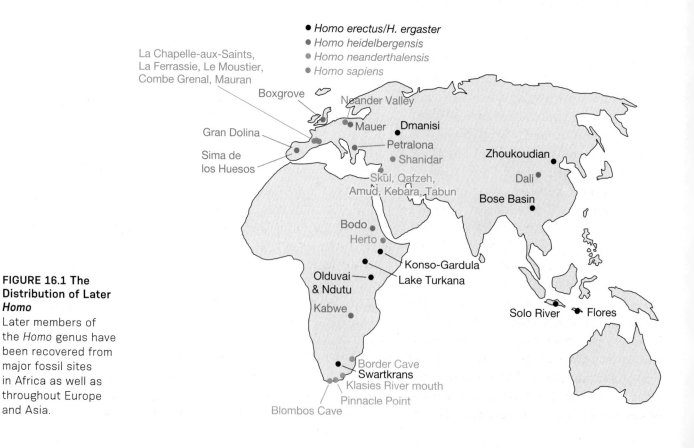

**FIGURE 16.1 The Distribution of Later *Homo***

Later members of the *Homo* genus have been recovered from major fossil sites in Africa as well as throughout Europe and Asia.

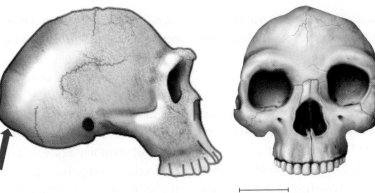

5 cm

**FIGURE 16.2 *Homo erectus***
*Homo erectus* had a long, low cranium with a large cranial capacity. It had large brow ridges and an occipital torus (arrow). It also had small teeth.

**brow ridge** a bony ridge located above the eye orbits

**occipital torus** a ridge of bone along the occipital bone that forms a small point when seen from the side

## Homo erectus

*Homo erectus* lived from about 1.8 mya to 300 kya (thousand years ago), during the late Pleistocene, in Africa and Asia, and the species lived in Europe from about 1.8 mya to 400 kya (if we include the Dmanisi individuals discussed at the start of this lab as part of the European group). Members of this species had larger cranial capacities (averaging around 950 cc) than prior species (**FIGURE 16.2**). Some very early individuals, such as the Dmanisi group, had smaller cranial capacities (600 cc) and some later individuals, such as the Zhoukoudian group in modern-day China, had even larger cranial capacities (1200 cc). *Homo erectus* crania were generally long and low, shaped like footballs when viewed from the side. These individuals also had pronounced **brow ridges**, relatively orthognathic (flat) faces, and an unusual projection at the back of the skull called an occipital torus. The **occipital torus** is a ridge of bone that runs along the occipital bone and forms a small point when seen from the side. In addition to these cranial traits, *Homo erectus* mandibles and teeth, particularly their premolars and molars, were much smaller than those of earlier species (such as the australopithecines). These features may relate to a shift in diet. Whereas australopithecines (especially robust species) relied on chewing, *Homo erectus* seems to have relied more on biting and tearing, so it did not require the larger chewing teeth seen in australopithecines.

One of the earliest and most famous *Homo erectus* specimens is nicknamed Nariokotome (or Turkana) boy, after the site in eastern Africa where the specimen was recovered. Nariokotome boy is a relatively complete skeleton from a single individual (**FIGURE 16.3**). It is believed to have belonged to a male who was around 8–10 years old when he died approximately 1.6 mya. This individual provides good evidence of *Homo erectus* postcranial traits. He had long legs and shorter arms, which indicate that he did not practice the arboreal locomotion that was still part of the repertoire of our earlier ancestors. This is further supported by his barrel-shaped rib cage, which is more similar to ours and less similar to that of arboreal nonhuman apes. Nariokotome boy also had angled femurs and various other lower limb traits that suggest he moved efficiently on two legs and could cover great distances with ease. Analysis of his skeleton also suggests he would have been close to 6 ft or 1.8 m tall in adulthood. Together, these lines

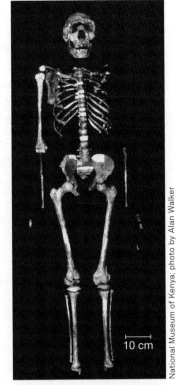

National Museum of Kenya; photo by Alan Walker

10 cm

**FIGURE 16.3 The Nariokotome Skeleton**
The nearly complete *Homo erectus* specimen nicknamed Nariokotome boy provides valuable information about the postcrania of this species. We can tell *H. erectus* was an efficient obligate biped with modern stature and limb proportions.

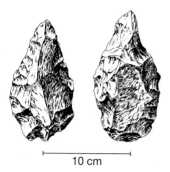

| |
|---|
| 10 cm |

**FIGURE 16.4 Acheulean Tools**
The Acheulean tool technology is characterized by handaxes. These tools required a slightly more complicated production process than Oldowan tools, and they were more standardized than Oldowan tools.

of evidence indicate that *Homo erectus* individuals, such as Nariokotome boy, were efficient obligate bipeds with **statures** and limb proportions similar to those of modern humans today.

Evidence from fossilized dental remains and stone tools suggests *Homo erectus* had a diverse diet that included more meat than those of earlier species, but it is unclear whether this meat was scavenged or directly hunted. As for its social life, it was originally believed that *Homo erectus* had less sexual dimorphism than earlier species. This would suggest a possible shift away from polygynous social structures. Recent evidence, however, suggests *H. erectus* may have maintained the higher degree of sexual dimorphism and likely polygynous social structures of earlier fossil species.

Early *Homo erectus* individuals used Oldowan tools (such as the choppers and flakes discussed in Lab 15), but around 1.5 mya, *Homo erectus* began to make and use new kinds of tools. These newer stone tools are considered

**FIGURE 16.5 *Homo erectus* Migration**
*Homo erectus* was the first member of our lineage to move out of Africa and settle in various areas of Europe and Asia. This migration was facilitated by the species' generalized anatomy and flexible technology.

to be part of the **Acheulean (Acheulian) technology** **(FIGURE 16.4)**. This technology was named after a site in Saint Acheul, France, where these tools were discovered in the mid 1800s. Tools called bifaces characterize this technology. A **biface** is a stone tool that has had flakes of stone removed from two sides. The most common biface in Acheulean sites is the handaxe. A **handaxe** is a biface tool that is shaped like a pear (or teardrop) with one end that is larger and rounded and another end that is more narrow and pointed. Most handaxes would fit neatly into the palm of your hand, and they were multipurpose tools that were probably used for butchering meat and/or digging up underground plant parts to be eaten. These versatile tools were useful in environments from Africa to Europe to western Asia, and they were effective enough that they remained largely unchanged for over a million years. Compared to the earlier Oldowan tools, Acheulean tools were manufactured through a slightly more complicated process that required more steps to produce the desired shape. In addition, the Acheulean tools were more standardized than Oldowan tools. An Oldowan chopper at one site can look very different from an Oldowan chopper at another site. However, Acheulean handaxes were the same shape and size from one place to another, across thousands of miles and hundreds of thousands of years.

One of the most significant aspects of *Homo erectus* is its geographic distribution. It was the first species of our genus to leave Africa, and within a few tens of thousands of years, *Homo erectus* was found as far away from Africa as southeastern Asia **(FIGURE 16.5)**. This migration into Eurasia between 1.8 mya and 800 kya (sometimes called **Out of Africa I**) was related to environmental shifts and changing food availability. Unlike many of the migrations in our recent history, *Homo erectus* did not consciously set out to move to a new place. Instead, the species probably moved a little further east with every generation. A group might settle in one region for a generation or two and take advantage of the wild animal herds and plant foods available in that area. As the environment

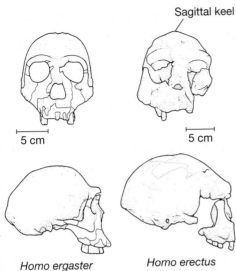

Sagittal keel

5 cm    5 cm

*Homo ergaster*    *Homo erectus*

**FIGURE 16.6 *Homo erectus* versus *Homo ergaster***
Some researchers argue that *Homo erectus* fossils can be divided into two different species. Compared to typical African specimens (*Homo ergaster*), non-African specimens (*Homo erectus*) have a more pronounced occipital torus, a sagittal keel, and a longer and lower cranium.

changed and the animal herds moved further east, the next generation of the *Homo erectus* group might follow and settle in a new region for another generation or two. Over many generations, *Homo erectus* was able to expand across Asia and up into Europe. Its ability to do this was likely facilitated by its generalized anatomy and flexible tool technology. Unlike highly specialized species (such as robust australopithecines), *Homo erectus* had a diverse diet and generalized anatomy that allowed it to do well in a wide range of habitats. Its more complicated but widely applicable stone tool technology may have helped it adapt to its varied surroundings as well.

As seen with the *Homo habilis* fossils discussed in Lab 15, there is significant variation within *Homo erectus* fossils, which suggests the African and non-African individuals (particularly from Asia) may form two distinct groups. The non-African fossils show more exaggerated versions of the traits seen in the African fossils (**FIGURE 16.6**). Specifically, members of the non-African group had thicker cranial bones, an even longer and lower cranium, more pronounced brow

ridges, a more pronounced occipital torus, and a unique cranial feature called a sagittal keel. The **sagittal keel** is a slight ridge of bone that runs along the midline of the cranium. Although it is located in the same position as the sagittal crest of a gorilla or robust australopithecine, it is much less pronounced and does not relate to chewing muscle attachment. In addition to these cranial differences, the members of the non-African group were a little shorter and stockier than their African counterparts. Some researchers believe these differences are significant enough to warrant classifying the African and non-African fossils into two different species. These researchers argue that the more generalized African group should be called *Homo ergaster*, while the more exaggerated non-African group should be called *Homo erectus*.

## Homo heidelbergensis

Around 600 kya (late Pleistocene), a new species called *Homo heidelbergensis* appeared in Africa and Europe (**FIGURE 16.7**). *Homo heidelbergensis* lived in these areas from around 600 to around 130 kya and in Asia from around 200 to 130 kya. Members of this new group had several traits in common with *Homo erectus*. They had long and low crania and large brow ridges. Some of the individuals even had a small occipital torus. However, *Homo heidelbergensis* also had some unique traits. For example, it had a larger cranial

**stature** an individual's overall body height

**Acheulean (Acheulian) technology** the second and more widespread stone tool technology that was characterized by handaxes

**biface** a stone tool that has had flakes of stone removed from two sides

**handaxe** a biface tool that is shaped like a pear or teardrop

**Out of Africa I** the migration between 1.8 mya and 800 kya of *Homo erectus* out of Africa and into Asia and Europe

**sagittal keel** a very slight ridge of bone along the midline of the cranium

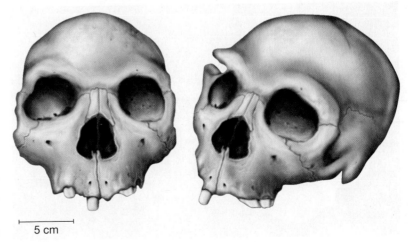

5 cm

**FIGURE 16.7 *Homo heidelbergensis***
*Homo heidelbergensis* had a long and low cranium, a large brow ridge, and a large cranial capacity. It also had small teeth that often show extensive wear on the incisors.

**Mousterian technology** a stone tool technology that used the Levallois technique to produce a variety of specialized flake tools

capacity (around 1200–1300 cc) and smaller back teeth (premolars and molars) than *Homo erectus*. Some of the European individuals in particular also had more tooth wear on their incisors. This indicates they might have been using their teeth as tools. Perhaps they held animal hides or plant fibers in their teeth while using their hands to scrape the material with a stone tool.

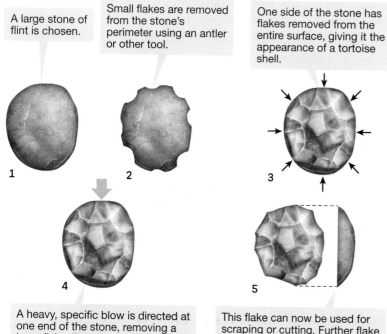

A large stone of flint is chosen.

Small flakes are removed from the stone's perimeter using an antler or other tool.

One side of the stone has flakes removed from the entire surface, giving it the appearance of a tortoise shell.

1   2   3

4   5

A heavy, specific blow is directed at one end of the stone, removing a large flake. This flake is convex on one side and flat on the other.

This flake can now be used for scraping or cutting. Further flake removal will produce a more specialized tool.

**A**

**B**

**FIGURE 16.8 Mousterian Tools**
Using the Levallois technique (A), Mousterian toolmakers produced regular flakes that were then modified into different tools (B).

As with the earlier members of the genus *Homo*, there is debate about how best to classify the *Homo heidelbergensis* fossils. A few researchers argue that these fossils share key features in common with modern humans, such as a very large cranial capacity. Based on this similarity, these researchers classify the *Homo heidelbergensis* fossils as members of our own species, *Homo sapiens*. Of course, these researchers acknowledge that these fossils are also different from us, especially in their cranial robusticity. To account for this robusticity, the fossils are considered to be *archaic* (or *early*) *Homo sapiens*, as opposed to *anatomically modern Homo sapiens* (humans of today). In contrast, other researchers emphasize the uniqueness of the fossil group. From their viewpoint, the robusticity seen in the fossil group is significant enough to distinguish the specimens from our own species, so they are classified as a separate species called *Homo heidelbergensis*. The large cranial capacity of *H. heidelbergensis* is believed to reflect a general trend toward larger cranial capacities that began with earlier members of the *Homo* genus, but it is not significant enough to warrant placing them in our own species.

*Homo heidelbergensis* had a diverse diet that included meat from big game animals. It is often unclear whether our earlier ancestors hunted or scavenged the meat in their diet. However, tools and other evidence recovered from *Homo heidelbergensis* sites suggest they actively hunted large animals. This hunting was likely facilitated by a shift in stone tool technology that occurred during this time. Early *Homo heidelbergensis* used Acheulean tools similar to those used by *Homo erectus*, but later members of *Homo heidelbergensis* used a new technology called the Mousterian technology.

The **Mousterian technology** is named after a site in France called Le Moustier, and it is very different from the earlier stone tool technologies (**FIGURE 16.8**). In both the Oldowan and the Acheulean technologies, a lot of emphasis was placed on core tools—the tools left when flakes had been removed. For a Mousterian toolmaker, the flakes themselves were the most important tools. These flakes were modified into a wide range of shapes that were each suitable for a specific task, such as scraping, drilling, and cutting. Whereas the Oldowan and Acheulean toolmakers used a few generalized tools to perform countless functions, the Mousterian toolmakers used a specific tool for each function. They even hafted (attached) stone points onto wood to make stone-tipped spears. To produce their specialized flake tools, Mousterian toolmakers used a much more complicated production process called the **Levallois technique**. In this process, the toolmaker first removed small flakes from around a core of rock, then created a platform at one end of the stone, and finally struck the platform to remove a precisely shaped flake. By repeating the process over and over, the same core could yield numerous flakes that all had roughly the same shape and size. After preparing these flakes, the toolmaker would then remove pieces of stone from the edge of the flake to form the specific tool desired. While the flake tools were shaped differently for different functions, these shapes were standardized across Mousterian sites. For example, a scraper tool in one area was very similar to a scraper tool in another area. While later *Homo heidelbergensis* did make Mousterian tools, the technology is most often associated with the Neanderthals; Mousterian tools are found at Neanderthal sites throughout Europe and western Asia.

## Homo neanderthalensis

*Homo neanderthalensis* is perhaps the most famous of our extinct fossil relatives **(FIGURE 16.9)**. The Neanderthals lived around 130 to 30 kya (late Pleistocene) in Europe and western Asia. They shared several traits in common with the earlier *Homo heidelbergensis* fossils. For example, they had a long and low cranium and large brow ridges. They also had small back teeth (premolars and molars) and highly worn incisors, suggesting they may also have used their front teeth as tools. In addition to these shared features, the Neanderthals also had several unique traits. They had incredibly large cranial capacities (around 1245–1740 cc). In fact, the average Neanderthal cranial capacity (1520 cc) was larger than the

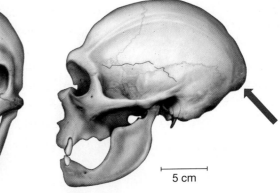

**FIGURE 16.9** *Homo neanderthalensis*
*Homo neanderthalensis* had an incredibly large cranial capacity, large brow ridges, a large nasal opening, and an occipital bun (arrow).

average human cranial capacity today (1400 cc)! However, when we take into account estimates of Neanderthal body weight, their brain to body ratio is lower than that of the average human today. The Neanderthals also had an unusual, round projection called an **occipital bun** located on the back of their skulls. When looking at this feature on a Neanderthal cranium, it almost appears as if a dinner roll (or bun) is stuck on the back of the head.

Neanderthals also had several adaptations that helped them in their extreme environment. During the time of the Neanderthals, the planet was experiencing a massive Ice Age. During certain times, much of Europe was covered in glaciers, and temperatures were considerably colder than today. The nonglaciated areas of southern Europe would have been bitterly cold habitats similar to what we find in Scandinavia, northern Russia, Alaska, or northern Canada today. Neanderthals in this extreme environment had large nasal openings that may have helped to warm the air when they inhaled. In addition, similar to Arctic human populations today, the Neanderthals had stocky bodies **(FIGURE 16.10)** that helped them to retain body heat (see Lab 8 for more information about climate adaptations in humans). In addition to their physical adaptations, Neanderthals also had cultural adaptations that helped them to survive in Ice Age Europe. They built fires, made use of caves as shelters, and probably had rudimentary clothing.

**Levallois technique** a process used to produce regularly shaped flakes that can then be further modified into different tools

**occipital bun** a large, round projection located on the occipital bone

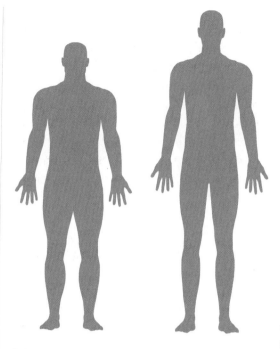

**FIGURE 16.10 Neanderthal Body Size**
Neanderthals (left) had stockier bodies than modern humans (right). This would have helped them to retain body heat in their Ice Age environment.

Similar to *Homo heidelbergensis*, Neanderthals had a diverse diet that emphasized big game animals. These animals were hunted using Mousterian tools, which required the Neanderthals to spear their prey at close range. This risky

Musée de l'Homme de Néandertal

**FIGURE 16.11 Neanderthal Burial**
Evidence of purposefully arranged burials from numerous sites (such as this one from La Chapelle-aux-Saints) suggests that Neanderthals regularly buried their dead.

hunting technique, along with other aspects of their life, resulted in a lot of physical injuries. Despite being stocky and robust, many Neanderthal fossils show evidence of traumatic injuries, such as broken bones. Interestingly, these injuries are often healed, suggesting the individual survived multiple injuries over a lifetime. In some cases, injured individuals would have been permanently disabled and may have required assistance from other members of the group to survive. In addition to possibly caring for their sick and injured, the Neanderthals regularly and intentionally buried their dead (**FIGURE 16.11**). These burials may reflect some sense of abstract thinking, such as a spirituality or consideration of an afterlife. Alternatively, the burials may reflect a more basic need to contain decomposition and avoid detection by predators and scavengers.

Neanderthals may have had aspects of culture and symbolic thought similar to those of modern humans. There is evidence that some Neanderthals made nonfunctional objects, such as decorated shells that may have been used as pendants or other personal ornaments. These types of artifacts are primarily associated with our own species, and the production of such things by Neanderthals support the idea that they may have been symbolic thinkers. There is also some evidence (both from the fossil record and DNA analysis) that suggests Neanderthals may have had the ability to produce language. Although that language may not have directly resembled human language today, it may still have been possible for Neanderthals to engage in complex forms of communication. The abilities and thought processes of Neanderthals are hotly debated, with some researchers arguing Neanderthals had abilities similar to modern people and other researchers arguing Neanderthals had far more limited abilities than humans.

The debate over Neanderthal culture and symbolism feeds into a larger debate about the relationship between Neanderthals and humans. Some researchers highlight the similarities between Neanderthals and humans and believe the two groups are closely related. These researchers often classify *Homo neanderthalensis* as archaic *Homo sapiens* (along with *Homo heidelbergensis*). In the classification debates about most *Homo* species, we must turn to the fossil record for evidence. This limits us to differences in the size and shape of skeletal features, as in *Homo heidelbergensis*. In the debate surrounding Neanderthal classification, however, we have another line of evidence available—ancient DNA.

As discussed in Lab 13, most fossils are mineralized remains that no longer contain organic materials and DNA. Some Neanderthals, however, have died recently enough that their skeletons have not fully fossilized. Therefore, in some cases, researchers have been able to extract trace amounts of Neanderthal DNA for analysis. Studies along these lines have examined both **mitochondrial DNA (mtDNA)** and **nuclear DNA**. The mtDNA evidence suggests that humans arose from a lineage in Africa that was separate from the Neanderthal populations living in Europe and western Asia. However, the nuclear DNA evidence suggests that when the humans arrived in these places from Africa, they interbred with Neanderthals that already lived in the region. When combined, these results indicate that while humans and Neanderthals are related and share minor genetic similarities, they are probably different species with unique evolutionary origins and histories (see next section for more information about human origins and dispersal).

### Homo sapiens

Our own species, *Homo sapiens*, first appeared in Africa around 200 kya, in western Asia around 90 kya, in Europe around 35 kya, and in the Americas around 12–15 kya (late Pleistocene). In general, early *Homo sapiens* individuals were much more gracile than earlier *Homo* species, especially compared to their robust Neanderthal contemporaries. However, these early members of our species were still slightly more robust than humans today. They had small, orthognathic (flat) faces with small brow ridges (**FIGURE 16.12**). They also had small front and back teeth and a pronounced chin on the front of the mandible. The overall cranial shape was tall and rounded, giving *Homo sapiens* a distinct, vertical forehead. They also had large cranial capacities (averaging at least 1350 cc) and a rounded occipital area (without any specialized structures such as an occipital torus or bun). Their postcrania were relatively gracile, with a long and lean body type that was generalized and suitable for a range of environments.

From the beginning, *Homo sapiens* had diverse diets that included a wider range of prey than those of other *Homo* species. They hunted and ate medium-sized game animals, such as ancient deer species, as well as smaller game, such as birds and fish. They also had more complicated cultural and symbolic behavior than seen with earlier *Homo* species. Humans made complex clothes, using needles, and they had complex shelters that required building, rather than simply taking advantage of naturally formed caves. Humans also engaged in a wide range of symbolic behaviors. Their burials were more ritualistic than Neanderthal burials, and they regularly interred their dead with special tools, jewelry, and other grave goods. They also produced a variety of symbolic objects, such as carved figurines

**mitochondrial DNA (mtDNA)** the DNA found in mitochondria that is passed from mothers to offspring

**nuclear DNA** the DNA found in the nucleus of the cell

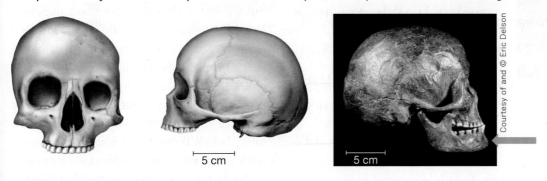

Courtesy of and © Eric Delson

5 cm

5 cm

**FIGURE 16.12 *Homo sapiens***
Early *Homo sapiens* can be distinguished from other species by its small brow ridges, tall cranium with a forehead, and pronounced chin (arrow).

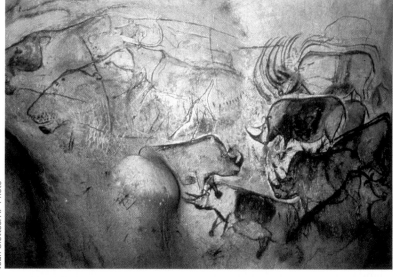

Jean Clottes/AP Photo

**FIGURE 16.13 Early "Art"**
*Homo sapiens* produced a variety of symbolic objects, including cave paintings, carved figurines, and personal ornaments (such as shell jewelry).

and cave paintings **(FIGURE 16.13)**. Although these symbolic creations are often referred to as "art," the actual purpose behind their production is unclear. In addition, while the European examples are the most famous, similar symbolic behavior was present in Africa and Asia before it appeared in Europe.

    *Homo sapiens* used a new stone tool technology that was not seen in other species. This technology is referred to as the **Upper Paleolithic technology** in Europe (based on its appearance during the Upper Paleolithic time period) **(FIGURE 16.14)**. The Upper Paleolithic period dates from about 40 to 10 kya. The term Paleolithic refers to the Stone Age, and the Upper Paleolithic is the most recent in a series of three stone ages—the Lower, the Middle, and the Upper. The Upper Paleolithic name roughly translates as "Late Stone Age," and in Africa the corresponding time period is referred to by this latter, alternate name. Similar technologies appeared in Africa, Asia, and elsewhere around the same time and can be clustered together under this heading. As with Mousterian tools, the Upper Paleolithic toolkit emphasized flake tools. However, Upper Paleolithic flakes had

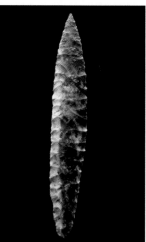

© David L. Brill, www.humanoriginsphotos.com

**FIGURE 16.14 Upper Paleolithic Tools**
The Upper Paleolithic tools made by *Homo sapiens* required the production of elongated stone flakes called blades. The blade shown here was then modified into a point.

a special elongated form, with the flakes being at least twice as long as they were wide. These elongated flakes are called **blades**. Producing stone blades required an even more lengthy and difficult process than the Levallois technique, and raw blades still needed to be further modified to make specific tools. As with Mousterian tools, Upper Paleolithic blade tools were specialized for different functions, and included scrapers, drills, knives, and stone arrow points. These tool types were standardized within a region, so, for example, multiple drills at a site had the same size and shape. However, the tool forms often varied from one region to the next, with each region having particular shape preferences and styles. Interestingly, Upper Paleolithic toolmakers were very selective about their raw materials, and these raw materials would be passed along long-distance trade networks across hundreds of miles. In addition, Upper Paleolithic toolmakers made a variety of objects from materials other than stone, such as harpoons made from animal bones, beads and pendants made from shells, and tools made from antlers.

    Interestingly, early *Homo sapiens* coexisted with other *Homo* species in various parts of the world. Most famously, humans coexisted with Neanderthals in western Asia for around 50,000 years and in Europe for around 5,000 years. It is unclear to what extent the two species interacted during these times. Based on the available evidence, it appears that the two groups probably did not engage in regular conflict on a large scale. Although Neanderthals were subject to frequent injury, these injuries cannot be clearly credited to attacks from the modern *Homo sapiens*. At the same time, the two groups may have engaged in more peaceful interactions. For example, some evidence suggests that Neanderthal technology may have been influenced either directly or indirectly by the more complicated techniques introduced by humans. Other evidence indicates the two groups interacted more directly through interbreeding (see information about the assimilation model below).

    Today, humans occupy most of Earth's continents year-round (with the exception of Antarctica). Where did we come from, and how did we get to all of these places? Many researchers have attempted to answer these questions, resulting in three popular explanations for the origin and dispersal of our species. The first explanation, often called the **replacement model** or **Out of Africa II** (to differentiate it from the earlier migration of *Homo erectus*, called Out of Africa I), argues that modern humans originated in Africa recently (**FIGURE 16.15**). From there, our ancestors spread into western Asia, Europe, eastern Asia, and beyond. On arriving in these regions, *Homo sapiens* replaced the earlier *Homo* species that occupied the territories, such as *Homo neanderthalensis* in Europe and *Homo erectus* in Asia. This view argues that all humans today have recent common ancestry in Africa, there was little to no interbreeding between humans and other species, and any variation in people today is superficial and evolved recently.

A second explanation for the origin and dispersal of humans is called the **multiregional model** (**FIGURE 16.16**). According to this view, *Homo sapiens* evolved from earlier species (such as *Homo erectus*) in multiple regions. Thus, humans in Asia evolved from *Homo erectus* in Asia, humans in Africa evolved from *Homo erectus* in Africa, and so on. This model also argues that populations in these regions interbred, which made them similar to one another through **gene flow**. This view argues that there

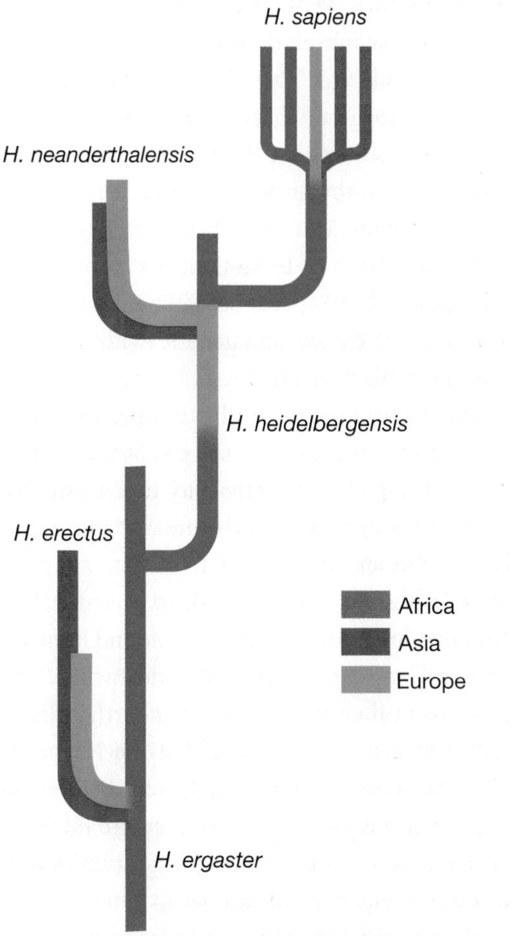

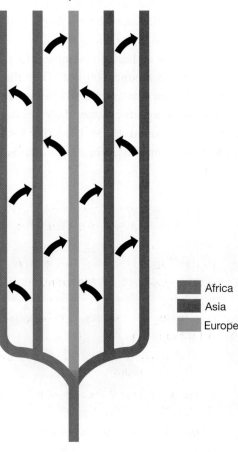

**FIGURE 16.16 The Multiregional Model**
According to the multiregional model, *Homo sapiens* evolved from earlier species (such as *Homo erectus*) in multiple regions. For example, humans in Asia evolved from *Homo erectus* in Asia, while humans in Africa evolved from *Homo erectus* in Africa. The populations would have remained similar across regions due to interbreeding (arrows).

**FIGURE 16.15 The Replacement Model**
According to the replacement model, *Homo sapiens* evolved in Africa. From there, *Homo sapiens* spread to other regions and replaced the species (such as *Homo neanderthalensis*) that lived there previously.

**Upper Paleolithic technology** a complex stone tool technology characterized by tools made from special stone flakes called blades and also included tools made from antler and bone

**blade** a stone flake with a special elongated form

**replacement model (Out of Africa II)** an explanation for the evolution of humans that argues the species evolved in Africa and then expanded to other regions, replacing related species as it went

**multiregional model** an explanation for the evolution of humans that argues the species evolved from local populations in separate regions around the Old World

**gene flow** the exchange of genes between previously isolated populations that begin to interbreed

**assimilation model**
an explanation for
the evolution of
humans that argues
the species evolved
in Africa and then
expanded to other
regions, interbreeding
with related species
as it went

**Y chromosome** the
smaller of the two
sex chromosomes,
having genetic
information that
codes primarily for
traits related to
maleness

**founder effect** a
special type of
genetic drift that
occurs when a
subset of a larger
population founds
the next generation
due to substantial
population loss or
population movement

are multiple points of origin for our species, and some variations in people today may go back hundreds of thousands of years to regional differences in *Homo erectus* populations.

The third explanation for human origins is called the **assimilation model** (FIGURE 16.17). This view has been proposed more recently and combines the African origin and interbreeding of the other two models. According to the assimilation model, *Homo sapiens* first evolved in Africa. From there, the species spread into other regions, such as western Asia and Europe. When settling in these regions, humans did not completely replace earlier *Homo* species. Rather, they interbred with local populations, such as Neanderthals in Europe. Current evidence supports the assimilation model more than the other two explanations.

Recall that the earliest *Homo sapiens* fossils appear in Africa around 200 kya. They then appear in western Asia around 90 kya, Australia around 40 kya, Europe around 35 kya, and the Americas around 12–15 kya. This fossil data suggest we originated in Africa and then dispersed to the rest of the world. The genetic data also support this hypothesis. Researchers have studied mitochondrial DNA (mtDNA) to track female lineages and **Y-chromosome** DNA to track male lineages. These two forms of DNA do not recombine, so they accumulate changes slowly and can be used to estimate when groups split apart and began separate evolutionary tracks. Analysis of both types of DNA in living humans shows that the greatest genetic diversity is found in Africa. This suggests African populations have had the most time to accumulate mutations (variations) in their DNA. In addition, genetic variation is increasingly limited the further one gets from Africa. This suggests that multiple **founder effect** situations occurred as humans moved out of Africa. With each migration further east, only a subset of the existing variation migrated onward. This pattern of decreasing variation suggests that people first migrated out of Africa along the South Asian coast. Subgroups then moved north and west into Eurasia. This genetic information matches nicely with the pattern of fossil data that shows East Asia and Australia being settled before Europe. Thus, both the fossil and genetic evidence support an African origin.

What about the possibility of interbreeding? DNA from partially fossilized Neanderthals is providing new insight into the possibility of interbreeding between humans and other *Homo* species. According to recent analyses of Neanderthal DNA, it appears that the last common ancestor of Neanderthals and humans lived as long ago as 800 kya. Meanwhile, the last common ancestor of all Neanderthals lived only 140 kya. This suggests that the Neanderthal and human lineages split long before the recent species evolved. Thus, they are likely to be two distinct species, rather than two closely related subspecies of humans. Interestingly, Neanderthal DNA is more similar to the DNA of non-African humans than it is to African humans. For example, Neanderthals and modern European humans may share between 1% and 4% of their nuclear DNA in common, but Neanderthals and modern humans from sub-Saharan Africa share 0% in common.

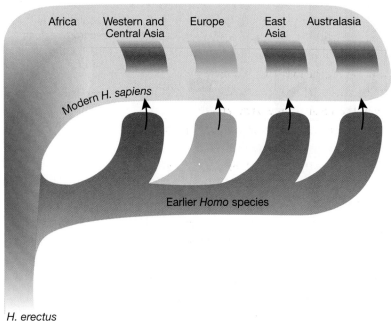

**FIGURE 16.17 The Assimilation Model**
According to the assimilation model, *Homo sapiens* evolved from a *Homo erectus* lineage in Africa. *Homo sapiens* then spread into other regions where they interbred with the species already present (such as *Homo neanderthalensis* in Europe). The arrows in the diagram represent this interbreeding between earlier regional populations and incoming humans.

The similarity between the Neanderthal and non-African genomes suggests that humans interbred with Neanderthals after they left Africa. Thus, recent genetic analysis supports the interbreeding element of the assimilation model.

### Homo floresiensis

We often emphasize the temporal and geographic overlap between *Homo sapiens* and Neanderthals, particularly the 5,000 plus years they both lived in Europe around 30 kya. However, recent evidence suggests that humans overlapped with another *Homo* species even more recently. Around 16–18 kya when *Homo sapiens* lived throughout Southeast Asia and Australia, an unusual species called *Homo floresiensis* occupied the Indonesian island of Flores (FIGURE 16.18). These individuals had small teeth and orthognathic (flat) faces, similar to other late *Homo* species, but they had somewhat more primitive locomotor adaptations, such as long arms and flat feet. They were also sophisticated hunters that made and used flake tools. Most interestingly, *Homo floresiensis* individuals had remarkably short statures (around 3 to 3.5 ft or 1 m tall) and small cranial capacities (around 400 cc). These unusual body proportions contributed to their nickname of hobbits.

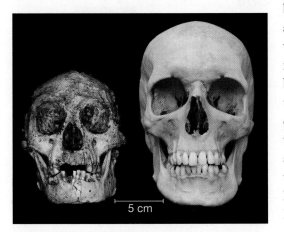

**FIGURE 16.18 *Homo floresiensis***
*Homo floresiensis* (left) had a much smaller stature and cranial capacity than modern humans (right).

Photograph courtesy of Peter Brown. From Brown et al. 2004. A new small-bodied hominin from the Late Pleistocene of Flores, Indonesia. *Nature* 431:1055–1061. Copyright © 2004, Rights Managed by Nature Publishing Group.

Researchers have hotly debated the reason behind their unusual size, and most argue that it is the result of an evolutionary process, rather than a type of pathology. The *Homo floresiensis* lineage appears to have been subject to a process known as **island** (or **endemic**) **dwarfism**. In this process, animals that are large on the mainland often become smaller on islands, which is an adaptation in response to the limited amount of available resources. *Homo floresiensis* was probably a lineage of early *Homo erectus* (or perhaps *Homo sapiens*) that became a dwarf population after settling on the island of Flores. The same island dwarfism process resulted in other dwarf animals on the island, such as dwarf elephants.

## THE NEWEST MEMBER OF THE *HOMO* GENUS?

In 2008, researchers working in a Siberian cave called Denisova discovered a fossilized hand phalanx fragment from a child. Because its archaeological context was dated to around 30–48 kya, the investigators hoped the fossil contained some organic material that had not fully fossilized, and they submitted it for DNA analysis. They assumed the mitochondrial DNA (mtDNA) analysis would indicate the bone had belonged to either a Neanderthal or a human, both of which lived in the surrounding area at that time. The researchers were astounded when the results came back, and the bone was identified as neither Neanderthal nor human, but something entirely different and previously unknown—a Denisovan. Since the initial discovery, two teeth have also been recovered from the same cave. Looking at both anatomical and genetic characteristics, these teeth appear to also belong to a Denisovan, rather than a Neanderthal or human. Researchers believe the Denisovans are more closely related to Neanderthals than to humans, and they diverged from the human lineage as long ago as 700 kya.

As with the *Homo floresiensis* finds, the Denisovan evidence suggests that our evolutionary past was a complex landscape, and that our species shared Earth with many other *Homo* species until very recently. This is further compounded

**island (endemic) dwarfism** a process where animals that are large on the mainland evolve to be smaller on an island as an adaptation for the limited amount of available resources

by genetic evidence that indicates Denisovans (like Neanderthals) interbred with humans. Some modern humans from Southeast Asian islands and Australia may share as much as 6% of their genome with Denisovans. Interestingly, Denisovan genetic markers have not yet been found in people outside this region. With such a limited sample of Denisovan data, many questions remain unanswered, but there is hope that as more fossil material is uncovered and analyzed, more will be learned about this newest group of extinct human ancestors.

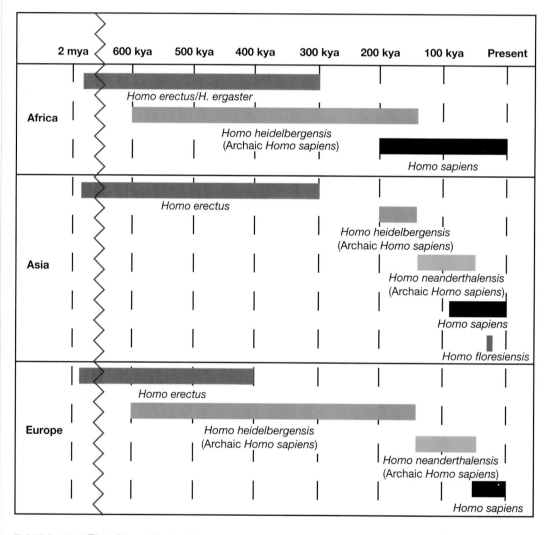

**FIGURE 16.19 Time Line of Later *Homo***
The fossil species discussed in this lab were distributed in Africa, Asia, and Europe within the last 1.8 million years.

# CONCEPT REVIEW QUESTIONS

Name: _____     Section: _____

Course: _____     Date: _____

Answer the following questions in the space provided.

1. Which of these species was the first to live outside of Africa?

    A. *Australopithecus garhi*
    B. *Homo erectus*
    C. *Homo sapiens*
    D. *Homo habilis*

2. True or false? Some researchers consider the African members of *Homo erectus* to be a separate species called *Homo ergaster*.

3. I lived in Europe around 200 kya. I had a long and low cranium, a large cranial capacity (around 1300 cc), and a very small occipital torus. What fossil species am I?

    A. *Homo neanderthalensis*
    B. *Homo erectus*
    C. *Homo heidelbergensis*
    D. *Homo sapiens*

4. True or false? Mousterian tools are made from stone flakes that have an elongated, blade-like shape.

5. Name *one* species that made Mousterian tools.

6. Why have we been able to recover ancient DNA from a few Neanderthals but not from our other extinct relatives?

7. Describe *one* physical adaptation Neanderthals had for life in a cold climate.

8. Compared to Neanderthals, early humans had

    A. a taller cranium and more vertical forehead.
    B. a more limited diet emphasizing large game animals.
    C. more physical adaptations for living in a cold climate.
    D. a more pronounced occipital bun.

9. Which *Homo* species has the largest average cranial capacity?

10. I lived on a small Indonesian island around 18 kya. I used stone tools to hunt animals, but I had a very small cranial capacity (around 400 cc) and a very small body. What fossil species am I?

   A. *Australopithecus afarensis*
   B. *Homo erectus*
   C. *Homo habilis*
   D. *Homo floresiensis*

# LAB EXERCISES

Name: _____    Section: _____

Course: _____    Date: _____

## EXERCISE 1   EARLY VERSUS LATER MEMBERS OF THE GENUS *HOMO*

Work in a small group or alone to complete this exercise. Review the mystery fossils provided by your instructor (or depicted in the lab Appendix) and answer the following questions.

1. Which of these mystery fossils is *Homo habilis*?

2. Which of these mystery fossils is *Homo erectus*?

3. Describe *two* traits you used to make these identifications. (Be sure to describe how each trait varies in the two fossils.)

## EXERCISE 2   THE EVOLUTION OF BIPEDALISM

Work in a small group or alone to complete this exercise. Use the *Australopithecus afarensis* and *Homo erectus* postcrania provided by your instructor (or depicted in the lab Appendix) to answer the following questions.

1. Describe *two* postcranial traits that differ between these two species. (Be sure to describe how each trait varies in the two fossils.)

2. What do these differences suggest about the two species' locomotion?

## *HOMO HEIDELBERGENSIS*

Work in a small group or alone to complete this exercise. Refer to the *Homo heidelbergensis* and *Homo erectus* crania provided by your instructor (or depicted in the lab Appendix) to answer the following questions.

1. Describe *one* trait that these two species share in common.

2. Describe *one* trait that differs between the two species. (Be sure to describe how the trait varies in the two fossils.)

## STONE TOOL TECHNOLOGY

Work in a small group or alone to complete this exercise. Examine the mystery stone tools provided by your instructor (or depicted in the lab Appendix).

1. Which mystery tool is a handaxe?

2. Describe the features of this tool that led you to identify it as this tool form.

3. What tool technology does it belong to?

4. Name *one* fossil species that may have made this tool.

5. Which mystery tool is a blade?

6. Describe the features of this tool that led you to identify it as this tool form.

7. What tool technology does it belong to?

8. Name *one* fossil species that may have made this tool.

## *HOMO NEANDERTHALENSIS*

Work in a small group or alone to complete this exercise. Review the mystery fossils provided by your instructor (or depicted in the lab Appendix) and answer the following questions.

1. Which of these mystery fossils is *Homo neanderthalensis*?

2. Which of these mystery fossils is *Homo sapiens*?

3. Describe *two* traits you used to make these identifications. (Be sure to describe how each trait varies in the two fossils.)

## EXERCISE 6  *HOMO FLORESIENSIS*

Work in a small group or alone to complete this exercise. Compare the mystery fossil crania provided by your instructor (or depicted in the lab Appendix), and complete the chart below. Place an "X" in the appropriate column to indicate which mystery fossils have the traits listed. *Note:* A trait may be found in more than one mystery fossil.

|  | Mystery Fossil A | Mystery Fossil B | Mystery Fossil C |
|---|---|---|---|
| Large Cranial Capacity |  |  |  |
| Orthognathic (Flat) Face |  |  |  |
| Low Cranium |  |  |  |

1. Based on this information, which mystery fossil is *Homo floresiensis*?

2. Based on this information, which mystery fossil is *Homo sapiens*?

3. Based on this information, which mystery fossil is an australopithecine?

# CRITICAL THINKING QUESTIONS

On a separate sheet of paper, answer the following questions.

1. This question may be completed independently or as a group exercise. Biological anthropologists disagree about the classification of *Homo erectus* fossils. Describe the *two* approaches to classifying these fossils. Which classification do *you* support? Why? (Be sure to support your decision with specific evidence.)

2. This question may be completed independently or as a group exercise. Based on what we know of their physical *and* cultural traits, how were Neanderthals adapted for their life in Ice Age Europe? Did early humans in Europe have these same adaptations? How might these adaptations relate to the extinction of the Neanderthals and the continuation of humans? (*Hint*: Is it possible to be too specialized?)

3. This question may be completed independently or as a group exercise. In Exercise 6, you examined the unusual cranium of *Homo floresiensis*. Why do most researchers believe *Homo floresiensis* had such a small cranium?

4. This question may be completed independently or as a group exercise. Consider the stone tool technologies discussed here and in Lab 15 (the Oldowan, Acheulean, Mousterian, and Upper Paleolithic). Describe the general trends in changes in tool form, tool specialization, and tool production techniques across these technologies.

5. This question may be completed independently or as a group exercise. In this lab, we discussed three explanations for the origin and spread of humans. Which model is probably the most accurate? Be sure to support your argument with evidence.

6. This question may be completed independently or as a group exercise. Consider the diversity of the later *Homo* species discussed in this lab. Why do you think our direct ancestor survived when the other species (or subspecies) went extinct? What physical and behavioral characteristics may have made our human ancestor better adapted than the other species?

7. This question may be completed independently or as a group exercise. Examine the list of general trends in human evolution below. Based on your knowledge of our fossil ancestry, list these trends in order from oldest to most recent. Place a "1" next to the trend that occurred first (is the oldest) and number the remaining trends in order to the most recent ("5"). For each trend, also note which fossil species is first associated with the change.

    _____ Increase in brain size to an average of over 1000 cc

    _____ Production and use of stone tools

    _____ Adaptations for bipedalism

    _____ Habitation (living) outside of Africa

    _____ Clear evidence of symbolic behavior ("art," elaborate and ritualized burial, etc.)

8. In this lab we reviewed many different fossil species and their defining characteristics. To help you make comparisons across these species and understand larger trends in our evolutionary history, complete the following Later *Homo* Chart.

## LATER *HOMO* CHART

| Fossil | Dates and Location | Cranial Traits | Postcranial Traits | Suggested Behavior |
|---|---|---|---|---|
| *Homo erectus* (*H. ergaster*) | | | | |
| *Homo heidelbergensis* | | | | |
| *Homo neanderthalensis* | | | | |
| *Homo sapiens* | | | | |
| *Homo floresiensis* | | | | |

# APPENDIX:
# LAB EXERCISE IMAGES

## Exercise 1 Early versus Later Members of the Genus *Homo*

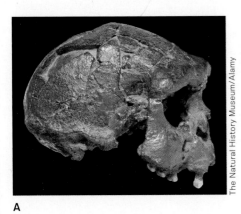

A

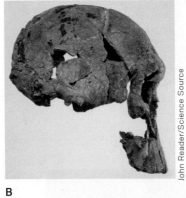

B

## Exercise 2 The Evolution of Bipedalism

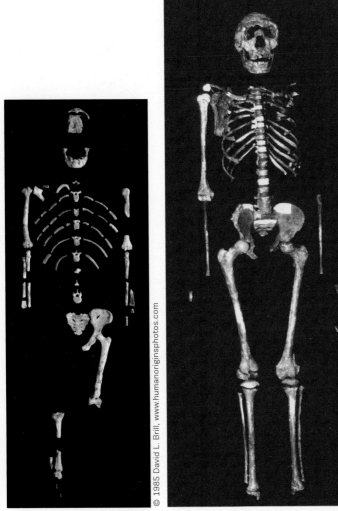

*Australopithecus afarensis*          *Homo erectus*

## Exercise 3 *Homo heidelbergensis*

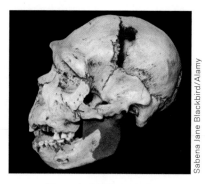

*Homo heidelbergensis*

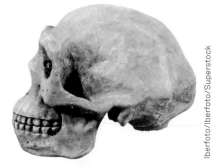

*Homo erectus*

## Exercise 4 Stone Tool Technology

A

B

## Exercise 5 *Homo neanderthalensis*

A

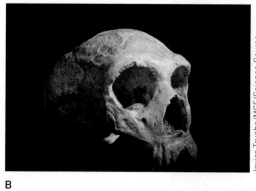

B

# Exercise 6 *Homo floresiensis*

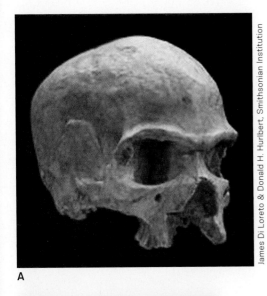

James Di Loreto & Donald H. Hurlbert, Smithsonian Institution

**A**

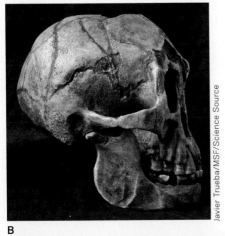

Javier Trueba/MSF/Science Source

**B**

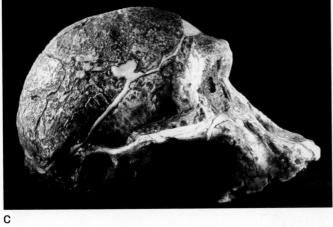

Philippe Plailly/Science Source

**C**

## A

**absolute dating**   also called chronometric dating, any dating method that provides a numerical age estimate for the dated material.

**acclimatization**   a short-term, temporary adjustment the body makes to better suit its current environmental context.

**Acheulean (Acheulian) technology**   the second and more widespread stone tool technology that was characterized by handaxes.

**adapiform**   one of a group of early primates that lived between 56 and 34 mya.

**adaptation**   a trait that has been favored by natural selection and helps a population be better suited to its environmental context.

**adenine**   one of the nitrogen bases in DNA; its complement is thymine.

**adult**   an individual that has reached physical maturity.

**affiliative behavior**   behavior that is generally cooperative.

**affiliative communication**   verbal or nonverbal communication that reinforces social relationships.

**aggressive behavior**   behavior that challenges, threatens, or harms others.

**aging**   the process of estimating an individual's age at death based on skeletal remains.

**alarm call**   a vocalization that indicates a particular threat.

**allele**   an alternate version of a gene.

**Allen's rule**   based on the principle that equiaxed shapes have less surface area than elongated shapes, long limbs are well adapted for hot climates because they have more relative surface to help vent extra body heat.

**analogy**   a trait that is similar across organisms due to similar adaptations.

**ancestral trait**   a trait that is shared by two organisms from a relatively distant common ancestor, also called a plesiomorphy.

**antemortem pathology**   pathology that developed at any time prior to an individual's death.

**anterior**   relative location toward the front of the body.

**anthropology**   the study of people.

**antibody**   protein that attacks antigens directly or marks them for attack by other parts of the immune system.

**anticodon**   a triplet of bases in transfer RNA.

**antigen**   (in ABO blood group system) the cell surface marker found on red blood cells that relates to an individual's ABO blood type and triggers antibody reactions to a foreign blood antigen.

**appendicular skeleton**   the bones of the appendages (arms and legs).

**arboreal**   living in trees.

**arboreal quadrupedalism**   a form of quadrupedal locomotion that is practiced in the trees.

**archaeology**   the study of the cultural life of past people, as seen through their material remains such as architecture, bones, and tools.

**argon–argon dating**   a radiometric dating method that relies on the ratio of two argon isotopes, used for material from similar time periods as in potassium–argon dating.

**articulation**   a meeting between bones in the body.

**assemblage**   a collection of material (such as bones and/or artifacts) recovered from a forensic context or an archaeological or paleoanthropological site.

**assimilation model**   an explanation for the evolution of humans that argues the species evolved in Africa and then expanded to other regions, interbreeding with related species as it went.

**atlas**   the unusually shaped C1, a vertebra that works with the axis to allow for head movement and rotation.

**auditory ossicles**   the three tiny bones that help form each middle ear.

**autosome**   a chromosome other than one of the sex chromosomes.

**axial skeleton**   the bones that lie along the midline (central axis) of the body.

**axis**   the unusually shaped C2, a vertebra that works with the atlas to allow for head movement and rotation.

## B

**bachelor group**   an all-male social group where multiple adult males live together, without females or offspring.

**balanced polymorphism**   a situation where different alleles for a trait are maintained in balance because natural selection favors the heterozygous condition, where different alleles are needed.

**Bergmann's rule**   based on the principle that volume increases more rapidly than surface area, a large, thick body is well adapted for cold climates because it has less relative surface that would vent vital body heat.

**biface**   a stone tool that has had flakes of stone removed from two sides.

**bilophodont molar**   a molar with four cusps arranged in two parallel ridges (or lophs).

**bioarchaeology**   the study of skeletal remains from archaeological contexts.

**biocultural approach**   research approach that recognizes the close relationship between human biology and culture and attempts to study these two forces simultaneously.

**biological anthropology**   the study of human evolution, including human biology, our close living and extinct relatives, and current similarities and differences within our species; also called physical anthropology.

**biological species concept**   the biological concept that argues two organisms are from the same species if they can produce viable (fertile) offspring.

**bipedalism**   a form of two-footed locomotion where movement occurs primarily through the use of the legs.

**blade**    a stone flake with a special elongated form.

**blunt force trauma**    injury caused by contact with a blunt object, such as a club, which often causes depressions in the bone that are surrounded by small fractures.

**bone remodeling**    the process of bone resorption and re-formation.

**brachiation**    a form of suspensory locomotion where movement occurs through arm-over-arm swinging.

**brow ridge**    a bony ridge located above the eye orbits.

## C

**canal**    a narrow tunnel or tubular channel in a bone.

**canine**    a pointy tooth between the incisors and premolars.

**captive primate study**    research conducted with primates in captivity (in laboratories or zoos).

**carpal**    one of the eight short bones of each wrist.

**cartilage**    a type of flexible connective tissue found at the joints between bones and in the nose and ear.

**cartilaginous joint**    a joint united by cartilage that allows some movement.

**cause of death**    the medical determination of the physiological reason for an individual's death.

**centromere**    the contracted area of a chromosome, whose position varies from one chromosome to the next, useful in distinguishing chromosomes.

**cervical vertebrae**    one of the seven vertebrae (C1–C7) that form the neck.

**cheek pouch**    a pouch in the cheek and neck area that can expand to store food.

**chopper**    a large, heavy stone tool with a sharp edge where small pieces of rock have been removed.

**chromatid**    a single chromosome fiber that duplicates and occurs in pairs when a cell is about to divide.

**chromosome**    a tightly coiled strand of DNA within the cell nucleus.

**chronometric dating**    also called absolute dating, any dating method that provides a numerical age estimate for the dated material.

**cladistics**    an approach to classification that emphasizes derived traits and deemphasizes ancestral traits, also called phylogenetic systematics.

**cladogram**    a diagram used to represent cladistic classifications, where lines are used to link organisms in different degrees of relationship to one another.

**class**    the level of classification that includes multiple related orders.

**clavicle**    a slightly curved bone that helps stabilize each shoulder, also called the collarbone.

**clinal distribution**    a distribution of trait variations that has a continuous gradation across a geographical area.

**coalition**    a group of multiple primates that work together against other members of their group.

**coccyx**    a small bone that articulates to the inferior end of the sacrum, also called the tailbone.

**codominant**    when multiple alleles are expressed in the phenotype, without one being clearly dominant over the other.

**codon**    a triplet of bases in DNA (or messenger RNA).

**comparative approach**    research approach that emphasizes the importance of comparisons across cultures, times, places, species, etc.

**comparative stratigraphy**    a relative dating method based on the assumption that things found in the same strata (or layer) will be from the same time period because they were deposited together.

**connective tissue**    body tissue made of cells, fibers (such as collagen fibers), and extracellular matrix.

**context**    the time, space, environment, historical circumstances, and cultural practices within which a subject of anthropological investigation is situated.

**continental drift**    the shifting of the continents that is caused by the movement of Earth's continental plates.

**cortical bone**    the compact tissue that forms the outside surface of lamellar bone.

**cranial capacity**    the amount of space available in the cranium for the brain.

**cranial suture closure**    the process of ossification where the cranial bones fuse together at the sutures, the extent of which can be used to age a skeleton.

**cranium**    the skull without the jawbone.

**crossing-over**    the stage in meiosis during which genetic information is exchanged between the two chromosomes in a homologous pair.

**cultural anthropology**    the study of the cultural life of living people, including their cultural practices, beliefs, economics, politics, gender roles, etc.; also called social anthropology.

**cusp**    a rounded (or slightly pointed) projection on a tooth's chewing surface.

**cut mark**    indentation left on bone by a sharp instrument, such as a knife or stone tool.

**cytosine**    one of the nitrogen bases in DNA; its complement is guanine.

## D

**Darwin, Charles**    often considered the father of evolutionary thinking, he devised the theory of natural selection to explain the process of evolution in the natural world.

**deciduous teeth**    the first set of teeth, also called baby teeth, that are later replaced by permanent teeth.

**dental caries**    areas of the teeth that have undergone demineralization and decay due to acid exposure, also called cavities.

**dental comb**    a tooth structure made of elongated and closely situated lower incisors and canines that project out from the front of the face.

**dental enamel hypoplasia**    a gap or horizontal line on a tooth that has less enamel than surrounding areas.

**dental formula**    a numerical count of the different tooth types in an animal.

**dental (tooth) wear**   the wearing down of tooth surfaces with continued use, the extent of which can be used to age adult skeletons.

**dentin**   a calcified tissue found inside a tooth, beneath the enamel surface.

**dentition**   the teeth.

**depression**   a hollow or depressed area of a bone.

**derived trait**   a trait that is a modification of an ancestral form, also called an apomorphy.

**diaphysis**   the central area of a bone that forms separately and fuses with the ends of the bone during growth and development.

**direct percussion**   the process of stone tool production where two rocks are hit directly together in order to break off flakes.

**dish-shaped face**   a somewhat concave face formed by a sloping upper face and protruding lower face.

**distal**   relative location farther away from the trunk of the body.

**diurnal**   active primarily during the daylight hours.

**DNA (deoxyribonucleic acid)**   the chemical that acts as the genetic blueprint for an organism.

**DNA replication**   the process whereby DNA is copied.

**dominant**   a dominant allele masks the effects of other alleles for a trait; may also be used in reference to dominant traits or dominant phenotypes.

**dorsal**   relative location toward the back of the body.

**Down syndrome**   a chromosomal disorder that results from an extra chromosome 21.

## E

**eburnation**   the polishing of a bone caused by repeated direct contact between bones at a joint.

**enamel**   the hard mineralized tissue on the exterior surface of a tooth.

**epiphyseal fusion**   the process of ossification where the shaft and ends of a long bone fuse together, the extent of which can be used to age a juvenile skeleton.

**epiphysis (epiphyses, plural)**   the area at the end of a long bone that forms separately and fuses with the middle of the bone during growth and development.

**estrus swelling**   the swelling of the female genital region around the time of ovulation.

**ethmoid**   the small, cube-shaped bone between the frontal bone and sphenoid bones in the cranium.

**eukaryote**   organism (such as a plant or animal) that is made of many cells that have cell nuclei.

**evolution**   change in allele frequency.

**evolutionary systematics**   an approach to classification that emphasizes both derived traits and ancestral traits.

## F

**family**   the level of classification that includes multiple related genera.

**femur**   the bone that forms the thigh of each leg.

**fibrous joint**   a joint united by irregular, fibrous connective tissue that allows for little to no movement.

**fibula**   the thinner and more lateral of the two bones in each lower leg.

**field primate study**   research conducted with primates in their wild habitat.

**fission–fusion**   a social organization that involves the fission of a large group into smaller groups to pursue sparsely distributed resources and the fusion of the smaller groups back into a large group at other times.

**flake**   a small piece of rock that has been removed from a larger rock and can be used as is or further modified into a specialized tool.

**flat bone**   a bone with a layer of trabecular bone sandwiched between two thin layers of flat cortical bone.

**focused observation**   the observation of a single individual at a time.

**folivory**   a diet that emphasizes leaves (foliage) and other plant parts.

**fontanelle**   a soft spot on a baby's head where the space at the suture joints is particularly big.

**foramen (foramina, plural)**   a hole in a bone.

**foramen magnum**   the large hole at the base of the cranium that allows the brain to connect to the spinal cord.

**forelimb**   the upper or front limb (commonly called the arm).

**forensic anthropology**   the application of knowledge and methods of skeletal analysis to assist in legal investigations.

**forward-facing eyes**   eyes that are positioned at the front of the face and point directly ahead.

**fossa (fossae, plural)**   a shallow depression in a bone.

**fossilization**   the process of fossil formation that occurs under certain conditions.

**fossil**   the rock-like traces or remains of an organism.

**founder effect**   a special type of genetic drift that occurs when a subset of a larger population founds the next generation due to substantial population loss or population movement.

**fracture**   a break in the bone due to a trauma (or injury).

**frontal bone**   the most anterior bone of the cranium.

**frugivory**   a diet that emphasizes fruit.

## G

**gamete**   a sex cell (in humans, sperm or egg).

**gene**   a section of DNA that codes for a particular trait.

**gene flow**   the exchange of genes between previously isolated populations that begin to interbreed.

**genetic bottleneck**   substantial loss of genetic diversity (as in many founder effect situations).

**genetic drift**   the changes in allele frequencies that occur randomly, due to factors like differential reproduction and sampling errors.

**genetic locus**   the location of a gene on a chromosome.

**genetic recombination**   the mixing of genetic information into new combinations that occurs during meiosis.

**genotype**    the specific alleles an organism has for a trait.

**genus** (**genera**, plural)    the level of classification that includes multiple related species.

**gracile**    having nonrobust, thin, light musculature and bone.

**grooming**    the removal of foreign objects (such as insects or plant parts) from another primate's fur.

**groove**    a furrow along the surface of a bone.

**group observation**    the observation of multiple individuals simultaneously.

**guanine**    one of the nitrogen bases in DNA; its complement is cytosine.

**gummivory**    a diet that emphasizes tree gums (or sap).

**gunshot wound**    injury caused by various small arms (gun) fire, which may cause holes or nicks in bone, depending on where the shot enters and exits the body.

## H

**habitual bipedalism**    bipedal locomotion that is practiced regularly (or habitually).

**half-life**    the length of time it takes for one-half of an amount of a radioactive isotope to decay.

**hallux**    the biggest and most medial of the toes on each foot.

**handaxe**    a biface tool that is shaped like a pear or teardrop.

**Hardy–Weinberg equation**    the equation ($p^2 + 2pq + q^2 = 1$) outlined by Godfrey Hardy and Wilhelm Weinberg to predict the probable genotype frequencies of a Mendelian trait in the next generation.

**heterozygous**    an organism's genotype for a trait when it has one dominant allele and one recessive allele for a trait (such as *Rr*).

**hind limb**    the lower or back limb (commonly called the leg).

**holistic approach**    research approach that emphasizes the importance of all aspects of the study subject and requires a consideration of context to gain an understanding of the broader picture.

**homologous pair**    set of matching chromosomes with similar types of genetic information, similar lengths, and similar centromere positions.

**homology**    a trait that is similar across organisms because the organisms share common ancestry.

**homoplasy**    the evolutionary development of similar traits in unrelated organisms.

**homozygous dominant**    an organism's genotype for a trait when it has two dominant alleles for the trait (such as *RR*).

**homozygous recessive**    an organism's genotype for a trait when it has two recessive alleles for the trait (such as *rr*).

**human biology**    the study of human genetics, variations within our species, and how our species is impacted by evolutionary processes.

**humerus**    the upper bone in each arm.

**hyoid bone**    the small, U-shaped bone suspended in the throat below the cranium.

**hypoxia**    a condition where one cannot take in enough oxygen to meet the body's needs.

## I

**ilium** (**ilia**, plural)    the large, blade-like area of each os coxa (hip bone).

**incisors**    the spatula-shaped teeth at the front of the mouth.

**infanticide**    the killing of infants or young members of the species.

**inferior**    relative location lower on the body's axis.

**inferior nasal concha** (**conchae**, plural)    one of a pair of scroll-like bones inside the nasal cavity.

**innominate bone**    one of the pair of bones that form the side and front of the pelvis, resulting from the fusion of the ilium, ischium, and pubis; also known as os coxa.

**insectivory**    a diet that emphasizes insects.

**iron-deficiency anemia**    a condition caused by a severe lack of iron in the body.

**irregular bone**    a bone with a complex shape that is not easily classified as long, short, or flat.

**ischial callosity**    a roughened patch of skin located in the ischial area (on the rump).

**ischium**    the bone that forms the underside (posteroinferior side) of an os coxa.

**island (endemic) dwarfism**    a process where animals that are large on the mainland evolve to be smaller on an island as an adaptation for the limited amount of available resources.

**isotope**    a variation of a chemical element based on the number of neutrons in its nucleus.

## J

**juvenile**    a physically immature individual whose body is still growing and developing.

## K

**karyotype**    the picture of an individual's stained chromosomes, arranged in homologous pairs and laid out in order from largest to smallest.

**kingdom**    the highest level of classification, which includes multiple related phyla.

**knife wound**    injury caused by a sharp, blade-like instrument, which often leaves telltale nicks or cut marks on bone.

**knuckle-walking**    a form of terrestrial quadrupedalism that involves walking on the knuckles of the hands.

## L

**lactase**    a protein required in order to properly digest the lactose in milk.

**lactose**    a sugar found in milk.

**lactose intolerance**    a condition common to all mammals where adults cannot properly digest lactose.

**lactose tolerance**    an unusual condition in some humans where adults can properly digest lactose.

**lamellar bone**    a type of organized, mature bone.

**lateral**   relative location farther from the midline of the body.

**law of independent assortment**   the particles (or genes) for different traits are sorted (and passed on) independently of one another.

**law of segregation**   the particles (or genes) for traits appear separately in the (sex cells of) parents and are then reunited in an offspring.

**law of superposition**   a principle that argues material from lower geological layers must be older than material from higher geological layers.

**Levallois technique**   a process used to produce regularly shaped flakes that can then be further modified into different tools.

**linguistic anthropology**   the study of how people make and use language.

**locomotion**   an animal's form of movement in traveling from one place to another.

**long bone**   a bone with an elongated middle shaft and distinct, slightly larger ends.

**lumbar vertebra**   one of the five vertebrae (L1–L5) that form the lower back.

## M

**mammary gland**   a milk-producing gland found in female mammals.

**mandible**   the bone that holds the lower teeth and is primarily responsible for chewing; also called the jawbone.

**mandibular symphysis**   the area where the two sides of the mandible are attached by cartilage in an unfused mandible.

**manner of death**   the circumstances surrounding death that may have contributed to death, such as traumatic injuries.

**mastoid process**   the bony projection located posterior to the ear that allows for the attachment of neck muscles.

**maxilla (maxillae**, plural)   one of the pair of bones that forms the face and holds the upper teeth.

**medial**   relative location closer to the midline of the body.

**meiosis**   the process of cell division that produces gametes.

**melanin**   a pigment that helps to give skin its brownish color.

**Mendel, Gregor**   a European monk who conducted tests on pea plants and identified two important principles of classification.

**Mendelian trait**   trait controlled by one gene (although there may be multiple alleles for that one gene).

**messenger RNA (mRNA)**   the RNA formed in the first stage of protein synthesis (transcription) that brings the genetic information from the cell nucleus to the ribosome.

**metacarpal**   one of the five bones that form the palm of each hand.

**metatarsal**   one of the five bones that form each foot.

**metric trait**   measurable trait on the skeleton that can be used to estimate ancestry.

**minimum number of individuals (MNI)**   the minimum number of individuals that could be represented by the skeletal elements recovered.

**mitochondria (mitochondrion**, singular)   cell organelles that produce energy for the cell and that contain their own DNA.

**mitochondrial DNA (mtDNA)**   the DNA found in mitochondria that is passed from mothers to offspring.

**mitosis**   the process of cell division that occurs in somatic cells.

**molar**   a large, multicusped tooth at the back of the mouth.

**monogamy**   a form of social organization where one adult male, one adult female, and their offspring live together.

**Mousterian technology**   a stone tool technology that used the Levallois technique to produce a variety of specialized flake tools.

**multimale polygyny**   a form of social organization where multiple adult males, multiple adult females, and their offspring live together.

**multiregional model**   an explanation for the evolution of humans that argues the species evolved from local populations in separate regions around the Old World.

**mutation**   change in the genetic code that creates entirely new genetic material.

## N

**nasal bone**   one of a pair of small bones that forms the bridge of the nose.

**natural selection**   the theory outlined by Charles Darwin to explain evolution: it argues that some traits are more suited to an organism's particular environmental context and are therefore passed on preferentially into the next generation, and these traits become more common in successive generations, resulting in evolutionary shifts in populations.

**New World**   the name traditionally assigned to the American continents (North and South America).

**nocturnal**   active primarily during the night hours.

**nonhuman primate culture**   group-specific, learned behavior in nonhuman primates.

**nonmetric trait**   nonmeasurable trait on the skeleton that can be used to estimate ancestry.

**nonradiometric dating**   any chronometric dating method that is not based on the principles of radioactive isotope decay.

**nuclear DNA**   the DNA found in the nucleus of the cell.

**nucleotide**   a set of linked phosphate, sugar, and nitrogen base molecules in DNA.

**nucleus**   the area inside a eukaryotic cell that contains most of the cell's DNA.

## O

**obligate bipedalism**   bipedal locomotion that is practiced all the time.

**occasional bipedalism**   bipedal locomotion that is practiced sometimes (or occasionally).

**occipital bone**   the bone that forms the back and base of the cranium.

**occipital bun**   a large, round projection located on the occipital bone.

**occipital torus**    a ridge of bone along the occipital bone that forms a small point when seen from the side.

**Old World**    the name traditionally assigned to the majority of the non-American continents, specifically Africa, Asia, and Europe.

**Oldowan technology**    this earliest stone tool technology is characterized by chopper and flake tools.

**omomyoid**    one of a group of early primates that lived between 56 and 34 mya.

**opposable digit**    a finger or toe capable of being positioned opposite the other digits (fingers or toes), which allows for the ability to grasp objects.

**order**    the level of classification that includes multiple related families.

**organelle**    a type of cell part with its own function, like an organ of the body.

**orthognathic**    having a flat face.

**os coxa** (**ossa coxae**, plural)    one of the pair of bones that form the side and front of the pelvis, resulting from the fusion of the ilium, ischium, and pubis; also known as the innominate bone.

**ossification**    the process of bone mineralization and fusion that occurs as an individual develops into a physically mature adult.

**osteoarthritis**    a condition where trauma or accumulated wear and tear on the joints results in the loss of their cartilage lining.

**osteoblast**    bone cell responsible for forming bone.

**osteoclast**    bone cell responsible for removing bone.

**osteocyte**    a bone cell responsible for bone maintenance.

**osteometric board**    an instrument used to measure bones.

**osteophyte**    spicule of bone that often forms around the margin of a joint surface when the cartilage at the joint is worn down.

**Out of Africa I**    the migration between 1.8 mya and 800 kya of *Homo erectus* out of Africa and into Asia and Europe.

## P

**Palatine**    one of a pair of bones that forms part of the hard palate in the mouth.

**paleoanthropology**    the study of the anatomy and behavior of humans and our extinct relatives.

**paleomagnetic dating**    a nonradiometric dating method based on changes in Earth's magnetic polarity.

**paleospecies**    an extinct species that is known through fossil evidence.

**parietal bone**    one of the pair of bones posterior to the frontal bone that forms the top of the cranium.

**pastoralism**    a lifestyle where raising domesticated herd animals is central to the diet and economy.

**patella**    the small, slightly triangular bone that helps form each knee joint, also called the kneecap.

**pathology**    the study of disease, particularly how it changes the body.

**pedigree diagram**    the method of diagramming inheritance that shows the phenotypes of individuals from multiple generations in a family.

**perimortem pathology**    pathology and trauma that developed around the time of an individual's death and may have contributed to that death.

**permanent teeth**    the second set of teeth, also called adult teeth, that replace the earlier deciduous teeth.

**phalanx** (**phalanges**, plural)    one of the 14 bones that form the fingers and toes on each hand or foot.

**phenotype**    the physical expression of an organism's genotype for a trait.

**phylogram**    a diagram used to represent evolutionary relationships that also accounts for the amount of change (and usually length of time) separating organisms.

**phylum** (**phyla**, plural)    the level of classification that includes multiple related classes.

**plesiadapiform**    one of a group of diverse primate-like mammals that lived over 56 mya and may be among the first primates.

**point mutation**    a mutation that occurs at a single point (nitrogen base) in a DNA strand.

**polyandry**    a form of social organization where one adult female, multiple adult males, and their offspring live together.

**polygenic trait**    trait controlled by alleles at multiple genetic loci.

**polygyny**    a form of social organization where there are multiple adult females for each male.

**porotic hyperostosis**    a form of bone destruction that usually presents in the cranial bones as porous and spongy bone surfaces, rather than the normally smooth surface.

**postcranial**    relating to the bones below or behind the head.

**posterior**    relative location toward the rear of the body.

**postmortem interval**    the time elapsed since an individual died.

**postorbital bar**    a bar of bone that sits lateral to the eye but does not fully enclose the eye in a bony pocket.

**potassium–argon dating**    a radiometric dating method that relies on radioactive potassium isotopes with a half-life of about 1.3 billion years.

**prehensile tail**    a tail with the ability to grasp tree branches and act like a fifth limb.

**premolars**    tooth with two cusps, between the canines and molars.

**primate ecology**    the study of the relationship between primates and their environments.

**primatology**    the study of living primates, particularly their similarities and differences and why these similarities and differences might exist.

**prognathic**    having a projecting or protruding face.

**projection**    an area of bone that protrudes from the main bone surface.

**prokaryote**    organism (such as a bacterium) that has a cell without a nucleus and is often made of only a single cell.

**protein synthesis**   the process of determining proteins from a DNA sequence.

**proximal**   relative location closer to the trunk of the body.

**pubis**   the bone that forms the front (anterior) of an os coxa, also called the pubic bone.

**Punnett square**   the method of diagramming inheritance where parent genotypes are used to estimate the probability of various genotypes in a potential offspring.

## Q

**quadrupedalism**   a form of locomotion that uses all four limbs.

**qualitative data**   descriptive data about the qualities that are observed.

**quantitative data**   focused and clearly measurable data.

## R

**radiocarbon dating**   a radiometric dating method that relies on carbon-14, an isotope with a half-life of 5,730 years.

**radiometric dating**   any dating method that uses the principles of radioactive isotope decay to determine numerical age.

**radius**   the more lateral of the two lower bones in each arm.

**recessive**   a recessive allele is masked by a dominant allele for a trait; may also be used in reference to recessive traits or recessive phenotypes.

**relative dating**   any dating method that provides the age of something relative to something else, rather than as a numerical age.

**replacement model (Out of Africa II)**   an explanation for the evolution of humans that argues the species evolved in Africa and then expanded to other regions, replacing related species as it went.

**reproductive success**   the successful production of viable (fertile) offspring.

**rhinarium**   a damp pad at the end of the nose.

**rib bone**   one of the 12 long bones that form each side of the rib cage (or thoracic cage).

**RNA (ribonucleic acid)**   a chemical that is similar to DNA, except it contains uracil instead of thymine; it plays vital roles in the process of protein synthesis.

**Robust**   having thick, dense, heavy musculature and bone.

## S

**sacrum**   the large, triangular bone at the base of the vertebral column and between the two hip bones.

**sagittal crest**   a ridge of bone along the midline of the cranium that allows for the attachment of extra-large chewing muscles.

**sagittal keel**   a very slight ridge of bone along the midline of the cranium.

**savanna environment**   open grassland interspersed with pockets of trees.

**savanna hypothesis**   an explanation for the evolution of bipedalism that argues bipedalism was selectively favored as open grassland environments expanded throughout Africa in the past.

**scapula**   a large, flat bone that forms part of each shoulder joint, also called the shoulder blade.

**scientific method**   a cycle of scientific practices that helps scientists to gain knowledge and sparks further scientific inquiries.

**scientific theory**   a scientific explanation supported by substantial evidence.

**semibrachiation**   a form of suspensory locomotion where movement occurs through the use of the arms and a specially adapted prehensile tail, which can grasp tree branches.

**septum**   the soft tissue between the nostrils.

**sex chromosome**   one of the two different chromosomes (X and Y) involved in the determination of an organism's biological sex.

**sexing**   the process of determining the likely sex of an individual based on skeletal remains.

**sexual dimorphism**   the physical differences between mature males and females of a species.

**shared derived trait**   a modified trait that is shared by two or more organisms, also called a synapomorphy.

**short bone**   a bone with a cube-like shape, with similar width and length dimensions.

**sickle-cell anemia**   a disease that results from the sickle-cell allele.

**sickle-cell trait**   a variation of a gene that results from a point mutation and causes misshapen red blood cells.

**single-male polygyny**   a form of social organization where one adult male, multiple adult females, and their offspring live together.

**social hierarchy**   the assignment and distribution of different social status positions in a group.

**social science**   a discipline concerned with the study of human society, such as anthropology, psychology, or sociology.

**solitary**   a form of social organization where adults spend most of their time alone; adult females (and their offspring) occupy separate territories, and an adult male occupies a territory that overlaps with that of several females.

**somatic cell**   a non-sex cell that makes up different body parts; also called body cell.

**species**   one of the most specific levels of classification uniting related organisms.

**sphenoid bone**   the butterfly-shaped bone between the cranial vault and face.

**stature**   an individual's overall body height.

**sternum**   bone formed by the fusion of three separate bones in the chest, also called the breastbone.

**strangulation**   the forcible choking of another individual, which often results in damage to the hyoid bone.

**stratigraphy**   the study of the deposition of geological and cultural layers (or strata).

**Suchey–Brooks method**   a method of aging adult skeletons that relies on changes to the symphyseal surface of the pubic bone.

**superior**   relative location higher on the body's axis.

**suspensory locomotion**   a form of locomotion where the body is suspended (or hanging) below tree branches.

**suture**   an immovable fibrous joint between the individual bones of the cranium.

**synovial joint**   a highly mobile joint held together by ligaments and irregular connective tissue that forms a fluid-filled articular capsule.

**systematics**   the study of the relationships between organisms.

# T

**tarsal**   one of the seven short bones that form each ankle.

**taxonomy**   the classification of organisms.

**temporal bone**   one of the pair of bones inferior to the parietal bone on each side of the cranium.

**terrestrial**   living on the ground.

**terrestrial quadrupedalism**   a form of quadrupedal locomotion that is practiced on the ground.

**thoracic vertebra**   one of the 12 vertebrae (T1–T12) that articulate with ribs in the chest area.

**threat display**   an action (such as flashing the teeth) that seeks to threaten others from a distance.

**threat yawn**   an opening of the mouth that displays the teeth in a threatening manner.

**thymine**   one of the nitrogen bases in DNA; its complement is adenine.

**tibia**   the larger and more medial of the two bones in each lower leg, also called the shinbone.

**tooth (dental) eruption**   the process whereby the deciduous teeth (and later the permanent teeth) grow into the mouth, the extent of which can be used to age juvenile skeletons.

**trabecular bone**   the spongy (honeycomb-like) tissue that forms the inside of lamellar bone.

**transcription**   the first step of protein synthesis where nuclear DNA is transcribed into messenger RNA that can leave the cell nucleus.

**transfer RNA (tRNA)**   the RNA that helps form the amino acid chains in the second stage of protein synthesis (translation).

**translation**   the second step of protein synthesis where RNA is translated (or read) to form a sequence of amino acids that forms a protein.

**Turner syndrome**   a chromosomal disorder that results from having a single X chromosome without another sex chromosome.

# U

**ulna**   the more medial of the two lower bones in each arm.

**unfused mandible**   a mandible (jawbone) that is made of two separate bones that are attached by cartilage along the midline.

**uniparous**   producing one offspring at a time.

**unique derived trait**   a modified trait that is unique to one group, also called an autapomorphy.

**Upper Paleolithic technology**   a complex stone tool technology characterized by tools made from special stone flakes called blades and also included tools made from antler and bone.

# V

**vasoconstriction**   the constriction (narrowing) of the blood vessels near the surface of the body to help maintain heat in the body's core.

**vasodilation**   the expansion of the blood vessels near the surface of the body to help heat escape the body.

**ventral**   relative location toward the belly of the body.

**vertebra (vertebrae, plural)**   an irregularly shaped bone that is part of the vertebral column.

**vertebral column**   the row of bones that form the backbone.

**vertical clinging and leaping**   a form of locomotion where the body is oriented vertically and movement occurs by leaping from tree to tree.

**viable offspring**   offspring that are capable of reproduction.

**vocalization**   a verbal communication.

**vomer**   a small, thin bone inside the nasal cavity.

# W

**woven bone**   a type of bone that is unorganized and primarily found in immature bone.

# X

**X chromosome**   the larger of the two sex chromosomes, having genetic information related to a wide range of traits.

# Y

**Y chromosome**   the smaller of the two sex chromosomes, having genetic information that codes primarily for traits related to maleness.

**Y-5 molar**   a molar in the lower dentition that has five cusps positioned such that a pronounced Y-shaped groove forms between the cusps.

# Z

**zygomatic arch**   cheekbone area formed by numerous small bones, allowing a space for the jaw muscles that attach to the mandible below and the temporal bone above.

**zygomatic bone**   one of the bones that forms the zygomatic arch.

Agarwal, S. C., M. Dimitriu, and M. D. Grynpas. 2004. Medieval trabecular bone architecture: The influence of age, sex and lifestyle. *American Journal of Physical Anthropology* 124:33–44.

Antón, S. C. and C. C. Swisher III. 2004. Early dispersals of *Homo* from Africa. *Annual Review of Anthropology* 33:271–296.

Arbib, M. A., K. Liebal, and S. Pika. 2008. Primate vocalization, gesture, and the evolution of human language. *Current Anthropology* 49:1053–1076.

Asfaw, B., T. White, O. Lovejoy, B. Latimer, S. Simpson, and G. Suwa. 1999. *Australopithecus garhi*: A new species of early hominid from Ethiopia. *Science* 284:629–635.

Balter, M. 2006. Radiocarbon dating's final frontier. *Science* 313:1560–1563.

Barsh, G. S. 2003. What controls variation in human skin color? *PLOS Biology* 1:19–22.

Bass, W. M. 1995. *Human Osteology: A Laboratory and Field Manual*, 4th edition. Columbia, MO: Missouri Archaeological Society.

Beall, C. M. 2001. Adaptations to altitude: A current assessment. *Annual Review of Anthropology* 30:423–456.

Beall, C. M. 2007. Two routes to functional adaptation: Tibetan and Andean high-altitude natives. Pp. 239–256 in J. C. Avise and F. J. Ayala, eds. *In the Light of Evolution, Volume 1: Adaptation and Complex Design*. Washington, DC: The National Academies Press.

Beall, C. M. and A. T. Steegmann Jr. 2000. Human adaptation to climate: Temperature, ultraviolet radiation, and altitude. Pp. 163–224 in S. Stinson, B. Bogin, R. Huss-Ashmore, and D. O'Rourke, eds. *Human Biology: An Evolutionary and Biocultural Perspective*. New York: Wiley-Liss.

Beard, K. C. 2002. Basal anthropoids. Pp. 133–149 in W. C. Hartwig, ed. *The Primate Fossil Record*. Cambridge: Cambridge University Press.

Begun, D. R. 2002. European hominoids. Pp. 339–368 in W. C. Hartwig, ed. *The Primate Fossil Record*. Cambridge: Cambridge University Press.

Benefit, B. R. and M. L. McCrossin. 2002. The Victoriapithecidae, Cercopithecoidea. Pp. 241–253 in W. C. Hartwig, ed. *The Primate Fossil Record*. Cambridge: Cambridge University Press.

Berger, L. R. 2013. The mosaic nature of *Australopithecus sediba*. *Science* 340(6129):163–165.

Berger, L. R., S. J. de Ruiter, S. E. Churchill, P. Schmid, K. J. Carlson, P. H. G. M. Dirks, and J. M. Kibii. 2010. *Australopithecus sediba*: A new species of *Homo*-like australopith from South Africa. *Science* 328(5975):195–204.

Berger, T. D. and E. Trinkaus. 1995. Patterns of trauma among the Neandertals. *Journal of Archaeological Science* 22:841–852.

Berra, T. M. 2008. *Charles Darwin: The Concise Story of an Extraordinary Man*. Baltimore: Johns Hopkins University Press.

Blau, S. and C. A. Briggs. 2011. The role of forensic anthropology in Disaster Victim Investigation (DVI). *Forensic Science International* 205:29–35.

Bloch, J. I., M. T. Silcox, D. M. Boyer, and E. J. Sargis. 2007. New Paleocene skeletons and the relationship of plesiadapiforms to crown-clade primates. *Proceedings of the National Academy of Sciences* 104:1159–1164.

Bouzouggar, A., N. Barton, M. Vanhaeren, F. d'Errico, S. Collcutt, T. Higham, E. Hodge, S. Parfitt, E. Rhodes, J.-L. Schwenninger, C. Stringer, E. Turner, S. Ward, A. Moutmir, and A. Stambouli. 2007. 82,000-year-old beads from North Africa and implications for the origins of modern human behavior. *Proceedings of the National Academy of Sciences* 104:9964–9969.

Brace, C. L. 2002. The concept of race in physical anthropology. Pp. 239–253 in P. N. Peregrine, C. R. Ember, and M. Ember, eds. *Physical Anthropology: Original Readings in Method and Practice*. Upper Saddle River, NJ: Prentice Hall.

Brothwell, D. 1981 *Digging up Bones*, 3rd edition. Ithaca, NY: Cornell University Press.

Brown, P., T. Sutikna, M. J. Morwood, R. P. Soejono, Jatmiko, E. Wayhu Saptomo, and Rokus Awe Due. 2004. A new small-bodied hominin from the Late Pleistocene of Flores, Indonesia. *Nature* 431:1055–1061.

Brunet, M., F. Guy, D. Pilbeam, H. T. Mackaye, A. Likius, D. Ahounta, A. Beauvilain, C. Blondel, H. Bocherens, J.-R. Boisserie, L. De Bonis, Y. Coppens, J. Dejax, C. Denys, P. Duringer, V. Eisenmann, G. Fanone, P. Fronty, D. Geraads, T. Lehmann, F. Lihoreau, A. Louchart, A. Mahamat, G. Merceron, G. Mouchelin, O. Otero, P. P. Campomanes, M. P. De Leon, J.-C. Rage, M. Sapanet, M. Schuster, J. Sudre, P. Tassy, X. Valentin, P. Vignaud, L. Viriot, A. Zazzo, and C. Zollikofer. 2002. A new hominind from the Upper Miocene of Chad, Central Africa. *Nature* 418:145–151.

Buikstra, J. E. and D. H. Ubelaker, eds. 1994. *Standards for Data Collection from Human Skeletal Remains: Proceedings of a Seminar at the Field Museum of Natural History*. Arkansas Archaeological Survey Research Series, no. 44. Fayetteville, AR: Arkansas Archaeological Survey.

Byer, S. N. 2010. *Introduction to Forensic Anthropology*, 4th edition. Upper Saddle River, NJ: Prentice Hall.

Cain, M. L., C. K. Yoon, and A. Singh-Cundy. 2009. *Discover Biology*. New York: W. W. Norton & Company.

Cann, R. L., O. Rickards, and J. K. Lum. 1994. Mitochondrial DNA and human evolution: Our one lucky mother. Pp. 135–148 in M. H. Nitecki and D. V. Nitecki, eds. *Origins of Anatomically Modern Humans*. New York: Plenum.

Cann, R. L., M. Stoneking, and A. Wilson. 1987. Mitochondrial DNA and human evolution. *Nature* 325:31–36.

Caspari, R. 2003. From types to populations: A century of race, physical anthropology, and the American Anthropological Association. *American Anthropologist* 105:65–76.

Chaimanee, Y., C. Yamee, P. Tian, K. Khaowiset, B. Marandat, P. Tafforeau, C. Nemoz, and J.-J. Jaeger. 2006. *Khoratpithecus piriyai*, a late Miocene hominoid of Thailand. *American Journal of Physical Anthropology* 131:311–323.

Chaplin, G. and N. G. Jablonski. 2009. Vitamin D and the evolution of human depigmentation. *American Journal of Physical Anthropology* 139:451–461.

Churchill, S. E., T. W. Holliday, K. J. Carlson, T. Jashashvili, M. E. Macias, D. J. de Ruiter, and L. R. Berger. 2013. The upper limb of *Australopithecus sediba*. *Science* 340(6129):1233477. doi: 10.1126/science.1233477.

Conroy, G. C. and H. Pontzer. 2012. *Reconstructing Human Origins: A Modern Synthesis*, 3rd edition. New York: W. W. Norton & Company.

Cooper, A. and C. B. Stringer. 2013. Did the Denisovans cross Wallace's line? *Science* 342(6156):321–323.

Covert, H. H. 2002. The earliest primates and the evolution of prosimians: Introduction. Pp. 13–20 in W. C. Hartwig, ed. *The Primate Fossil Record*. Cambridge: Cambridge University Press.

Cruciani, F., R. La Fratta, P. Santolamazza, D. Sellitto, R. Pascone, P. Moral, E. Watson, V. Guida, E. Beraud Colomb, B. Zaharova, J. Lavinha, G. Vona, R. Aman, F. Cali, N. Akar, M. Richards, A. Torroni, A. Novelletto, and R. Scozzari. 2004. Phylogenetic analysis of haplogroup E3b (E-M215) Y chromosomes reveals multiple migratory events within and out of Africa. *American Journal of Human Genetics* 74:1014–1022.

Dart, R. A. 1925. *Australopithecus africanus*: The man-ape of South Africa. *Nature* 115:195–199.

Deacon, T. W. 1997. What makes the human brain different? *Annual Review of Anthropology* 26:337–357.

Dean, M. C. and B. H. Smith. 2009. Growth and development in the Nariokotome youth, KNM-WT 15000: A dental perspective on the origins and early evolution of the genus *Homo*. Pp. 101–120 in F. E. Grine, J. G. Fleagle, and R. E. Leakey, eds. *The First Humans: Origins of the Genus Homo*. New York: Springer.

Deino, A. L., P. R. Renne, and C. C. Swisher III. 1998. $^{40}$Ar/$^{39}$Ar dating in paleoanthropology and archeology. *Evolutionary Anthropology* 6:63–75.

DeSilva, J. M., M. E. Morgan, J. C. Barry, and D. Pilbean. 2010. A hominoid distal tibia from the Miocene of Pakistan. *Journal of Human Evolution* 58:147–154.

Dunsworth, H. and A. Walker. 2002. Early genus *Homo*. Pp. 419–435 in W. C. Hartwig, ed. *The Primate Fossil Record*. Cambridge: Cambridge University Press.

Estrada-Mena, B., F. J. Estrada, R. Ulloa-Arvizu, M. Guido, R. Méndez, R. Coral, T. Canto, J. Granados, R. Rubí-Castellanos, H. Rangel-Villalobos, and A. Garcia-Carrancá. 2010. Blood group O alleles in Native Americans: Implications in the peopling of the Americas. *American Journal of Physical Anthropology* 142:85–94.

Eunice Kennedy Shriver National Institute of Child Health and Human Development, NIH, DHHS. 1997. *Understanding Klinefelter Syndrome: A Guide for XXY Males and Their Families* (97-3202). Washington, DC: U.S. Government Printing Office.

Fleagle, J. G. 1999. *Primate Adaptation and Evolution*, 2nd edition. San Diego: Academic Press.

Fleagle, J. G. and M. F. Tejedor. 2002. Early platyrrhines of southern South America. Pp. 161–173 in W. C. Hartwig, ed. *The Primate Fossil Record*. Cambridge: Cambridge University Press.

Fossey, D. 1983. *Gorillas in the Mist*. New York: Houghton Mifflin Company.

Fragaszy, D., P. Izar, E. Visalberghi, E. B. Ottoni, and M. G. De Oliveira. 2004. Wild capuchin monkeys (*Cebus libidinosus*) use anvils and stone pounding tools. *American Journal of Physical Anthropology* 64:359–366.

Franzen, J., P. D. Gingerich, J. Habersetzer, J. H. Hurum, W. von Koenigswald, and B. H. Smith. 2009. Complete primate skeleton from the middle Eocene of Messel in Germany: Morphology and paleobiology. *PLOS One* 4(5):e5723. doi:10.1371/journal.pone.0005723.

Galik, K., B. Senut, M. Pickford, D. Gommery, J. Treil, A. J. Kuperavage, and R. B. Eckhardt. 2004. External and internal morphology of the BAR 1002'00 *Orrorin tugenensis* femur. *Science* 305:1450–1453.

Gebo, D. L. 2010. Locomotor function across primates (including humans). Pp. 530–544 in C. S. Larsen, ed. *A Companion to Biological Anthropology*. Chichester, UK: Wiley-Blackwell.

Gebo, D. L. and K. D. Rose. 2002. Adapiformes: Phylogeny and adaptation. Pp. 21–43 in W. C. Hartwig, ed. *The Primate Fossil Record*. Cambridge: Cambridge University Press.

Gebo, D. L., M. Dagosto, K. C. Beard, T. Qi, and J. Wang. 2000. The oldest known anthropoid postcranial fossils and the early evolution of higher primates. *Nature* 404:276–278.

Gilbert, C. C., E. A. Goble, and A. Hill. 2010. Miocene Cercopithecoidea from the Tugen Hills, Kenya. *Journal of Human Evolution* 59:465–483.

Gray, T. 2004 [1998]. A brief history of animals in space. Garber, S. (web curator). National Aeronautics and Space Administration. http://history.nasa.gov/animals.html.

Green, R. E., J. Krause, A. W. Briggs, T. Maricic, U. Stenzel, M. Kircher, N. Patterson, H. Li, W. Zhai, M. H.-Y. Fritz, N. F. Hansen, E. Y. Durand, A.-S. Malaspinas, J. D. Jensen, T. Marques-Bonet, C. Alkan, K. Prüfer, M. Meyer, H. A. Burbano, J. M. Good, R. Schultz, A. Aximu-Petri, A. Butthof, B Höber, B. Höffner, M. Siegemund, A. Weihmann, C. Nusbaum, E. S. Lander, C. Russ, N. Novod, J. Affourtit, M. Egholm, C. Verna, P. Rudan, D. Brajkovic, Z. Kucan,

I. Gušic, V. B. Doronichev, L. V. Golovanova, C. Lalueza-Fox, M. de la Rasilla, J. Fortea, A. Rosas, R. W. Schmitz, P. L. F. Johnson, E. E. Eichler, D. Falush, E. Birney, J. C. Mullikin, M. Slatkin, R. Nielsen, J. Kelso, M. Lachmann, D. Reich, and S. Pääbo. 2010. A draft sequence of the Neandertal genome. *Science* 328:710–722.

Goodall, J. 1986. *The Chimpanzees of Gombe: Patterns of Behavior.* Cambridge, MA: Harvard University Press.

Goodall, J. 1996. Foreword: Conserving great apes. Pp. xv–xx in W. C. McGrew, L. F. Marchant, and T. Nishida, eds. *Great Ape Societies.* Cambridge: Cambridge University Press.

Goodman, M., C. A. Porter, J. Czelusniak, S. L. Page, H. Schneider, J. Shoshani, G. Gunnell, and C. P Groves. 1998. Toward a phylogenetic classification of primates based on DNA evidence complemented by fossil evidence. *Molecular Phylogenetics and Evolution* 9:585–598.

Gunnell, G. F. 2002. Tarsiiformes: Evolutionary history and adaptation. Pp. 45–82 in W. C. Hartwig, ed. *The Primate Fossil Record.* Cambridge: Cambridge University Press.

Harcourt-Smith, W. E. H. 2007. The origins of bipedal locomotion. Pp. 1483–1518 in W. Henke and I. Tattersall, eds. *Handbook of Paleoanthropology.* New York: Springer.

Harmon, E. H. 2013. Age and sex differences in the locomotor skeleton of *Australopithecus.* Pp. 263–272 in K. E. Reed, J. G. Fleagle, and R. E. Leakey, eds. *The Paleobiology of Australopithecus.* Dordrecht: Springer.

Harrison, T. 2002. Late Oligocene to middle Miocene catarrhines from Afro-Arabia. Pp. 311–338 in W. C. Hartwig, ed. *The Primate Fossil Record.* Cambridge: Cambridge University Press.

Hay, R. L. and M. D. Leakey. 1982. The fossil footprints of Laetoli. *Scientific American* 246:50–57.

Jablonski, N. G. 2002. Fossil Old World monkeys: The late Neogene radiation. Pp. 255–299 in W. C. Hartwig, ed. *The Primate Fossil Record.* Cambridge: Cambridge University Press.

Jablonski, N. G. and Chaplin, G. 1993. Origin of habitual terrestrial bipedalism in the ancestor of the Hominidae. *Journal of Human Evolution* 24:259–280.

Jablonski, N. G., M. G. Leakey, C. Kiarie, and M. Antón. 2002. A new skeleton of *Theropithecus brumpti* (Primates: Cercopithecidae) from Lomekwi, West Turkana, Kenya. *Journal of Human Evolution* 43:887–923.

Johanson, D. and M. Edey. 1981. *Lucy: The Beginnings of Humankind.* New York: Simon and Schuster.

Kay, R. F., C. Ross, and B. A. Williams. 1997. Anthropoid origins. *Science* 275:797–804.

Kay, R. F., J. G. Fleagle, T. R. T. Mitchell, M. Colbert, T. Bown, and D. W. Powers. 2008. The anatomy of *Dolichocebus gaimanensis,* a stem platyrrhine monkey from Argentina. *Journal of Human Evolution* 54:323–382.

Kelley, J. 2002. The hominoid radiation in Asia. Pp. 369–384 in W. C. Hartwig, ed. *The Primate Fossil Record.* Cambridge: Cambridge University Press.

Kimbel, W. H. and L. K. Delezene. 2009. "Lucy" redux: A review of research on *Australopithecus afarensis. Yearbook of Physical Anthropology* 52:2–48.

Krause, J., Q. Fu, J. M. Good, B. Viola, M. V. Shunkov, A. P. Derevianko, and S. Pääbo. 2010. The complete mitochondrial DNA genome of an unknown hominin from southern Siberia. *Nature* 464:894–897.

Larsen, C. S. 2014. *Our Origins: Discovering Physical Anthropology,* 3rd edition. New York: W. W. Norton & Company.

Leakey, M. G., C. S. Feibel, I. McDougall, and A. Walker. 1995. New four-million-year-old hominid species from Kanapoi and Allia Bay, Kenya. *Nature* 376:565–571.

Leakey, M. G., F. Spoor, M. C. Dean, C. S. Feibel, S. C. Antón, C. Kiarie, and L. N. Leakey. 2012. New fossils from Koobi Fora in northern Kenya confirm taxonomic diversity in early *Homo. Nature* 488:201–204.

Lewontin, R. C. 1972. The apportionment of human diversity. *Evolutionary Biology* 6:381–398.

Livingstone, F. B. 1958. Anthropological implications of sickle cell gene distribution in West Africa. *American Anthropologist* 60:533–562.

Livingstone, F. B. 1971. Malaria and human polymorphisms. *Annual Review of Genetics* 5:33–64.

Long, J. C., J. Li, and M. E. Healy. 2009. Human DNA sequences: More variation and less race. *American Journal of Physical Anthropology* 139:23–34.

Lordkipanidze, D., T. Jashashvili, A. Vekua, M. S. Ponce de León, C. P. E. Zollikofer, G. P. Rightmire, H. Pontzer, R. Ferring, O. Oms, M. Tappen, M. Bukhsianidze, J. Agusti, R. Kahlke, G. Kiladze, B. Martinez-Navarro, A. Mouskhelishvili, M. Nioradze, and L. Rook. 1997. Postcranial evidence from early *Homo* from Dmanisi, Georgia. *Nature* 449:305–310.

Lovejoy, C. O. 1981. The origins of man. *Science* 211:341–348.

Lovejoy, C. O. 2009. Reexamining human origins in light of *Ardipithecus ramidus. Science* 326:74e1–74e8.

Lovejoy, C. O., G. Suwa, L. Spurlock, B. Asfaw, and T. D. White. 2009. The pelvis and femur of *Ardipithecus ramidus*: The emergence of upright walking. *Science* 326:71e1–71e6.

McGraw, W. S. 2010. Primates defined. Pp. 222–242 in C. S. Larsen, ed. *A Companion to Biological Anthropology.* Chichester, UK: Wiley-Blackwell.

McGrew, W. C. 1998. Culture in nonhuman primates. *Annual Review of Anthropology* 27:301–328.

Mintz, S. W. and C. B. Tan. 2001. Bean-curd consumption in Hong Kong. *Ethnology* 40(2):113–128.

Moura, A. C. A. and P. C. Lee. 2004. Capuchin stone tool use in Caatinga dry forest. *Science* 306:1909.

National Institute of Environmental Health Sciences. 2012. Dry Bones (or Skeleton Bones). http://kids.niehs.nih.gov/games/songs/childrens/dry_bonesmp3.htm.

Nepomnaschy, P. A., K. Welch, D. McConnell, B. I. Strassmann, and B. G. England. 2004. Stress and reproductive function: A study of daily variations in cortisol, gonadotrophins, and gonadal steroids in a rural Mayan population. *American Journal of Human Biology* 16:523–532.

Nishida, T. and K. Hosaka. 1996. Coalition strategies among adult male chimpanzees of the Mahale Mountains, Tanzania. Pp. 114–134 in W. C. McGrew, L. F. Marchant, and T. Nishida, eds. *Great Ape Societies*. Cambridge: Cambridge University Press.

Nystrom, P. and P. Ashmore. 2008. *The Life of Primates*. Upper Saddle River, NJ: Pearson Prentice Hall.

Peng, Y., H. Shi, X-b. Qi, C-j. Xiao, H. Zhong, R-l. Z. Ma, and B. Su. 2010. The ADH1BArg47His polymorphism in East Asian populations and expansion of rice domestication in history. *BMC Evolutionary Biology* 10:15. doi: 10.1186/1471-2148-10-15.

Pruetz, J. D. and P. Bertolani. 2007. Savannah chimpanzees, *Pan troglodytes verus*, hunt with tools. *Current Biology* 17:412–417.

Relethford, J. H. 2009. Race and global patterns of phenotypic variation. *American Journal of Physical Anthropology* 139:16–22.

Remis, M. J. 2000. Preliminary assessment of the impacts of human activities on gorillas *Gorilla gorilla gorilla* and other wildlife at Dzanga-Sangha Reserve, Central African Republic. *Oryx* 34:56–65.

Richmond, B. G. and W. L. Jungers. 2008. *Orrorin tugenensis* femoral morphology and the evolution of hominin bipedalism. *Science* 319:1662–1665.

Rightmire, G. P. 1998. Human evolution in the Middle Pleistocene: The role of *Homo heidelbergensis*. *Evolutionary Anthropology* 6:218–227.

Rose, K. D. 2006. *The Beginning of the Age of Mammals*. Baltimore: Johns Hopkins University Press.

Ruvolo, M. 1997. Genetic diversity in hominoid primates. *Annual Review of Anthropology* 26:515–540.

Ruwende, C. and A. Hill. 1998. Glucose-6-phosphate dehydrogenase deficiency and malaria. *Journal of Molecular Medicine* 76(8):581–588.

Sapolsky, R. M. 2006. Social cultures among nonhuman primates. *Current Anthropology* 47:641–656.

Schneider, T. D. 2010. Placing refuge: Shell mounds and the archaeology of colonial encounters in the San Francisco Bay Area, California. Ph.D. dissertation, University of California, Berkeley.

Semaw, S. 2000. The world's oldest stone artefacts from Gona, Ethiopia: Their implications for understanding stone technology and patterns of human evolution between 2.6–1.5 million years ago. *Journal of Archaeological Science* 27:1197–1214.

Shoshani, J., C. P. Groves, E. L. Simons, and G. F. Gunnell. 1996. Primate phylogeny: morphological vs. molecular results. *Molecular Phylogenetics and Evolution* 5:102–154.

Simons, E. L., E. R. Seiffert, T. M. Ryan, and Y. Attia. 2007. A remarkable female cranium of the early Oligocene anthropoid *Aegyptopithecus zeuxis* (Catarrhini, Propliopithecidae). *Proceedings of the National Academy of Sciences* 104:8731–8736.

Smith, F. H. 2002. Migrations, radiations and continuity: Patterns in the evolution of Middle and Late Pleistocene humans. Pp. 437–456 in W. C. Hartwig, ed. *The Primate Fossil Record*. Cambridge: Cambridge University Press.

Smith, F. H. 2010. Species, populations, and assimilation in later human evolution. Pp. 357–378 in C. S. Larsen, ed. *A Companion to Biological Anthropology*. Chichester, UK: Wiley–Blackwell.

Soligo, C., O. A. Will, S. Tavarré, C. R. Marshall, and R. D. Martin. 2007. New light on the dates of primate origins and divergence. Pp. 29–49 in M. J. Ravosa and M. Dagosto, eds. *Primate Origins: Adaptations and Evolution*. New York: Springer.

Spencer, F. 1997. *History of Physical Anthropology: An Encyclopedia*. New York: Garland.

Sponheimer, M., Z. Alemseged, T. E. Cerling, F. R. Grine, W. H. Kimbel, M. G. Leakey, J. A. Lee-Thorp, F. K. Manthi, K. E. Reed, B. A. Wood, and J. G. Wynn. 2013. Isotopic evidence of early hominin diets. *Proceedings of the National Academy of Sciences* 110:10513–10518.

Stoneking, M. and J. Krause. 2011. Learning about human population history from ancient and modern genomes. *Nature Reviews Genetics* 12:603–614.

Strait, D. S. 2010. The evolutionary history of the australopiths. *Evolution: Education and Outreach* 3:341–352.

Strier, K. B. 2010. *Primate Behavioral Ecology*, 4th edition. Upper Saddle River, NJ: Prentice Hall.

Strier, K. B. 2010. Primate behavior and sociality. Pp. 243–257 in C. S. Larsen, ed. *A Companion to Biological Anthropology*. Chichester, UK: Wiley-Blackwell.

Susman, R. L. 2005. *Oreopithecus*: Still apelike after all these years. *Journal of Human Evolution* 49:405–411.

Swallow, D. 2003. Genetics of lactase persistence and lactose tolerance. *Annual Review of Genetics* 37:197–219.

Takai, M., F. Anaya, N. Shigehara, and T. Setoguchi. 2000. New fossil materials of the earliest New World monkey, *Branisella boliviana*, and the problem of platyrrhine origins. *American Journal of Physical Anthropology* 111:263–281.

Tannen, D. 2003. Gender and family interaction. Pp. 179–201 in J. Holmes and M. Meyerhoff, eds. *Handbook on Language and Gender*. Oxford, UK, and Cambridge, MA: Blackwell.

Tishkoff, S. A., F. A. Reed, A. Ranciaro, B. F. Voight, C. C. Babbitt, J. S. Silverman, K. Powell, H. M. Mortensen, J. B. Hirbo, M. Osman, M. Ibrahim, S. A. Omar, G. Lema, T. B. Nyambo, J. Ghori, S. Bumpsted, J. K. Pritchard, T. B. Wray, and P. Deloukas. 2006. Convergent adaptation of human lactase persistence in Africa and Europe. *Nature Genetics* 39:31–40.

Trinkaus, E. 2005. Early modern humans. *Annual Review of Anthropology* 34:207–230.

Trinkaus, E. and P. Shipman. 1993. Neandertals: Images of ourselves. *Evolutionary Anthropology* 1:194–201.

Trotter, M. 1970. Estimation of stature from intact long limb bones. Pp. 71–84 in T. D. Stewart, ed. *Personal Identification in Mass Disasters*. Washington, DC: Smithsonian Institution, National Museum of Natural History.

Ubelaker, D. H. 1989. *Human Skeletal Remains: Excavation, Analysis, Interpretation*, 2nd edition. Washington, DC: Taraxacum.

Van Schaik, C. P. and J. A. R. A. M. Van Hooff. 1996. Toward an understanding of the orangutan's social system. Pp. 3–15 in W. C. McGrew, L. F. Marchant, and T. Nishida, eds. *Great Ape Societies*. Cambridge: Cambridge University Press.

Van Schaik, C. P., M. Ancrenaz, G. Borgen, B. Galdikas, C. D. Knott, I. Singleton, A. Suzuki, S. S. Utami, and M. Merrill. 2003. Orangutan cultures and the evolution of material culture. *Science* 299:102–105.

Vekua, A., D. Lordkipanidze, G. P. Rightmire, J. Agusti, R. Ferring, G. Maisuradze, A. Mouskhelishvili, M. Nioradze, M. Ponce de León, M. Tappen, M. Tvalchrelidze, and C. Zollikofer. 2002. A new skull of early *Homo* from Dmanisi, Georgia. *Science* 297:85–89.

Walker, A. and R. Leakey. 1993. *The Nariokotome* Homo erectus *Skeleton*. Cambridge, MA: Harvard University Press.

Ward, C., M. Leakey, and A. Walker. 1999. The new hominid species *Australopithecus anamensis*. *Evolutionary Anthropology* 7:197–205.

Ward, S. C. and D. L. Duren. 2002. Middle and Late Miocene African hominoids. Pp. 385–397 in W. C. Hartwig, ed. *The Primate Fossil Record*. Cambridge: Cambridge University Press.

Watson, J. D. 1968. *The Double Helix: A Personal Account of the Discovery of the Structure of DNA*. New York: Atheneum.

Wheeler, P. E. 1991. The thermoregulatory advantages of hominid bipedalism in open equatorial environments: The contribution of increased convective heat loss and cutaneous evaporative cooling. *Journal of Human Evolution* 21(2):107–115.

White, T. D. 2002. Earliest hominids. Pp. 407–417 in W. C. Hartwig, ed. *The Primate Fossil Record*. Cambridge: Cambridge University Press.

White, T. D., B. Asfaw, Y. Beyene, Y. Haile-Selassie, C. O. Lovejoy, G. Suwa, and G. WoldeGabriel. 2009. *Ardipithecus ramidus* and the paleobiology of early hominids. *Science* 326(64):75–86.

White, T. D., M. T. Black, and P. A. Folkens. 2011. *Human Osteology*, 3rd edition. San Diego: Academic Press.

Whiten, A., J. Goodall, W. C. McGrew, T. Nishida, V. Reynolds, Y. Sugiyama, C. E. G. Tutin, R. W. Wrangham, and C. Boesch. 1999. Cultures in chimpanzees. *Nature* 399:682–685.

Williams, B. A., R. F. Kay, and E. C. Kirk. 2010. New perspectives on anthropoid origins. *Proceedings of the National Academy of Sciences* 107:4797–4804.

Wolpoff, M. H., A. G. Thorne, F. H. Smith, D. W. Frayer, and G. G. Pope. 1994. Multiregional evolution: A worldwide source for modern human populations. Pp. 175–199 in M. H. Nitecki and D. V. Nitecki, eds. *Origins of Anatomically Modern Humans*. New York: Plenum Press.

Wood, B. A. 2010. Systematics, taxonomy, and phylogenetics: Ordering life, past and present. Pp. 56–73 in C. S. Larsen, ed. *A Companion to Biological Anthropology*. Chichester, UK: Wiley-Blackwell.

Yuasa, I., K. Umetsu, S. Harihara, A. Kido, A. Miyoshi, N. Saitou, B. Dashnyam, F. Jin, G. Lucotte, P. K. Chattopadhyay, L. Henke, and J. Henke. 2006. Distribution of the F374 allele of the SLC45A2 (MATP) gene and founder-haplotype analysis. *Annals of Human Genetics* 70(6):802–811.

Zilhão, J., D. E. Angelucci, E. Badal-Garcia, F. d'Errico, F. Daniel, L. Dayet, K. Douka, T. F. G. Higham, M. J. Martínez-Sánchez, R. Montes-Bernárdez, S. Murcia-Mascarós, C. Pérez-Sirvent, C. Roldán-Garcia, M. Vanhaeren, V. Villaverde, R. Wood, and J. Zapata. 2010. Symbolic use of marine shells and mineral pigments by Iberian Neanderthals. *Proceedings of the National Academy of Sciences* 107:1023–1028.

Zimmer, C. 2013. *The Tangled Bank: An Introduction to Evolution*, 2nd edition. Greenwood Village, CO: Roberts and Company.